COSIMA
WAGNER

Da Capo Press Music Reprint Series

MUSIC EDITOR
BEA FRIEDLAND
Ph.D., City University of New York

❋❋❋❋❋❋❋❋❋❋❋❋❋❋❋❋❋❋❋❋❋❋❋❋❋

RICHARD COUNT DU MOULIN-ECKART

COSIMA
WAGNER

Translated from the German
by
CATHERINE ALISON PHILLIPS
And with an Introduction
by
ERNEST NEWMAN

VOL. I

Introduction to the Da Capo Edition
by
GEORGE J. BUELOW

DA CAPO PRESS · NEW YORK · 1981

Library of Congress Cataloging in Publication Data

Du Moulin-Eckart, Richard Maria Ferdinand, Graf,
  1864-1938
  [Cosima Wagner, English]
  Cosima Wagner.

  (Da Capo Press music reprint series)
  Reprint. Originally published: New York: Knopf,
1930.
  Includes index.
  1. Wagner, Cosima, 1837-1930. 2. Wagner, Richard,
1813-1883. 3. Opera producers and directors —
Germany — Biography. 4. Wagner family. I. Title.
ML429.W133D83 1981   782.1'092'4 [B] 81-1500
ISBN 0-306-76102-5   AACR2

This Da Capo Press edition of *Cosima Wagner*
is an unabridged republication of the edition
published in New York in 1930, supplemented
with a new Introduction by George Buelow.
It is reprinted by arrangement with Alfred A. Knopf, Inc.

Published by Da Capo Press, Inc.
A Subsidiary of Plenum Publishing Corporation
233 Spring Street, New York, N.Y. 10013

Manufactured in the United States of America

INTRODUCTION TO
THE DA CAPO EDITION

COSIMA WAGNER (1837-1930), the second of three children by Franz Liszt and the Countess Marie d'Agoult, was a figure of immense significance to the history of German music in the nineteenth and early twentieth centuries. Her life had nothing of the commonplace about it. Out of a childhood totally subjugated to her father's strangely remote will, she developed into a woman of impregnable strength of character, who ruled imperiously over interpreters of Wagner's music. Liszt's children grew up having little contact with their parents in the upper middle-class societies of Paris and Berlin. The composer directed Cosima's education by proxy first through his own mother and then through various governesses. He seemed to feel his one responsibility to her, other than financial support, was to make certain her education would attract a suitable husband.

But Destiny, to invoke that convenient abstraction so favored by nineteenth-century historians, had another future in store, and the course of Cosima's life progressed with few hesitations to Richard Wagner and Wagnerism. Her marriage to her father's gifted piano student Hans von Bülow was the first crucial step in that progression into Wagner's life, first as wife of his close friend and admirer, then as his lover, and finally as his wife, protectress, and surrogate. Without her indomitable will-power, coupled with the intelligence and practical skills she drew upon to assist Wagner in countless complex matters involving his career and personal life, he would never have had the time or the physical strength to complete his great works, notably the *Ring* operas and *Parsifal.* In addition, he could not have accomplished the building of the Bayreuth theater without her constant support and labor, nor could he have produced the first summer festivals at which the premier performances were given of *Der Ring des Nibelungen* in 1876 and *Parsifal* in 1882. And after Wagner's death in 1883 the widow dedicated herself totally to continuing the festivals, a career extending through 1908 when she turned over the direction to her son Siegfried. During these years as festival director she imposed her concepts of staging and performance of Wagner's operas with a jealous protectiveness and dictatorial control that made her as much hated as beloved by the musical world. Although Bayreuth today has weathered other crises since Cosima's death, it is no exaggeration to state that the annual Wagner performances in this small Franconian town would not have survived if she had not sacrificed all of her widowed years to the building of that remarkable monument to her husband's genius.

Everything about Cosima Wagner's life was portentous. In many ways she resembled a figure out of a nineteenth-century romantic novel. Her life, governed by atypical mores, was a succession of dramatic conflicts and hyperbolic experiences. The sensationalism accompanying many episodes has left behind controversies that are still unresolved, the most argued, undoubtedly, being the circumstances surrounding her liaison with Wagner while still Hans von Bülow's wife, and her bearing three of Wagner's children. During her long life and career she became friend and often enemy of a large number of great and complex personalities, and many of these relationships have left behind a maze of factual and interpretive problems. It is hardly surprising for these reasons alone that no one has written a completely successful, impartial, accurate biography of this extraordinary woman comparable, for example, to Ernest Newman's four-volume *Life of Wagner*. Such a biography remains a priority not only for research into the life and music of Richard Wagner, but also for a clearer comprehension of German musical developments in the rapidly and often tragically changing cultural configurations of the late nineteenth century.

The work in hand, by Count Richard du Moulin-Eckart (Munich, 1929; English translation by Catherine Alison Phillips in two volumes, New York, 1930), has major significance for several reasons. Most important, it was the first biography of Cosima, written with her guidance and approval. The inner circle of Bayreuth was open to Moulin-Eckart, and the musical world considered his book an official documentation of the *Meisterin's* life, as he often refers to her. For the first time important and previously well-guarded papers in the family archives became available to Moulin-Eckart, including the now famous Cosima Wagner *Diaries*.[1] The richness and uniqueness of this material made his biography a primary source of information for most subsequent writing about both Richard and Cosima Wagner. All later biographies of Cosima repeat more

---

[1] Cosima Wagner kept a daily diary in which she recorded intimate details of her life with Wagner from the year 1869. This record was to serve, she stated, as a testament for her children. Moulin-Eckart and the Wagner biographer Carl F. Glasenapp were the first to be given access to the diaries. They later became the property of her daughter Eva, who eventually presented them to the city of Bayreuth on the condition they be sealed for thirty years after her death, which took place in 1942. Various legal processes kept these invaluable documents locked in a bank vault until the summer of 1975. They were published in two volumes as *Cosima Wagner, Die Tagebücher*, ed. Martin Gregor-Dellin and Dietrich Mack, Vol. I, 1869-1877 (Munich, 1976), Vol. II, 1878-1883 (Munich, 1977). Subsequently a two-volume translation by Geoffrey Skelton has appeared (New York, 1978-1980).

or less exactly the details of her life as first recorded by Moulin-Eckart.[2]

Richard Maria Ferdinand, Graf du Moulin-Eckart (1864-1938) was not a musician by profession, although his father Eduard was an amateur composer and conductor. Eduard had been an early supporter of Wagner, organizing the first fund-raising campaign in his home city of Regensburg for the building of the Bayreuth theater. Wagner became the godfather of Richard Moulin-Eckart. According to Richard, his father had been a student and close friend of Franz Liszt and later of Liszt's mistress, the Princess Carolyne Wittgenstein. The father, according to Cosima Wagner's *Diary*,[3] was a frequent visitor at Wahnfried, the composer's home in Bayreuth, and this relationship undoubtedly extended later to the son.

Count Richard du Moulin-Eckart was a historian, having studied at the universities in Würzburg, Leipzig, Munich, Breslau, and Heidelberg. He received the doctorate from the last named in 1891, and became a professor of history at the Technische Hochschule in Munich in 1894. In addition to the Cosima Wagner biography he published a life of Hans von Bülow (Munich, 1921), and edited a collection of Bülow's letters (Munich, 1927). A brief book of considerable interest entitled *Wahnfried* (Leipzig, 1925), presents an intimate and colorful picture of Wagner's home, family, and friends, all based on first-hand experiences. He wrote a large number of articles and books on various aspects of German politics and history, in-

[2] The more important biographical studies of Cosima Wagner include: Max von Millenkovich-Morold, *Cosima Wagner* (Leipzig, 1937); Walter Siegfried, *Frau Cosima Wagner—Studie eines Lebens* (Stuttgart, 1930); Lilian Scalero, *Cosima Wagner* (Zürich, 1934); Alice H. Sokoloff, *Cosima Wagner, Extraordinary Daughter of Franz Liszt* (New York, 1969); Douglas Sutherland, *Cosima. Eine Biographie* (Tübingen, 1970).

[3] See *Die Tagebücher*, Vol. II, pp. 57, 224, 254, 691.

cluding *Bismarck, der Mann und das Werk* (Stuttgart, 1915), *Englands Politik und die Mächte* (Munich, 1901), and *Luitpold von Bayern, ein historischer Rückblick* (Zweibrücken i. Pfalz, 1901). In 1929 he published an extensive *Geschichte der deutschen Universitäten* (Stuttgart).

In the preface (p. xxi) Moulin-Eckart expresses the hope he will continue this biography beyond the conclusion with the death of Richard Wagner. The sequel, presumably to end with Cosima's death, was never written, and his failure to fulfill his plan is puzzling and difficult to explain. Although the published biography had the approval of Cosima, the book nevertheless quickly fell out of favor among those in the Bayreuth circle after Cosima's death. The German writer on music and Wagner authority, Hans von Wolzogen, who lived next door to Wahnfried until his death in 1938, called the book an "exemplary work of trash,"[4] apparently because he thought Moulin-Eckart had quoted excessively and carelessly from the personal papers of Cosima. This is a strange criticism, for these very quotations, often of considerable length (which today can be confirmed to be highly accurate when compared with the original *Diary* entries), were the very reason subsequent writers found the biography valuable and which even today gives the work a flavor of authenticity and relevance.

Moulin-Eckart's fall from popularity in official Bayreuth was probably the result of reasons connected to the turbulent political climate in Germany in the early thirties. Both he and his son Karl Leon had active associations with the Nazi party in its early history. Graf Richard was arrested though not prosecuted for his part, together with his friend Ernst Röhm, in the Beer Hall Putsch of 1923 in Munich. His son became head of

---

[4] As reported in Winfried Schüler, *Der Bayreuther Kreis von seiner Entstehung bis zum Ausgang der Wilhelminischen Ära* (Münster, 1971), p. 79, fn. 3.

the SA Intelligence Service in Munich, but in 1934 found himself a victim of the infamous Röhm Putsch in which Hitler ruthlessly murdered or imprisoned those members of the Party posing a threat to his own power. Karl Leon served two years in Dachau. To what extent his father's reputation was tainted by his son's political disgrace can only be conjectured, but it is perhaps not surprising that his biography of Cosima was soon condemned in Bayreuth, where Hitler was already a welcome guest, and that Count Richard published nothing further before his death.

The English translation by Catherine Alison Phillips[5] reflects a remarkable degree of fidelity to the original German, and yet it is highly literate in its own right. This is not an easy biography to appreciate, and readers today will be distressed if not dismayed by Moulin-Eckart's verbosity and his frequently unbearable panegyric tone. He writes as a prostrate worshipper before the shrine of Cosima. He sees her as the "greatest woman of the century," the Mistress of Bayreuth, always noble, always brilliant, always wonderful. She is without flaws, and if we should believe Moulin-Eckart, her goodness radiated out to touch all those who came with the proper attitude of admiration and devotion. That a university-trained intellectual, a historian in his thirties, could have succumbed to such an unreal image of this great but clearly imperfect woman is in itself a fact worthy of reflection. For the picture created by this book is

[5] The translator was the wife of British historian Walter Alison Phillips, chief assistant editor of the *Encyclopaedia Britannica*, 11th edition. Mrs. Phillips had a remarkable career in translating biographies of composers, all of them for the American publisher A. A. Knopf. They include the lives of Schumann, by Victor Basch (New York, 1931), Chopin by Henri Bidou (New York, 1927), Purcell by Henri Dupré (New York, 1928), Brahms by Walter Niemann (New York, 1929), and Puccini by Richard Specht (New York, 1933). With her husband she translated Mörike's fictionalized account of *Mozart on the Way to Prague* (Oxford, 1934).

not only an "official" account sanctioned by Cosima; it is also the very substance of the woman as seen by the large number of disciples who came to Bayreuth seeking musical inspiration and ideological sustenance. Functioning as high priestess, and in collaboration with family and friends, she nourished this cult with utmost personal care and volumes of written propaganda.

If this work has a questionable tone of adulation often bordering on sycophancy, if it is meant to absolve Cosima of the slightest human weakness, and if at times Moulin-Eckart uses facts carelessly, why then reprint the biography? The reasons are several. First, it remains a major document for Wagner research. While at times we must read between the lines to find the truth, Moulin-Eckart nevertheless clearly understood much about Cosima's personality and achievement that was not based on idolatry. Her life was full of paradoxes: her education reflected her father's rampantly male-supremacist attitudes, yet she fought through the middle-class suffocation of women's rights to become a woman of striking accomplishment in the totally male-dominated world of the musical arts. Her devotion to Wagner, while apparently consistent with the German attitude towards the role of the wife, took an unusual turn when, as a widow, she assumed domination over the musical world to rule single-handedly in all matters involving Wagner and his music.

Especially pertinent is Ernest Newman's introduction to the English translation. Often critical of Cosima Wagner in his own voluminous biography of her husband, he nonetheless found in Moulin-Eckart's work an important rectification of the facts regarding her life and relationship to both Hans von Bülow and Wagner. The notoriety and, to nineteenth-century bourgeois society, the immorality of the affair had led naturally to a sizable literature condemning Cosima. According to Newman "the great value of the present book is that it lifts the whole Wagner-Bülow-Cosima story out of the old commonplace atmosphere of a mere struggle of two men for the possession of a woman, and shows us the inner significance of the amazing story."

"Significance" means, of course, Cosima's unswerving faith that spiritual forces had brought her to Wagner, and that his mission in life could only be fulfilled with her aid. In the midst of Wagner's darkest hours, without apparent hope for the future, bankrupt, crushed, she took upon herself his salvation. And just as in each of Wagner's music dramas a self-sacrificing, noble woman saves the hero, so too in real life Wagner was rescued from defeat by such a woman. If these facts seem larger than life, indeed resemble a Hollywood scenario, they are no less true. For the life of Wagner, his musical accomplishments, and the interacting personalities were all part of a reality which most of us read about with initial disbelief.

Another aspect of the continuing value of Moulin-Eckart's work is the well-informed discussion of the complexities of Cosima's childhood and adolescence. There is ample material here for psychiatric analysis, and certainly a psychological study of Cosima would be instructive. Whatever she became, Cosima's life was shaped or, one might say, warped by her appalling childhood. This was not because of physical deprivation or a poor education, but rather because of the total absence of any relationship with either parent. Liszt, in his rather brief alliance with the Countess d'Agoult (who later became a somewhat successful writer under the pseudonym of Daniel Stern), had three children: Blandine, Cosima, and Daniel. He seems to have felt no emotional attachment to his offspring, and the same attitude prevailed on the part of the mother. For many years the children were the sole responsibility of Liszt's mother Anna, who raised them in Paris, while Liszt paid the bills. They

were expressly forbidden to have any contact with their own
mother, an arrangement she seemed to find totally satisfactory.
Although it is incomprehensible to us, years would often pass
without a single visit from the father, and the pleas of Cosima
and Blandine in letters to their father asking for a visit are
heart-rending to read. As the girls approached their teens, and
after Liszt had begun to live with the Princess Carolyne Wittgenstein in Altenburg, he summarily dismissed his mother
from the guardianship and, upon the advice of the Princess,
appointed her former Russian governness, Madame Patersi.
In 1855, however, when Liszt thought the Countess d'Agoult
was beginning to show too much interest in the girls, he had
them removed to Berlin where they were placed in the household of the mother of Hans von Bülow—a fateful decision
Liszt must often have remembered as he watched his daughter
become involved with Wagner through Hans von Bülow. This
whole strange story is told by Moulin-Eckart with compassion
and vivid details.

The biography also has considerable information about those
brilliant, unsettled, fascinating decades in the center of the
nineteenth century. The work is as much a cultural history
as it is a personal account of one life. It is packed with information regarding Wagner's own tumultuous career. Not
all of what we learn is pleasing to remember. We see, again
often between the lines, how much the author believed in a
concept of German nationalism that would soon affect the future of Germany and Europe with multiple disasters. Cosima's
world planted the seeds of political and cultural evil. Anti-
Semitism, while never overtly advocated, is touched upon
here and there as a perfectly normal concept. To have been
Jewish, as for example in the case of Hermann Levi, famous
conductor of Wagner's first *Parsifal* in Bayreuth, was viewed
as having "had a heavy burden laid upon him by fate"!

Curiously, none of the subsequent biographies, not even the more recent one in English by Alice H. Sokoloff, present an any less idealized, more truthful picture of Cosima as a person and as a central figure in the history of nineteenth-century German musical culture. Her strong, willful personality still overwhelms authors. Perhaps this book can suggest to others to look more objectively, with less prejudice, into her life and times. The task is difficult. In Moulin-Eckart's study the cast of major characters is enormous, and they were all giants in the nineteenth century: The Countess d'Agoult, Franz Liszt, Princess Sayn-Wittgenstein, George Sand, Berlioz, Hans von Bülow, Bismarck, Nietzsche, Lenbach, Hans Richter, Mathilde Wesendonck, numerous members of the German aristocracy, not the least being King Ludwig II of Bavaria. These are only a few of the influential and creative giants who belong to the foundations of the history of Wagner and his extraordinary cultural epoch in Germany.

GEORGE J. BUELOW
School of Music
Indiana University
November 1980

COSIMA WAGNER

RICHARD COUNT DU MOULIN-ECKART

COSIMA WAGNER

VOL. I

Translated from the German
by
CATHERINE ALISON PHILLIPS

And with an Introduction
by
ERNEST NEWMAN

NEW YORK · ALFRED · A · KNOPF · MCMXXX

This book is dedicated to the memory of
HOUSTON CHAMBERLAIN
Richard Count du Moulin-Eckart

✳✳✳✳✳✳✳✳✳✳✳✳✳✳✳✳✳✳✳✳✳✳✳✳✳✳✳✳✳✳

COSIMA WAGNER

TRANSLATOR'S NOTE

The translator would like to express her most grateful thanks to MR. ERNEST NEWMAN *for his generous assistance in elucidating a number of difficult points; also to her husband for his unfailing help, and especially for his verse renderings of the poems.*

FOREWORD

I

VOLUMINOUS as the Wagner documents are, they are still
far from complete, and until many more of them are in our
possession an authentic biography and a finally reliable psychological study of the man as distinct from the artist are alike impossible. But with the publication of Graf Du Moulin Eckart's
Life of Cosima, of which the present volume forms the first in-
stalment, we enter into possession of a vast amount of new and
fascinating material. Cosima's diaries were apparently used by
Glasenapp for his biography of Wagner, but only to the extent
that they bore on the outer life of the composer. Now for the first
time we have the diaries practically at first hand, and the result
is that our former opinion of both Wagner and Cosima has to be
revised on more than one point.

Criticism of Wagner as a man took a sharp turn after the
publication of *Mein Leben* in 1911. There was so much that
was unpleasant in that book, and Wagner's accounts of people
and events were so often at variance with his own letters, that
the world had reluctantly to accept the disagreeable truth that
noble music does not necessarily proceed from a noble character. Mrs. Burrell, who obtained a copy of the privately printed
edition as early as 1892, was so shocked at the contents of it
that she jumped to the conclusion that for " this miserable
book " " Richard Wagner was not responsible." She declared
that its language " is not the German of a German " — the infer-
ence being, of course, that it was the work of Cosima, " the unmistakable purpose of the book " being " to ruin the reputation

of everyone connected with Wagner." Mrs. Burrell maintained that " Wagner consented under pressure to the book being put together, that he yielded to the temptation of allowing everyone else's character to be blackened in order to make his own great fault [i.e., his association with Cosima] pale before the iniquities, real or invented, of others." Mr. George Ainslie Hight, in his *Richard Wagner, A Critical Biography* (1925), opined that " possibly much has been expunged in preparing it for publication." His own belief was that " the great bulk, at least of the earlier part, is certainly by Wagner." " At the same time," he continues, " I believe the text to have been effectively ' edited ' before it was published, often in such a way as to destroy the sense, and I think it likely that much has been added to and much excised from the original draft."

The campaign against Cosima inaugurated by Mrs. Burrell went on merrily for some years, the climax of it being reached in an ill-informed, malicious, and foolish book by Messrs. Hurn and Root, bearing the facetious title *The Truth about Wagner*. We were given to understand that this egregious volume was founded on " Wagner's suppressed autobiography." Cosima was pictured as the evil genius of Wagner's life. She was answerable for much that was vile in *Mein Leben* and for the garbling of the original in the public issue of 1911; and although the gifted authors of *The Truth about Wagner* contradict themselves liberally on the subject, they were clearly not unwilling for the reader to believe that the fourth part of *Mein Leben* (dealing with the years 1861–1864), which is not included in the private imprint of the 'seventies, was not Wagner's work but Cosima's.

All this nonsense has been blown to the winds once for all by Dr. Julius Kapp in an article in the Berlin *Lokal-Anzeiger* of 30th March, 1930. Dr. Kapp had a copy of the privately printed edition placed at his disposal by the Wagner family. An examination of it revealed that between this edition and the public issue of 1911 there are only fourteen small discrepancies in the whole 870 pages. Only one of these — a matter of about a dozen words — can be regarded as a " suppression " in the full sense of the term. In the original, Wagner relates how, on the 28th November, 1863, he and Cosima swore with sobs and tears to

COSIMA WAGNER
Photograph by A. v. Gross

belong to each other alone; but as we had already guessed something of the kind from what *is* told us at this point in *Mein Leben*, the " suppression " is not very serious. For the rest, eight of the " garblings " are merely softenings of Wagner's regrettable virulencies against the Wesendoncks, and the remaining five are passages of no concern to the general reader that have been omitted out of consideration for the descendants of the parties on whom Wagner was venting his spleen. But the most crushing blow to the calumniators of Cosima comes in connection with the fourth part of *Mein Leben*. It is true that this does not appear in the privately printed edition of which Mrs. Burrell managed to obtain a copy — the said copy having been an extra one struck off for his own use by the wily Bonfantini, the Basel printer of the first three volumes. Apparently Wagner had come to have his suspicions of the good Bonfantini, and so he had the fourth part printed *in Bayreuth* in 1881. It thus becomes clear that Wagner is responsible for the whole of *Mein Leben*, including the fourth part, and that as between the private and the public editions there has been no suppression whatever of the slightest importance by Cosima, if we except the line I have quoted above, referring to November 1863.

I give these facts, though they are not strictly relevant to the present volume, because they indicate how little truth there is in the charges brought against Cosima by one writer after another during the last twenty years or so. Apparently she was too proud to trouble to refute them, as she could so easily have done; she had gone through too much in the years between 1864 and 1883 to be surprised at any baseness on the part of average humanity, or to care in the least about combating it.

II

Wagner biography can be written from more than one angle, especially when the data have been so incomplete as we now see them to have been. To the German public of the 'sixties and 'seventies the Wagner-Cosima-Bülow affair was merely the usual matrimonial triangle; and even recent biographers can be forgiven for insisting unduly on this aspect of the case. It should be a warning to us all never to sum up before the whole of the evidence is before the court. Not that the evidence is even yet complete. We remain in ignorance of many letters of Bülow that would probably throw still further light on the matter; and the letters that passed between Cosima and Wagner are wholly lacking. But thanks to the present volume, and especially to the extracts therein from Cosima's diaries, we know enough now to see the situation more from the inside than we could a few years ago. No one can doubt now that Cosima threw in her lot with Wagner from motives that were in the main not only disinterested but of the loftiest kind, and that had she not taken the decisive step she did it is almost certain that the world would never have had the completed *Ring*, or *Parsifal*, or Bayreuth. If other testimony did not point in this direction, Wagner's, at any rate, ought to convince us.

To understand what the union with Cosima meant to Wagner we must examine the previous history and the character of each of them. There were times in Wagner's life when the artist in him receded into the background, and the man seemed to be heading for destruction. So highly-charged a personality could hardly be expected to run his life intelligently along normal lines; and it need not surprise us to see him now and then completely losing his bearings. It was so during the Jessie Laussot affair; it was so again during the Vienna years (1861–1864) that ended with his rescue by King Ludwig. (The Wesendonck affair is in quite another category: his infatuation in that case was merely the by-product of the incandescence of the *Tristan* that was taking shape within him. He was not writing *Tristan* because he was in love with Mathilde, as the world naïvely supposes; he was in love with Mathilde because he was full of *Tristan*). In the Vienna period in particular he seemed to all his friends to be making for total shipwreck: disappointment at not being able to produce *Tristan*, rage over the baseness and stupidity of ordinary humanity, and his uncontrollable passion for luxury all combined to drive him into a reckless course of living that could have only one end. What would have become of him had not King Ludwig stepped in at the critical moment it is impossible to conjecture.

The Munich days, at first so full of promise, brought him before long to something probably not far from madness. His disappointment was all the greater because of the hopes with which the generous idealism of the young King had originally filled him. Caught up against his will in the stream of Bavarian politics and intrigue, he saw all his plans being frustrated by what could only appear to him as the incurable blindness and Philistinism of the type of men through whom alone, unfortunately, the artist can realise himself in a Court opera house. The years 1865 and 1866 were the darkest in his life. Through all the unyielding strength that was the basis of his artistic character there ran a curious human weakness: he could not exist without a love and devotion from others amounting to complete self-sacrifice on their part. Many of his friends had shown him a fidelity and a generosity at which the world now wonders; but this was not enough. Nothing but utter self-sacrifice would satisfy him; he knew what treasures for humanity were locked up within him, and, forgetting that this is after all a real, not an ideal world, he expected of his friends more than even the truest friendship could be expected to supply. The saying of one of them in the later Vienna days, that Wagner " could not be helped," rankled in him for years afterwards, and is answerable for much of the bitterness of his autobiography.

III

Cosima alone not only saw that he *could* be helped, but was willing to help him at any cost to others or even to herself. There is something almost mystical in the rounding off of their common story. On the occasion when, as a girl of not quite sixteen, she first met him, he read to the company his drama *Siegfrieds Tod* — the original form of the work that, after many years' interruption, he was to bring to its triumphant conclusion under her care. As Cosima von Bülow she was at Zürich during the Mathilde Wesendonck catastrophe of 1858, and it is tolerably clear that as early as that the pair felt subtly drawn towards each other; Cosima had even then not only a profound pity for the unhappy man but a kind of sixth sense of the fundamental cause of all his unhappiness and of his inability to make a success of his life, and an instinct that she could " save " him. It was not till years after their union that Liszt, after a good deal of misunderstanding and estrangement, recognised the vein of fatality that had run through the long story. " *C'était une mission,*" he said when some one spoke to him of his daughter's taking charge of Wagner as she had done. Cosima herself had been in some mysterious way conscious of her " mission " from the earliest days.

By nature and by training she seemed pre-destined to regard life in general and her own life in particular as a mission. She had in her all Liszt's lofty idealism, together with a strength of character, probably derived from her mother and her maternal grandmother, that is not always discernible in Liszt, who allowed himself to be dragged this way and that by people who were both intellectually and morally his inferiors. Cosima was brought up as a child in a hard school, by elderly women who took the severest Nineteenth Century views of duty. Her marriage with Bülow, who, for all his excellent qualities, had some in addition that made him anything but an easy person to live with, still less one in whom so strong and resolute a character as Cosima's could sink itself, gave her an early sense of life as a struggle of idealism against harsh and ugly reality. By Bülow's own testimony, in the letter he wrote her before the final parting, she had acquitted herself nobly of her " mission " with regard to him as an artist. Her final resolve to throw in her lot with Wagner was due in part to the attraction of a greater personality than Bülow's, partly to her instinct — now seen to have been extraordinarily sound — that Wagner, after the Vienna and Munich experiences, more than ever needed someone to save him from the brutal world and from the weaker part of himself, and that she alone could play the part of saviour.

IV

The great value of the present book is that it lifts the whole Wagner-Bülow-Cosima story out of the old commonplace atmosphere of a mere struggle of two men for the possession of a

THE YOUNG LISZT

woman, and shows us the inner significance of the amazing story. The reader will discover for himself how conscious she was of the injury she had done Bülow, and how her heart ached over him to the end. But she was convinced also that in devoting herself to Wagner she was fulfilling the mission for which she had been sent on earth. Bülow also had no doubt that in the interests of something greater than the mere domestic life of all concerned it was his duty to stand aside and let Cosima devote herself to nursing the bruised spirit of Wagner back to artistic creation. Bülow himself told Klindworth, in 1869, that " if Wagner ever wrote another note it would be due to Cosima "; and even without the direct evidence of the as yet unpublished Wagner-Cosima correspondence it is clear that she had risked all and fled to him because he had assured her that without her he was " finished." The reader of the following pages will be able to see for himself, from the composer's own utterances, how indispensable she was to him. His great regret, as he told her again and again, was that he had not found her earlier. Without in the least disparaging poor Minna, who also had sacrificed herself to him in the only ways she understood, the world can now share that regret.

For all his self-pity and his unshakable belief that his life was one long renunciation, Richard Wagner was among the luckiest of men: he asked more both of his circle and of the world than any other artist has ever done, and in the end got everything he wanted, even to that theatre of his own that must have appeared at first to his contemporaries as the mere dream of a hopelessly unpractical idealist. But his supreme stroke of luck was Cosima. All his life he had looked to women, rather than to men, for " salvation "; in Cosima he found a woman who not only shared to the full his own theory that women are sent on earth to devote themselves to great men, but was no less convinced than himself that the worthiest object on earth for a woman's devotion was Richard Wagner. The world has long been familiar with the story of Wagner's " egoism." But we need to recognise now that, all in all, this egoism was more pitiful than censurable. He simply could not live without the devotion of others; it was as necessary to him as sunlight to a flower. The slightest failure on the part of a friend to live up to the doctrine that when Richard Wagner wanted anything Richard Wagner must have it, was enough to poison the unhappy little man's life for weeks. He could not merely not forgive, for instance, he could not even understand, how Cornelius and Tausig, instead of coming to him when he had expressed a desire for their company, could prefer to take a little holiday in Switzerland — an excursion " no doubt of a more important and more agreeable nature," he says with bitter irony. " Without the slightest expression of regret at not being able to meet me this summer," he tells us in *Mein Leben,* " I was simply told that they had just gaily ' smoked a splendid cigar to my health.' When I met them again in Vienna, I could not refrain from pointing out to them the offensiveness of their conduct; but they did not seem to understand that I could have had any objection to their preferring the beautiful tour in French Switzerland to visiting me at Biebrich. They obviously thought me a tyrant." That he obviously was a tyrant never seems to have occurred to him.

V

In Cosima he had the good fortune to meet a being whose view of Richard Wagner, and of humanity's duty to Richard Wagner, was in every respect Richard Wagner's own. She was possessed with the same inflexible idealism where matters of art, culture, duty, and so on were concerned, and, like him, she saw all these things centreing in Richard Wagner. Her intellectual interests and tastes were the same as his. It was not that she deliberately took her cue from him; the extraordinary thing was that, thinking for herself, she invariably saw life and art from the same angle as he. For the first time in his life he found himself in daily communion with a woman, and a beloved woman at that, who was perfectly tuned-in to himself. They read together and thought together. To the irreverent there is a slightly comic side to it all; but Nature had mercifully deprived Cosima of a sense of the comic where Wagner was concerned. The pair lived in a constant state of intellectual high pressure: Wagner, like some mighty tree that knows instinctively what will nourish it and what is useless for its growth, had no eyes or ears for anything in the world that could not minister to his own inner development; it comes as something of a shock to the reader to find that for a time he took a certain interest in anything so low-brow as a murder story! He needed solitude for the terrific concentration involved in the creation of the great works of his last period, but the solitude had to be a solitude à *deux;* and by a miracle he found in Cosima all he desired — unquestioning love and obedience and perfect understanding. How necessary it was for him that he should be the sole sun in his own planetary system is shown by his strange jealousy even of Liszt; he could not bear that Cosima should give a particle of her love even to her own father.

She had intellect enough to enter into all his ideas, but not intellect enough, or at any rate not the kind of intellect, to see round them or beyond them and criticise or question them — a course of action that would assuredly have hurt him and hindered him in his work. She shared his contemptuous opinion of " Professors " — the people who, with a specialized training of their own, failed to theorise upon art and culture and politics along Wagnerian lines. She could live, like him, for ever upon the highest slopes of the mind: she was as incapable as he was of stooping to such minor or lighter products of civilisation as *Carmen* or the operettas of Offenbach. His world was in every respect her world. Further — and in no respect is she more wonderful than in this — not all his patent defects of character could soil the vision she had of him. She knew, at any rate in outline if not in every detail, the often murky story of his dealings with other women. She saw him, by the malicious publication of the " Putzmacherin " letters in 1877, held up to the gleeful ridicule of the world. She suffered agonies from his uncontrollable temper and from what he himself has admitted to be the wounding scurrility of his language in moments of anger. She knew him to be ungrateful and unfair to friends who had done their best for him according to their light. But nothing either in him or reflecting upon him from the world without could shake her belief in him as not only a great artist, whom at all costs it was necessary for her to cherish for the world's good, but a great man; and if posterity cannot quite share her whole-hearted admiration of him as a man, it must give us food for thought when we find that for her, from whom none of his weaknesses were hidden, and who, living with him day by day, suffered more under them than friends at a distance could ever do, he was fundamentally great and good. It may be that she saw him thus only because of her own fundamental greatness and goodness; but whatever the explanation, the fact remains that she could say of this, to the world at large often repellent character, " Whoever is used to his company, whoever has had his mind penetrated by his, is indifferent to everything else; the cleverest people seem to me in comparison as flat as a field, since I have given myself up to his pure and glacier-high being." The important point for us is not whether she was justified throughout in her view of him, but that she held that view; for had she not done so it is a reasonable certainty that the world would have lost part at least of the greater Wagner of the later years. Whatever the final verdict of the world may be upon the total activities of Cosima, this credit at any rate can never be taken from her. And no one knew better than Wagner himself what he and the world owed to her. To no one but Cosima would the proud egoist have said, as he did in 1877, " We two will live together in the memory of men."   ERNEST NEWMAN

PREFACE

THIS book speaks for itself. It was a sacred obligation to raise a monument to the greatest woman of the century by giving an account of her life, which was so rich, so great, and so fine. At the same time it was a bold undertaking to write such a book, since only by becoming entirely engrossed in the life, activity, and work of this great and remarkable woman, her thoughts and her feelings, was it possible to do justice to her. It would scarcely have been possible for anybody who had not known her, and seen the sway which she exercised, to draw a portrait of her. For this reason the duty was not one that could be left to a later generation, which could no longer possess that complete impression of her which was requisite in order to get all that was to be got out of the rich treasures of material placed at my disposal. It has been my privilege to see her in the days of her commanding influence, and myself to acknowledge it. What is more, I have also had the good fortune to stay with her frequently in her old age, to marvel at her soaring intellect and to learn much from her in person that was of the deepest significance, not so much for this book as for forming my conception of her personality. Every moment that I was able to spend at her side, every word that she spoke, bearing witness at once to her rich intellect and great soul, and revealing the significance of men, actions, and events, not only produced a stimulating and elevating effect upon me, but gave my work itself its inspiration and directed its course. I shall never forget how, in words which revealed the full goodness of her heart and her wonderful kindliness, she herself granted me permission to use her diaries for my work. It goes without saying that I have made the most comprehensive use of them, though the treasures contained in them can never be fully exhausted. But they provided me with the main lines of my account of her unique relation with Richard Wagner and enabled me to recognize how, with the eyes of a loving woman and a kindred soul, she discerned his genius. This daughter of Franz Liszt and the Countess d'Agoult was herself so richly endowed with distinguished qualities that she would undoubtedly have been capable of playing an important part in the intellectual life of two nations. But, like a true and wonderful wife, she placed her life at the service of a duty which was in itself of historical significance for the world; for but for her sacrifice Richard Wagner would never have been capable of bringing his work to perfection. Thus this book is the story of a wonderful woman and a wonderful love, and artistic propriety seemed, as it were, to demand that it should close at the moment when her head was bowed in ineffable sorrow over him who was dead. It had been her wish to die with him. But the very sense of duty that was so intimately bound up with her love kept her alive. And when she vanquished grief and once more raised her head, she did so that she might enter upon her beloved husband's heritage in full self-reliance, grandeur, and significance and carry out his great ideas. This must be reserved for a separate account. " The Lady of Bayreuth (*Die Herrin von Bayreuth*) " is not the same woman as she who dedicated her life to the creator of the art-work of Bayreuth, watching over its fulfilment as she did over the life and works of her beloved husband. From the chamber of mourning she stepped out into the world, revealing herself in her grandeur, with a power that dominated both artists and their works. This calls for a description that must find its place elsewhere than in the study now offered to the public, which is based upon the inexhaustibly rich material placed at my disposal, with an unexampled display of confidence, by the house of Wahnfried. The richness of the material was often positively overwhelming. But this was a case for the most unflinching candour, combined with a clear and trustworthy account of the deepest inward emotions. It was immaterial to me whether I was repeating what was well known and had often been told before. The sole purpose which my material had to serve was that of doing justice to the revelation contained in it and of placing this in its due order in time. This was only possible if I used the material placed at my disposal quite unreservedly. I therefore assume unqualified responsibility for the whole book and all that is related in it, no restrictions of any sort having been imposed upon me from any quarter whatsoever. I regard this as a sacred obligation, which I assume all the more gladly because of the pride which I feel at the confidence reposed in me. This in no way detracts from the gratitude which I owe to the house of Wahnfried, to Siegfried Wagner and his wife, Frau Winifred, the daughters, Frau Geheimrat Daniela Thode, the Countess Blandine Gravina, and Frau Eva Chamberlain. I have next to acknowledge my great obligations to the town of Bayreuth, and especially to Herr Oberbürgermeister Preu and Herr Rechtsrat Keller; in connexion with whom I would also mention the Richard Wagnerarchiv and its directress, Fräulein Wallem. I also owe a special debt of gratitude to Herr Geheimrat Ritter Adolf von Gross, whose wise kindliness and kindly wisdom have accompanied the book from its very inception. I have dedicated the book to the late husband of Frau Eva. Perhaps something of Houston Chamberlain's deep comprehension of the qualities of this unique and noble woman may have been communicated to this book. For me the hours which I have spent upon it have been hours of consecration, and I hope to have strength to write the sequel to it in the same spirit and with the same feelings. It has at least been my endeavour to reveal to the German people and to the world one whom I esteem the greatest woman of her century. May all good spirits watch over the memory of her who, like a second Titurel, survived in her greatness into our age, and whose every breath was beyond price. But she belongs to history, and her greatness looms above the present age from the towering heights of a mighty epoch of the past.

CONTENTS

❋

ILLUSTRATIONS

✳

INTRODUCTION

THREE times during my childhood did I meet Franz Liszt. The first time was at Munich, in the garden of the Hotel Marienbad, where he was sitting waiting on a seat. The unique personality of this remarkable man, with its suggestion of something hardly of this world, exerted an instinctive attraction over the boy not yet six years old. I began playing about the bench, and, by a variety of skilful evolutions, I managed to have a good look at his face from behind. " You are a pretty little fellow," he said, stroking my hair. " What is your name? " " Richard," was my reply. " A fine name. And who is your god-father? " " Richard Wagner." Upon this he picked me up in his arms, and, recognizing my mother, who had meanwhile come out into the garden, he carried me towards her. It was my parents for whom he had been waiting. Shortly afterwards my father appeared with an extraordinary little lady on his arm, who made a strange and positively terrifying impression upon me, quite different from that produced by the appearance of Franz Liszt. This was the Princess Carolyne Wittgenstein. My father had been to call upon Liszt, who had, however, mean-while come to see us.

When I next met him, I was somewhat older. It was at the Beethoven Festival organized by my father, at which he directed a performance of Liszt's *Beethoven Cantata*. Liszt sat in our box, and when a symphonic poem of my father's, dedicated to the memory of Beethoven, was performed, he took me upon his knee and said that I must pay attention now, for I was listening to something by my father; and he held me fast in his arms during the whole piece.

Several years went by before he appeared again, this time to hear his new *Saint Cecilia* in the Cathedral. I became his almost invariable companion. He spent his evenings at our house, and there I would see him sitting playing at the grand piano, his hands moving over the keys as though he were musing, or, as I remarked at the time, as though he were writing a book. He accompanied his own songs, which my mother sang. It was then that I received my fullest impression of him, which was an abiding one: that of the wonderful gentleness of a man who had attained serenity of mind and looked out upon his contemporaries with his fine, flashing eyes, which radiated forth nothing but the kindliness and gentleness which in the course of his long life had become his true nature. Only later did I learn that this was the expression of a deep and inexpressibly suffering resignation, and, in a sense, the ultimate outcome of his great and wonderful life. Add to this that, next to that of Richard Wagner, his name was the one most often mentioned in my parents' house, and always in connexion with the great artistic questions with which my father was concerned throughout his whole life. Starting from these first impressions, I have never regarded Liszt from any point of view save that of an artist's son, and all that I afterwards learnt of him grew, like a true and good tradition, out of these beautiful and, in their way, unique beginnings. I can never think of Liszt except as an embodiment of infinite goodness of heart. Even while still a child I often had a feeling that he was a sort of apostle, entrusted with a subsequent mission and charged by his Master to make good what had previously been left undone in the Church.

I naturally became more mundane in after days and began to look upon Liszt, too, with mundane eyes, but always with awe! And when I myself became an initiate, my understanding was increasingly alive to that faint suggestion of martyrdom which I had only instinctively divined at my first meetings with him. Consequently no biography of Liszt has ever succeeded in arousing in me any feeling but one of infinite annoyance, and often, I am bound to say, of deep anger. When I read the first volume of Ramann's biography, shortly after its appearance, my comment was: " But this is quite a different man from the one whom I knew," upon which my father remarked with a smile: "Prescient innocence! (*Du ahnungsvoller Engel du.*) " Even so did Gretchen detect Mephistopheles. He said no more, but I felt that something was wrong with the book, and my opinion has not changed in the least today, now that I know the genesis of this so-called biography; for this lady, whom I met in Munich once, and once only, has, so to speak, dramatized it, treating it as a great drama of situations, but with none of the humour and stage attractiveness possessed by Scribe's plays. Thus I have arrived at a clear conception of the whole development of this great and wonderful man from his youth up, and, since I would have nothing but the truth, I have had confidence only in what I have heard from trustworthy persons or discovered and felt for myself. It was no easy task, while still seeing in my mind's eye that fine, venerable head, to picture to myself the artist's youthful beauty of expression during his years of development. But I naturally felt impelled to trace the process by which that noble and lovable old man had become what he was.

It was a never-failing pleasure to me, who had also spent the fairest years of my childhood in a country village, to picture him there in the village of Raiding, in the cosy little home of his parents, who had always loved the boy beyond expression, and continued to do so till their death. This village of Raiding, where he was born, and where the first premonitions of his musical destiny made themselves felt and were revealed to him, had already become unspeakably precious to me even while still far away, and I was not disappointed in it when I visited it, though this was not possible till after he had gone to his last home in Bayreuth. I felt a sort of kinship with his devout and fervent character when he was a child, and, as the son of an artist, I took his musical development as a matter of course. I now watched him — for I visualized it all, as in a series of pictures — arriving in Vienna and taking lessons there from a pupil of Beethoven's, at the same time coming into touch with a man who had played a part in the life of Mozart. The names of Czerny and Salieri appeared to me, so to speak, as those of secondary personages in that wonderful dramatic scene in which the boy appeared before Beethoven, and Beethoven kissed him upon the brow. To me this was the real and great, but no less obvious, experience, compared with which young Franz's playing seemed to me of but subsidiary importance; for I saw in it only a part of his power. Already a celebrated pianist, he next went to Paris with his father, and there the stirrings of a sort of dæmonic power began to make themselves felt about him. But I already entered into all this in the spirit of the great new age of Germany which had been developing since 1871. I asked, to be sure, whether Liszt was a Hungarian, and already heard his smiling " No! " " No, he is not, even if he sometimes imagines that he is." It was quite immaterial to me that his mother's family should have come from Krems, a place of which I afterwards became unspeakably fond, and in the sound of whose name I can hear the rushing of the Danube; or that his father was connected by name, and also, perhaps, by birth, with the List family of Swabia, from which the famous economist drew his origin. As I say, this was a matter of complete indifference to me then, and still is today. But in the rebuff with which he met in Paris, at the hands of the composer Cherubini, when he tried to enter the Conservatoire, I saw the expression of an absolutely outrageous hostility to Germany, which I cannot get over, in spite of all the attempts of German scholars to reconcile the German public with Cherubini, and in spite of the fact that he made a strong impression on me at an early age, while, at a momentous hour of my destiny, my heart was deeply stirred by his great *Requiem*.

But now the vision of Liszt's development was mingled with French connexions and conditions, with which I became acquainted for other reasons and as a result of other states of feeling, in no way connected with music. Paris was intimately bound up with my family traditions. Thus it was easy for me to picture him to myself as playing a part in the *salons* there, and all that I heard about his successes was in keeping with the impressions of Parisian life which I had gained from other sources. I saw him in the *salons* surrounded by ladies, or else at the piano, but always as a figure which produced a strongly individual impression. His tender youth had matured; the child had become a boy, the boy a youth, who had to go alone to Boulogne to attend his father's funeral, but, instead of returning to the peaceful spot where his mother lived, sent for her to Paris, in order that he might provide her with a pleasant home there and a peaceful old age at his side.

I interpreted this period in the light of the feelings with which one grows up oneself from boyhood to youth, full of glad hopes and proud projects, yet, above all, of such humility before all that is great. Later, indeed, it interested me particularly to picture Liszt not only as the autocrat of the *salons,* not only as the wizard at the piano, but as henceforth dedicating himself to the development of his inner nature in his quiet and secluded retreat. I need only think of those hours in the Cathedral at Regensburg, and recall how his eye glowed with deep and heart-felt piety, to feel how thoroughly permeated he was at that time with a deep and exalted religious feeling, which very nearly impelled him to become a priest. I heard of his predilection for the *Imitation of Christ* of Thomas à Kempis. This again was in no way surprising to me, for everyone during his youth has a certain predilection for this book, which occupied him so much, and at times exclusively. But he was living in Paris, which had passed through the terrible Revolution, through whose streets Napoleon's regiments had marched, first as victors and afterwards as vanquished, and where Louis XVIII, who had once faithlessly deserted his brother's side, had become king by the grace of England, and was now followed by his brother Charles X. It was in this Restoration atmosphere that Liszt grew to maturity, and it was obvious that the impressions of every kind to which he was exposed were bound to produce their effect upon him. It has been said that he became a democrat at this time and, being imbued with a certain interest in social questions, associated with the advanced spirits in Paris, who spent their lives fluctuating between socialistic romanticism and romantic socialism, yet could not always tear themselves away from the old fascination which looked out from the mirrors of the *salons* like some spectral image of the past. Paris will never forget this strange mingling of past and present, of aristocracy and democracy, or, to express it in terms of topography, of the faubourg Saint-Antoine and the faubourg Saint-Germain. But now that his mother had joined him, Liszt, who had been, with Chopin, the most famous, beloved, and fêted virtuoso in Paris, lived entirely unto himself and for his studies. Not that this remarkable woman brought any sort of religious pressure to bear on him. She was far too pious to be at all fanatically bigoted; she was too much of a woman to inspire her child with any horror of the world or tempt him to solitude, and far too much of a mother to grudge him any joy or success or any healthy self-development. Perhaps if he had not had his mother at his side — and, be it remembered, he was only twenty-one — those years would have produced quite a different effect upon him from that which they did. But, as things were, he rose superior to everything — the retirement and painful struggles in which he hoped to find self-realization, and afterwards a deep and silent affection which remained in his thoughts during his whole life — though it must be admitted that it was only later that a particularly rosy glow was cast over this youthful love by the efforts of the great lady of the Vatican. We refer to the young Countess Caroline Saint-Cricq, who undoubtedly returned his love. The young teacher's feelings were observed, but no rupture or scandal was desired, and the young lady was "simply" married to someone of suitable rank, though she would gladly have taken refuge in a convent, there as a nun to cherish in silence her memories of the handsome young artist.

But the result was that Liszt fell seriously ill, and his recovery was despaired of. His death was even announced, and officious hands had already prepared his obituary notice. But he recovered, and ended by overcoming his desire to seek peace and oblivion in a monastery.

Now came the Revolution of 1830, which in reality only changed Paris superficially. The various intellectual coteries continued to exist alongside of one another. In almost all of them Liszt found personalities who aroused his admiration, just as the great figures of the French past had a strong attraction for him. From Jean Jacques Rousseau he had turned to Voltaire, and in Montaigne he at last found a man of learning whom he would perhaps have taken as his leader had not the present and its figures exerted too strong an influence upon him. Thus he took an interest in Chateaubriand and Lamartine, who attracted him as a man, too, and made as deep an impression upon him, both as artist and as musician, as Victor Hugo did later. He even frequented the assemblies of the school of Saint-Simon, which had a profound influence in Paris even after the death of its founder; though a close association with this sect, with its peculiar ethical tinge, did not involve a whole-hearted adhesion to it. But it was above all the Père Lamennais who produced the greatest impression upon him — an impression which lasted for years and even influenced his life — for he became personally intimate with Lamennais, and this stout fighter in the cause which he espoused, who did not hesitate even to break with Rome, was Liszt's confidant in his own personal questions of conscience and the heart. A great deal has been said about Liszt's *Revolutionary Symphony*. It was not the product of the July Revolution, but arose out of the storm and stress of his own development and is thus a sort of volcanic explosion of this strong and powerful nature. Yet in it he cannot help giving musical expression to the great revolutionary movements of the age. In this symphony he makes use of the *Hussitenlied* (*Song of the Hussites*), as well as of Luther's *Ein' feste Burg ist unser Gott* and the *Marseillaise*. Thus in three movements he gives expression, as it were, to three great upheavals, which seem akin to one another outwardly, but, for all their similarity in appearance, arise from quite different motive forces.

But the progress made by Liszt as a musician during this period, or, rather, the reaction now produced by music upon his inner development and destiny is quite another question. Much has been made of the point that the advent of Paganini stirred him to the very depths, and that this dæmonic artist's individual method of handling his musical material suggested to him the great secret of how to establish a close relation between the piano — of which he was master — and all the great music of the day — which he wanted to master — though he did not become conscious of this all at once. The piano now became in some sort his comrade, both as teacher and as performer, and the great interpreter, not only of his own compositions, but, it may be said, of the whole of music, from Beethoven down to Meyerbeer, to whose operatic airs he gave, as it were, a musical backbone in his arrangements for the piano.

His development proceeded on quite peculiar lines. There was as yet no immediate transition to purely creative production. In the first place, he had become too much identified with his instrument for this. He had, as it were, to learn by experience how to work towards a balance between giving and receiving on his instrument, and, though an incomparable improviser, he was forced to place this side of his art at the service of his instrument and of others' compositions. This formed the protecting shelter beneath which the whole of his great inner development went on. In spite of all the apprehensiveness and nervous impatience which were characteristic of him, while causing him, at the same time, a sort of happiness — though, for obvious reasons, our sources tell us comparatively little about this — we see him growing to maturity and awaiting the moment when the great final mystery of his being, the creative faculty, was revealed in its full power.

For not in vain did Beethoven kiss him upon the brow. That kiss was not for the virtuoso, nor even for the musician as such, but for the creator of the symphonic poems. He had to travel by new paths and embody new impressions in his work before he discovered anew in a great form that relationship with the orchestra which Beethoven himself had carried to the utmost limits of possibility in his Ninth Symphony. But before Beethoven's kiss produced its effect, another kiss, from lovely lips, opened his eyes to the meaning of life, just as Kundry's kiss did to Parsifal. In a Paris *salon* he met the young Countess Marie d'Agoult, who had followed a development all her own, consisting in a curious blend of the prevailing intellectualism of the *salons* with a tendency to visionary mysticism, which had accompanied and directed her path from her earliest childhood until this meeting. A veil has been drawn over this noble and

lovely figure, too, in the biography written by the Princess
Carolyne Wittgenstein's attendant. We recognize the Princess's
own hand in the section of that work devoted to this young and
wondrous figure. It is now established beyond a doubt that the
Princess herself wrote that part of the biography and attempted
to exclude this beautiful figure from the circle of those upon
whom Liszt cast his spell. The memorable correspondence between the Princess and her faithful Ramann is deposited in the
Weimar Archives and is not to be opened till fifty years after
the Princess's death. It will provide a complete elucidation of
the relation between the Princess and this strangest of all
biographies. It is no wonder that others have concurred in this
judgment, with even greater severity. It has taken long enough
for justice to be done to this remarkable woman, for her to
receive, in general, such treatment as it has been impossible to
refuse to similar romantic figures, such as Karoline Schelling,
though these are not comparable to her. The book cannot be ab-
solved from the charge of calumny, in spite of the attempts that
have been made to defend it in some inessential points. There
can be no personal or other reason for concealing anything, or
for refusing to allow the figure of this beautiful and original
woman to produce its effect upon us without suppression or
prejudice. For not only was she, too, both beautiful and original,
not only did she move, as befitted her many talents, on the highest human plane, but, thanks to these very talents, it was her
lot to play a part in French literature, and that no ephemeral
part, but a lasting one. Her friend and biographer Ronchaud
has justly assigned her a place in some sort intermediate between Madame de Staël and George Sand. Towards the end of
her life she herself published her memoirs, the first volume of
which deals with her childhood and marriage and closes with
the moment at which she made the acquaintance of Franz Liszt.
This book decidedly merits attention. It not only reveals to us
the nature of this highly gifted woman, but gives us, in some
sort, a picture of the deep and powerful connexion that had
grown up between the French society of pre-Revolution days
and that of the Restoration — relations which have to some extent lasted till today, if not altogether in Paris itself. The magic

of the *ancien régime* will not allow itself to be entirely banished from French history; and though the faubourg Saint-Germain still seems desolate, and we have an impression as though all these old palaces were shuttered up, yet something of its spirit still survives. We cannot understand the figure of the Countess d'Agoult apart from this distinctive atmosphere. She is in a double sense the child of these conditions, but at the same time, too, a product of the age and of all the transformations which had taken place in France, with the addition of an individual attribute in that, through her German mother, she brought into the exclusively noble atmosphere of her own and her husband's families something of the Huguenot spirit derived from her mother's parents in Frankfurt am Main. Not only was she a French aristocrat — who none the less felt strangely drawn towards democracy — but a strong German strain always made itself felt in her; and it was precisely owing to this admixture, as well as to the strongly patrician traditions which influenced her life from the Frankfurt side, that she acquired those qualities which we must recognize and undoubtedly admire in her, both as the mother of her children and as the celebrated and notable authoress Daniel Stern.

In the days of the French Revolution there arrived in Frankfurt am Main a certain Monsieur de Flavigny, who had been brought up wholly in the tradition of the old French *noblesse*. His forefathers had all been soldiers, but, almost without exception, they had combined with their military efficiency that marked literary tendency which, intuitively rather than consciously, informed the whole of that class of society with a creative gift. The father of this Count de Flavigny who had come to Frankfurt am Main had suffered on the scaffold during the Terror, and his wife with him, for his fidelity to his King. But in the year 1797, while in Frankfurt, where he had undertaken to recruit troops for the army of the *émigrés*, the young Count formed a friendship with the Bethmann family, and in particular with a daughter of the house, Maria Elisabeth, who, while still little more than a child, had married one Bussmann, but had been left a widow when only eighteen years of age. A daughter had been born of this marriage, with whom we meet again in the life-story of Clemens Brentano. But her mother, Maria Elisabeth, felt that her perfect happiness depended upon the young Frenchman, and achieved her desire, which was a marriage with the homeless and impoverished nobleman. It is most touching to picture her entry into the young French officer's cell in prison; and even her parents had to yield before the determination of so strong a passion.

Of this marriage was born Marie Catherine Sophie de Flavigny. The fact that her father had once been a page to Marie Antoinette left a lasting impression upon her. She was born during the night of December 30–1, and it was to the hour of her birth that in her visionary way she attributed a whole series of deep emotional experiences and ideas, which continued to exert an influence over her life and cast a shadow over it up to an advanced age.

In the year 1809 her parents returned to France and bought a property in Touraine. Here they lived, far from the imperial court, refusing all the inducements which were offered to them to enter the service of Napoleon or of Queen Hortense. Their home was the beautiful estate of Mortier, with its fine park and charming surroundings, in which hill and stream alternated with vineyard and forest. Here they lived a life quite in harmony with the age when Marie Antoinette had played the shepherdess at the Petit Trianon. Marie lived here in a completely secluded world, quite in the spirit of past days, when a nobleman's little daughter was already treated like a little chatelaine. Her family were attached, heart and soul, to the Bourbons. The lily that shone resplendently on the banner of the Bourbons was their sacred flower, and their opposition to the usurper had a strong tinge of hostility. In later days Marie philosophized a great deal about this period and the æsthetic conceptions of the *noblesse*, who referred everything back to their past and set up their altars in the temple of tradition. Indeed, she always felt it to be of importance that the same house whose walls had witnessed her mother's last blessing should hear her child's first broken words. But she grieved to see these nobles who had survived the Revolution and the Empire only to die of the wounds that they had received, like the butterfly, which, with the pin transfixing its body, flutters up once again into the air with its damaged wings, only to sink dying upon the flower it loves.

All the same, everything was grander and more distinguished than what she had known in the house of her maternal grandparents in Frankfurt. There everything had been " respectable and tedious, a medley of wooden virtues, narrow abilities, and clumsy elegance," and she asks herself: " Must one always be forced to choose between the effete softness of aristocratic manners and the clumsy strength of democratic ones? " Her own inclination was towards the latter, but she wanted to reconcile the two and saw in the attempt to do so the mission of woman. Yet she still bore within her something of the bourgeois pride inherited from a grandmother who had ruled her house like a noble lady of the *ancien régime*. And one thing, too, remained a living memory in her and added, as it were, a sort of consecration to her life: just as Franz Liszt had received a kiss of consecration from Beethoven's suffering lips, so she, too, felt herself to have been hallowed by another great man — Goethe. One day the splendid old man appeared in the garden of the Bethmanns' country-house, and little Marie approached him among the rest. Overcome with shyness, she gazed up at his great, flashing eyes, and her glance rested upon the poet's radiant brow. On taking his leave he passed his hand caressingly over her fair hair, and she was deeply moved and hardly dared to breathe. " I felt indeed," she writes, " that in that magnetic hand there was a blessing and a promise for me. I cannot express it. All I know is that more than once during my long life I have bent in spirit over that hand of benediction, and at these times I have always felt myself to be stronger and purer." We may bear in mind the fact that in this little admirer of Goethe a feeling had already been awakened which was afterwards to draw her with such inexpressible force to Franz Liszt. These ideas always dominated her mind during the period of her education, which she received from the Abbé Gaultier, who taught the children of the French *noblesse,* and from whom, as a matter of fact, she learnt a great deal. She was initiated, if only superficially, into German and French literature and into all branches of knowledge, thanks to which knowledge she was afterwards able to play a part in the *salons*. She was next sent to the Convent of the Sacré-Cœur. This was the lot of almost all the daughters of the French *noblesse*. They were bound to pass with the nuns the period before they were allowed to enter society, and she herself describes these days, sometimes in rather lurid colours. But though the conditions prevailing there did not and could not suit her, yet the religious life and education made a deep impression on her. It was something of the same nature as what afterwards made itself felt so strongly in Franz Liszt and caused him, too, as a young man, to hesitate between the world and the cloister. It consisted mainly in inducing a state of ecstasy, which was exploited for purposes of worship and instruction. She played the organ in the little chapel there, while the nuns and her little friends sang sacred songs, and she felt a certain dread when the world was talked of. She would fall into states of ecstasy, as the nuns desired, and her piety assumed an almost morbid tinge. But those days, too, came to an end, and the noble young lady, now educated and quite ready to enter the world, returned to her mother. She was reluctant to leave the convent; for she had moments of exalted spiritual agitation, when what she would most have loved was to have had her lovely fair hair cut off and to spend her life as a nun, far from the dangerous stir of life, a deep dread of which had been inculcated in her.

Home and society now claimed her. And, as was natural, the next thing was to find her a suitable match. She herself tells us how for a time she was decidedly attracted by General de Lagarde, who, on his side, felt a strong and chivalrous devotion for her. But another alliance was in view; negotiations were opened, in which her confessor took part, and in which even the court took a hand; and so she was betrothed to the Count Charles d'Agoult. It was an imposing wedding that took place on May 16, 1827, at which King Charles X, with the Dauphin and his consort, signed the register, together with the Duchess of Berry and Marie Amélie, Duchess of Orleans, and Louis Philippe, Duke of Orleans. With this marriage she entered a new world, in which she was fitted to play a leading part, but in which, none the less, she found nothing but infinite disillusionment. In that part of her memoirs which cover the years from 1833 to 1854, and which her grandson Daniel Ollivier published in 1927, she expresses this state of feeling quite otherwise than in the closing years of the first part. But she also describes how the world into which she entered was dominated, not exclusively by the old ways of thinking, but also by the new spirit of poetry, and the ideas awakened in society by leading clericals, as well as by the spokesmen of other tendencies. This was the period when Chateaubriand had written his *Génie du christianisme*, which made a deep impression on her. Those were the days when an equal enthusiasm was felt for Ossian, Shakspere, and *Werthers Leiden*. Goethe's *Faust* and Byron's *Manfred* found their imitators. All questions affecting society were discussed, as well as all questions concerning social misery; and they stirred men's souls.

It was at this time that she came in contact with Liszt and learnt to know and love him. Indeed, she could not but love him. There could be no question here of guilt or innocence, but only of destiny, which bore its own justification in itself and was afterwards glorified in the children. " Passion is eternal in the hearts of man. To those possessing the soul of a Sappho, an Héloïse, a La Vallière, a Lespinasse, or a Madame Roland, a Petrarch or a Dante, love will always be the mightiest god." With her eyes fully open she indulged this passion with its poignant sufferings, for she considered that a day would come that would justify and hallow such emotions. But she did not need to wait for it; for Gustav Freytag's fine saying applies to her: " He who stakes his life in order to prove his fidelity to the loved one has for ever the right to set himself apart, above the common herd of the simple." She acted in accordance with a true morality, based on a conjunction of the spirit of the age, freedom and necessity. She does not blink the fact that she was the wife of a noble-hearted and honourable man, and the mother of two sweet and attractive children. But all the outward brilliance of her existence aroused in her nothing but grief for the betrayal of her youth. Even when she gazed into her children's eyes, she felt none of the happiness which might have been hers in a true love-match. She strove with herself and strove in prayer with God. She went to communion in order to find consolation and peace, yet all was in vain. " Not even prayer, not even the deepest union with God in His sacrament gave my heart peace, and my spirit light. My conscience was never at rest, though it had nothing with which to reproach itself." She scorned to descend to the standards of French society, which knew but one commandment: to avoid scandal and keep up appearances.

And now Franz Liszt entered her life. Among her friends there was an aged Marquise who was bringing up in her house a beautiful young niece to whom young Franz Liszt was music-master. At that time he had withdrawn from society and limited the number of his pupils to what was necessary for the support of himself and his mother. But up to that time he had continued to frequent this house, and here it was that she met him. It had been the old lady's intention that Marie should hear him there and admire him, perhaps for the last time before he retired from the world. She herself describes it as follows: " When, about ten o'clock, I entered Madame de L. V.'s drawing-room, where the whole party was assembled, Liszt was not yet present. Meanwhile they were preparing to sing a chorus by Weber. Then the door opened, and a wonderful apparition appeared before my eyes. I say an apparition, for I can find no other word for the extraordinary emotion which stirred me at the sight of the most extraordinary man I ever saw. A tall and extremely slender figure, a pallid face with great eyes of the deepest sea-green, which flashed fire, a suffering and yet powerful cast of countenance, a gliding step which seemed to float along the ground rather than tread firmly upon it, and a distracted and restless impression, like that of a phantom at the moment when the bell tolls that summons it back to darkness: thus did I see before me this young genius, whose retired life aroused at that moment as lively a curiosity as his triumphs had once excited envy." He spoke with her as if he had long been intimate with her, and at his words she sank, as it were, into a deep reverie. It was this first emotion that dominated and impelled her in what followed. It is true that she was the elder, for he was only twenty-three. But she was still a child, in spite of the social position that she occupied, and he represented to her something new and mysterious, which exerted a powerful attraction over her. She was drawn to him, in spite of everything, by her passionate longing and thirst for love, and when obstacles presented themselves at a later stage, when fate knocked warningly at her door and she was crushed by the death of her beloved child, she clung fast to him. These were indeed terrible days through which she had to pass, and her description of how her child died in her arms is written, not only with dramatic power, but with the whole strong emotion of her mother's heart. Liszt himself avoided her, not through any lack of love, but out of a feeling like that of Tristan, who saw the highest loyalty in braving matters to the utmost (*höchste Treue im kühnsten Trotze*), and had retired to the Père Lamennais, yet could not break with her. He wanted to take leave of her in his mother's house. "Poor mother!" he exclaimed to the Countess, "how you have suffered!" He was determined to leave France and Europe. But now Marie asked him: "What have you decided? What have you to say to me, and what do you mean to say to me? Are you going?" "*We* are going!" he cried, and his eyes, "which had not moved from mine, besought me with such ardour, such hope, and such love that I could not support his gaze. 'What are you saying, Franz?' I said, averting my eyes. 'I say,' he replied in a steady voice, 'that we cannot live like this. I had resolved to leave you. But I thirst for life, I have had enough of suffering for what is nothing worth. We must make great mistakes, or express great virtues in our life. We must acknowledge the sacredness or the impiety of our love before Heaven. Do you understand me now? Do you grasp my meaning now?' And his arms clasped me to him and closed round my trembling form. 'Great God!' I cried aloud. 'Your God is not my God,' cried Franz, laying his hand on my mouth. 'There is no other god but love.' And thus it happened, thus were all ties severed, all things cast away, for our love's sake. The unknown god, the mightiest god, took possession of us and of our destiny."

And the great love came, and all the great plans came into being. They travelled by way of Basel and Bern to Geneva, and from Basel he wrote to his mother: " Beyond all our hopes, we arrived today in Basel at ten in the morning. Longinus " — for so he called the woman he loved — " is here, and her mother besides. I know nothing definite yet. We are both in good spirits, and it never occurs to us to be unhappy." And so they went to Geneva, and that great and wonderful love of theirs began. We cannot say, as so many biographers have done, that it was the spirit of the age that carried them away, and, above all, turned Liszt aside from his path. He was not a weak-willed man, nor was he the man to surrender himself to a passion except with all his being. This passion had overwhelmed them, and they had no choice save either to retire into the cloister, or, like the Wälsungs, to fall passionately into each other's arms. Though Liszt himself may have thought differently about this period later, one thing is certain: Marie d'Agoult was ready to sacrifice herself for the good of this god-like genius, who had nothing in common with the rest of humanity and should not have been subject to the ordinary laws. " In these ecstasies of love, which no doubt arose from my German blood, nothing seemed to be left save one desire and one will — love; there was no duty, no conscience, that I should not have been bound to sacrifice for him. I should have been ready to be a saint for love. In moments of extreme tension and ascetic fervour I blessed my agony."

And when the first traces of indifference began to appear in Franz, she kept silence, for there was no part of her heart which was not filled by him. " I have a lover," she would think at such times, " but no friend to share my sorrow." A tinge of the deepest mysticism lies over her life in Geneva and afterwards in Italy as well as at Nohant, where she stayed with George Sand. And throughout all her life and love one thing, above all, is clear in her relations with Liszt — the hope and the will that through her love he should rise to the greatest heights as an artist.

At Geneva Blandine was born, and it was by his child's cradle that Liszt composed his first song, *Angiolin dal biondo crin*, the words of which, by Cesare Bocelli, may be translated as follows:

Angel fair with golden hair,
Thou hast seen two springs take flight,
May thy days be pure and bright!
Angel fair with golden hair,
May soft summer gales caress thee,
Friendly stars on thee are shining,
Rays of light about thee twining;
Angel fair with golden hair,
Lovely image of a flower.
Softly wafts a breath of love
From thy lips when thou art sleeping,
Knowest naught of pain and weeping,
Angel fair with golden hair,
Image of a lovely flow'r.
Joy to thee and happiness
By thy mother's smile be given,
May thine eyes to her be heaven!
Angel with the golden hair,
Image of a lovely flow'r.
Learn from her the kindly spell
Art and nature each possesses,
Never learn how care oppresses.
Angel fair with golden hair,
Image of a lovely flow'r.
If thou learn to lisp my name,
Often let thy lips repeat it,
That thy mother's heart may greet it,
Angel fair with golden hair,
Image of a lovely flow'r.

This song, like so much else of what he wrote at that time, is among his finest compositions, and perhaps Madame d'Agoult's mistake was that she failed to recognize in this little song the greatness of her Franz's creative art.

It must be left to someone else, who can devote himself entirely to the development of this wonderful woman's character, to follow the strange course of this exalted love. We must hasten to continue our picture of her life and development. In Geneva a world apart formed itself round these two. We see him always striving and struggling, and growing intellectually; and in these emotions can perhaps be found the first stirrings of the young man who could bear no constraint, but felt urged to go forth and take the world by storm. We find the pair on Lake Como, in Florence and in Rome. Everywhere he was learning, everywhere he was taking in impressions; and when he stood before the picture of St. Cecilia at Bologna, he felt her to be the patron saint of his art and his life. There were many times when these great days of their love resembled the moments of passion spent by Chopin and George Sand on the island of Majorca. Here, too, there was bound to be that excess of emotion which perhaps inevitably ends in antagonism. None the less, we find scenes of the greatest charm: for instance, one evening at Nohant, the country-house of George Sand, who describes the impression made on her by this extraordinary woman as follows: " That evening, while Liszt was playing the fantastic songs of Schubert, the Countess was walking up and down in shadow below the terrace. She was dressed in some light-coloured garment, and her head and almost all her slender figure were shrouded in a great white veil. As she paced along with measured tread, her foot scarcely seemed to touch the sand. Plunged, like all nature around us, in a mood of melancholy joy, we could not turn our eyes away from the magnetic circle described before us by the mute sibyl in the white veil. Her step became slower and slower, as the artist modulated through harmonies of a strange melancholy into the gay melody of the song *Sei mir gegrüsst!* Her every movement was as full of grace and harmony as though she herself were pouring forth melody like a living lyre. She seated herself on a hanging bough, which scarcely bent, as though it were supporting an elf. And now the music ceased. It was as though the life of these sounds were bound up by some mysterious bond with the life of this fair, pale woman. Next moment we saw her glide past the lights of the *salon,* near at hand. Her fair hair blazed like a golden aureole, and in the light movements of her proud gait her white veil surrounded her figure as with a cloud. The singing fingers wandering over the keys were hushed, and the vision vanished into night."

We need only transport the scene of this wondrous nocturne to Bellagio, on Lake Como, to know what a world it was into which, on December 25, 1837, the daughter was born to whom Liszt gave the name Cosima, in joyful remembrance of the lake and of the hours which he had passed there — though also of a work of George Sand's, and not least of St. Cosmas. It was here that the parents read Dante's *Divina Commedia* together, and thus the daughter is, as it were, associated with her father's deepest, richest work, the *Dante Symphony*. Cosima was born, and they could now sing to her too the cradle-song that he had written for Blandine: *Angiolin dal biondo crin*.

Next came Rome, and here Daniel was born. The Countess bore Liszt three children: fair, lovely children, the fruit of a true and mighty love, of a noble mother and a great father.

Yet a fate hung over this love. It was actually George Sand, their kindly hostess at Nohant, though she seemed to be united by the deepest friendship with the hot-blooded and talented Countess, and loved and venerated Liszt, who in some sort profaned the period of this great love, not in any work of her own, but by drawing the attention of one of the greatest of French novelists to this "material." In after days another took his place by the fireside at which Franz and Marie had sat and mused: it was Balzac who heard from the lips of the jealous woman and writer all the remarkable details relating to Liszt and her, his great and loving mistress. In his famous novel *Béatrix* he used these to draw a portrait of the pair, and especially of Marie, which, for all its wonderful artistry, is even closer to the life than is usual in his works, true as they are to nature. This was the snake already lurking in the grass and threatening their love with its deadly venom.

But this was not till later. The children, with Marie herself, came to stay with Liszt's mother in Paris, where he, too, always returned in triumph from his travels, which carried him very far afield, and after which, year after year, he would spend beautiful and wonderful summers with his lovely wife and charming children, especially Cosima, at Nonnenwerth on the Rhine. Perhaps it was at the very moment when his fame had risen with new power that he felt the waning of this love most strongly. There, as everywhere, he was fêted. All Germany, Austria, and Hungary rang with the enthusiasm aroused by his playing. And there on the Rhine, by this lovely woman's side, the great river stirred in him anew a deep and mighty emotion, and this was due to his feeling for the beauty of Marie d'Agoult, self-named the Lorelei; for it was now that Liszt set Heine's *Lorelei* to music, and a wealth of songs had their origin here, while one of his best and truest friends, Prince Lichnowsky, himself composed a poem at Nonnenwerth, which Liszt set to music. It was in the year 1843 that he dedicated to the Countess the poem entitled *The Cell of Nonnenwerth.*

Lone, alas, the cloister now
Stands amid the waters' flow,
And I see, with grief unspoken,
That for me its spell is broken.
Vineyards fair nor castles high
Work on me such wizardry,
Not the lovely hills and meads,
Nor the tale of Roland's deeds,
Nor the landscape that I see,
Cradle fair of Germany.
For the autumn's chilly breath
And the winter's icy death
Made assault. She had to flee,
She who wrought this wizardry
Upon the cloister cell, whose charms
The Rhine enfolds with loving arms.
So must I bear my grief alone
And lonely with the cell make moan.
But if some hope return to me,

Thenceforth my songs shall silent be,
And this one with its dying strain
Cries out: Come back! Come back again!

This poem was, as it were, a foreboding that this was their last stay at Nonnenwerth, and that for these two there was to be a parting of the ways.

In referring to this poem dedicated to the Countess, the Princess Wittgenstein makes her faithful creature say that with it the cell of Nonnenwerth was closed for ever. She might have added that another one awaited the composer of the song, less sunny than that on the lovely Rhine, where Franz Liszt's love for Marie d'Agoult had had such a wonderful epilogue, both in art and in reality. Never again did he compose such beautiful songs, so full of deep feeling, as during the three summers which he spent with the mother of his children at Nonnenwerth; and essentially they are all inspired by her. This is particularly true of the original and melodramatic *Ich weiss nicht, was soll es bedeuten,* and no less so of the tone-poem *Am Rhein im schönen Strome,* which tells of the miraculous image exactly resembling his beloved; but it is particularly true of his setting of Goethe's *Mignon.* In short, through her influence over the creative artist, which was apparently on the wane, the Countess now achieved the object which had been, on the whole, the only selfish motive in the feeling which caused her to follow him and belong to him for years.

But these days were at an end. Liszt was seeking new paths, and thus the rupture with the Countess came about of its own accord. She heard of his relations with that remarkable courtesan Lola Montez and now turned from him. And so, when Ramann's biography says that his complete rupture with the Countess was an act of self-preservation, this is the expression of a hypocrisy which did not originate in the heart of Franz Liszt. And it is equally false when it says: " And had not the world-famous figure of the artist, with its brilliance and beauty of character, drawn the eyes of the world to this affair at that time and surrounded it with an erotic glamour, it would have remained a local affair, a liaison like a hundred others." Liszt's relations with the Countess d'Agoult are as little to be described as a liaison as those with the Princess Wittgenstein. In both the union of hearts was on the same lofty plane, except that the Graces hovered over his connexion with the Countess d'Agoult and showered their fairest gifts upon it.

However that may be, the two parted. But how noble Marie d'Agoult's feelings were, in spite of all her agitation, disillusionment, and resentment, is clear from the poem in which she commemorated this parting:

> *Non, tu n'entendras pas de sa lèvre trop fière,*
> *Dans l'adieu déchirant un reproche, un regret.*
> *Nul trouble, nul remords pour ton âme légère*
> > *En cet adieu muet.*
> *Tu croiras qu'elle aussi, d'un vain bruit enivrée,*
> *Et des larmes d'hier oublieuse demain,*
> *Elle a d'un ris moqueur rompu la foi jurée*
> > *Et passé son chemin.*
> *Et tu ne sauras pas qu'implacable et fidèle,*
> *Pour un sombre voyage elle part sans retour;*
> *Et qu'en fuyant l'amant dans la nuit éternelle*
> > *Elle emporte l'amour.*

(No! In these heart-rending farewells neither reproach nor regret shalt thou hear from her proud lips. No trouble nor remorse shall afflict thy shallow soul in this wordless farewell. Thou wilt believe that she, too, carried away by vain rumour, and forgetting tomorrow the tears of yesterday, has broken her plighted faith with a mocking laugh and gone her way. Thou shalt not know that, implacable in her fidelity, she is starting upon a gloomy journey which has no return; and that in fleeing from her lover she bears love away with her into eternal night.)

COSIMA WAGNER

CHAPTER I

YEARS OF FORMATION

THE BREACH between Franz Liszt and the Countess d'Agoult was now an accomplished fact. If it cannot be said that this was a foregone conclusion, it was, as a matter of fact, inevitable, and it would be entirely false to throw the brunt of the blame upon this proud, beautiful, noble, and most ill-fated woman, as has been done. At any rate, it is quite futile to search for causes when temperament will explain everything. The very essence of Liszt's nature was such that he could not have acted otherwise; he longed for freedom. And the words, " I am not my own master," that he wrote to his friend Schober in Vienna were only too true. Of course, as we have already seen, he was affected by those symptoms of violent nervous agitation which are, in the nature of things, inseparable from such a parting between two people who have given themselves to each other utterly. His will was bent upon the rupture; his very nature would have demanded it even had this not been so. It must not be forgotten that Marie was older than he was, and that she was developing in a different direction from that followed by the young Liszt's great nature, for he had something of Wotan in him and could have applied to himself at this very time the words: " *Als junger Minne Lust mir verblich, begehrte nach Macht mein Mut* (As youthful love's delight from me fled, my soul grew athirst for power)." [1]

It is curious that at this very period of doubts and hesitations he sent for a work on Ahasverus (the Wandering Jew) from his library. He was, indeed, filled with an immense unrest, and

[1] *The Valkyrie*, II, ii (Newman's translation, Breitkopf edition).—Tr.

3

the urgent longing which he felt at once to display his powers as a virtuoso before the world with éclat was heightened by this nameless temperamental unrest, which could only be appeased by almost daily exercise of his lofty and unique art, which he wished once more to bring to its full consummation. Though the Countess had been known as the "Lorelei" while the sunlit days at Nonnenwerth still lasted, there was one thing that she found impossible, in spite of all her wondrous and almost magical beauty — that is, to bind to her the man whom she loved in her own fashion; and the desire to do so was ever present in her. But love was no longer her motive. Other feelings were already rising to the surface in her and were slowly transmuted by her poetic faculty into the emotions which produced the authoress Daniel Stern.

But the rupture was final. She withdrew from the house of Liszt's mother, which had for so long been her refuge and the home of her children. And such was the fascination of her personality that she was able to go her way in Parisian society without assuming any penitential sackcloth and ashes or making demonstrations of contrition before the hypocritical society of Paris. Liszt had paved the way for her return to her family, and so the parting took place in Paris itself, without in any way attracting public attention. Even the children, who remained behind with their grandmother, felt as yet only the outward effects of the parting and were still young enough not to trouble their heads about it. Perhaps it was a good thing that just at this time Liszt avoided Paris as much as possible. In this way the children were left to his mother alone. His wonderful *Lobgesang des erwachenden Kindes* (*Hymne de l'enfant à son réveil*) was, as it were, his farewell to them. His setting of Lamartine's verse: "*O père qu' adore mon père* (Father, whom my father adoreth) . . ." is full of the deepest emotion. It was in some sense a pendant to his beautiful song to Blandine *Angiolin dal biondo crin*, which he had composed during the happiest days of his great love.

The mother's feelings were otherwise. But those to which she gave expression in dedicating to her daughter the fine dialogue *Dante and Goethe* were much the same: "Your birthplace and

4

your name are Italian. Your desires and your destiny have
made you German. I was born on German soil; my star shines
in the Italian sky; and so it was my wish to dedicate to you
these reminiscences, in which Dante and Goethe are brought
together: a twofold confession of faith in which our souls meet,
an ideal home in which love indissoluble unites us, come what
may and though all things upon earth part us."

Her love for Franz had been turned to hatred by her perfectly justifiable jealousy. Brünnhilde's feeling on detecting
Siegfried's breach of his troth was no stranger to her heart:
"*Ratet nun Rache, wie nie sie geras't! Zündet mir Zorn, wie
noch nie er gezähmt* (Teach me a vengeance too dire to be told,
Stir me to wrath that may never be stilled)!"[1] And indeed all
kinds of rumours — both true and false, but no doubt for the
most part true — had come to her ears about Liszt's concert
tours and the love-adventures which accompanied them. His
whole life at that time might be regarded as one monstrous
breach of faith. Another woman, it is true — one who not only
was equally clever, but also had a little more heart — might
have forgiven him, if only for the sake of his piano-playing.
But it must not be forgotten that Liszt was then abandoning himself to these adventures somewhat wantonly and was entangled
so deeply that people even talked of a marriage with creatures
who, like Lola Montez, were bound to be abhorrent to this
woman whose inmost nature was, in spite of all, infinitely pure.
For a great gulf lay between her and that dæmonic woman,
and, if any criticism is permissible in matters of love, it is
inconceivable that any man should have crossed it. But his
heart burnt with yet other flames, and his mother in Paris
had no little difficulty in shielding her son from the catas-
trophes that threatened to ensue from his reckless amours.
But all this was of no account in comparison with the inward
conflict which drove him into such paths — which, for the rest,
had no lasting effect upon his essential nature. In a certain measure his whole being, his temperament, in whose inmost depths
raged such fearful storms, required this outlet. We know from
his own avowals that he shunned Paris and went on prolonged

[1] *The Twilight of the Gods*, II, iv (Newman's translation, Breitkopf edition).—TR.

concert tours in order to escape the influences connected with Paris. Thus, on March 3, 1845 he wrote from Gibraltar to his friend Franz von Schober, Franz Schubert's faithful comrade: " I do not know what will happen to me this spring and summer. In no circumstances shall I go to Paris. You know why. It is perhaps my unspeakably melancholy relations with . . . that had indirectly most to do with my tour in Spain and Portugal. I have no cause to regret it, though my best friends tried to dissuade me from it. At any rate, it seems to me that my mind is maturing and my sorrows growing old before their time beneath this lovely, powerful sun of Spain." But he was determined to visit the Rhine again that summer with his mother and Cosima.

Though one feels the deepest sympathy with Marie at this period, yet one is bound to admire Liszt as a father; for his thoughts hovered with infinite tenderness over the glorious trio in Paris. His care was for them. He knew that they were in good keeping, with his mother, and tried to arrange things so that their bringing-up should be as good and free from taint as possible, both spiritually and intellectually. For this reason he was extraordinarily pleased with his mother's good reports. On the other hand, a certain jealousy of Marie's interference in the arrangements for the children is apparent. He was determined to bind them wholly to himself and thus to guide their destiny entirely according to his own views. He had now attained to full maturity, for at his age the expression is legitimate. And even later, when his mother admonished him, he replied with great decision: " I cannot enter upon any other path, I cannot change my convictions and habits. The errors which I commit are not serious, they are more easily repaired than those into which I should fall as a result of other people's promptings. So far I cannot seriously be reproached with having steered the ship of my life badly. I can find none among my fellow-artists who has succeeded any better. I see, it is true, that if I do not mean to be a fool or an imbecile, I must exchange this vessel for a better one, more comfortable and roomy. Very well, then! A lot of cumbersome ballast will go overboard; but I shall make my landing where and when I choose."

But the first thing was gradually to estrange the children from their mother, without making them too conscious of the rupture and separation. Blandine had been sent to Madame Bernard's boarding-school, where he knew that she was in safe keeping; notwithstanding, he wrote to his mother: " As regards Blandine, I must enjoin upon you the greatest discretion. Only let me know all that goes on; as soon as I come to Paris, I shall manage to arrive at the most fitting decision. Without any special instructions, you have complied with my wishes so well and naturally that I need no longer give you any further explanations. Only observe the same propriety in future, the same moderation and goodwill. In case of need, consult Madame Bernard about how to dispose of the holidays, and keep me informed of what happens. Sooner or later we must settle matters more definitely; for the present we can only be patient."

He was very glad when he received news that Madame d'Agoult was returning to her husband. For anxiety as to what designs she might have regarding the children occupied his mind incessantly during his travels. But he saw in a return to her old ties the wisest and most proper course. This was hard, and perhaps heartless; but, as he said: " Sooner or later it is bound to come. In this way, too, the question of the children would be simplified appreciably. In the mean time I rely upon you to see that no steps are taken contrary to my views and wishes concerning them." He was willing to see the Countess again in Brussels, but not in Paris. In this his paternal sentiments were affected by those of the injured lover and ardent young artist. For at the very time when he broke with the Countess d'Agoult, he had had a meeting with the young and lovely Countess de Saint-Cricq, now Madame d'Artigaux, who was living down in the south, at Pau, and had not forgotten him. He gave her a beautiful bracelet as a talisman, set with a large blue turquoise, which had come into his possession in St. Petersburg. He was still an incorrigible romantic, and it was only in what concerned his children that he was on firm ground. For as early as May 1845 he sent his mother a copy of " a splendid memorandum drawn up by a lawyer on the subject of the children," which put an end to all his uncertainties. " Show it to Massart and keep it by you. I shall expect your answer, as well as Massart's, at Lyons, and hope that both will be satisfactory, so that I may be spared a journey to Paris at a time when I have nothing to call me there."

But in the mean time Cosima's education had also begun. I have before me a remarkable childish letters of hers in verse, probably the first lines traced by a hand which was so diligent for a whole lifetime. It is a letter to Frau Anna Liszt on her name-day.

My DEAR GRANDMOTHER,

Whom alone have I to thank for life's delights? Who is it that approached me so lovingly with tender glances? I feel it and shall never forget it. For all my happiness — are you.

COSIMA LISZT

And at the very moment when Liszt was taking steps to secure his three children's future by legitimizing them, Cosima wrote him the first of her letters to which I have had access:

My DEAR PAPA,

Thank you a thousand times for finding time to write me such a sweet letter. I shall take pains to follow your good advice. Mademoiselle Camille is pleased with me, and when you return to Paris, you will be able to see that I have profited by my piano-lessons.

For it is worthy of note that the piano already played a great part in the child's life.

But she flourished in spite of all. Thus her grandmother wrote in September: " I hesitate to send Cosima to boarding-school; I think of keeping her myself for another year. She does her lessons nicely at home and has certainly missed nothing yet. She is still delicate and is growing fast. Her *nourriture* consists of cutlets, ' biff tea,' and leg of mutton. She does not need much food, but it must be nourishing. But if you absolutely desire me to send her to boarding-school in October, I will do so; but

I think I should soon have to take her away again on account of her health, and the money would be thrown away." Such a grandmother, whom we may well compare with Frau Aja, is really touching. But Cosima herself longed with all the vehemence of her nature to join her sister Blandine at school. On October 8 her grandmother was already writing to Liszt: " I hereby inform you of my decision with regard to Cosima, at which I did not arrive till a week ago. I sent her to school at Madame Bernard's on the 5th of this month. She went back with Blandine at the end of the holidays. The little mad thing (*cette petite folle*) demanded it of me *à grands cris* (with loud cries), and Blandine never stopped trying to make her stay with me. She was better than I ever saw her before, and so too were Blandine and Daniel, who has now also gone to a tutor. At Madame Bernard's Cosima at once had lessons from a Mademoiselle Chazarin, who had just become a mistress there. She requested me to ask you what method you wish Cosima to study with her. She is awaiting your answer." Liszt was highly delighted at this turn of affairs: " I cannot but approve in every way your decision to board out Cosima and Daniel. It is impossible for you to keep Daniel any longer — except at night, when he is asleep — and I think Cosima will be very happy at Madame Bernard's. Please convey my thanks to Mlle Chazarin, whom I hope to thank in person in the course of the next year. Tell her that I am sure she is directing Cosima's musical studies in the right way. All I wish is that Cosima should practise reading music and gradually learn to play from memory." He also sent some music for the children, who were nearer than ever to his heart; and he received very nice letters from them, especially from Cosima, giving him a detailed account of the progress of her studies. The harmony between the three children was touching. They were three regular cherubs, who were never seen apart. The relation existing between these four — grandmother and grandchildren — was a wonderful one. Yet all their dreams and thoughts turned upon their father. A line from him transported them with ecstasy. Franz Liszt's mother described the reception of their father's letter as follows: " Blandine and Cosima were quite beside themselves with joy at getting a letter from you. Daniel, too, already

takes far more interest when I get a letter from you, so when
you write next, do add a few lines specially for him. The poor,
beautiful little fellow! I wrote to you once this summer that I
found him *stoique,* because he took so little interest in many
things at which the girls would weep — it might be at a conversation or at something they read or at a letter from you — but
now I take back my words. He is not *stoique;* he showed that
on parting with his sisters, when I took them away to school. I
was afraid that I should have him ill. He longed for them and
kept saying that he wanted to go to Cosima and Blandine; we
represented to him that that could not be, because it was a girls'
school. '*Eh bien,*' he said, ' dress me in one of Cosima's dresses
and put one of her hats on my head, and then I shall be like a
girl too ' — and so on. I went oftener than usual to see the girls
and took him with me. Once I asked Madame Bernard whether,
supposing Daniel were to ask her to take him into her school,
she would say to him herself that this was impossible; and so
she did. Since then he has said no more about it and is sensible
on the subject."

The Liszts' home in Paris, which it was their father's intention to expand into a house of their own — at least, for a long
time he was occupied with plans for building one on the boulevard Montparnasse — formed the background of a remarkable
existence. A succession of his friends went in and out of the
house in the rue Louis-le-Grand. Some of them were old acquaintances, whom Liszt's absence did not prevent from maintaining friendly relations with his mother, and who, as time went
on, exerted a great influence over the children too. In the first
place there were the Seghers, Érard, and Kroll families, and all
Liszt's acquaintances who came to Paris sought out this house.
In the year 1847, again, he wrote: " My household in Paris,
which consists of you and my three children — with the addition
of Belloni as your adviser — ought to run like clock-work. My
position in Europe is more complicated, for there I depend upon
some hundred persons. All the same, do not be alarmed — I
shall soon make them dance to my piping, however much they
try to resist. And in order to preserve my full freedom for
the development of my career and my future, I must be able to

count upon it as a certainty that, though I cannot direct it myself, my Paris establishment is kept up in fitting style."

Before this letter, it is true, nothing had been heard from him for a long time. But all this time the children's education had been going on quietly. Cosima in particular had always turned towards her father. The older she grew, the more ardently she longed for him, with a touch of waywardness that was characteristic of her. Thus she wrote to him as follows: " It is a long time since I wrote to you, and the New Year is drawing near, and I hope that it will be a good one for you and for our whole family, and that God may grant you health for long years to come. Belloni holds out the hope that we may see you again in March, and it will be a great joy for the whole family when you return. At present I am learning Weber's *Invitation to the Waltz* as a solo. It is quite a hard piece for me, for I am not very strong, but I shall take pains to play it without a mistake." And she gave an account of her progress — how she had not won any prizes, but hoped to bring home several next year, " for it would be a disgrace if I did not win any. During the holidays we went to Havre and bathed in the sea, which did us a great deal of good, except Daniel, who was ill, but has now fortunately recovered his health." The children were brought up in an atmosphere of the deepest piety, and Cosima in particular was a remarkably devout child. On May 3, 1847 she wrote to her father: " In this letter I inform you of the greatest event in my life; that is, I am to take my first communion on June 21. I am very anxious for you to be present, and in the interval I shall expect you impatiently. I hoped that you would already have arrived on the 15th of the present month, but we have been disappointed in our expectations for so long past." And she informed him that she was playing Mozart's sonatas. She seemed indeed to be making great progress on the piano.

But her hope of welcoming her father on that solemn day was not fulfilled, and a short time afterwards she wrote: " Thanks for answering my letter so quickly. I am writing this to inform you of a solemn event — no more nor less than my first communion. I was confirmed a week after receiving Jesus Christ into my heart for the first time. I was very happy during those beautiful days, which seemed only too short. Nothing was wanting to my happiness but you. For at such moments it is a great joy to have all those one loves about one. Grandmamma came every time, and this was a great joy to me. I hope that I shall become worthy of the grace which God has vouchsafed to me. I prayed earnestly for you, and above all for Monsieur Bucquet, my confessor. He takes a great interest in us and is very kind to us — his good counsels will support us in our efforts to lead a good life. Now the holidays are beginning; shall we see you during this time? You have too long postponed this visit, which would make us so happy, but I am sure that this is not your fault, and that you, too, cherish the desire to see us."

Quite a vigorous strain runs through this young creature's letters, and in relation to her father she quite plays the Erlkönig: "*Und wenn du nicht willst, so brauch' ich Gewalt* (And art thou not willing, I'll take thee by force)." This attitude grew more marked as years passed by, during which her understanding of him increased. For it was no secret to the children — especially to Cosima — that their father was one of the greatest artists and grandest men of the day.

It should be understood that Frau Anna watched carefully over the children and prevented any cause of dissension from arising between their father and mother. For from the very beginning Liszt laid down as the watchword of their education: "Honour thy father *and* thy mother." But the children were not to mention their mother in his presence. This was naturally hard and, had it not been for the influence of Frau Anna, might perhaps have done harm. But she was on the alert, and her nature almost always inclined her rather towards the children's side than her son's, though she loved him beyond everything and, so long as he lived, did not abandon her motherly tutelage, however much he might struggle against it.

But in the interval he had, so to speak, placed himself under another tutelage. We see how his mother observed the great artist's silence with a certain uneasiness. She followed his progress, it is true, in the papers, which brought almost daily reports of his prodigiously brilliant successes and his more and more extensive tours. There could be no question of material anxieties, for the faithful Belloni remitted handsome sums for both Liszt's mother and his children. But she felt, as it were, a secret anxiety about his destiny, together with a slight touch of jealousy and mortification at the fact that he did not write to her, for she wanted to be assured that her own tender affection was reciprocated.

And then there was the political unrest, which, however, left their home untouched. Cosima writes that on account of the disturbances in Paris she had gone to her grandmother, but that, in spite of the unrest, the teachers had continued their lessons. Meanwhile the condition of affairs in Paris was far from clear, and Frau Anna regarded the whole situation with a certain dissatisfaction: " The Republic is to all appearances in rather a bad way," she writes, " and God knows what will happen next in France, or in other countries either, for the whole of Europe is in a ferment. What have our children still to go through — the Seghers family were *enchanté* with the Republic in February, like many others, but to hear them now they are something other than *enchantés*. They see the future in even darker colours than the present. I will not *attrister* (grieve) myself too much prematurely. God watches over his own and often saves them in their greatest need."

But now, after much inward perplexity and confusion, and a period of effervescence which we can pardon in the darling of all the women in Europe, Franz Liszt was approaching a new turn in his destiny. He had not been without sympathy for the Revolution. Yet at this time he felt himself a Hungarian before all things and took a pride in wearing the Hungarian cockade. But, much as he hoped, from the intellectual point of view, that an era of truth and justice was now dawning — and in this respect he went much further than his former teacher and friend the Père Lamennais — yet this revolution was no more than the background for a vast upheaval and revulsion which now took place in his inner nature and above all, too, in his destiny.

In the course of his concert tour in February 1847 he had arrived in Kiev. The city produced a profound and pleasing impression upon him. It was rich in colour and bore every outward mark of the Orient. He gave a concert there, at which one lady sent him a hundred-rouble note for her place. This lady, unique in her kind, was the Princess Carolyne von Sayn-Wittgenstein, who owned estates in that region. A Pole by birth, she was at the same time a Russian subject. Her father was Peter Ivanovsky, a great landowner and a vastly rich man, who had married Pauline Podoska, the daughter of a neighbouring landowner. Carolyne was their only child. Born on February 8, 1819 at Monastyrzyska, she was a creature as passionate as she was imaginative, possessing at the same time most forceful qualities of mind and will. She was the true daughter of a man who held sway over thirty thousand subjects, in a state of slavish dependence upon him, and who seldom laid aside the knout. Carolyne, too, seemed to be both uncontrolled and uncontrollable. Governesses without number were found for her. They came and went, for they could not master this untamable creature. At last an elderly woman was found, Madame Patersi de Fossombroni, who really gained an influence over this girl who was like an unbroken colt. Carolyne was devoted to this governess up to her death, and in later days entrusted her with one of the most important of missions — the education of Liszt's daughters.

Perhaps Madame Patersi's authority was principally due to the positiveness of her social ideas; she was avowedly *ancien régime*, and we find that in later days she made, as it were, no concessions to the life around her, but looked life itself, and what life brought with it, boldly in the face. She was a highly energetic person. It cannot be said that she had anything of the abbess about her, though she had to a certain extent taken religion as the basis of her educational method. She did not keep her first pupil aloof from the life of the world; on the contrary, she recognized it as necessary for a woman's development that she, too, should take up an attitude of her own towards the course of events and important personalities. With such a wealthy heiress this came about naturally. From the outset her father had looked upon her as the mistress and ruler of his broad estates. But Madame Patersi's young pupil was intelligent and clever and, what is more, unusually eager to learn. She took possession, so to speak, of books and their contents as though they were parcels of land. While still quite young, she was re-

garded throughout the whole of Poland and far into Russia as
a woman of exceptional learning and was nicknamed Miss Cato
or Miss Scipio; but when she was presented to the Emperor
Nicholas I, she infuriated rather than charmed him. She seemed
to him the very type of Polish womanhood, of which he used to
say: " I should soon have disposed of the Poles if only I could
first subdue the Polish women." But when her father tried to
steady her by entrusting her with the administration of his great
estates, her spirit aspired towards something more than this. In
the year 1836, indeed, while still young, and with a heart all
unconscious of what awaited her, she was married to Prince
Nicholas von Sayn-Wittgenstein! A child of nature and at the
same time a learned woman, she was vastly superior to her
young and insignificant husband in all personal qualities and,
what is more, in breeding and education, while financially, too,
she was the real mistress. Her spendthrift husband made havoc
of his wife's great fortune. But now, in her disconsolate and
embittered state, comfort came to her. In February 1837 she
gave birth to a daughter, whom she intended to bring up according to her own ideas and after her own heart and whom she
sought to remove from this atmosphere. She retired with the
" child," as Richard Wagner afterwards called the little Princess when she was growing up, to a distant estate, Woronince,
where she administered the property and devoted her life to
educating herself in all branches of learning. She became a
Hegelian and was thus directed towards the arts. She studied
Goethe and was inspired to write a commentary on his *Faust*.
From Goethe she was led to Dante. These were the two poles
between which the intellectual and spiritual experiences of
Marie d'Agoult also gravitated, and to which she remained true
till death.

It was Dante who had the most profound influence upon Franz
Liszt's soul and imagination, though in a different way from
Marie; but under the influence of Carolyne, Liszt's interpretation of him was essentially modified. He made the Princess's
acquaintance at Kiev and was fascinated by her qualities, while
she too was quite absorbed in him and the type which he
represented. She did not approach him and his performances

uncritically. As we know, she at once drew a distinction between his qualities as a virtuoso and as an artist. But when for the first time she heard one of his compositions — it was his *Pater noster* — she was profoundly affected by it, and henceforth she was inseparable from him. They met again at Odessa and were mutually fascinated, she attracting him at least as much as he did her. She invited him to her estate at Woronince, where she commissioned him to compose music for her. It was at this time that Frau Anna waited in vain for news of her son and wrote reproachfully that she had heard nothing from him for more than four months. But here it was that the whole subsequent course of his life was decided, and the place of the lovely fair-haired Lorelei was now taken by the Princess, who completely dominated him. Many were the discussions and consultations that took place on this lonely estate. She undoubtedly acquired an influence over his art and his artistic ideas and desired to lead him to the very greatest heights in music; and it was, in fact, there, in the profound solitude of that remote estate, that the first sketch of his *Dante Symphony* came into being, and much besides. A poem echoed in his memory, as from afar: "*Ce qu'on entend sur la montagne.*"

It was by Victor Hugo, in whom Marie d'Agoult, too, was so intensely interested at that very time. The Princess herself, passionately though she loved him, and passionate as was his feeling for her, inclined his thoughts and sentiments more and more towards clerical and Catholic ideas. Once at Bologna he had stood with Marie before Raphael's picture of St. Cecilia, and there he was so touched by the infinitely spiritualized charm of Raphael's creation that his sense of the unity of religion and music had become extraordinarily intensified. It was now quite another muse that he had at his side, earnest, indeed, but inspiring him with her flashing eyes — yet leading him to a deeper and more sombre outlook upon life and emotional experience.

It cannot, however, be said that their love was mainly influenced by any theoretical considerations. The discovery of their passion was mutual, and they determined upon flight and marriage. The difficulties which stood in the way of the latter were, indeed, endless; but the intention of both was great and pure, and Liszt faced all opposition in a spirit of chivalry. He brought the Princess to the Altenburg at Weimar, and there they established the home to which he himself came only later and in defiance of the small-minded society of Weimar. The Altenburg became a supreme focus of intellectual and artistic life, where Liszt ruled; and perhaps his rule would have been even more brilliant and resplendent had it not been for the strong constraint exerted over him by the Princess. But we must not cavil; her intentions at least were great, and she desired the highest from the man whom she loved. And now Frau Anna too heard of this metamorphosis of her son. On September 15, 1848 she wrote in the margin of her letter: " My humble respects to the Princess." As a matter of fact, the Princess was bent upon establishing relations with Liszt's mother at once, and even invited her to Weimar forthwith; but this fresh turn in the life of her son, whom fortune had so strangely guided and exalted, did not move the old lady overmuch. To one with her direct and simple nature, which was yet so strongly tinged with fancy, it was only natural. And when the Princess wrote her letters addressing her as " Mother," she wrote to her son as though nothing unusual had happened: " Present my thanks to the good Princess for her affectionate letter to me. Though I often have news of you from her, I should so much like to have a few lines from yourself. Your health is better, *La Princesse* told me; I can quite understand it — with these sad things which have happened in so many countries and have now gone on for nearly a year, and which still appear to offer no reassurance for the future. How many of your acquaintance and friends must have met with misfortune! — this may have had much to do with your ill health; how could you have remained indifferent, with your sensibilities? Belloni told me that you have written something definite to J. Janin about your marriage with the Princess, which is apparently to take place in April, when you will pay us a visit. Is this true? Do tell me too." She gently reminded him of the children and their progress and seems to lay stress upon this point for the express purpose of not losing her influence for the children's sake. She had watched over everything, she said. Under her wing, as we have seen, Cosima had taken her first

communion, and in writing to the Princess, too, she speaks about
the children in a way that seems decidedly pointed. Thus she
writes: " Noble Princess, I thank you heartily for your affectionate letter of the 13th, which was so sympathetic and full of
kind wishes, on the happy occasion of the great step which
Cosima took on the 21st at the Church of St. Sulpice, and of
which I was a deeply moved spectator. My son's letter to Cosima
caused great joy, the children love their father beyond words.
When I talk of him to them, I always see tears in their eyes,
they are tender-hearted creatures. Your health, noble Princess,
is fairly good now, is it not? God be praised. Try to bear up —
with philosophy to aid you, and time and circumstances often
change so much, and such will be the case for you too, and you
will gain your ends. My son is well, too, and is working indus-
triously, so I understand from your most valued letter. In times
like the present, when there is so much to afflict one, health is a
possession above all price, and occupation serves to distract one,
so that one does not think so much of the universal misery that
prevails in so many countries. I kiss you in thought, noble Princess, and my son too, and am, with the highest esteem and respect, your most devoted mother, A. Liszt." In August she
describes to the Princess how they had celebrated the Feast of
St. Anne, which she had spent quite merrily with her three children: " They are very good-natured and good. The two girls
recited beautiful verses to me in German, Blandine about St.
Augustine, and how he wanted to solve the mystery of the Holy
Trinity by the sea-side (*am Bord de mer*), and how an angel
appeared to him; and Cosima about heaven. Daniel came, too,
bringing his own compositions in German, in which, as you can
see for yourself, *Madame la Princesse,* the phrases are more
français than German. You see, noble Princess, that I am not
afraid of boring you with my chatter about the children, because
I have entire trust in your tender heart and am confident that it
cannot be unpleasant to you to hear about all that concerns me
or my son." Thus she places, as it were, the Princess's future
duties as a mother to Liszt's children quite definitely and clearly
before her eyes. But even before this she had already touched
upon deeper matters and, so to speak, sounded her from the re-

ligious point of view too on the subject of her future marriage. All this was of the highest importance for the children's future. She herself was too pious, and at the same time realized that a religious conflict in her son's heart could give rise to nothing but unrest and trouble; and so she writes: "Noble Princess, I am ashamed to suggest any doubts in this matter about which you have sent me such a prompt answer in reply to the question I addressed to my son. Forgive me, I should never have ventured to put this question to you, noble Princess. But since you have answered me, and so decisively, I am heartily glad and thank you very much. The Catholic religion, in which the laws regulating these things are so extraordinarily strict, is somewhat less severe in Poland. What a joyful hope for me! — though it will indeed cost you some struggles yet to gain your end. But since the possibility exists, ah! then I have no further doubt that you, noble Princess, with your great force of character and firm will, can accomplish it. So may God grant my son the grace to make you happy, thoroughly happy, to transform the sufferings you have endured into joys, and I, noble Princess, who esteem you so highly and love you without having the honour to know you personally, though I have a great desire to do so — but your letters tell me what a noble soul dwells in you — I will always continue to pray to the Almighty for your health and happiness."

Meanwhile, however, the children were developing quite brilliantly, and it is particularly astonishing how fast they progressed in music. They played Haydn, Beethoven, and Weber duets. The whole of music passed before them, and Seghers had a really splendid influence, especially on the younger daughter's understanding of music. He invited her to one of his concerts, so as to bring her into even closer contact with music. And now something further was added. "We have just been given a dancing-master. His name is Strauss and he is a brother of the one who composed the waltzes. I shall work very hard, for Madame de St. Mars tells me that in the street I look thoroughly Austrian," wrote little Cosima, rather impishly.

They worked at everything. They read German, even Pyrker's out-of-the-way poem *Die Perlen der heiligen Vorzeit,* and then Schiller's *Die Kraniche des Ibykus* and Tieck's *Epilog auf*

19

Goethe. Cosima recited *Die Teilung der Erde* and translated a
a fable of La Fontaine into German. In English they read the
Midsummer Night's Dream and Lord Byron's *Roman Daughter;*
so the children were undoubtedly in the best of hands, while
Liszt's destiny and that of the Princess were beginning to develop into a tragedy, thanks to the envy of men and the un-
propitiousness of circumstances.

And now Frau Anna's noble and sound sense proved itself in
her attitude towards the Princess. She discussed financial conditions with her son and pointed out how her own husband had
married her without any financial provision, and how money
in no way ensures happiness. There is something infinitely
touching in hearing this simple-minded woman speaking thus.
But to the Princess herself she writes: " I beg you yourself, noble
Princess, not to be at all disturbed or offended at these odious
questions of property which concern you. Take care of your
health, which is the greatest good in human life. With great love
on both sides it is possible to be happy even with little — perhaps, indeed, with far less than you possess — love makes helpful. My son can and will earn so as to make your life as pleasant
as possible, put your trust in him, you do love him, and time
often changes many things, and I believe it is not impossible that
in this way fate may be kinder to you after a few years; and,
if not all, at any rate a large part of your fortune may come back
to you. Even if this hope prove vain, rise superior to it, and
call philosophy to your aid — and, besides, I repeat that love
endures much, very much."

But meanwhile Liszt had come to a forcible decision with
regard to the children's education. A letter of Frau Anna to her
son may have had some influence upon this: " A dark cloud is
hanging over me, I hope and pray that it will pass away. Belloni
told me that Madame d'Agoult sought him out and talked to
him about the children, whom she wanted to see; she even
wanted the girls to be removed to another school, with an *institu-
trice* to themselves. Belloni observed to her that this would add
very much to the expense, upon which she said that she would
contribute towards it. I beg you not to consent to this proposal,
let things remain as they are, a change of schools is seldom ad-

vantageous. Besides, I am afraid that she may give the children tastes (*gout machte*) which may be very detrimental to them later on. Pains have been taken to bring them up simply. Madame Bernard is a very sensible woman and understands her business. She brings the children up in good ways of virtue and piety, and if, as is perhaps not far distant now — for so you yourself tell me — you are one day the Princess's legitimate husband, then I hope, too, that you will no longer be so far away from the children, or from me either; Perhaps the children and I may even live in the same house as you and your wife. Such are the dreams I cherish, then you could come to their aid with advice (*conseils*) which would have great influence with them, because they love you so much. The Princess, too, would not disdain to help them with her lofty intelligence, for she has great ability of soul. I repeat, that I often dream such beautiful things about it, do you think this dream can ever be fulfilled? Madame d'Agoult is quite well able to find distraction without assuming any share in the education of these children. She is always writing, it could only be an interruption to her. I meant to tell you, besides, how she also told Belloni that she will provide for these children, each of them receiving a sum of 20,000 francs after her death. But I do not believe a word of it. Five months ago she spoke of 20,000 francs, which each of them was to receive after her death. No, it was 10,000, now it is 20,000, eight years ago it was 100,000. Adieu, dear child! "

It is clear that Frau Anna, too, considered their mother's influence rather more objectionable than it was. However that may be, it was while in Weimar that Liszt definitely decided to entrust the education of his children, and especially of his daughters, to Madame Patersi. She was summoned from St. Petersburg, and travelled straight to Paris by way of Weimar. The old lady did not consider the railway quite *comme il faut*. She was still accustomed to the dashing carriages of Russia and considered it absolutely improper to lean back against the cushions of a railway carriage; so she actually made the long journey from St. Petersburg to Weimar — in so far, that is, as it could be made by the railway — sitting bolt upright. It was no wonder that she arrived in Weimar seriously ill and had to let herself be nursed for two months by her pupil the Princess. But during this time she won Liszt's heart as well, though he felt a strong antipathy, and even mistrust, for certain of the old lady's eccentric qualities. But he recognized that in this energetic personality would be found a strong ally in counteracting any influence on the part of Madame d'Agoult. It was quite certain that any attempts of the mother's would make no impression upon Madame Patersi. He was mainly induced to adopt this almost hostile attitude by Marie's recently published novel *Nélida*, which bore only too evident witness to a love transformed into hatred. Far too much importance has been ascribed to this novel, however, even by Liszt himself. It is by no means the best of her works, and it must be admitted that the book had better not have been written; but we ought not to forget from what emotions this highly gifted and remarkable woman, the course of whose life had been so utterly deranged, had to recover before she could find herself. From a purely human point of view this was only possible if she could, so to speak, clear up her position, though in an exaltedly poetical and even distorted fashion, towards the man who was everything to her. This is a psychological problem which ought not to be judged by everyday standards. *Nélida* is a mediocre novel and a tactless book. But Marie's strength, without any doubt, lay chiefly in her treatment of historical and æsthetic questions, and especially in the delineation of character. However that may be, the book appeared, and, moreover, all sorts of malicious reports had reached Weimar, which only confirmed the antagonism. When she heard of the new establishment at the Altenburg, she is said to have remarked — in allusion to earlier relations — " Then she will indeed have to make the desert blossom like the rose (*Da wird sie Rhododendron in Alkai's Einöden pflücken müssen*)." She had supposed herself to have been mistaken in Liszt; and that he was only a virtuoso, not, as she had desired and intended, a creative artist. But now news reached Paris that he was meditating great new works, and that the Princess's influence had awakened the genuine artist in him. It was this that cut her to the soul. But Liszt, too, was most deeply wounded, and under the influence of this feeling he wrote to his mother on October

COUNTESS MARIE D'AGOULT

After a painting at Wahnfried

25, 1850: " I should have preferred that these lines should be delivered to you by Madame Patersi, to whom I request you to hand over both my daughters, since I desire to entrust her with their education from now onwards. I thank you with all my heart for all the love with which you have taken charge of the children during the last few months, and they too, as well as myself, will always be grateful to you for the care which you have bestowed upon their early childhood. Unfortunately Madame Patersi fell ill immediately on arriving here and cannot reach Paris for a fortnight to come. But since you are moving, her sister, Madame Saint Mars, who will live with her and my daughters at No. 6 rue Casimir-Périer, faubourg Saint-Germain, will be so good as to fetch the children away and keep them with her until the arrival of Madame Patersi. On receipt of this letter, therefore, will you hand over Blandine and Cosima to her care? Will you also be so kind, dear Mother, as to have such furniture as I have indicated, together with everything else necessary for housekeeping, which you assure me you can spare, removed to the above-mentioned residence of Madame Patersi. I hope that you will often give my daughters the pleasure of joining them at their meals, and I wish Daniel, too, to visit Madame Patersi's house frequently. They will also require table-silver for six persons, glass and china, table- and bed-linen. I should have to buy all these new and should be much obliged if you could let them have as much of them as you do not require yourself. I have requested Madame Patersi to call upon you frequently with my daughters, and to escort them everywhere. I am sure that on closer acquaintance you will esteem her, and even be fond of her, when you see that she has a good influence on the children. It is for her alone to decide what they are or are not to be allowed to do. She knows my ideas on their education and future, which are in complete accord with her own. Under her influence I hope that the evil effects of their education as directed by Madame Bernard, which are so distressing to me, will soon disappear."

And so, even before the arrival of the Russian governess, the children were handed over to her relative Madame Saint Mars. It was not till later that the great instructress herself arrived,

this time with another letter to his mother, which may be regarded as in some sort a sequel to the fundamental laws laid
down by Liszt for his daughters' education: " Madame Patersi
brings you my wishes for the happy celebration of October 22.
I hope that you have stood the troubles of moving splendidly
and are enjoying flourishing health. Where exactly are you living now? Have you moved nearer to the children or farther off?
Write me in more detail about this in your next letter, so that I
may know where and how you have found a nest. Since Madame
Patersi naturally requires a number of books, I beg you to place
the whole of my small library at her disposal. I should even be
glad if the greater part of the books were sent to her house, so
as to furnish the children's schoolroom. It gives me great satisfaction that my daughters are growing up in normal and in
every way satisfactory conditions. Madame Patersi's distinguished character and ripe experience give me the justifiable
hope that my earnest endeavour to assure them a fitting future
will be crowned with success. I have no doubt that you will enter
into pleasant relations with her and welcome the new state of
affairs, which I trust, with God's help, will last until the girls
marry." The Princess too set, as it were, her seal to this significant document. " By October 22 of next year I hope to have the
happiness of belonging to you as a daughter in name too, for I
have felt for long past how entirely my heart was yours. I need
hardly tell you how I greet every return of this day [1] with exalted
thanks to God for all the happiness that your son gives me, for
not a day passes without establishing our happiness even more
securely, and uniting us still more intimately in the bonds of
mutual affection. May you pass the day, dear Mother, in the
happy consciousness that God's blessing rests upon your children. I am glad that, during the two months that Madame Patersi has spent with us, your son has come to know her thoroughly and has entrusted his daughters to her with absolute
confidence. It fills me with a deep joy, and I hope that you, too,
rejoice to know that they are under such wise and tender
protection."

Frau Anna was by no means overjoyed at this sudden turn

[1] Liszt's birthday. — Tr.

of affairs, and the children, too, were alarmed at first, while a certain opposition undoubtedly made itself felt in Cosima to these categorical stipulations of her father's, against which certain feelings of her child's heart protested. But in the end she could not but bow to her father's wishes, nor did she wish to do otherwise. How hard she found it is clear from the following words: " I want to make up for the injustice I did you in thought by an entire submission to your will. The letter you wrote caused me pain, but it also made me feel to the full how wrong I was. I am of course full of grief at leaving Mademoiselle Laure, whom I love dearly and who has taken such a great interest in me. But since I know that you have reasons for separating me from her, I submit to my fate. I am most eager to see you again, but while waiting for this happy day I submit, and we are working so as to do credit to your name, as you say in your letter to me." And a few days later she sends an even fuller answer to her father, who was now somewhat mollified: " This letter, which I so longed to receive, gave me great joy, and I am answering it for your birthday. I wish that all heaven's blessings may descend upon you and make you happy. Your letter gave me food for thought. You are dissatisfied with the vagueness of my letter, in which I lay too little stress upon what happens. I shall take pains not to give you cause for dissatisfaction again. In future I shall endeavour always to keep you informed of the course of my studies, and I ask your pardon for my negligence. I have a request to make, that I hope you will not refuse. Fräulein Kautz has stopped our musical studies for the present, since she does not know whether you approve of her giving us lessons. She has always shown the greatest zeal for us, and it would be very painful to me to leave her. I have started Hummel's concerto; it is a very fine piece, which has given me pleasure for some time past. I am redoubling my zeal, so as to learn to play it as best I can, for the piece is, of course, far beyond my powers. When I play it, I always think of you, for Grandmamma has told me that you have played it at your concerts.

" Madame de Saint Mars has produced the effect upon me that you had reason to expect. She is full of good feeling and virtues and is nicer to us every day, but I tell you frankly that I

felt great grief at leaving Grandmamma. It seems to me that it
would be the greatest ingratitude to feel no grief at leaving a
grandmother who has shown us so much kindness. But Madame
de Saint Mars is so kind that I am already quite accustomed to
her and am really fond of her. I am perfectly ready to feel the
same towards Madame Patersi, whom you praise so highly. In
order not to waste all our time, we have shared the lessons of
Madame Patersi's niece till she arrives. After her arrival everything will naturally have to be arranged. This niece, who is
called Mademoiselle Ducoudray, is very well educated, she has
passed two examinations, which I think of taking too later on.
She gives us instruction in grammar, geography, arithmetic, and
history. This is the subject which interests me most. I have started
modern history again, as well as mediæval. I have worked up
Roman history from the middle of the Republic onwards, for I
know quite well that this is the best way to begin. I am now reading Boileau's *Satires*, which I find charming. I prefer the ninth
Satire, in which the author apostrophizes his own wit (*esprit*)
and in which he disposes so wittily and subtly of the authors
whom he wants to make fun of. I have finished the epistle which
he dedicated to the King on the joys of peace. I think I like this
even better than the *Satires*. I have also read an epistle which
he dedicated to Racine, to comfort him for the intrigues which
so weighed upon the great writer's spirits when he saw that the
works of lesser writers were preferred to his own. I consider this
section very beautiful, written in a very finely wrought and
finished style. It also contains a parallel which touched me
deeply — namely, with Molière: I like that best. I have also
read Augustin Thierry's *La Conquête de l'Angleterre par les
Normands*, which interested me very much and was very useful
for understanding the history of England. I like the Saxons far
better than the Normans, but I have never liked Harold. I do
not consider it a good action to swear to free one's country and
then not to give it freedom. At Grandmamma's I had a dispute
with an Englishwoman on this point, who preferred the Normans,
which I could never understand. In English, too, I am now reading several pieces by Shakspere, such as *King Lear, Henry V,
Henry IV, Henry VI, Coriolanus, Macbeth*, and *Julius Cæsar*.

All of them interested me enormously, but I prefer *Macbeth* and have learnt by heart the passage in which the hero sees a dagger before him — that is the finest in the whole piece. I prefer Shakspere to Corneille, but I like Racine better than either.

" Last time I was at the Invalides Madame Petit asked me to recall her to your memory and to ask if you would let us pay her a visit. I hope that you will allow this. The General has always shown us great kindness, and it is a pleasure to us to see him. And now, dear Papa, I hope that you will not be dissatisfied with this letter. I am very depressed. All my life long I will always do everything to give you pleasure, and I hope that you will always find in me a daughter who comes up to your expectations."

So, willy-nilly, the daughters had to get used to Madame Patersi, and as a matter of fact the education which this lady gave them was no mean one. It is true that she also had recourse to the aid of the clergy and once even took them to the Père Ventura, who had a great reputation in Paris at that time. What Blandine writes about this is not without interest: " He received us with quite particular kindness, and when Madame Patersi spoke to him about the great fault which we had committed, he said that that was past now, and no more need be said about it. But he then added: ' Now, children, you must obey your father blindly, even if you do not understand the reasons by which he is guided. You will know them much later, and then you will see that he has never acted save in your best interests.' We then asked him for his blessing, which he gave us in the most solemn fashion, besides which he gave us and Madame Patersi a cross, and medals which had been blessed by the Pope." On their father's name-day they went to the Madeleine, where the Père Ventura preached to a large congregation. Before he started his sermon there was a terrible uproar and a crush which almost amounted to a tumult. But the sermon itself, so Blandine relates, was brilliant. He preached on the necessity of good works and ended by venturing into the domain of politics.

Besides this the children had also to attend many concerts. We hear of them going to those of Reinecke and Berlioz. In general, instruction in music, as well as in literature, played a great part in their education. Cosima made rapid progress in languages. Proof of this is a letter of June 5, 1851, which is already written in English. In it she describes to her father her progress both in speaking and in writing English. But there is a certain charm when in her English chatter she also tells of her German studies, and especially of Schiller, whose works her grandmother had procured for her: " I find great beauties in this author. I particularly like *Wilhelm Tell,* and I reflect that this was written for the Swiss, who have been delivered from the misfortune of servitude. In a word, this Schiller has in-comparable qualities."

Their father could indeed feel nothing but joy at such letters; but his daughters also took the liveliest interest in his creative work. Even before they had been placed in charge of Madame Patersi, Cosima wrote that she had seen in the *Gazette musicale* how he was seriously engaged in composition, which had not left him a moment to write to her. " I regretted that very much, but I hope to have news from you very soon." For the rest, she was still further initiated into world literature. She was introduced to Shakspere and Scott. Cosima learnt by heart *Die Kraniche des Ibykus* and performed a scene from *Hamlet* with Blandine. To this were added various biographies to which Madame Patersi introduced her: for instance, the lives of Lord Chesterfield, Barnave, Fénelon, and Chateaubriand. As we see, all this was a little promiscuous, but it was a good sign that the new governess made them especially familiar with French affairs. During the holidays they went to Versailles, to see the Museum there, and admired the pictures of Horace Vernet. Next they went to Sèvres, to visit the porcelain factory. In Paris they saw Michel-angelo's *Il Penseroso.*

As was natural, Madame Patersi, who was so proud of her pupils, did not fail to use all her influence on behalf of their future stepmother, and it looked as if she were succeeding, though their remarks on the subject — on Cosima's side, at least — sound a little conventional. Thus she writes, for in-stance: " I hope that God will hear our prayers, and that we may soon be able to call the *Frau Princesse* mother, for she already occupies this place in our hearts." But the value of this education was undoubtedly great. The children learnt to know the Paris museums, where they had their attention directed to the various artists, while the rest of their life, too, passed away joyously enough. Cosima in particular made good progress, and by the beginning of 1852 she was already writing German letters in German script. They saw and took part in everything. They were interested in *Mardi gras* (Shrove Tuesday), and watched the carnival procession, about which Cosima wrote: "The ox was very fine, but the *char* (car) was hideous." The young ladies were also taken to the grand opera and heard Meyerbeer's *Les Huguenots*, which was so much praised and fêted in Paris at that time.

Meanwhile their grandmother had made the journey to Weimar to visit her son, and Madame Patersi's influence consequently became even more absolute. Of course Cosima longed greatly for Frau Anna, as is evident from her affectionate and childlike letters; but she was very thoroughly occupied with her studies, and even at that time, in her piano-playing in particular, her deep understanding of music, which grew ever stronger, was plainly evident. In July 1852 she wrote in one letter: "Herr Seghers has given us the Overture to *Don Giovanni* to play. We are very fond of this piece, and the great beauties in it give us a thrill every time we play it." Thus here she is already expressing what Richard Wagner says so grandly about this overture, and, indeed, about the whole first scene of this work of Mozart's.

But most touching is their interest in their brother's successes at his college, which were, moreover, remarkable. In earlier days their father had rebuked his son for his failures, with some severity and force, and Daniel had drawn the necessary conclusions. But Cosima gives a delightful description of the distribution of prizes, at which they had been present: "The prize-distribution started sharp at midday. It opened with a speech on the uses of reading good books. This speech, delivered by Rousset, the professor of history, left nothing to be desired, and after two more speeches, one by Monsieur de Roillet, who took the chair, and the other by the examiner, the names of the boys

who had won prizes were read out. They had just got as far as the
second class when it came on to rain, at first a very fine rain,
which soon, however, turned into a cloud-burst, and everything
was flooded, both in the courtyard and under the little colonnade,
where we sought safety, as the professorial dignitaries had done.
For our part, dear Papa, we had scarcely a dry thread on us,
from our outer garments down to what we wore next our skin.
We did not care a bit, being determined not to leave our places.
You understand, dear Papa, that the scene of the gathering was
only a great courtyard, over which had been stretched a canvas
awning, which was by no means watertight, but transparent
enough so that not only drops of rain reached us through it, but
regular deluges. The crowd of pupils jumped up on the benches
as best they could, and laughed at the stampede caused among
the audience by the rain. This little episode lasted twenty minutes. Then order was to a certain extent restored, and the
distribution of prizes began again — this time for the third
class. And now the name of Liszt was announced as having won
the first prize in the first division, and next the second prize in
Latin, and next — but you know the rest, dear Papa. After shiv-
ering with cold, we went with our *moutard* (brat) to visit Herr
Seghers, who lived opposite the college, and shared in our
delight." The rest followed naturally. They sent for a cab, drove
home, and there hung up the wreaths received by Daniel over
the portraits of their father and grandmother, but only provisionally, for they intended to send them home. Cosima's touching interest in Daniel's destiny runs through the whole of her
life, up to his premature death. There is something infinitely
moving about the way in which she clung to her younger
brother, and in the infinite love with which he requited her.

But now something of her mother's disposition showed itself
in Cosima too, in the form of a strong grasp of history and a
deep bent for it. At the age of fourteen she was reading Mignet's
History of the French Revolution, after which she was taken
by Madame Patersi to the Hôtel de Ville, which had been the
scene of an important part of this revolution. On this occasion
she showed that the names of those who had lost their lives here
were fresh in her memory. This blend of what she had learnt

for herself with the effect produced on her young mind by ideas is of peculiar importance, and shows us a side of Cosima which developed still more in the future; for her understanding of character and of political events made itself felt on all occasions. It is curious how, in her prematurely awakened intelligence, she managed to combine this clear grasp of the ways of the world with an equally deep-seated religious sentiment. We may instance one scene: Madame Patersi took her to church to be present at the conversion of a young friend who was leaving the Reformed Church to become a Catholic and was now baptized by Cosima's confessor, the Abbé Bucquet, Cosima and her sister having been chosen as *" filles spirituelles."* Her account of this is full of delicate tact, and she had no feeling save that of the deepest and most heart-felt piety. Or we have another scene, again described in English. They visited the Musée d'Artillerie, in order to see Abd-el-Kader, who was in Paris; and it was with great interest that they gazed upon this remarkable man.

Thus there was no lack of events to leave an impression upon her. But the deepest of all was that which she received from Beauchesne's book, presented to her about this time by the Abbé Bucquet — a work on the ill-fated Dauphin, describing his fate, his death-agony, and his death. "We went through all the horrors of the Revolution," she writes, " and saw how great was the resignation of the royal family."

She now proceeded to Beethoven and Haydn, whose gay and charming symphonies she played on the piano. These were true artist's children, growing up in no Bohemian surroundings, but in serious and, it must be admitted, intelligent hands.

It might almost be considered that the two young women's minds and feelings were overloaded with material. We are often conscious of a certain Eastern tinge in the character of Madame Patersi's instruction. On the whole, these young girls produce the impression of two princesses, whose lot it was to be endowed with all this fine and elegant breeding, as well as with the widest possible knowledge, in order to attain the goal of the princely education of that day: to yield to no weakness, and to shine.

Thus religion offered a by no means negligible counterpoise,

31

and sermons from such men as the Abbé Gabriel made the deepest impression on the girls. When Gabriel said that a woman's whole life ought to be nothing but a sacrifice, and that she was nothing but a living Host, the saying directly appealed to the whole of Cosima's nature. It arrested the child's attention, just as she had grasped the full implication of the words that had once been uttered at Versailles: " Kings are made for peoples, and not peoples for kings." We can see that, after all, something of her mother's nature and essential character survived in her. Thus she could say: " I do not like Chateaubriand's character. For me his soul is too arid (*trocken*) and cold, and, what is more, too egotistical."

For the rest, her whole sensibilities and emotional nature inclined rather towards music. When she went to concerts — whether those of some important artist such as Vieuxtemps, or of her own master Seghers — she always listened with her whole soul. She championed the cause of such young artists as Fräulein Kraus, a protégé of her father's, and hence of the Princess's. She observed, indeed, that his young lady was particularly applauded at her concerts by the Germans, and she considered that the success obtained by her was principally due to the work which she had interpreted — namely, *Les Patineurs*, a highly effective arrangement of her father's. She also went to hear Cossmann, a member of the Liszt circle, as was also Fräulein Kraus, who had found her way to the rue Casimir-Périer and met with a friendly reception there. But the strongest musical influence was still that exerted over her by Seghers, who not only supervised the young ladies' piano-playing, but guided and directed it. It was through him that she learnt to know Weber and Beethoven. The awakening of the girls' interest in their own father's art is quite remarkable. Gradually they were introduced to his works, which became known to them through the *Gazette musicale*. But Seghers did more than this: he, so to speak, established musical contact between father and children. And on going in person to Düsseldorf to a great festival performance in which Liszt was to take part, he suggested the idea that the children might meet their father again there. For to the children their father's successes were a very great thing, though they went without saying;

and in writing to their grandmother at Weimar for her birthday, they said that they could bear the separation patiently, " when we think of the happiness that you will have at seeing all our father's successes and enjoying them. You will write us a long letter, won't you, Grandmother dear, and tell us all the details, so that we can associate ourselves with our father's fame from afar. This is our greatest joy, and our consolation for being so far away."

But there was one strong curb upon their relations with their father. Madame Patersi allowed no letter to be sent off to him which she had not read, and when she could not do so, the letters simply had to lie and wait, often for weeks on end. She exercised a regular dictatorship over them, and did not hesitate to change their teachers. Thus instead of Blachta, who had taught the children German literature, another was appointed, named Stephens, who laid more stress upon style and composition than upon the interpretation of literature. But the children were bound to submit, and submit they did, and this, indeed, may have had a great influence on their letters. For the rest, the society in which they mixed was highly interesting, and in this respect Madame Patersi imposed comparatively little restraint upon them, for she considered that, as the daughters of a famous father, they ought to associate with famous people. Thus she took them to the Érard family's villa at La Muette, where they made the acquaintance of a whole succession of artists, such as Léon Fauche and his wife, the two Gutmanns, and Krieger, who, naturally, all played there, but it was also expected that the two young ladies should be heard. At first they were reluctant, but their governess thereupon interposed her authority. She held that it was right for them to play, provided it was understood that they aspired to be no more than amateurs and had no need to aim at perfect finish; and she added: " You may perhaps play badly, but play! " " We played," continues Cosima. " Blandine played a study of Czerny's and a Russian air of an ecclesiastical character, for those were the only pieces that she knew by heart, and I played the Third Hungarian Melody and *Lob der Thränen*. Daniel played too, the *Alexander March* without the Variations." They were heartily applauded. With the subtle humour

33

that came out in him so charmingly even as a boy, Daniel said that he " was afraid that he might ruin Monsieur Érard's piano for him." But the latter rejoined that " nothing of Liszt's can hurt a piano," and two days later, in fulfilment of an old promise, actually sent the two young ladies a new instrument. And it was needed, for under the direction of Seghers they continued to make greater and greater progress. " That means, my dear father, that we are already attacking your works, which are creating a furore among our friends, and which we play, though still, perhaps, very defectively."

The young ladies took the liveliest interest in everything, and Madame Patersi went the right way to work to increase it. She had the earliest specimens of Gutenberg's printing shown them at the Bibliothèque de l'Arsenal, besides Henry II's journal, with its wonderful drawings, and that of Charles VII. They were also shown the old Bibliothèque Sainte-Geneviève by one of their friends. Besides this they visited the Jardin des Plantes, where they delighted in the wonderful show of flowers. Next they read Walter Scott, and Augustin Thierry's *Histoire du Tiers État*. The description given by Blandine of the baptism of a young Jewess is not without interest: " She was baptized by the Abbé Ratisbonne, also a Jew, who turned Catholic and became a notable priest, his brother too being a convert. This ceremony took place in a little religious house founded by these two priests in order to further the conversion of the Jews, for which reason it has been called Notre Dame de Sion."

But they were glad to learn, for in the rue Casimir-Périer promises were already being held out which filled them with a great joy. From this time — July 1853 — onwards a note of new animation, as it were, is noticeable in their letters. This was evident in a description by Cosima of the Salon, where what they most admired were Gallait's two pictures, *Tasso* and *Egmont in Prison*. Their circle of friends increased, and they were attentive spectators of the public festivities which they witnessed in Paris — and, above all, of the great celebrations of August 1853. They saw the flaming apotheosis of Napoleon I, the illumination of the various churches, and also explored the surroundings of Paris; and both of them, Cosima in particular, had much to tell of these walks to Saint-Cloud and Versailles, where they visited the camp and were filled with enthusiasm by the spirit that prevailed there.

But now came the great event. After this long time they were to see their father again. After the Musical Festival at Karlsruhe and the now historic visit to Basel, where Liszt and his pupils had a joyous meeting with the lonely Master of Zürich, he and the latter came to Paris. And now the children, too, made the acquaintance of their father's great friend, at whose service Liszt had for some years past placed all the resources of his personality. About this meeting Richard Wagner writes in his autobiography: " One day Liszt invited me to spend an evening *en famille* with him and his children, who were living a retired life in Paris with a governess. It was something new to me to observe my friend with these girls, who were already growing up, and in his relations with a son who was also developing from a boy into a young man. He himself seemed astonished at his position as a father, of which he had for long years experienced only the cares, without the emotions which compensate for them." Here, as usual, Wagner proceeded to read them his works — in this case the last act of *The Twilight of the Gods* — that is to say, the close of the whole work which he had longed to accomplish. Berlioz and the famous feuilletonist Jules Janin were also present. Wagner met the children on two other occasions, once at Érard's and afterwards at the Palais-Royal, about which he writes: " Here I again met his children, the youngest of whom in particular, his son Daniel, made a really moving impression on me, owing to his great vivacity and his resemblance to his father, while all I had to notice in his daughters was their insuperable shyness." This was the first meeting between the mature man and the young girl who, though still developing, was already more deeply intimate with his works than Richard Wagner suspected.

Madame Patersi would not allow the children to write to their father again at once, giving as her reason that he would have other things to do at Weimar than to read their letters. Then Cosima wrote: " At last the seal is removed, and we can now tell you how very happy your presence in Paris made us, not only because we had the pleasure of seeing you, but because it has transformed things enormously for us. We now understand better what is good, and with our gratitude at bearing your name is mingled the inexpressible desire to see you made happy through us. The perfect motherly goodness of the Princess and of her daughter, who regards us as sisters, and Daniel as a brother, all this, my dear father, gives your three children a feeling of infinite happiness. We must repeat this to you, and will you tell the Princess that we already love her like a mother, and that she has said things to us that we shall never forget? Give us both your blessing, my dear father. For our part, we pray God that he may leave us nothing more to desire, and that we may soon give the name of ' Mother ' to her who will receive all her happiness from you, as you will receive all yours from her." And in the same spirit they wrote to the Princess herself how confidently they both counted on the marriage. Curiously incongruous with this was the visit of Madame d'Artigaux, their father's first love, who, on bringing her sick child to consult the famous Paris doctors, came to see them and gave them handsome presents.

Their musical studies had gained intensity from Liszt's presence, and Seghers in particular was now more anxious than ever to advance them, as well as to increase their interest in musical things. Thus he sent an inquiry to Liszt through his daughters as to whether Mendelssohn had made any cuts in Schubert's symphony. He next asked for a catalogue of Liszt's works, all of which the children were now to learn one after the other. And here Cosima cites an imposing list of those which she had already played: the Illustration to *Le Prophète*, the fantasias on *Lucia, Robert the Devil,* and *Les Huguenots,* the *Galop chromatique* and the *Consolations.*

Soon, too, the residence of the two young ladies was sought out by many German artists. Thus we find Fräulein Spohr, the daughter of Ludwig Spohr, frequenting their society, and many others. But, as early as this, Liszt had discussed various plans for his elder daughter. He wanted to marry her as soon as possible, and for this purpose an interview was arranged in her confessor the Abbé Bucquet's waiting-room between Blandine and a certain "Monsieur Ld." in the presence of several persons. The second meeting took place at the Jardin d'Hiver. The impression which he made was by no means favourable: " In no way," writes this young girl, who already had a mind of her own, " does he possess the distinction which I desire in my husband, if I am to consider him worthy to be your son-in-law. It cannot be said that he is altogether common, but neither can he be called *distingué*. I grant that everything is in his favour from the point of view of morality and the knowledge which he requires for his learned profession. Ld. is a man with a future. But I do not feel that this is enough. For the present I could have desired a little charm as well as intellect, to beguile the period of waiting for this future which is prophesied as a result of his learning. Since I am confident of your fatherly affection, my dear father, and am equally confident that you will never compel me to marry against my will, I told Monsieur Bucquet and Madame Patersi the whole truth, and there's an end of it. It was all done without any fuss."

This letter is highly interesting and shows how resolute and independent the two children had already become, yet how life was closing in upon them more and more. For the rest, everything seems to have been postponed till after Liszt's anticipated marriage with the Princess, which was expected to take place shortly. On April 3 the daughters wrote a joint letter to the Princess, addressing her as " *Madame (ou plus tant bien chère Mère)*," in which they thanked her for the motherly affection expressed in the Princess's letter: " Yes, madame, you are our mother, you have been so for a long time past. The charming watches which you gave us on our father's name-day told the first hour in which we rejoiced in a happiness free from bitterness, such as we had not enjoyed for long past, and they will enable us always to understand our father's value. All the suggestions that your letter makes to us, dear Mother, have long since been laid before us by Madame Patersi. We are fully alive to Madame Patersi's remarkable qualities; she does not spoil us in any way, but we are none the less grateful to you for having entrusted us to her care. She often talks to us about your sufferings. Be sure, dear Mother, that our hearts have accustomed

themselves to sharing in them, and that the day which ends them
will be blessed a thousandfold by us, as by all those who love
you." This was saying a great deal, even if we allow for the
strong and dictatorial influence of Madame Patersi.

Next they saw Daniel depart for Weimar, and both of them
shared without a trace of envy in the good fortune of the brother
whom they loved so devotedly, and they prepared him thoroughly for his journey to Germany. They read Madame de
Staël's *De l'Allemagne* with him and talked German with him
diligently, so that he should be to some extent prepared for his
arrival in Weimar beforehand. They also received more pocket-
money and were now treated in some respects like grown-up
daughters. The future which was held out to them was entirely
on the French model, and Cosima herself now wrote that they
were perfectly aware of how their present training was preparing them to be good and honourable women.

At the same time their education now proceeded on even
broader lines. Cosima went with Madame de St. Mars to attend
one of the sessions of the Chamber of Deputies. She reported
with a slight touch of irony that it had not been in any way
stormy, that P. had spoken against the revision of the Constitu-
tion, and that Henry de la Moskowa had spoken for more than
an hour and a half on the subject of " *crédits fonciers.*" This was
more than enough for them: they had been there and it had not
been so very interesting.

Meanwhile their studies began to draw to their close, and even
Madame Patersi now considered both of them fit to be " emeri-
tus professors." The chief stress was now really laid upon music
and religion. So soon as a new preacher came into prominence
— such as the Père Hermann at Saint-Sulpice, who was, moreover, a musician and a friend of their father's — the first to
attend his sermons were Madame Patersi and her two charges.
The summer of 1854 was, however, marked for both of them by
rather serious illness which rendered very careful treatment
necessary, so that they welcomed it almost in the light of a cure
when they received an invitation from their father to go and
meet him at Brussels under the escort of Madame Patersi and
the excellent Belloni. On the evening of July 18 they met their

father at the Hotel Bellevue. He had arrived from Rotterdam and Antwerp and was waiting there for the children. He was obviously delighted: " They are good, their looks are pleasing, and they have good hearts. We will talk over everything in detail in a few days; at present I am entirely at their service. I chat with them, or, rather, hold forth before them and for their benefit. Madame Patersi is as excellent and perfect as ever, and the being whom we know and love. She always keeps perfect order, even among the cross-currents of a whole series of confused ideas. I feel that I am at one with her on all points of importance." Thus he writes to the Princess, rather in the spirit of a friend and, as it were, a trustee for them than of a father. But during this journey the last-mentioned side of him appeared in full force: " Yesterday we went to Antwerp and spent a very lovely day at the Zoological Gardens, which are the most famous in all Belgium. We amused ourselves by passing in review lions, tigers, vultures, and ostriches. From there we went to the picture-gallery to see the superb Rubenses: the *Piercing of the Side,* the *Adoration of the Magi,* and the *Trinity,* all brilliant works. Then we dined with the Schotts at Kufferath's. After dinner I played, for Kufferath is a celebrated composer of piano-works in Brussels, a pupil of Mendelssohn's. This evening we are to repeat this session, and play the Ninth Symphony with Rubinstein." He speaks of his longing for the Princess and of how bored he is without her. " We are constantly talking of you apropos of everything." Yet we see that here he stood between two worlds, and another thing, too, seems to have occurred to distract him. He learnt, that is to say, that the learned " Diotima," as he ironically nicknamed Daniel Stern, had been in Brussels, to consult General Beudon for her history of the Revolution of 1848. The daughters returned to Paris, and Cosima sent him a wonderful account of their return journey, of the sufferings endured by Belloni in the heat, and also of the state into which the unfortunate Madame Patersi once more relapsed on this same journey. But in Paris they received a visit from young Louis Berlioz, who was full of the warlike doings in the East. He had arrived from Kronstadt, on his way to Sebastopol. He formed a complete contrast with the unhappy Belloni, who, in despair at the bad season, bankruptcies among the publishers, and the distress which seriously threatened, had devoted himself entirely to botany and become a disciple of Linnæus. The way in which she describes them both and manages to contrast the swashbuckling Berlioz with the inoffensive Belloni is most charming. She also gives a delicious picture, drawn with a touch of irony, of their grandmother, whose new abode was opposite the police-station, so that she could see malefactors being given in charge and then read the account of it in the paper next morning. Her grandmamma, she says, was already able to tell from their appearance whether they were innocent or guilty.

The most important event of the season was the concert of Hector Berlioz, who had meanwhile found in Liszt a champion and interpreter in Germany. It was a great concert, which the two young ladies attended under Seghers's escort, to hear *The Flight into Egypt, Herod's Dream, The Arrival at Sais,* and *Les Devins.* The concert made a great impression on the young ladies, as on the whole public. Cosima's description of her brother's enthusiasm is delightful: " Daniel acted as *claque* for the whole family and acquitted himself honourably in this capacity, with unflagging zeal, enthusiasm, and propriety. The march with which the first part opens is indeed a fascinating thing and produced an extraordinary effect. There was no falling off in this, especially in the scenes of *Les Devins,* in which Berlioz makes use of cabbalistic ideas in an extraordinarily fine and wonderful way. The whole hall was stirred to its depths by the massive power of his instrumentation. The *Flight into Egypt,* which had been heard in Paris before, had to be repeated. In a word, Berlioz's works achieved a gigantic success."

But the fateful event at this concert was their meeting with their mother. Cosima writes of it frankly — almost in a slightly trenchant tone: " Madame Patersi will have told you, my dear father, that our mother was present at Berlioz's concert last Sunday, and that she arranged with us there to fetch us on Tuesday at one o'clock and bring us back at nine. And this has actually taken place. She drove us to her house and first took us up to her study, where she left us alone for a moment, asking us to choose ourselves something there. Over the bookcase, dear

COSIMA LISZT

(in the background) with her sister BLANDINE, and
her brother, DANIEL, the grandmother ANNA LISZT,
and the governess SAINT MARS. Paris, 1853

father, we saw the bronze medallion of you, and your portrait *en face* by Ingres, which was hanging all by itself on one of the walls. Then she came back and asked whether we thought the house pretty. She made minute inquiries about the arrangement of our life, our work, social relations, and habits and said that she found Daniel extraordinarily charming. In accordance with the wish which she expressed of becoming acquainted with Wagner's works, we took her *Lohengrin* and *The Flying Dutchman*. We could not give her *Tannhäuser* yet, as Daniel has it at school. This shall be done another time, and with it we shall take your pamphlet on the two works, in which she displayed great interest. She was extremely charming to us, full of tenderness, love, and motherly care, showing nothing but happiness and joy, without any sort of *arrière-pensée*. We talked a great deal about you, dear Papa, in the way that one can. Among other things she said that, if the money she offers us is in the least displeasing to you, she would say no more about it, or about the Italian master whom she would like to give us, because he is a very distinguished man, who would teach us Italian splendidly, and whom she thinks we should find agreeable. But she expressly insisted that she would abandon the idea unconditionally if it did not suit you, and added that the most essential thing to her was to see us, and that as soon as you had given your consent to this, she did not wish to complicate matters in any way. Today she is going to see Daniel, where we are to join her. She also said that she would be heartily glad to give us such books as might interest us. On the whole, our relations with her are very good, very tender, very heart-felt and affectionate on both sides. She shows a high esteem for Madame Patersi, and all we have said to her could only confirm her in this. She gave us to understand that a little later she would invite us to dinner with Madame Patersi, asking a few persons at the same time, but only some of her friends, not people in society."

This event marked a decided epoch in the lives as well as in the ideas and feelings of the two young ladies. But it is evident from their correspondence that the Princess regarded this turn of affairs in Paris with a certain nervousness and sought to hinder any further development of the relations between mother

41

and daughters. As a matter of fact, on the Countess d'Agoult's side, too, all her hatred and aversion had been diverted from Liszt to the Princess, in whom she saw, on the one hand, the rival who had robbed her of the affection of the man she loved, and, on the other hand, the domineering woman whose influence was taking her children from her, and of whom she said in later days: " This mother who was chosen for them was a woman of Jewish race, 'who spends her life on the backstairs (*dans les coulisses*) of the Vatican." Though these words reveal a certain misunderstanding of the Princess, whose love of domination was undoubtedly always inspired by great aims, and never by purely egotistical ones, yet this remarkable woman's antagonism for the Princess was perfectly understandable; and it is indeed regrettable that owing to her unreservedly Catholic point of view, which was never free from a strong tinge of fanaticism, as well as of the most extreme doctrinairism, the Princess exerted a strong pressure upon the children's consciences in all circumstances. How rigid was this constraint, which, while they were in charge of Madame Patersi, made them hardly able to write their father anything about their mother before the winter of 1854, can be seen from a letter which Blandine had written to her father even before the arrival of the Princess's emissary: " I hasten, dear Papa, to let you know how happy we are at this moment and to confide to you how we managed to obtain this happiness, which has been so long denied us. We have seen Mamma again, and the joy is so great and makes us forget the pain of such a long parting. During all these past days I had felt the sorrow of not seeing her, and I tried to have news of her from time to time and was never happier than when I heard her name spoken. During the New Year holidays her address was mentioned in my presence. On the very next day we went out, and, entirely engrossed as we were in what we had heard, the inspiration to seek her out came to us suddenly as we went along, and this is how it happened that we saw her again. We only stayed with her a moment. She was deeply moved, and almost alarmed, at seeing us again, and she exhibited great joy when she learnt that our feelings towards her were still as lively and as deep as ever. On returning to Grandmamma we said nothing of what we had ventured to do. We were afraid that she would be angry at our having done anything without her advice. But now I hope that she is not angry with us and will share in our happiness as she has always done. Mamma longs to see us more often. She questioned us about our studies and looked at our exercises, and she seemed pleased with them. We are trying to prolong her visits, and we always feel great pain at parting. The ladies were so kind as to let Daniel go out several times, for they want to give us the chance of enjoying this great pleasure. He is coming on Monday, and Mamma too, in order to see all three of us together and enjoy the happiness of being with all her children. All these joys which I feel in the presence of Mamma, I shall feel in the same way with you and Grandmamma, and do not think that we do not feel your absence with grief in these days of happiness. My happiness will be complete when I see you and divide my affection between you and Mamma. I hope, my dear father, that you will not delay much longer to see your children, who have so long been deprived of your presence." The feeling in this came straight from Blandine's heart, and Cosima shared it to the full.

But it looks as though this letter had actually prompted the dispatch of Madame Patersi, besides which the recent appearance of their mother in Weimar had aroused very mixed feelings. It should not be forgotten what a wonderful figure this mother was, who had now, after a long and hard struggle, won an important position in Paris. Her mother had died in the year 1847. Two years later her daughter Claire married the Comte de Charnacé. She was now free and bought herself a house at the top of the Champs-Élysées — that Maison Rose, a gem of the Rennaissance, which was the resort of intellectual Paris. It was naturally an event for the children when they entered this house. As a matter of fact, their intercourse with their mother could not now be interfered with. Blandine, in particular, was now a marriageable young lady, and Cosima, too, was already quite mature enough to face life, and so rich in talent that she grasped these great and important questions of life with all the moral resources of a strong character. The first remonstrance that came from Weimar seems to have had reference to material advantages expected by Blandine, and her answer was very diplomatic, but very firm: " You surely understand so fully the joy which we felt at seeing our mother again that I need add no more, but I would beg you on my knees to have a good enough opinion of us and never to believe that our joy can have been accompanied by any ideas of material interest. I am sure, Father, that I am in no way uneasy about my marriage, and husband-hunting, as you so rightly call it, seems to me utterly ridiculous and no less immoral. There is no burden whatever upon my mind and heart and I seek ever to turn my thoughts upwards."

It was suspected — and the Princess seems to have laid great stress upon this — that the children might inherit a large fortune from their mother. To counteract this she now tried to work upon the children by means of presents. She sent them souvenirs of her estate at Woronince and supplied them bountifully with dresses. The way in which the children dealt with the situation is interesting, and in this connexion the two young ladies bore themselves like true Parisians. They followed in all things the advice given them by their mother, who said outright of certain costumes that young ladies ought not to wear such things in Paris. A curious situation arose out of Liszt's writings on the subject of Richard Wagner, which Marie d'Agoult now asked urgently to read. We know that the article on *The Flying Dutchman* was written by the Princess, and I do not believe that this was unknown to the children, or to the Countess either. It therefore reveals a certain irony, not on the part of the children, but on that of their mother, that she should have asked for these articles. She wanted to see the extent of the Princess's literary influence on Liszt, who had once been so strongly influenced by herself. The Princess seems to have sent a very acid reply; at any rate, Cosima simply had to apologize to her father, but her remarks on her mother's influence, which was being combated at Weimar, are remarkably independent and tactful: " I perfectly well understand that our mother must address her request to you alone, that the answer must come from you alone, and that in this matter we can have no vote in the conclave, in favour of either consent or refusal. Finally, my dear father, all the

errors that were committed were due to me, for my mother used
no such expressions; she only said that she awaited a reply from
you, and that she in no way desired to disturb the relations
which had been established between us. The expression of dissatisfaction originated with me alone, and I quite see that there
is something unseemly in it and apologize to you for having
used it. Last Sunday our mother called to take us to luncheon
with her. We saw nobody at her house but her daughter, and at
one o'clock she took us to the Museum. It had been arranged
beforehand that she should take us for a drive, but since the
weather was abominable, we were forced to give up this plan,
and so we decided to go to the Louvre. This visit interested
us in the highest degree. Mamma explained all the pictures
to us, pointed out all their beauties, and also told us a few
particulars about the lives of the painters. We saw the room set
apart for the French school, in which are the three famous
pictures by Gros, and then the great Salon Carré, where she
compared the various schools and pointed out to us the especial
beauties of each separate painter, and the points of resemblance
existing between the artists. About three o'clock we left the
Louvre, and she accompanied us home, where we found Grandmamma. On the following day Mamma sent Blandine a little
basket of fruit. On Wednesday she brought back Richard Wagner's poems and begged us to play your arrangements. She
considered them very fine, but our piano was extraordinarily
out of tune, and she asked us to repeat the pieces on another day.
We are to take her the Preface to your symphonic poems as soon
as we get it back. I am very glad that no secrecy prevails on
any side in the relations which now once more exist between us.
In view of our sentiments, all calculations based upon things
of this character seem entirely out of place, and I felt real joy
at the fact that our mother does not regard our relations from this
point of view at all. Had she done so I should have been deeply
pained, but I am able to say that on all our visits we have seen
nothing but happiness, without any *arrière-pensée,* and without
any taint of antagonism. She talks of you very much, dear
Father, and that in a way in which I love to hear you spoken of,
and she misses no opportunity of repeating to us over and over

again that we owe you everything, that we cannot thank you enough, dear Father. So far we have seen nobody at her house but her daughter, and we shall always take pains, too, to make precise inquiries about all persons we meet there; for we will never entertain the idea that the return of our mother to us should be a source of mysteries and intrigues and of things that are even worse and sillier."

Meanwhile Daniel had returned from his visit to Weimar, full of enthusiasm and delight, and the two daughters made him tell them all about it. We can see from their account how deep was the affection that united the three children. They did all they could to celebrate his arrival, and went to the Comédie-Française together. It is interesting to see that, even to Daniel, the only shadow that lay upon his visit to Weimar was the postponement of *Tannhäuser*, which was not performed till he had left.

All the same, it is noteworthy that precisely at this time the Princess tried to take charge of all questions concerning the dress of Liszt's daughters. For with a true woman's perception she perceived that it was precisely in these questions that the children might most easily be affected by their mother's influence. A certain note of dissatisfaction runs through all the Princess's letters, and the children had to justify every visit to their mother; and it really seems that in this the Princess was lacking in nice feeling and even in the most essential delicacy. They were forced positively to defend themselves, and they both do so adroitly but firmly, though, it is true, under a certain constraint; but the latter can be directly attributed to Madame Patersi, who now felt in her element, though she could not evade the duty of accompanying the children to their mother's house. There is a significant remark in a letter from Blandine to the Princess: "We have never been able to regard our mother's return to us in the light of an attempt to alienate us from our father. It is he who promotes our welfare, and will always do so, and we desire nothing else, and this is so firmly rooted in us that it seems to us impossible that our mother could have any other point of view. She is always very calm and reticent, always very full of courtesy to Madame Patersi, of which we are very glad. We belong, dearest, inseparably to our father, and I do know nobody who would possibly be capable of changing our feelings in any way. As you most justly say, one receives one's feelings from nature, but an age comes at which one sits in judgment on them. I think our mother sees quite well that we show her every mark of respect and love as daughters. But on her side, too, there is a reserve which shows that she judges things aright. There are no secrets between us, and this has always been our way of looking at the matter. There can be no such secrets. But, my dear, a thousand times dear, how can you possibly think that you can be an intruder? Never, in no circumstances and at no time will you be an intruder. Where love prevails, as it does between us and you, there can be no talk of intrusion. All the questions which Madame Patersi put to you are in reality the product of her foresight, for our mother has in no way taken exception to them. When we left her in the evening lately, she never even asked when we should meet again. She only asked that Daniel should take his meals with her on Sunday."

Among such feelings and antagonisms as these, then, they now entered upon the fateful new year, in which their mother's influence was almost wholly in the ascendant. But it is particularly attractive to see how charmingly the children write to their father, thereby — perhaps without themselves being aware of it — checkmating the Princess's influence. Thus Blandine begins her letter of January 19 as follows: " I am writing to you, my dear father, while Cosimette is playing Schubert's glorious trio, replacing the fiddle and 'cello, which are lacking, by her voice, yet I do not feel that the work suffers from it, and I find it sufficiently poetical and inspiring. Since everything beautiful naturally turns towards you, I cannot resist telling you all my love. It is a fortnight today since we went to see our mother. We went to hear Verdi's *Il Trovatore*." She draws a most ironical picture of this work, culminating in a description of the scene in which Leonora throws herself into the Count's arms, because she thinks him to be the troubadour. " For it is night-time. From this we drew the conclusion that the moral of the work, in general and in particular, is that people ought to provide themselves with lanterns." She next relates how on

Sunday their mother again called for them. " She talked a great deal to us about the libretto of *Tannhäuser,* which she considers wonderful, finer than both the others, and she begged me to play her the song (*Romanze*) '*O, du mein holder Abendstern.*' "

This learned and intellectual woman now tried to direct the children's attention to architecture in particular. Thus she visited the Sainte-Chapelle with them, and there showed them the delicacy of the Gothic. Next she went with them to the *Comédie-Française* to see Molière's pieces, especially *L'Avare* and *Les Précieuses ridicules;* while at home she now read them the *Prometheus,* followed by the Œdipus trilogy.

It is, moreover, interesting that, in spite of everything, the Princess was ready to profit by Madame d'Agoult's acquaintance with the painter Ingres, and the children were accordingly commissioned to open negotiations with a view to the acquisition of a drawing.

In fact, thanks to Madame d'Agoult's appearance on the scene, a new animation had come into their lives. One evening they saw Rossini's *Barber of Seville* at the Italian Opera, and thoroughly enjoyed themselves; while now something of the literary spirit which reigned in the house of Daniel Stern was communicated to the children. Quite apart from considerations of architecture and Greek poetry, they were directed mainly towards what was modern, and their mother brought to their notice the English novelist Dickens, who occupied quite a unique position at that time.

In any case, it was of decisive importance for Cosima that now, shortly before leaving Paris, she was once again able to enter into intimate relations with her mother. This can even be detected to a slight extent in her style. A new and individual note runs through her letters, and it is curious to find her saying: " I write to you amid the universal silence of nature in Paris; snow is falling in great flakes and keeps everybody within doors, not a sound disturbs my thoughts, which, it goes without saying, turn towards him who is their noblest inspiration. The great city lies in gloom, the sun breaks through the mist and produces a positively fantastic light, which reminds us quite involuntarily of the sombre shades of the *Flying Dutchman.* Thanks to the wonderful articles on it, this poem has impressed itself so profoundly upon our feelings that we can dream of nothing else. We are going to lend it to our mother, as we did the others, and we shall also take her the pamphlet on Wagner as soon as we have received it." Their mother liked the children to play to her, and especially Cosima. Indeed, both the young ladies' playing had advanced to such a point that Seghers, their master, asked Liszt to give him permission for them to take part in the trio-playing which he was getting up in the evenings. On this occasion Liszt gave his entire consent, which is really surprising in view of his attitude later, when he absolutely refused to allow Cosima to make any appearance in public.

But the Princess could find no peace. Again and again did she manage to insinuate some bitter thought into the hearts of Liszt's daughters. Thus Cosima writes on one occasion: " Dear one, I answer your letter at once, to say what I did not think it would be necessary to say to you, that in all these matters we have never obeyed our father merely passively. As regards your reproach, which makes us out to be mere nonentities, I prefer to believe that it is neither just nor well founded. For, the very first time, our mother told us that Madame de Charnacé would like nothing better than to escort us home. But we replied that that could not and must not be. Last time our mother asked us to dinner she was unwell and begged Madame Patersi to come and fetch us, and since Madame complained of being tired, our mother proposed Madame de Charnacé. I forgot to say that Madame Patersi had expressly declared that she would never call for us in the evening again. And now as regards the matter of the 1200 francs, we expressly told our mother that we accepted nothing and refused nothing, that she must refer to our father, who alone decides such questions. She mentioned the matter to us two or three times, and we always gave the same answer, and since then she has said no more. For the rest, I think she is equally convinced of the eternal and unchangeable love and gratitude which we bear our father, and we hope we have never in any way shown that we have forgotten what he is to us, or that we are not convinced that, so far as he is concerned, right, justice, nobility, and devotion prevail." This was plain speaking.

For the rest, however, we see how strongly both of them had set their course towards music. In their letters they speak like true artists. They were well informed about all the artists, about Mendelssohn and his works no less than about Berlioz. Like their father himself, they championed Wagner's cause if the conversation turned upon him, and in this connexion they wrote to Liszt, very beautifully, that genius is never understood by its own age. Nor did they allow their good spirits to be in any way dashed by the Princess, who had absolutely no sense of humour. It is delicious to hear, for instance, how she sent her adopted daughters to see the painter Popelin, to look at his pictures and admire them. They managed to extricate themselves with éclat and played off Popelin's master, Scheffer, against him. Their description of the parrot to which their grandmother had treated herself is delightful. She had soon become rather tired of the bird and its free concerts. Cosima closes her remarks on the parrot with an allusion to Matthias Claudius's ass, which kept repeating the words: " I have nothing to be pleased with. I am stupid and mis-shapen. Ah! Nature had a grudge against me. She gave me nothing but a lovely voice."

But for Cosima, at least, the hours in Paris were numbered. It looks as if their mother felt this and wanted to have as much of them as possible. She introduced them to artists and poets and showed them the Oriental sections of the Museum of the Louvre, not without preparing them suitably beforehand by giving them important books to read. It may also have been at this time that Cosima's mother entertained the poet Lamartine at tea. Indeed, they now entered a new atmosphere, for the rest of their father's friends, such as Belloni, for instance, were, after all, people of minor importance; but in the Countess's *salon* they learnt to know the whole brilliant world of Paris. It is true that just at that time Cosima was in rather bad health, which gave frequent cause for anxiety; but in her letters we see her speedily developing and growing. When she describes the acquaintances who frequented her mother's house or the rue Casimir-Périer, she knows how to make fun of them delightfully: for instance, of one Rosti, who was then saying his farewells before leaving for Düsseldorf. " He has at last found his vocation there. As a flautist? Oh, no! As an engineer? Not even that. A philosopher? No. A geologist? Not that either. A writer? Not at all. A sailor? Not a bit. He is, or he wants to be, or, better, he is beginning to be — guess what. A photographer! " For he thought that on a journey to China which he was just intending to undertake he would be able to record everything and reproduce it better by that means than any other.

Next came a period of sickness for Madame Patersi, which caused no small anxiety in Paris and still more in Weimar. The children had to send the Princess constant reports of the course of their governess's illness and did so in a really tactful and discreet way. For a considerable time their only subject of correspondence is Madame Patersi's condition. It was nothing but a nasty abscess that troubled her, which ultimately proved not to be malignant. But, for all their good-heartedness, a slight irony runs through these reports, especially from the moment when it became apparent that the whole sickness was not dangerous.

What really fascinated them was their mother's *salon,* where they now met Jules Simon, the new Academician, Renan, and many others. Their mother initiated them more and more into literature, thereby perfecting the education which they had obtained during this time of preparation in Paris, which had now lasted for ten years.

Meanwhile in the high conclave of Weimar the idea had been hatched of transplanting the children from Paris to Germany. It had at first been intended to receive them at Weimar, in the Altenburg; but the idea was utterly rejected by both sides, and so Liszt was considering to whom he could entrust his two daughters. He had first thought of the Ritter family at Dresden. Frau Ritter was a noble and remarkable woman. It was she who had intervened in Richard Wagner's life at the decisive moment and enabled him to enjoy at least a few years of creative work free from anxiety. Her son was closely connected with Liszt and Richard Wagner, but was also a very intimate friend of Liszt's favourite pupil, Hans von Bülow. But it was quite on his own initiative that Liszt now thought of the latter's mother, who had always made a remarkable and even striking impression on him. Though her son and her husband had both suffered considerably from her character, and especially from her vehemence and severity, yet in the many transactions which he had had to conduct with her on Hans's account, Franz Liszt had always felt a particular liking for her.

Accordingly, in July the Princess set out for Berlin to visit Frau von Bülow, and she, too, recognized that this undoubtedly remarkable and original woman was fitted to assume the further charge of the children. It was a curious decision to take with regard to these two grown-up daughters who were then beginning to shine in their mother's Paris *salon,* Blandine no less than "La Cigogne (the Stork)," as Blandine had christened her sister. Their appearance was attractive, and the second daughter's golden hair, in particular, was already much admired. There had previously been a curious dispute about it. Cosima's hair had been falling out badly, and the doctor accordingly said that it must be cut off, so that it might grow again more strongly. Thereupon Cosima appealed to the Princess in her sweetest way and asked her to decide the point; so that they ceased preparing her, as it were, for the cloister — though Madame Patersi's house had rather a conventual atmosphere! Indeed, the type of piety in which the two young girls were still being brought up was by no means in accordance with their father's way of thinking. He was essentially pious and a believer, but the whole of his religious emotion and observances amounted to no more than hearing a low mass. But the girls' education, which had assumed a strongly religious tinge under Madame Patersi's supervision, was of quite a different character. Hence the counteracting influence exerted by Madame d'Agoult's entry into her daughters' life was altogether a good one; for though she was allowed to alter nothing in the course of their bringing-up, and with fine tact did not even interfere, yet, through the extraordinary charm of her character and attainments, she was able to give her children something quite out of the ordinary. I might almost call this half-year, during which Cosima had the joy of closer intercourse with her mother, the period during which she reached the culminating point of her education. It was a sort of Academy, and it would thus be entirely false to omit this influence of Daniel Stern in the story of Cosima's development. Its short duration only made it all the more intense; for now it was the mother who reacted upon her child, and since she was unable to do so in other ways, she effected it by way of culture, or even learning. However that may be, during this latter period Cosima obtained a glimpse of the great and important world of Parisian culture and through her mother came to some extent in touch with most of the leading men. It was a new world for her; but it was her fate to depart from it, and that at the right moment, for she had a mission which she could not have fulfilled as a Frenchwoman, but only as a German.

But there can be no doubt that the migration of Liszt's daughters to Germany was the direct consequence of this return of their beautiful mother into their lives. At this time, in particular, as well as subsequently, all questions concerning Madame d'Agoult were dealt with at the Altenburg with a certain nervousness, so the father's decision came in the first place, not from his own heart, but from the brain of the Princess. This also explains Liszt's remark that he could certainly bring his children to Germany, but never permanently to the Altenburg. How deeply he was prejudiced against their mother again at that time is most clearly evident from a letter to his " unknown friend (*Freundin*)." [1] On July 7, 1855 he wrote to her: " The day before yesterday in the evening I travelled to Dresden and in a few hours' time was on my way back to Berlin. You know the reason for this excursion, and Frau Ritter will probably take charge of my daughters for a year or two, after which it may be assumed that they will marry. The Parisian atmosphere is becoming more and more harmful to them. Their mother — in parenthesis — is just publishing in the *Revue contemporaine* a long fragment of a history of Holland, which is announced under the title of *Pouvoir et liberté*. Madame d'Agoult's *nom de guerre* is, as you know, Daniel Stern. On the other hand, I cannot and will not have my children under my roof at the Altenburg. Only I think it would be a good thing for them to spend some time in Germany, and

[1] Mrs. Agnes Street. — TR.

53

Dresden or Berlin seems to me to be the most suitable city for them for this purpose. I have said nothing to them of this plan as yet and shall not enlighten them until I see them again, in order to avoid all superfluous comments and explanations. There are already enough things that are unavoidable and necessary, without adding to them."

The visit to Dresden was indeed, as we have seen, without result. The Princess, on the other hand, went to Berlin to set up a sort of temporary *salon* after her own fashion. She eagerly discussed with Liszt all the intellectual, literary, and artistic connexions which might be made there, from Alexander von Humboldt to Varnhagen von Ense. He wrote to her that his daughters would certainly be settled in Berlin, for, owing to the question of a lodging, Dresden would not be possible till the following spring. "And I should not like to delay their liberation from Paris too long, for it is absolutely worthless to them in present circumstances. It is therefore my duty to consider what may be natural and useful for my daughters, who will find far better chances of marrying in Germany than in France, my relations with which have been too broken for me to be able to take any measures to further their future prospects to advantage."

And now, so it would seem, it was Hans von Bülow who first set the matter afoot on his visit to Weimar. In the same letter of July 21 in which Liszt mentions the arrival of his favourite pupil, there occurs the remark: "My daughters will be settled with Frau von Bülow this autumn in Berlin." It was a curious relation which now sprang up between the Princess and this undoubtedly intellectual, remarkable, and energetic woman, who throughout her whole life exerted an extraordinary influence upon her son, and that not always of a helpful kind. The form which it took, indeed, was that at decisive moments she raised a number of difficulties for him — not from lack of heart, but out of a kind of boundless motherly solicitude, of the sort which lays more stress on the mother's own care than on its object. There were undoubtedly a number of similarities and traits of resemblance between her and the Princess, and the two ladies came to a thorough understanding at the Altenburg. The Princess liked her, while upon her the Princess produced a deep and positively commanding impression. For this very reason the Princess undoubtedly succeeded in improving the relations between mother and son, and one of this gifted woman's witty sayings was to write to the anxious mother that her son was advancing with seven-leagued boots. The Bülows were no strangers to the house in the rue Casimir-Périer in Paris or to Liszt's mother either. Hans von Bülow himself looked with marked interest in the direction of this retired and mysterious dwelling, and he also took a lively interest in the grandmother, both when she met with an accident at Weimar and in connexion with her activities in Paris. It so happened that in the year 1854 his sister had gone to Paris, when he insisted that she should call upon Liszt's mother and his children. For this purpose she received a letter of introduction from the Princess, which did not meet her wishes at all, for she thought that a few lines from the father would carry greater weight. But her brother now set her right: "You are wrong," he wrote, "in supposing that the Princess's letter to Liszt's daughters is not as good a recommendation as a letter from their father. On the contrary; if only for the reason that the children's governess — a certain Madame Patersi, I believe — brought up the Princess Wittgenstein too and possesses her unbounded confidence, while it is she too who has established them where they are. Have you been to see Liszt's mother? Pay your court to the old lady a little, and you may speak German with her, for she is fond of a little local Austrian gossip (*gerne Österreichisch lokalisiert*). Get Liszt's daughters (the Erlkönig's daughters), of whom I beg you to give me accurate silhouettes, to take you to see her." And she did as her brother desired.

It is interesting to see how the Princess now stayed on in Berlin, no doubt in order to make her personality widely felt and to win a wide influence in all circles. It was not till now that the children were carefully prepared and invited to Germany, all three of them. Their joy was complete, especially as the silence which had preceded it had made them all uneasy. Daniel had again ended his school year with a whole series of prizes and was hoping not only for his father's approbation, but also for an invitation to Weimar. And now all three of them received one. They were overjoyed, and Cosima wrote to the Princess:

"Dear one, I only write a line to say that we are starting on Saturday. These words sum up our whole idea — that we shall see and embrace our father again." Neither cares nor presentiments weighed upon them. Their infinite love for their father made them forget everything else. None but their grandmother saw through this move; for the very letter which notified her of her grandchildren's migration had something of the Princess's character: " Since you cannot decide to leave Paris, and I cannot arrange to come there, I should like at least to see my children again and spend a week with them. Frau von Bülow is so kind as to fetch them from Paris and accompany them to Weimar, where I will prepare a welcome for them which will leave a pleasant memory behind it. Perhaps it is not particularly pleasant to you to offer hospitality to Frau von Bülow. All the same, dearest Mother, I beg you to put her up as comfortably as possible during the three or four days of her stay in Paris, until all preparations for the journey are complete. You know how greatly I esteem Frau von Bülow, and how fond I am of her son, whom I consider the best fitted of my pupils to carry on my activities in the world of art and to occupy a position which he honestly deserves. So give Frau von Bülow a friendly welcome, and, even if her presence is necessarily rather burdensome in your small household, do not let it be apparent to her. That is the simplest way of showing hospitality."

So Frau von Bülow came. The effect was not at all gratifying. On the contrary, the old lady felt herself deeply injured and wrote to her son: " I was delighted to receive your letter from Madame de Bülow. It is quite a rare thing for me to receive a few lines from your own hand. On Saturday, before Madame de Bülow arrived, I learnt from Madame Patersi that you want to have the three children with you for the holidays, for which purpose Madame de Bülow will be so good as to fetch them and escort them to you. I was quite astonished at this, for once or twice while I was in Weimar I heard you say: ' I cannot let Cosima and Blandine come to Weimar.' It is true that two years have gone by since then, and time changes many things. This journey will be very good for the children in every respect, and it will also be very useful, both for the present and for the

future, for them to spend some time with you. I myself would
have undertaken to escort the children to you and back again
too. And I repeat here what I wrote to you long ago, as well as to
the Princess — that it grieves me to neglect everything like this,
and to waste the property I possess as I have done since the children have been here. A husband may very well be found for Blandine soon, and my idea has been to give her the better part of it
then with your consent, afterwards selling the rest, and, if you
wanted me, to stay with you at the Altenburg, and I would move
there. Or else, as soon as Daniel, who has still another year of
his studies or college, starts on some other career according to
his training — if Blandine is already provided for, I might
have Cosima and Daniel to myself, and the *frais* (expenses)
would certainly not be too high, for so far the charge has been
too great for you, and, believe me, it has often grieved me when
I thought about it. Only you would have it so and not otherwise.
It hurt me to see the children in other hands, for I was well and
still very active. Since then I have met with the accident to my
foot, yet I still feel myself capable of managing a small household and supervising the children, who are devoted to me. I
could manage with a sensible person, but not too *précieux*, because I cannot go out as I should like, and one servant or a
femme de ménage, which would be ample and is less expensive.
I want the children to come up to your expectations, and you
to feel that they are some compensation to you for your cares.
They often see their mother, as you already know from
Madame Patersi, but I do not think her influence has been harmful to the children yet, though Madame Patersi feared that it
would be. A great deal might be said about this, but I cannot
write it all, you will be able to convince yourself by seeing the
children; people's opinions are so different on the subject of
the children having seen their mother lately, so I learn from
Madame Patersi, for I see very few people. Some say: ' What
happiness for the children to see their mother! ' But others say:
' What a misfortune for those children to have been deprived
for so long of others,' who might have been a good match, but
it is over now, and so forth. You did not want to injure them in
any way as regards their *dot* when they should marry, and you

therefore acquiesced in their mother's desire to see the children. I should have been better pleased if things had remained as they were, and if she had wanted to do anything for the children at any time, she could always have done so. If only you had spoken with her yourself, last time you were here, she came here for that very purpose, I do not know from where, in order to talk to you. Now adieu, my dear child, I cannot do much for Madame de Bülow, since I am infirm, but I think she is not dissatisfied with me. I did not know her very well in Weimar; now I know her better and have become fond of her. She is a very good and accommodating woman, it is a pity that she is so delicate. Since she has been here, she has suffered badly from headaches."

CHAPTER II

AWAKENING

THE CHILDREN now started out on their journey under the escort of Frau von Bülow, who had been to Weimar to get the necessary instructions. The Princess and her daughter had left for Paris on August 19 by way of Brussels, and Liszt's children arrived in Weimar on the 21st. Liszt gives the following detailed description to his " unknown friend ": " My daughters spoke very nicely about your visit to the rue Casimir-Périer. I shall have more to say to you on this point. My daughters lack neither wit nor intelligence, and I think they are turning out well, without any falling off. They are perceiving and buoyant enough, and with this is combined a touch of youthful and lively mischief which becomes them well. I shall keep them with me for about ten days before sending them on to Berlin. I have received proposals on the subject of two prospective husbands for Blandine, but probably neither of them will meet her views." And a little later he wrote: " My daughters monopolize two thirds of my day. They are enchanting young creatures, intelligent, lively, and even a little inquisitive. They take after both Papa and Mamma. It appears that Blandine will not hear of her two or three offers of marriage, though they are all suitable, and even good. The girls do not much care about settling in Berlin, though this would be far the best and most advantageous course for them; for Madame de Bülow possesses admirable qualities, not only as regards character, manners, and intellectual culture, but also for the task which I have entrusted to her. So I hope that, having sent my daughters to every sort of devil for their visionary and wrong-headed arguments — as has

already happened several times during the last three days —
they will be fully convinced of the single-mindedness and wisdom of my efforts on their behalf and will acquiesce whole-
heartedly in my intentions; for they have a great fund of affection for me." Meanwhile news arrived from the Princess in
Paris which pleased him greatly. It appeared that there were a
number of excellent proposals of marriage for the girls there;
but his daughters were astonishingly indifferent, and he had to
content himself with treating them as *" précieuses ridicules "*
and leaving them their freedom of action. " What they require
as a husband would be something in the nature of a Beethoven
or a Raphael doubled with a nabob." It seems, indeed, that on
this journey to Paris the Princess had assumed, among other
things, the diplomatic mission of arranging marriages for them.
But her behaviour towards Liszt's mother had produced, on the
whole, a by no means pleasing impression. On September 3
the latter wrote to her son: " I can wait no longer, but must write
to you, I am so upset since hearing the latest decision about
Blandine and Cosima ten days ago. The Princess told me about
it with the greatest indifference, that they were to be sent to
Berlin under the charge of Madame de Bülow, who is to be with
them always and *gouverner* them. I could find nothing to say but
that the children are too big to make another change. The Princess replied that otherwise there would never be an end to Madame d'Agoult's scribbling, as she had been very impertinent
in her letters to you for some time past. But consider, dear child,
to hand these children over to strangers in a strange land, where
they do not know a soul, is certainly no indifferent matter for
them, and I am afraid that if this happens, one or the other of
them will fall ill. It would have been better if the Princess had
left Madame Patersi in Poland or in Russia and not entrusted
these children to a woman who was, moreover, already in her
seventy-second year when they were handed over to her charge.
She was already too tired. When I was in Weimar for the first
time and saw her portrait, I said to the Princess: 'This lady is
too old for such an undertaking,' but she rejoined at once: ' *Ah,
elle est encore bien verte* (She is still full of vigour) '; but I was
sad for the children, and perhaps you may still remember that

I cried a good deal. But when I got to Paris, I saw that I must resign myself, and God gave me the grace to do so. I prepared the children for their new residence and had to say a great deal that went against my feelings — and it was all right (*es ging*). They became reconciled to this old lady, who never felt any affection for them, for when she arrived here she had *la tête monter* (been filled with prejudices) against their mother by the Princess; she had an antipathy for Blandine and greeted her with the words: ' *C'est sa mère* (She is her mother's daughter),' in that tone of hers which you know. To Blandine, who had been under the gentle guidance of Madame Laure Bernard, this seemed very unfriendly. She cried a great deal, and the only reply was: ' *C'est de l'eau* (Tears are only water),' and more to that effect. Oh, my dear child, it was a good thing I was here too. I talked to her, and in time things went fairly well. Now these two ladies have taken a dislike to Cosima (*en grippe genommen*) because she has the misfortune to be like her mother. These two ladies want rest. They know quite well that the Princess will not abandon them, and I would gladly take upon myself the trouble of which they are trying to be rid, but above all it would have been necessary to have confidence in me. On your side, at least, nothing has ever been wanting. The children are good and must be guided by love, for they have proud, sensitive hearts. Madame de Bülow seems to me to be a kindly disposed woman, but to send the children away to Prussia on account of their mother! Look into the matter if you think it necessary and if you fear any bad influence over the children. You have them with you now, they will listen to you and take things from you that they would not take from others, because they love you and feel that they, too, are loved by you. Do not believe all the nasty things that have been told you. Madame Patersi told me on several occasions that their mother sent for the children five times — I do not know, it is possible, of course, while Madame Patersi was ill and they saw that St. Mars was much occupied with the sick woman — perhaps it happened once or twice, to give their *réponses* about a marriage. Ask the children, they will tell you the truth. You will see whether they are not better than they are painted. I have received a letter from

61

all three of them, full of happiness and joy at being in your society. I am embarrassed when I write to them, since I know what is before them. But I heard from Madame Patersi, with much mystification, that two offers of marriage are just being made for Blandine, in connexion with one of which Popelin *pére* is in Weimar at present to ask for Blandine for his son. I do not think a better match will offer itself again; the second, it seems, is a lawyer here, who is making his *chemin* (way in the world) very well, and, it is hoped, will get on even better in time, for he is very active and intelligent. He is thirty years of age and is called Dafour, I do not know if I am spelling his name properly. He often met Blandine at General Petit's house and was much taken with her. Blandine knows nothing about it. He has never said a word to her. And now, dear child, supposing that a marriage for Blandine were soon arranged to your liking, is it worth while to arrange a change for the children? Think it over, I beg you. I am still on most harmonious terms with Madame Patersi and St. Mars, you have nothing to worry about in that respect. The Princess had *déjeuner* with me twice and I dined once with her at her hotel to meet young Popelin and Monsieur de Metz." However, this prospective marriage broke down, because Blandine was unwilling. She considered that he was lacking in good "sense." Her grandmother was very much vexed at first, but after a while she wrote that she was very glad Blandine had rejected him, for she had heard that the young man was consumptive, and had personally convinced herself of the truth of this.

Meanwhile, however, the two young ladies were extraordinarily happy in Weimar, and, as was his kind-hearted way when not misled by the Princess, Liszt was quite carried away too, for they were both lively enough to dominate their father. From the very moment of their arrival they upset the game of whist, which was *de rigueur,* and had, as he puts it, borrowing an expression of Jean Jacques Rousseau, set up a regular court of misrule or "tapageocratie" (*Lärmherrschaft*). They filled the Altenburg with a spirit of rebellion and exultantly inaugurated a new time-table; for once, on coming home after midnight, he found the drawing-room still lit up and the two young ladies still occupied in reading, and let himself be drawn into chattering with them for another hour. He promised to tell the Princess by word of mouth what they had chattered about. At seven o'clock the very next morning Blandine appeared at his bedside to wake him up; but Liszt, who was notoriously no early riser as a rule, remarked: " I have stipulated that I am not to have breakfast with the clan (' *Sippschaft* '), and that for the whole of their stay, whatever happens, I reserve to myself the morning hours up to second breakfast."

It is particularly charming to observe how, at her father's suggestion, Cosima gave the Princess detailed descriptions of certain pictures in the Paris Exhibition. In this she was, as it were, her father's collaborator, for he gave the Princess detailed hints about all the leading personalities in Paris, as he had done for Berlin. Thus he advised her among other things to go and see Heinrich Heine, though the latter had notoriously exhausted all the resources of his mordant wit at the expense of Franz Liszt, and, in obedience to a particular charge to do so, the Princess called upon Liszt's old friend George Sand. He could not refrain from announcing the noble lady's arrival to the Lady of Nohant in rather a formal fashion. His old friend was indignant at being addressed as " Madame " and wrote to him: " I am most astonished at the ' Madame ' with which your letter begins, my dear Franz. I am at a loss to know the cause of it, and the Princess assured me that it was no doing of hers, and I am confident that this is so. It is true that when people have not seen each other for a long time, many things come between them and their pleasant memories. So far as I am concerned, I have not changed in any way." She sang the Princess's praises and was delighted because the latter had held out a hope that Franz would visit her, even if it meant going as far as Nohant. And now, too, the Princess was once more reminded of Madame d'Artigaux: everything, that is, that was opposed to " Nélida," as he now called the Countess d'Agoult.

Meanwhile preparations were completed with a view to his daughters' departure for Berlin; and on September 4 Liszt actually travelled with them as far as Merseburg, where Frau von Bülow was ready to receive them and escort them to Berlin. But he had reckoned without his daughters' temperament. As they were leaving the Cathedral at Merseburg, Blandine begged so hard to be allowed to spend a few more days at Weimar that, willy-nilly, Liszt decided to take them back to the Altenburg.

It was not till the 8th that they finally left Weimar, this time to begin a new life in Berlin. Liszt decided — and this is characteristic of him — that his daughters were to write to him in turns and only every fortnight. This seems very seldom when we think that he called the Princess's letters his " daily manna." The parting was a very painful one, but Liszt was glad to be rid of the interruption, and return to his work. Two days later he wrote to the Princess that she would find him a little ashamed of himself for having worked so little during her absence, but it had been really impossible to work while the children had been there, as well as his cousin Eduard Liszt and Frau von Bülow.

But the singular fashion in which the children had been transferred to Germany shows that the Princess's influence was not altogether in conformity with the feelings of his own heart. While Liszt settled the affair — though he did so, it is true, in harmony with her views — she went to Paris, her train, so to speak, passing the one which was bringing the children from Paris to Weimar. Her intention was to play the same part in Paris as she had done in Berlin; for it was her habit to seek the acquaintance of famous people everywhere, and in Paris, too, she made a number of visits to sculptors and painters, poets and writers, in order to increase the circle of her acquaintances. It was indeed fortunate for the childen to be so entirely their own mistresses at the Altenburg, and this perhaps made it easier for them to reconcile themselves to going to Berlin, where Frau von Bülow now proved a truly motherly friend to them, in so far as she was able. She esteemed their father and found the children really very lovable and attractive; and she seems to have contemplated the possibility that her son might find a wife in one of them and found the idea not unwelcome, though a little later she seems to have rebelled against it. Her own temperament inclined her rather in the direction of Leipzig and the school of Mendelssohn, and it was with some irony that at this very time, when the " new music," and especially that of Richard Wagner, was meeting with a run of success, she adopted the Princess's opinion that it would soon be necessary to be a Wagnerian in order to make a career. There was still a good deal of irony in this saying, but at the same time it showed a dawning comprehension of the greatness of Richard Wagner, who, once he had carried the first positions, went on from victory to victory in concert-hall and theatre with a sort of elemental power. It is true that the public and the critics did not follow the same paths. But now that the two daughters had arrived in Frau von Bülow's house, and their instruction in piano-playing had by their father's express desire been entrusted to his young pupil Hans, the atmosphere in which the young ladies lived was a thoroughly musical one.

The attitude of Hans von Bülow towards the "Erlkönig's daughters" now becomes highly interesting. The letter which he wrote Liszt as early as September 30 is quite a little idyll: "Fräulein Blandine has just borrowed my inkpot, in order to work at musical theory under the direction of Ehlert, who seems to be just the right teacher of harmony for your two daughters and has undertaken not to bore them and to give them a thoroughly sound training. You ask me, dearest master, for the latest news of your daughters. I should have found this impossible earlier, in view of the degree of ' stupefaction,' admiration, and even exaltation, to which they have reduced me, especially the younger one. As regards their musical endowments, they possess not only talent, but genius. They are true daughters of my benefactor, quite extraordinary beings. It is in an uplifted mood that I busy myself with their musical education — and they are superior to me in acuteness of mind, fineness of taste, and so on. But it will not be possible to make them work regularly until we have moved to our new home in the Wilhelmstrasse, which will take place on October 4 or 5; then they will have a piano to themselves, and we shall not inconvenience one another. Yesterday evening Fräulein Blandine played Bach's Sonata in A, and Fräulein Cosima Beethoven's Sonata in B minor, and with Laub too, who will very often make music with the young ladies. I have also had arrangements for piano duet made for them from the scores of the works to be performed at Stern's concerts. I give them an analysis of each work, and I am pedantic rather than otherwise in my supervision of their studies. In the exchange of ideas which arises out of this occupation and brightens the boredom of my days, it is I who am a hundredfold the gainer in pleasure. They cause me to make quite remarkable progress, for they are at my side while I am playing. I shall never forget the exquisite evening on which I played them your Psalm over and over again. The two angels were, so to speak, lost in adoration of their father. You would indeed have been most happy had you been present at that moment unseen. They understand your masterpieces better than anyone else, and in them you have a public provided by nature. I was affected and deeply moved at recognizing in Fräulein Cosima's playing the ' *Ipsissimum Lisztum* ' (very manner of Liszt). To my mind she resembles Scheffer's picture of you, and Fräulein Blandine the bust by Bartolini. The similarities and differences apparent in their two characters and individualities are in accord with this. Meanwhile they are not indulging in overmuch excitement in Berlin, as you seem to fear, but they are a long time becoming acclimatized to their — Jersey. They have only been to the theatre three times, to *Tell, Egmont,* and a ballet. Since my mother and I live a very retired life in Berlin, they have seen very few people, except Marx, Stern, Ehlert, Groll, and Herr von Bronsart, who spent an hour with us on each of his two visits to Berlin and will be able to give you the latest news direct from your children."

As a matter of fact, this was more than Liszt had expected. For he had had very much less than this in view in entrusting Bülow with the instruction of his daughters in piano-playing: " Allow me to tell you what great importance I attach to the fact that you are making them work seriously. For I believe them to be far enough advanced in their musical studies to be well able to profit by your lessons. So turn them into splendid propagandists for the music of the future, as it is their duty to be; no indulgence, then, and do not pass over any superficiality or slovenly playing. They start with a due respect for you, and you will not find it hard work to knock things into their heads as you should."

This language had quite a different ring, and we feel in it

something of the severity of the Princess, whose mouthpiece he was. But, for the present, Bülow had her full approbation, and from her letters to his mother we can see how happy she was to be the patroness of this young nobleman and eminent artist. She was well aware that none of Liszt's pupils or disciples were able or willing to do such service to his cause as friend Hans. But the role which she allotted him, for more or less utilitarian reasons, naturally influenced the girls in a very different way. Through this fidelity to their father he had won their confidence from the outset, and Liszt was quite right when he spoke of their respect for him, for on entering the narrow circle of the Bülows' house in Berlin they both brought with them an esteem for his capacity. But more than this: they had found it hard to leave Paris — though not Madame Patersi — and the parting with Weimar and their father, whose company they had been able to enjoy unreservedly in the absence of the Princess, was painful to them. They were entering a world which was quite new and entirely strange to them. And now their education and training stood them in good stead. They came to Berlin with a complete intellectual equipment, and just the right one. For at that time there was no place in which so much value was attached to knowledge — almost more than to capacity — as in the Prussian capital. Thus from the very beginning they were able to carry all before them; and their quickness of wit, their social gifts, and the wonderful charm by which they delighted everybody were an especial recommendation to them everywhere. They were indeed true daughters of Liszt, in touch with all that is highest in intellectual life, and with a deep intuitive comprehension of all that was great and true in art and life. Moreover, both of them, and especially Cosima, possessed the true artist's nature, but the latter had also a strong womanly devotion for what was great and significant in genius and character. To this was added a touch of the elfin in her character, which was attractive to every noble nature.

And now they saw the much-vaunted musical life of Berlin, in which, in spite of his youth and nerves, Bülow undoubtedly played a commanding part, and was furthermore the most distinguished figure, both intellectually and artistically. The progress of his development was not unknown to them. They knew how he had suffered, struggled, and worked, and recognized what he had achieved at such an early age. And there was yet another thing: lying on his piano they saw a ballade which had come into being before their very eyes; and having newly arrived from Paris, the very focus of the Chopin cult, they knew the significance of this. For it was widely held at that time — and the saying had even been coined into an idly repeated maxim — that nobody could write ballades again after Chopin — in spite of which, Bülow had dared to write one, and Liszt had pronounced it one of his best works. " It is a brilliant piece, full of fire, well proportioned, and, like all you write, powerful and aristocratic in style." And the man who was capable of such things was their teacher, and they were quite conscious of the master hand that directed them — a master chivalrous and gay, precise to the verge of intolerance in all musical matters, but full of delight in their ability and unusual gifts, and great and distinguished to a pre-eminent degree. And in this master, their father's favourite pupil, they found, so to speak, a playmate. Even Bülow's mother had changed quite beyond recognition. All her strictness and theories were swept away by a revival of the strong feeling for art which she had always possessed; and for Liszt's daughters she was full of motherly solicitude. There was, indeed, a certain inward antagonism which she was powerless to surmount. Though there was nothing of Madame Patersi in her, she had a certain love of predominance, of which there were repeated outbreaks in her relations with her son, even in the days of her blindness and approaching death. And so Cosima did not feel by any means so much attracted to her as Frau Franziska desired and had, indeed, a right to expect. A certain reserve persisted, and Cosima felt herself robbed by Frau von Bülow's presence of all dæmonic power and so constrained that it became almost impossible to play before her.

But there was one thing that Bülow's mother understood better than almost any other woman, and that was how to introduce them into society. She entertained considerably in her own house, which was frequented by all musical Berlin: besides Marx and Stern, of whom her younger son was a colleague at the Conservatoire, the girls met Liszt's pupils and her son's young friends, above all Hans von Bronsart, who, of all those who had served their time in the musical garrison at Weimar, was for long one of Hans's dearest friends and at any rate remained one of the most faithful and honourable of them. But more than this: though they took no personal part in the musical activities of Berlin, they were able to look on at this unending *mêlée* as though from above and observe this wild game of profit and hazard from quite close at hand. Above all, they could observe their young friend himself as he constantly entered the lists bearing their father's colours; and if he could not always carry them to victory, the daughters were none the less bound to admire his courage and imperturbability. As a man, too, he gained their confidence more and more, for he surrounded them with the most devoted care and touching delicacy of feeling. It is most moving to see how, while honouring their father in them and observing the rare intellectual and spiritual affinity existing between him and his daughters — a wonderful phenomenon of nature which often struck him — he used his influence with their father on their behalf and tried to commend them to his heart: " Your daughters are sad that you do not concern yourself with them in any way — but sad in a spirit of truly Christian resignation. For a week past they have waited in vain for news from Paris. They were bewailing their disappointed hopes. I asked them with as discreet a sympathy as possible why they did not complain straight to you of their lack of direct news. Upon which Fräulein Cosima replied that she never complained of what hurt her most deeply."

But during the whole of his stormy life he, too, met with a sympathy and understanding from them which were full of humour and even of gay mischief. In them he found, indeed, two fascinating partners. For the mordant wit with which the fairies — both good and bad alike — had endowed him in the cradle kept coming out, and he developed more and more into a " Percy *Heiss-sporn* (Hotspur)," as he had been nicknamed. But his heart was always ready to redress the balance. His caustic side belonged to his everyday life and, while running parallel with his other achievements, forms in the best sense of the word a sphere apart, full of wit and power, though doubtless carried to excess. In short, all that the girls saw and heard marked him out as a dominant personality alike as man and artist; but in either capacity he was always an aristocrat. This had a direct appeal for them, for the aristocratic element in him had in many respects a similarity to that in their mother, who had followed the path of democracy in both speech and thought and, like him, was convinced that none but a nobleman could be a true democrat. So here was another point of contact, both intellectually and spiritually. But the uncompromising directness of such an infinitely high-strung creature as Cosima caused her to be drawn to him by a profound sympathy. She was no novice in the musical world, having learnt to know both music and musicians in Paris, and could tell him more about Berlioz, for whom he had such a veneration, than he himself suspected. She had heard all the leading artists play there, and spoke of Shakspere and the French writers with full personal knowledge, if not as dogmatically as a professional literary man. She took an interest in everything — in architecture and especially in the Gothic style — and if some historical question was introduced, she knew the works dealing with the subject and had her own views, not only about the ideas of the day, but about those of the historian who treated of them. And in all this there was no trace of pedantry or of a lesson learnt by rote. She showed herself natural and true, as, indeed, everything about her was. To this was added the profound goodness of her heart, her understanding, permeated with a spiritual quality which was unspeakably winning, though accompanied by a gentle and reticent strength which always goes with the deepest and noblest capacity for self-surrender. She saw him struggling, and rejoiced in his efforts; but the sight of his sufferings aroused in her not only pity, but love. Perhaps at the same time she divined that Bülow's controversial activities and propaganda in favour of the new music were distracting him too much from the paths by which he ought to scale the heights of Parnassus; this was exactly what Richard Wagner meant when he warned him to resist this tendency and give free scope to his inmost nature by producing creative works as a composer. Wagner wrote this at a time when he was himself feeling the same need — during the days of his concerts in London. The letter arrived just at the right moment, for Bülow was making preparations for the performance of the Overture to *Tannhäuser* — perhaps with all the more zest since Cosima loved this work above all others, with one of those deep and mysterious instincts which commonly accompany great souls throughout life and often guide their destiny. The evening of the concert arrived. Though the Overture to *Tannhäuser* was no longer new, yet, in view of the short-lived career of musical works in Berlin, it was as yet little known, and its performance was a positively unheard-of event; and, since it was the work of the innovator, it was hissed. This was too much for Bülow, and, though he was usually well able to stand his ground against his enemies in the concert-hall, he fell into a dead faint. Cosima saw both composer and interpreter "*versungen und vertan*[1] (forsung and fordone)," but not in her own eyes. She had known the work ever since she was a child; she had already played it in Paris as a duet; she possessed the piano-score and carried on a warm propaganda in its favour. But her deep delight in the music and her disgust with the undiscriminating and prejudiced public only served greatly to enhance her sympathy for their friend. As soon as he recovered, he found comfort among the artists; but on reaching home Cosima said to Frau Franziska and Blandine that after such an event it was their duty to wait up for him and say a word of consolation to him on his return. They would not listen to her, so she waited for him alone. Liszt himself writes: "Towards two o'clock in the morning I pushed Hans in at his door in the Wilhelmstrasse. The house was still lit up, but I did not go in, and shall not present myself to '*ces demoiselles*' till this morning about ten o'clock." But Cosima was still keeping vigil. When the others refused to keep her company, she waited for him alone. And now she felt how, from her faith in him, his talent, and his mission, a great and mighty love was arising in her heart. And he came: depressed on his master's account, hopeless of any result from his own efforts, but exalted by the presence of this wonderful being, who appeared to him that day as a good angel — and a loving one.

[1] *The Mastersingers*, I, iii. — Tr.

That is what she was prepared to be to him in future, and both of them knew that they were destined for each other. That was the true moment of their betrothal. Her friend's apparent defeat showed her and him that she not only valued and esteemed him, but loved him; and amid the storm through which he was steering the ship of his life, she was prepared to come on board with him, in the strong but quiet hope that through storm and breakers she might pilot him to the bright shores of happy creation. In this she shared the feelings of the great man at Zürich, about whom propitious news was now arriving from Weimar and London. Liszt wrote about the first two acts of *The Valkyrie:* " To me they are like a miracle."

Bülow poured out his heart to his master without delay. As soon as the latter arrived for the rehearsals in November, Bülow asked him for Cosima's hand, and Liszt was deeply delighted and contented. He was ready to give him his daughter without more ado, and wrote at once to the Princess to this effect. But he considered a marriage premature and decided that they must wait a year. Cosima's youth and the short time for which they had known each other seemed to require this.

The delay was doubtless painful to Bülow, but he none the less proceeded to prepare with fiery energy for the performance of the great Liszt Concerto. It was a good idea of Bülow's to invite the former darling of the Berliners, who had greeted his playing with rapturous applause, to introduce some of his own compositions to them and to commend them by the magic of his personality; and Liszt entered into it not only readily, but with peculiar eagerness. This was an achievement in the fullest sense of the word, which showed that Bülow's influence was already considerable. The two daughters watched these preparations with joyous exaltation. The universal sympathy for Liszt was palpable to the " Erlkönig's daughters," too; and a few days before the concert Blandine draws an enthusiastic picture of the tense expectation prevailing in Berlin: " My father will presumably arrive on Sunday evening. You can imagine our joy; all Berlin is waiting for him; I believe that a surprise is being prepared for him and that he will be received in state at the station — it would make you so happy, dear Grandmother, to see how highly esteemed and loved my father is in Berlin, where people are usually so cold and critical. This enthusiasm cannot be gainsaid, they are very fond of us too, and people are extraordinarily kind to us."

Of course there was still " the old disputes, the old distress (*die alte Zwist, die alte Not*) ": [1] while the public was full of sympathy, the critics were full of venom and bitterness. The court was extremely friendly to Liszt, and now to Bülow as well, and by the King's express wish he was commanded to play at the court concert. Before this, Bülow had spoken jestingly to Liszt of his ambition to become court pianist, but the latter had purposely taken his words quite in earnest. Not so his daughter Cosima. In her merry way she called Hans " *un vil courtisan* (base courtier)," whose talent for this role had been an unexpected revelation. Her energy now began to show itself in every way. She forcibly refused to continue her attendance at Stern's concerts, because, in spite of his promise, her father's name was no longer to be found on the program. On the other hand, she attended Marx's lectures on musical history and also took lessons in Italian. But her influence on her future husband was obviously a good one, tending, indeed, to his emancipation. He actually went so far as to go with her to balls, where he danced; and this busy man even found time for theatricals, proving his talents as an actor, together with Cosima and Blandine, in Musset's *Un Caprice.*

To her, too, all this was only play, a social duty to which she submitted smilingly. To her lover she stood for more than this. She was no constraint upon him in his battles, but cheered him on and gave him heart, studying only to alleviate the tragic sting left by all his activities. She was deeply moved by his fidelity to her father, as well as to Wagner, and he found in her a deep understanding of all his cares and tribulations; for she felt that the greatness of the two men made all the conflict and exertion not only worth while, but a sacred duty. And now it was his turn, too, to come out in his full strength. On January 14, 1856 she had attended with him the first performance of *Tannhäuser* in Berlin. This was an event for her; for now, for the first time,

[1] Cf. *The Valkyrie*, II, i: *"Der alte Sturm, die alte Müh'."* — Tr.

she heard the whole work, of which she had already acquired so thorough and intimate a knowledge. In spite of this, she secretly shared Bülow's discouragement at the artistic deficiencies of the performance, which upset him so violently that they almost made him ill, especially as he saw his own efforts frustrated, for he had carried on an ardent propaganda and at the later performances even provided the *claque* out of his own very limited means. From Cosima he met with a noble understanding in all things, and her lucid, highly cultivated intelligence was a stimulus to him, so much so, indeed, that he felt a certain consciousness of her superiority. The elfin element, which was so deeply rooted in her nature and led him to divine in her a genius rare in women, often aroused a feeling of humility in him. Thus he wrote to his friend Jessie Laussot: "These wonderful girls have indeed a right to bear their name; full of tact, intelligence, and affection, they are interesting figures such as I have seldom come across. Another man than I would be happy to associate with them. But I am embarrassed by their obvious superiority, and the question of how I am to appear sufficiently interesting to them prevents me from appreciating the charm of their society as I should like." But, in spite of their betrothal, he had no idea how near Cosima's soul had drawn to his, albeit unconsciously, and the real, deep mystery of her nature remained, both now and in the future, a closed book to him.

Moreover, Liszt had not yet given his final decision. In his every letter Hans could, indeed, be sensible of his affection and kindliness; but Liszt's mind, too, was distracted by the question whether the marriage would be a happy thing for these two, both of whom he loved in their different ways. In December, after his return from the great performance in Berlin, he had written by way of warning that he felt sure Hans would desire nothing but to carry out the will of a father whose sole object was to do what was best in every situation. In March Frau von Bülow still did not know what was really going to happen. Hans certainly suffered from this agonizing suspense. On April 20 he remarked with characteristic tact at the end of an interesting letter to Liszt: "My forlorn condition here is terrible. I should be glad to go back to Weimar, so as to work a little, my poor capacities are completely dormant in Berlin." Liszt now invited him to Merseburg or Weimar, where they could talk everything over at their ease. We can see what was to be discussed from Blandine's birthday letter of May 7 to her grandmother: " Cosima will surely have told you about her marriage. My father has asked Herr von Bülow to meet him on the 11th of the month at Merseburg, presumably he means to settle everything with him there." Bülow responded to the call and stayed at Weimar for a week. They now arrived at an understanding, though there was no lack of obstacles and delays; but it looks as though Liszt was rather more reserved towards his favourite pupil than he had been previously, for as early as April 2 he had written to his mother: " Daniel will probably not arrive in Paris till this evening. I hope he will bring you the best of news from Berlin, where the little girls are flourishing splendidly. They have been fairly well amused this winter, and their character seems to be more equable. If by some miracle a little reason could be got into their mother, one might augur the best for their future. However, I shall do everything that is feasible for them. I tell you in confidence that there is much talk of a marriage between Hans von Bülow and Cosima. She seems to be very much attracted by him. I have nothing against it, but I stand by my intention of not influencing my daughters' choice; that is the most convenient and at the same time the wisest course for me in this situation, which is not of my making, but has been thrust upon me, and whose drawbacks I should like to obviate both for myself and for my daughters. Daniel will certainly have acted as intermediary between the mother and daughters. I am not letting him stay in Weimar, so as not to embarrass him in this role, which, I fear, he will handle somewhat clumsily. It would have been disagreeable to me to see him just now, for, with the best of intentions, the good fellow is naïve enough to burden his heart with all sorts of nonsense which exhausts my patience." There is a strong echo of the Altenburg in this. But Frau Anna would not let herself be misled, and replied in her wonderful way, which was at once motherly and strong: " Your letter of April 2 made me very happy. On the same date I too posted you a letter, which you will probably have received at the same time as I received yours. Just as two people who love each other often have the same thought, isn't it? — and that is really beautiful. In spite of the fact that you did not want Daniel to visit you on his way to or from Berlin, it happened all the same, and it was a good thing. If it were possible, I wish he could see you as often as his sisters do, it would do him, too, the greatest good; but since it cannot be, I beg you to converse with him more often by letter. In him the spirit is willing, but the flesh is weak. He is still so young and inexperienced. He must and ought to be reminded of his gratitude and filial duties to you. He will listen to you, because he loves you — and he loves you very much. But he also loves his mother, and he sees her more often than he does you. Care ought therefore to be exercised lest her words produce a bad influence on him, so I again beg you to write to him oftener. Yesterday evening he went to see the Abbé Bucquet. I am very anxious that he should not disregard the Abbé, who gives him good advice and is very fond of Daniel. Yet for the last few months he has not visited him so often." She goes on to say: " The news of a marriage between Monsieur de Bülow and Cosima does not surprise me. For a girl *tête à tête* with a young man for a long time past — and he her professor too — friendship may well be kindled, and from friendship, love. And now, supposing this marriage were really to take place, it does not seem to me *brillant*, but it is not always marriages which appear brilliant that are the happiest. I always heard it said at Weimar that Bülow was very intelligent, that is always a *ressource*. Even if there is no fortune, he can earn it if he has health. But unfortunately I heard from his mother here that he is often in poor health. One good thing about it would be that in him you would have a son-in-law who understands you and is able to appreciate you. Besides his professorate, too, he has another little post, so his mother told me here, and he is still young and can *avancer*. Besides, this *mariage* gives Madam d'Agoult an opportunity of making some sign, her house, or even two small houses belonging to her, so the children say, next door to each other, are to be *demoler* (pulled down) in a little while, and the avenue de St. Marie is going to be turned into a boulevard."

YOUTHFUL PICTURE OF COSIMA LISZT

About 1855 — *After a drawing by Claire Charnacé*

But a long time was still to elapse before the prudent Liszt gave his full assent. And so the summer went by. Bülow went for a cure to Baden-Baden, where he found a number of dear friends and in particular made the acquaintance of a noble woman, Madame de Kalergis,[1] who afterwards became a friend of Cosima's. Liszt himself went to Gran for the performance of his Festival Mass. But his daughters had started for Paris, to surprise their grandmother, who heartily rejoiced at their presence. " They were greatly pleased with Paris again," she wrote to her son in October, " and God be praised, they are still well, in spite of the oppressive July heat which we have had, which has often reminded me of the year '11. After two months Cosima returned to Berlin, where she was already living in spirit more that she was here, and Blandine stayed with me."

And so, externally at least, the lives of the two sisters were separated. For Blandine, too, was now to meet her great and splendid fate, which lasted, alas, for so short a time. Her sentiments towards her future brother-in-law were gay and tinged with humour — for in this latter sphere her gifts were remarkably great. Liszt himself had observed this with joy when he had been in Berlin in November of the past year and seen " *ces demoiselles.*" " They are most presentable (*passabel*), dainty and Parisian. Among other entertaining ways, Blandine has one which is to mimic Philarète Chasles. She really made me absolutely split with laughter by her lifelike imitation of the gestures, carriage, and even style of this professor's teaching and academic eloquence. She hit off the language and phraseology of professorial style in a way all her own. Hans assured me that shortly before I arrived she had already kept up this sort of entertainment for more than an hour. The Chasles lectures are very popular, and Monsieur Philarète is making quite a sensation here. I shall attend his next one." Blandine now wrote to thank Hans for a composition which he had sent her from Berlin by the hands of one Herr Gotheimer. She had been highly delighted on opening the packet and finding the *Mazurka* in print.

[1] *Née* Nesselrode, afterwards the Marie Monchanoff who figures so much in the later part of the book. — TR.

She teases him a little and reminds him of certain moments in their life together, and how he had got it into his head that his master's daughters might be a little supercilious. " I dream of our charming evenings, uninterrupted by impatient or malevolent enemies. I think of our disputes about Taglioni, et cetera. I think of so many things that I should almost have forgotten the excellent Gotheimer, had he not reminded me by an opportune sigh." And she continues: " Now that Gotheimer has gone, I can thank you without infringing the laws of politeness for your charming present, my dear Hans. And while I am thanking you, I shall scold you at the same time. Do you know that it is very naughty of you not to write to me? I know that you are very busy, and that you have been playing a great deal in public. But could you not have found a little quarter of an hour to think of me? Ah, I know the reason. It is not all your work or all those people who are responsible for your silence, but a certain lady who successfully usurps my place in Berlin, whose acquaintance I only made at the concert at the Tiergarten, but whose name also begins with a B, and who by her conversation and her wit consigns me to utter oblivion, does she not? — now haven't I guessed right? " This seems to have been a most charming and teasing allusion to Bülow's veneration for Goethe's old friend Bettina. It is true that at Weimar he had also paid attentions to her daughters for a time.

Cosima had now returned to Berlin. She had archly hinted to Bülow's mother that she might make her return to Berlin less burdensome by coming half-way to meet her; and Frau Franziska had accordingly gone to meet her at Cologne. But even now their suspense was not at an end. Liszt still could not make up his mind to give his final consent to the marriage, for he could not quite come to an agreement with Bülow's mother. Yet Cosima still stayed in her house, while Hans had long since moved to a lodging in the Eichhornstrasse. And so this year, too, was filled with the joys and sorrows of an engagement. But Bülow's future wife was already his good comrade, who by no means exercised a timid restraint over him, but herself possessed such a fund of energy that fighting and striving, far from alarming her, gave her a certain pleasure, so long as they did not affect his health.

She had soon felt at home in the musical world of Berlin, so that she was also perfectly familiar with the questions which had to be fought out. And so Bülow found in her, if not a companion-in-arms, at any rate a friend with a full understanding of the joys and sorrows connected with his work. Concerts and controversies became, so to speak, almost indistinguishable. He felt compelled to have a perfect set-to with the representatives of the various newspapers, in spite of the fact that Wagner advised him against it. But out of this tragicomedy there arose a comedy in which Cosima played the leading part. She had heard that the well-known critic Rellstab intended to stay away from a concert of Bülow's on the pretext that he had to go to the ball at the Opera. This was the second time that he had tried to evade the difficulties of criticizing Liszt's compositions. " And now," so Bülow himself relates, " Fräulein Cosima took it into her head to punish the old Incorruptible and did so by a charming letter in which she said all sorts of flattering things to him about the wit and charm of his articles and begged him to give a hearing to one of her father's masterpieces, promising him that it would produce a very strong impression on him. And Rellstab came, ' in full dress,' found the Sonata very interesting — very beautiful, indeed — and had what was to all appearance a fearfully moving interview with Liszt's daughter, which ended in a cordial handshake." Thus one of Bülow's opponents was placed *hors de combat* by the shrewdness of his future wife.

Next came his concerts abroad, his experiences in Leipzig, and, above all, the Musical Festival at Aachen, where he had gone with his young pupil and friend Eduard Du Moulin. They shared the same ground-floor room, and so long as the festival lasted, Bülow was in the wildest spirits during the hours in which he could withdraw from the general activities, though there was, indeed, something forced in his gaiety. But he was not given to moping, and, whether at the concerts or elsewhere, he displayed a gaiety and a sense of deep happiness which proved how sure he was of his ground. For the more laurels they won, the fiercer were the attacks of their enemies, and Richard Wagner wrote about this festival in utter bitterness of spirit: " The devil take you all with your swinish musical festivals (*Sau-musikfesten*) and musical horse-races. You allow yourselves to be pelted with flowers on the one hand and muck on the other. What can ever come of such doings, where it is not even possible to get really good performances? Nothing of real worth, and a lot of beastliness to boot." This was what Bülow felt too, when he returned home and read the hostile reports of the Aachen Musical Festival: "I feel as sick as if it were the end of all things (*ein weltuntergangsmässiger Katzenjammer*), the mephitic bath of eau-de-Cologne with which we have been drenched was hardly calculated to freshen us up much."

All the same, the Musical Festival had one advantage, in that Liszt felt how true Hans had remained to him even in these days of struggle: his heart was softened, and now at last he gave his consent to the marriage.

It is profoundly interesting to watch Liszt's attitude towards his daughter Cosima's marriage during these days which followed the Aachen Musical Festival, with all their hard battles and subsequent insults of a vile press. He had retired to the mineral springs at Aachen to take the cure, though from the first he was determined not to submit to it fully. Perhaps he hoped to acquire from his stay in the old imperial residence a certain attitude of mind towards his daughters, akin to that which had characterized Charlemagne, the great ruler of Aachen. But, besides this, his head was now full of two themes, which were working out, not musically, but in feelings, ideas, and even actions. It was just at this time, when he was about to release his children from his tutelage — for Blandine's marriage too was pending — that there began to stir within him a sense of antagonism between his affection for his children and his great feeling for the Princess Wittgenstein. If something of Wotan was uppermost in him at that time, it was not as the All-father who loved his children, but as the god who, in the spirit of the Greek Heracles, felt that he was under obligations to the Frigga of Weimar. It is significant that in informing the Princess of the date of the wedding he added the words: " if you consent to it." There was a deep conflict of emotions within him, though at the same time he tried to be just to his daughter

Cosima. On July 28 he writes to his mother: " Towards the end of next week I hope to be rid of my indisposition and shall go to Berlin with Hans von Bülow for Cosima's wedding. The banns have already been published. Their exuberant youth is, I believe, settling down into a happy union. Their characters are admirably suited to each other, and I foresee a distinguished artistic career for Hans. I esteem and love him for his rare talent, his keen intelligence, and the great rectitude and nobility of his character. I am greatly pleased with Cosima, too. She was always my favourite and has gained both in bearing and in intellectual distinction. She seems to me to have a better and more competent grasp of things than her sister, who is too much inclined to let herself be guided by vain and sentimental fancies. I do not know how marriage will affect Blandine. Her ideas are very different from mine; they have too much resemblance to those of her mother, who abandoned herself entirely ' *au vogue des passions*' (to the tide of passion). This was why I feared that I might not be able to be as helpful to her as I wished." He had no presentiment of the hard fate that hung, sinister and menacing as a dark cloud, over this sunny figure and the happiness which she both gave and enjoyed. He would, indeed, have had to stay the wheel of fate if he had wished to be his daughter's protector. But, for all his power, round the altar at which this daughter was married hovered the figure of the Dance of Death, which at this time, just before and after the marriage of his daughters, had such a strong fascination for him and pervaded both his imagination and his works.

In other respects his daughters went firmly and surely on their way, in spite of the elfin mischief of their nature. Their grandmother saw things with a simple, truly feminine intuition. It was at this time that she wrote: " Now he is off to Berlin for Cosima's affairs, in connexion with her *mariage* to Monsieur de Bülow. May God's blessing be upon it. They have known each other long enough, so each knows the other's weaknesses, love bears much with patience." This latter quality existed to a wonderful degree in Cosima. Her long engagement, which had lasted almost two years, had, indeed, redounded only to her good and to their mutual understanding. Thus, though on other occasions Bülow had spoken of marriage with the forced and sardonic humour of opinionated bachelordom, he could say on the eve of his wedding: " For the rest, I am indeed fortunate — if I think of the possibility of any other marriage for myself than this, I feel revoltingly disgusted. My wife is such a perfect friend to me that it is impossible to imagine anything more ideal." But even in these words there is a curious tone, which sounds rather coldly analytical in a young man of six-and-twenty speaking of such a marvellous fiancée. But it was his way to say nothing of what he felt most deeply.

Yet he was right in using this language, though it expressed only part of the infinite richness of this unique being. She was his perfect friend, and, we may add, his discriminating comrade-in-arms. And if there was anyone besides Liszt and Wagner who had a full, deep, and warm understanding of him, it was his future wife, who formed, or, rather, was capable of forming, a wonderful complement to him, as much by her intellectual as her spiritual endowments. She was also welcomed with sincere sympathy by his relatives. His mother had become more and more reconciled to the idea of accepting her as a daughter-in-law, and it no longer seemed to her so disagreeable as it had done to see Liszt's daughter the wife of her son; but a certain prejudice, worthy of a woman of the middle classes, still persisted on her side.

But Cosima felt drawn by a strong sympathy towards her husband's stepmother, Luise von Bülow, the daughter of Field-Marshal Bülow von Dennewitz, who had dispelled the shadows and brought sunshine into the closing years of the life of Hans's father. This lady possessed a certain faculty of clairvoyance, and on first meeting the beautiful daughter-in-law who in later days clung to her so touchingly, she received a singular impression, which remained somewhat tragically imprinted on her memory. When the young couple first entered her room, she saw, by a sort of second sight, another form than that of her stepson at his young fiancée's side. At the time she took pains to suppress the emotion — nay, terror — which she felt at the vision that she supposed herself to have had. She wrote down this deep presentiment, thus showing how seriously she took it. It was particularly serious to her because she loved her stepson, and because his future wife had made an unusual and striking impression on her.

But now the last difficulties which had stood in the way of the marriage were surmounted. Bülow had at last, with great difficulty, become naturalized as a Prussian subject. All his friends and relations had to bring their influence to bear in order to effect this. The obstacles which prevented him from becoming a Prussian subject were due to a curious idea of his father's, who, with a lofty disregard of all questions of domicile, wanted to be neither Dessauer, Saxon, nor Prussian, but simply a German. The day of the marriage was fixed by Liszt for August 18, on account of his cure at Aachen. He desired a Catholic wedding, and Bülow responded to this wish with all his heart. In doing so he was not merely complying with his master's desire, which was to him a command, for his own sympathies were with the idea. At any rate, he would not hear of repeating the ceremony in a Protestant church, "for," as he wrote to his father-in-law a few days previously, "so far as my personal opinion on the matter is concerned, apart from my inclination towards Catholicism, I think more highly of a church which regards marriage as a sacrament, and so I could feel no personal satisfaction in the blessing of a Lutheran pastor." At that moment this saying was quite after the heart of Cosima's father; for during that very summer his old taste for Catholic church-music — not as it was, but as it had been, and as he wished to remodel it on the basis of Palestrina and his school — was working in him with especial force. It is curious, too, how much he thought and wrote about such problems and projects during these days.

The ceremony was to have taken place very quietly; but the newspapers had for a long time past seized upon this *cause célèbre* — even, as Bülow trenchantly observed, without being authorized to do so by receiving a fee for inserting their comments. And so the couple were married in the Hedwigskirche on the morning of August 18. It is curious to read the announcement which Liszt sent round on the occasion:

I have the honour to announce herewith the marriage which took place today at the CHURCH of ST. HEDWIG, BERLIN, between my daughter

COSIMA LISZT

and

HERR VON BÜLOW

BERLIN, August 18, 1857.   FRANZ LISZT.

Here, as in all his dealings with the various "black-robed gentlemen," to use an expression of Gustav Freytag's, we find curious evidence of his love of form and formalism in the affairs of life, though he had himself managed to cast them aside so boldly. The Princess did not appear at the wedding; but Bülow wrote to Liszt on August 15: "I should have liked to write a few lines offering Her Serene Highness the Princess Wittgenstein my profound respects. For to her, too, is due part of the gratitude which I owe for my life's happiness. For it was she who had the idea of sending your daughter to Berlin and so enabled me to discover that angel, in both mind and soul, whose name is Cosima." There is something strange in these words, and indeed in the whole ceremony, which was celebrated, for the rest, solemnly and quietly. On the very same day the young couple accompanied Liszt to Weimar, but without stopping there. They continued their journey to Baden-Baden, where they were received by Richard Pohl and his wife. There were other friends, too, to greet the newly-married pair; but their next destination was Bern and the Lake of Geneva.

There was no merely symbolical significance in the fact that Frau Cosima wanted to visit this wonderful lake, which had been so fateful for her father and mother. It was in Geneva that Franz and Marie had spent their days of deepest passion, and that Blandine, the " angel with the golden hair," had been born; and at this very time the beautiful Countess, with her daughter Blandine, who seems to have taken her mother's side entirely, had made her way to this lake, in order to start from thence for Italy. Frau Cosima, too, was anxious to see her sister and mother and confide to them her own deep emotions. But, as

Liszt wrote, almost with a sigh of relief, " the pair found that the mother and daughter were no longer in Switzerland." And so, apart from their common enjoyment of the wonderful and characteristic scenery of this mysterious and sublime lake, Bülow had the better of the bargain, for he found his old friend Karl Ritter in his curious little house at Lausanne.

Meanwhile there was no lack of outward adventures, culminating in the losing and finding of the trunk in which Bülow had packed his " monies (*Moneten*)." But these were wonderful days, and Frau Cosima was filled with supreme ecstasy at the beauty of this unique spot. And now came the visit to Richard Wagner at Zürich, as a result of repeated invitations and of their own wishes. Bülow succumbed to a severe attack of rheumatism and had to keep his bed in the little hotel " Zum Raben " for two days, which his master brightened by presenting him with *The Valkyrie*. It was not till a week later that they could move to the " Asyl." Their happy host was suffering at that time from a superfluity of visitors, and Eduard Devrient had just appeared on the " Green Hill," having secured a certain measure of official and financial support for the Master's new project, which he intended, or at least promised, to turn to account in his own sphere of activity at Karlsruhe.

But Wagner was delighted with the young couple. His Zürich period came to its climax in this house, which this much-enduring and much-travelled man regarded as a refuge (*Asyl*), which he hoped never more to leave. It had been placed at his disposal by the friendship of a noble pair, the Wesendoncks; but all this is a well-known story which I have no intention of repeating. The most interesting picture which these days have to offer us is the meeting between the two noble women Mathilde and Cosima. Both were wonderfully favoured by fortune. One of them walked in the full sunlight and thus was better able to radiate forth an inner warmth. But the other was emerging from the shadows of her youth and possessed, as it were, a radiance of her own; we see here, in some sense, the contrast between moon and sun. On the one hand we have the pure and noble effulgence of the young, intelligent woman, stirred to her depths by those artistic emotions which she also aroused, and possessing a perfect understanding and the noblest womanly sympathy for the Master's creative work and for the whole of his pre-eminent nature; and on the other hand we have the young woman who was now to see her newly-wedded husband's teacher and ideal. Not to push the comparison too far, the whole situation was permeated by something of the atmosphere of Hebbel's *Gyges und sein Ring*. But at the time the interest and emotion of them both were engrossed by the Master's works, and under Bülow's magic hands the piano-scores of *The Rhinegold* and *The Valkyrie*, which Karl Klindworth had completed, came to life. We may, if we please, regard this as one of the first performances of *The Rhinegold* and *The Valkyrie*, as well as of the first two acts of *Siegfried*, which Bülow succeeded in clothing with their form from the Master's pencil-sketches. All the guests were deeply impressed, especially Cosima, who listened in silence, and when the Master turned to her with a question, burst into tears. It was by her husband's own hand that the great veil was lifted before her eyes, and the work of the future Master of Bayreuth appeared before her in all its grandeur.

But not only did she hear what was already in existence; she also saw with her own eyes the completion of the new poetic creation which Richard Wagner had derived in the plenitude of his creative powers from the great love-scene in the third act of *Siegfried*, but from which his constructive power evolved a world apart: *Tristan and Isolde*. When the young couple arrived, the first act of the libretto was already finished. When they left, after some weeks, the whole was complete. There is a singular and wondrous charm in watching these two women as they listened, like two Leonoras, to the work of this Tasso. As each act was completed, Bülow at once prepared a fair copy of it, and then it was read out act by act to the little circle. Finally there came the "collective reading (*Kollektiv-Vorlesung*)" of the whole great burning poem, that wonderful song of night and day, as it has been called, interpreting it in the sense of Wolfram's opening recitative in Act III of *Tannhäuser*, though by a misapprehension of its true and profound significance.

Wagner's account of the impression made by this scene, as he afterwards dictated it at Triebschen to Cosima, who had been present as a listener at the time, is characteristic: " When Frau Wesendonck seemed particularly affected by the last act, I said consolingly that there was no need to mourn over it, for this was the best *dénouement* in such grave circumstances — in which Cosima agreed with me." Both these women had, as it were, held the fatal potion in their hand and yet were destined by their fate to live.

Wagner could not wonder enough at Cosima and her husband too. He wrote to his friend Julie Ritter that the visit of the young Bülows was the most pleasant event for him that summer. " I have seldom felt so agreeably and delightfully stimulated as by this intimate visit. During the morning they had to keep quiet, for I was then writing *Tristan,* of which I read them a fresh act every week. Then for all the rest of the day we almost always made music, which was faithfully attended by Frau Wesendonck every time, and so we had our appreciative public immediately at hand. Bülow's command of the instrument is enormous; in addition to his unerring musical intuition, his incredible memory, and all the wonderful facility which is peculiar to him, his indefatigability and unfailing readiness were of splendid service to me.

" If you know Cosima, do agree with me, too, in considering the young couple as happily endowed as possible. With all their great intelligence and real genius there is so much that is light and buoyant in both the dear little people (*Leutchen*) that one cannot feel anything but happy with them. It was with great regret that I let them go in the end, but only in return for a faithful promise that they would come again next year."

And now they started on the journey home, first passing through Saint Gall, where the young wife wanted to look at some lace, to Ötlishausen, which had once been a refuge for Bülow's father and his wife Luise. Bülow was in the most magnificent spirits, and in this mood they arrived in Munich, where they stayed a few days, " naturally," as Bülow wrote, " without exposing ourselves to a surfeit of plastic delights *à la* Wittgenstein." " For the rest," he added exuberantly, " I seem to myself so little like a married man that I feel as free as is good for my peace of mind." They next went on to the Altenburg, where they spent a few weeks together, Cosima then returning alone to Berlin, while Hans still stayed on with his father-in-law. " Her husband," as Liszt observed not without gratification, " left her the trouble of arranging their winter quarters in Berlin, a task from which Cosima would extricate herself very well. She is in every respect a right-thinking, clever, and very practical young woman."

And so, on his return to their home in the Anhalterstrasse, Bülow was able to experience the magic charm of a young *ménage.* He was welcomed there by his pupils, and one of them, my father, presented him with a composition, entitled *Feiergesang.* After more than eighty years it has come back into my hands, and I cannot deny myself the pleasure of reproducing a strophe or two of it here:

> All joyous the songs that now greet you!
>   As envoys of heaven's high throne
> The Muses have sent them to meet you
>   And hail you a son of their own.
> The Muses who carried you singing
>   To earth in a bright aureole
> And laid their sweet tones, clearly ringing,
>   Deep into your heart and your soul.
> They vowed you a care never-ending,
>   If you do to their service no wrong,
> And with flashes of genius blending
>   Their song ever rise from your song.
> The songs that you here have been singing,
>   Inspired by their kisses divine,
> To heaven's high throne have gone winging
>   And there with heaven's music combine.
> As echo they now are descending,
>   With a sweetness infused from above,
> And as love was their theme never-ending,
>   So now are they singing to love.

Such was the song sung by the young man of three-and-twenty to his friend and master on his entry into this hospitable house, which he was now to see Frau Cosima ruling with her fairy hands.

✳✳✳✳✳✳✳✳✳✳✳✳✳✳✳✳✳✳✳✳✳✳✳✳✳✳

CHAPTER III

HOPES AND SORROWS

L ISZT was right in supposing that his daughter would set up
her new household in Berlin like a good, shrewd, worldly-
wise woman. After the short and brilliant visit to Weimar, filled
with festivities in honour of the young couple, she had returned
to Berlin transformed and matured by a few weeks of newly-
married life. The elfin element in her nature, which she still
preserved up to her extreme old age, formed a mystic accompaniment to this new sphere of existence in Berlin, and produced
an effect as of something exceptional upon all who came in
contact with her, both men and women. The great fuss made by
the papers about the marriage between Liszt's daughter and
Hans von Bülow was a purely superficial affair, such as has
always been and always will be the custom of the sensational
press. The public loves to have any event of importance served
up to it, as it were, in the form of an anecdote. But now a strange
flutter ran through the intellectual world of Berlin. The new
home, though not rich, was not poor either and was maintained
on a high level owing no less to Frau Cosima's social relations
than to the efforts of her husband, inspired as they were by a
sense of honour at once artistic and aristocratic; and in spite of
their quiet and reserve it became in a few weeks' time an object
of general interest in society.

But her chief preoccupation was to be a true wife to her
husband, which was her aim, as well as a good comrade, which
was his desire. This was the underlying motive of her efforts
from the first, and with her undoubted genius she was able to do
justice to it in every respect. She was at once clever and high-

minded, and when there was any question of economizing, she did it at her own expense only. She was indeed a pattern for all women, combining in herself all the good German qualities, but surmounting all weaknesses and pettinesses — especially those of the women of Berlin — by the polished and charming animation which she had acquired in Paris, and which was in no way studied. She was perfectly conscious of what was her right course: her task was to lead upwards to dazzling heights the husband whom she already saw shining as a star of the first magnitude in the firmament of Berlin. But to do so it was above all things necessary to guarantee him security for his own creative work, even amid the crushing burden of toil which was piled upon him, and which, in his restless activity, he had increased almost beyond his strength. Thus alone would he be able to realize himself and devote himself to creation in the fullness of those powers whose existence his two masters, in Zürich and Weimar, had more than once proclaimed, and in which she herself believed with all her woman's intuition. It is wonderful how, without imposing any restraint upon her husband's temperament otherwise than by her smile and the calm which emanated from her being, she sought in the first place to free him as much as possible from the worries of the Conservatoire. On his return Bülow had been completely at loggerheads with his Director and colleague Stern, but she succeeded in so managing things that the greater part of the morning was set apart for his own work, and Bülow was thoroughly convinced that in this lay the sole possibility of further development for him. It did not entirely square with Frau Cosima's views when her father told his favourite pupil that he ought to devote himself that winter not so much to his piano-playing as to an attempt to make himself a sort of musical field-marshal in Berlin. In itself this was certainly a just idea and encouraged her husband in a course in which he was to achieve the highest things. But in this respect she was her mother's daughter too, and Marie d'Agoult had gone wrong about Liszt for the very reason that she had not perceived early enough the great transformation which was taking place in him from a virtuoso to a creative artist. Without being in the least pedantically opinionated, her daughter now wished to take measures in advance. She knew, too, that no change could be brought about overnight, but that it was necessary to produce a general atmosphere, in which Hans von Bülow should become not merely a virtuoso or a leading conductor, but a composer as well.

She herself was so eager for knowledge and self-development that she not only preserved what she already had, but carried it still further; and this Parisian now adapted herself to Berlin conditions in an absolutely brilliant fashion and, through her French education, succeeded in securing for her husband a position of his own in a world which was far from insignificant and, what is more, was full of emulation. It is attractive to follow these first beginnings, and the charm is greatly enhanced by the fact that soon absolutely everything was at her feet. This young wife, schooled and experienced in all the arts of hospitality, profited brilliantly by her husband's old circle of friends, in which she at once drew a distinction between those who might be of value to her husband intellectually and spiritually, and those who were really nothing but pretentious people, who, taking advantage of her husband's great nobility of character, exacted disproportionate services, involving real sacrifice, in return for the slight ones they had themselves rendered. She was on friendly terms with Kroll, Laub, who had been her master for a time, and the amiable little Jew Fischel, who both as a man and as a writer maintained till his last breath that truly touching devotion of which a Jew is capable. He entered the lists on behalf of his friend and his great cause selflessly and with a wisdom genuinely prompted by the heart, and for this reason was honoured in Bülow's house by his wife, too, as one of their trusty friends. Among these were also Mützelburg and, above all, Karl Tausig. Perhaps their relations with the latter — the only one of Liszt's pupils who was a serious rival to Bülow — were the most exceptional. Shortly after his return to Berlin the young couple had him to stay with them in their young *ménage,* and Bülow made him play at one of his own concerts, thus opening up the road to triumph before him. The episode also reveals Frau Cosima in her unique relations to her father. She loved him and revered his art, and while her mother, Marie d'Agoult, had longed in vain for works of his own creation, the daughter came to know them while still very young; and Bülow tells us himself how his wife could sit beside him at the piano while he was practising and, so to speak, coach him in Liszt's symphonic poems and compositions for the piano, not theoretically, but with a wonderful intuitive comprehension of her father's works. For it must be established from the outset that even at that time she already stood on the highest level of musical capacity, and knew neither rest nor peace till she had developed it still further; and it cannot be too often emphasized that in her Frau Clara Schumann might have seen the rise of a rival had not Frau Cosima had loftier artistic duties, and ideas too, than those of an executant. Much to the annoyance of Stern, the director of the Conservatoire, she took lessons in composition from a friend of her father and husband, Karl Friedrich Weitzmann, who after a long life spent in moving about between Riga, Reval, St. Petersburg, London, and Paris, had arrived in Berlin in the year 1847. Musically, he had a very stimulating personality, and he now became a friend of the family, to whom she owed a great deal. For she wanted not only to join in the discussion of all musical questions, but also to offer advice and take an active part in them, all the more so because, in her deep affection for Hans von Bülow, she wanted to further his progress. During her stay in Zürich she had come to know the man to whom her father did homage. And she had chosen as her husband the man who did homage to them both. But supremely high as she already rated Richard Wagner's art — and, indeed, she could not have done otherwise — she had it equally at heart that her husband should not remain one among the crowd of mere musical journeymen; on the contrary, she adopted as her own her father's saying that Hans, and no other, should one day enter into possession of his artistic and musical heritage. It was at Zürich that Bülow's relation to both Liszt and Wagner had been defined in the most cordial and magnanimous terms by the Master himself, who greeted him, not as a pupil, but as a friend and artist with a marked individuality of his own. It was known to Frau Cosima that the Master was always trying to exert an influence over him and his creative work, but that his wishes had so far been frustrated by a sort of humility on the part of Bülow himself. Thus Bülow had for a long time been engaged on the composition of music for *Romeo and Juliet,* and had had much discussion and correspondence with Wagner on the subject; but he had not arrived at the point of putting the idea into execution, perhaps because Wagner had directed his attention to a still greater conception — that of composing an *Oresteia* symphony, not in the old style, but by the method of writing an overture to each separate drama of the trilogy, which together would form a symphony on the new model. There is no doubt that this idea of Richard Wagner's was taken up by Frau Cosima on her husband's behalf. In order to give him the literary and poetic foundations for such a work, she even seems to have made a summary of the *Oresteia* as a " program " on the lines of which Bülow was to construct his symphony. The study of hers which is extant under the title " Oresteia " cannot be interpreted in any other way, nor can it have served any other purpose than that of leading Bülow by her gentle hand and deep understanding into the distant realms of antique tragedy, while at the same time pointing him clearly and surely towards the artistic form which she had already recognized in Richard Wagner's *The Ring of the Nibelung.*

This study is important for the understanding of Frau Cosima's method of work. At the same time it is a sign of how she not only aspired and strove, but derived ideas and images of her own from this grandiose work of the tragic muse. She had a definite conception of classical antiquity and in this study [1] she gives in her clear language, which is already quite adapted both to poetic style and to her own sensibility, a striking and heart-stirring picture of the great tragedy.

There is no doubt that she had a marked literary tendency, which, it must be said, Bülow not only encouraged, but highly esteemed. For from the first he had rightly recognized the commanding greatness of her character and talent and even during their engagement had been somewhat nervously conscious of her surpassing qualities.

A room in the new home was assigned to her, he wrote to the

[1] See Appendix, page 441. — Tr.

Princess, as her sanctum, embellished by the latter's wedding-
present, Deger's Madonna, which, he explained, was its only
adornment. Here she lived for her ideas and her work. But her
literary activity did not lack stimulus, and the result of this was
not only to awaken, but also to increase her existing tendency.
In this respect her mother was her model from the first. There
is no question whatever that, in spite of all her inward reticence
— which arose chiefly, and quite involuntarily, out of her sensitiveness on her father's account and is a psychological mystery
with which we have no right to meddle — her mother's literary
activity also acted as a sort of spur to Frau Cosima, and that
this met with her husband's full approval. He was an enthusiastic
admirer of Daniel Stern's *History of the February Revolution;*
and, indeed, the whole personality of this remarkable woman
had exerted a strong influence over him, both as the mother of
his wife and as an independent creative artist, even before he
became personally acquainted with her. As a young wife, Frau
Cosima now saw the disappearance of the obstacles which had
been placed in her way by the Altenburg; her relations with her
mother had now become freer, and the marriage of her sister
Blandine, especially, had done nothing but improve them. For
almost at the same time as she had married Bülow, Blandine,
too, had become engaged. Among the many suitors who flocked
round the lovely, gentle, merry Blandine — who, according to
Wagner's description, had a certain witty self-possession, yet
very quick intellectual perceptions — she had chosen the young
lawyer Émile Ollivier. It was about this time that Liszt wrote
to their mother on the subject of his daughters: " In order to
satisfy me completely, they must, at any rate, not be content to
go through the world idly and drowse along from day to day.
They must be born again in the spirit of what is best in me; not
till then will they be wholly mine." When Liszt gave his consent
to the marriage, which seems to have come about entirely under
the mother's auspices, he had not yet made Ollivier's acquaintance. His attitude of reserve towards this daughter's marriage is
curious. He writes, it is true, that the young advocate had
approached him in the most correct way, and that the accounts which he had received of him were satisfactory in every

respect; but his remarks in connexion with the marriage of this daughter have a curiously bourgeois tone. Not so those of his mother. She wrote with a certain feeling of satisfaction: " You have now the joy of knowing that your second daughter, too, will soon be provided for, and reasonably happily; and according to her own *goût* (taste) too, which pleases me very much, as also Cosima. For all the difficulties that attend the married state are more easily borne if one can attribute the choice of one's husband to oneself alone, and such is the case with both your children."

Even the wedding had an almost adventurous character, for Blandine and her mother made the journey to Florence in order to have her married on Italian soil. This decision originated in some sort in the Countess's memories of the past, when she had given birth to this child. It was this which influenced them far more than any social difficulties which might have arisen in connexion with a wedding in Paris, though these too should not be exaggerated. They would have been of a personal nature only, for in Paris it would hardly have been possible to avoid a meeting between the father and mother. It is curious, however, that even her grandmother did not know Blandine's future husband. For she says: " Blandine wrote to me ten days ago that she wants to be married on October 22, if possible, and if the papers on both sides arrive in time. I think her wishes in the matter will be gratified. I do not know Émile Ollivier, but I hear from many quarters that he is a talented, distinguished, honourable young man of thirty-two and has a promising future before him. May God grant His blessing on this union! "

And the marriage was actually solemnized in Florence on October 21, as Liszt himself relates. By this means yet another obstacle to the intercourse between Frau Cosima and her French relations was removed. And now that the ice was broken, it was obvious, too, that the mother's literary activity could produce its full and untrammelled influence on Frau Cosima. To this was added the stimulus of literary circles in Berlin itself. Her relations with Varnhagen von Ense and Adolf Stahr, in particular, were of decisive importance. Bülow had inherited these connexions from his father, the romantic, who was a friend of

Tieck. Varnhagen von Ense in particular took him and his young wife under his especial protection. He was at that time quite the most famous political publicist and was greatly feared, on the one hand for his caustic wit, and on the other hand for his indiscretion, which this former Prussian envoy at the court of Baden, now a leading celebrity in Berlin, used as a weapon, in so far, that is, as it was not part of his very nature. Varnhagen has been both overrated and underrated. At any rate, he exercised a far-reaching influence, and everybody strove to gain admission to his *salon*, though often with mixed motives. The young couple had no occasion for any such feeling, for towards them Varnhagen and his household showed a certain consideration. Before every one of his parties he even wrote to ask them what people would be pleasing or unpleasing to them. It was in this connexion that they made the acquaintance of Morin, a Frenchman who was staying in Berlin at the time. He had only come to Germany with the object of spending a day at Weimar, where he had a brief meeting with Liszt and the Princess; but he went on to Berlin and was detained there for a long time. He had been editor of the *Revue de Paris*, and people said that he was studying German affairs; he was also suspected of having written the letters from Berlin which had appeared in the *Revue germanique*. It is curious that these reports were first brought to Frau Cosima's notice by the Princess Carolyne, who had already in her possession the first volume of this review, which had just appeared, and it is significant that Bülow begged the copy of her. We may conclude from this that his young wife intended from the first to write for this review, as she afterwards did very extensively.

The activities upon which Frau Cosima now resolved were to be of a twofold order: she meant to translate German poems for this review, but also to act as a correspondent, like Morin himself. She was eager, too, to express her views on politics. This is a most remarkable phenomenon at that period and is not to be attributed entirely to her association with Bülow's friends. It is true that Bülow had a great friendship for Ferdinand Lassalle. This clever and undoubtedly remarkable man, who had become a close friend and to some extent an associate of Lothar Bucher, had taken a great liking to Bülow, and above all to the art and the artists for whom he stood. Lassalle had a remarkable and grandiose personality. His philosophical works are of deep import, his poetry shows power, and — what is quite remarkable in a Jew — a robust candour and an open and honourable allegiance to all things German, to which he was also true both as a politician and as the protagonist of Social Democracy. The Bülows' house was frequented by Lassalle and Lothar Bucher alike, while Bülow was particularly fond of attending this striking and remarkable man's reunions. But Frau Cosima at the last moment always found a pretext for staying away from these seances and regarded Lassalle's influence over her husband with a certain anxiety, though not for political reasons. It was to please Lassalle that Bülow, under the pseudonym of W. Solinger, had set to music Georg Herwegh's *Arbeiter-Marseillaise* (*Workers' Marseillaise*), which was used as the labour anthem of the German trade union, the Allgemeine deutsche Arbeiterverein. Frau Cosima was more intimate with the poet and found him more sympathetic. She had made his acquaintance before, in Zürich, and was on intimate terms with his family. She was godmother to Herwegh's son and esteemed the father highly, so much so that in the year 1858 even Richard Wagner felt a trace of intellectual jealousy of him. As early as the summer of 1857 he had written the following verses in her album, which echo the deep, striking, and bracing impression made upon him by the young bride. She appeared to him at first sight as the important figure that she was.

> Lo, every human countenance
> Is with soft light irradiate,
> Reflected from the radiance
> Of the high stars that guides its fate.
> The genius of harmony
> Shall hold thee evermore unfurled
> In wingèd tones, nor canst thou be
> Attuned to a discordant world.

This was fine homage, which certainly made a deeper impression upon Frau Cosima than the joyful verses with which Hoffmann von Fallersleben greeted the young couple at the Altenburg on October 3, on their way back from their wedding-journey. There is a certain interest in comparing the two.

> The Festivals are at an end,
> And Weimar is itself again.
> But other guests now hither wend,
> A bride and bridegroom in their train.
> Two branches of the Lisztian stem,
> The best of all we offer them:
> All the goodwill our hearts contain.
> For — these two festivals are blest
> All other festivals above:
> Whene'er two hearts are joined in love,
> And one for another prays the best.

Thus Frau Cosima had no political reservations to make with regard to the founder of the German Labour party, who actually laid so much stress upon the word " German " that a few years later Bismarck even thought of entering into an alliance with him, to crush German democracy between them, as it were — or, rather, its representatives, the German Radicals. It is characteristic of them both that his faithful Lothar Bucher, who brought about the alliance between him and Lassalle, should have been one of the circle of friends who met at the Bülows' house.

There was another, too, who was a welcome guest there: the well-known and famous theologian Bruno Bauer, who in spite of his notoriety was honourable at heart. Frau Cosima has herself described to the present writer the impression made upon her by this singular controversialist during those days in Berlin. He frequented their house a great deal, and it is characteristic of her that Frau Cosima, who at all times preserved her deep and even childlike piety, should willingly have entered into searching discussions and controversies with him. But for the very reason that he approached everything from a doctrinaire point of view, he could obtain no influence over her. This would have been much easier for Lassalle, had not her true womanly intuition dictated to her a certain reserve towards this remarkable man. Lassalle was clever enough to feel this. He was hardly ever received by Frau Cosima alone, and she always managed to evade his invitations. But he, too, was among those who reverenced Frau Cosima most deeply. He tried every means of attracting her, such as inviting her to meet French visitors; but, as we have said, she remained inexorable. She had, indeed, a further reason: she thoroughly distrusted his influence over her husband, and since the well-known experiment with hashish she felt an openly avowed antipathy for him. But during the whole time she spent in Berlin she was very much concerned with politics, and at the beginning of the Bismarckian era wrote accounts of them for the *Revue germanique.*

Meanwhile she took a lively and spirited part in the musical life of Berlin and particularly in her husband's great and growing activities. Shortly after their return from their wedding-journey they had to go to Dresden, to be present at the concert for the benefit of the court orchestra. Some works of Liszt's were performed there, and Cosima rejoiced at the success of this festival. She also formed a close friendship with Johanna Wagner, Albert Wagner's famous daughter. But one thing is obvious at once: she was trying to convert this remarkable singer, whose reading of the part of Elisabeth was so fine, from her coldness towards her uncle. But in this she was no more successful than her husband and Alexander Ritter.

But through all her efforts there runs a clear and definite tendency. When, at the cost of heavy sacrifices to himself, her husband wanted to give a great orchestral concert as propaganda for the new art, she was prepared to enter into this cheerfully and to meet the considerable deficit out of her housekeeping money, though, as Bülow himself writes, they were forced to deny themselves in consequence. But Bülow had the positive joy of watching the steady rise of his position in Berlin, due, no doubt, to his own merit, but also to the vigorous collaboration of his wife. She stood at his side unperturbed, with the faint, exquisite smile that was characteristic of her, always on her lips, ready at any moment to parry hostile and spiteful insinuations by an energetic and pregnant saying. By this means she won her husband a friend of the greatest importance, who became very intimate with them. This was Ernst Dohm, the editor of the *Kladderadatsch,* a man of extraordinary ability in the sphere of pure journalism and possessed of a true poetic gift as well. What is more, he was a thoroughly faithful and straightforward friend, who remained faithful both to Cosima and to Hans up to his latest breath. He too belonged to the number of those who revered that wonderful woman; indeed, Frau Cosima found in him a good and sterling ally in her plans and projects. She made full use of this noble and honourable man's enthusiasm for the benefit of her husband.

In after years she would still recall a lady who was already quite old even in those days, but who made a most pleasing impression upon her. This was Hedwig von Olfers, who, after much moving about, had set up her home in Berlin, and, what is more, her *salon,* which was frequented by more than one generation at the beginning of the nineties. Frau Cosima cherished a particularly affectionate memory of this lady.

She shared with Hans a great taste for the theatre, which, as we have seen, had attracted her ever since her childhood. While still a child she had gained deep and lasting impressions from the English Shaksperian company which had visited Paris, and in addition to this she remembered all the tragic actresses in Paris in their chief roles. By no means the least of these was Ristori, of whom she had been especially fond. In Berlin, too, the drama was the object of her liveliest interest. At that time Marie Seebach was the star at the court theatre, and her readings of the parts of Julia and Gretchen were feats which have hardly been paralleled since. This clever and sweet-natured woman frequented the Bülows' house, as did also Fräulein Franz, with her delicate and thoroughly artistic sensibilities, who afterwards, as the Baroness von Heldburg, became the wife of George, Duke of Meiningen, and remained a particularly faithful friend to Frau Cosima to the end of her days.

In one of his letters to the Princess Wittgenstein, which are so valuable in establishing the sequence of events, Liszt describes an evening party given by his daughter in his honour. He passes in review the guests who were present: " When I appeared at Cosette's house about nine o'clock in the evening, I found, among the ladies present, Fräulein von Jasky, Mdlle Ney, who had made a delightful medallion of Cosette, Mama Bülow, Frau Dohm, Frau Herwegh, Fräulein Franz, a fascinating English-woman, Frau Stahr, Frau Bulyowsky, and the Genasts. Among the men were: Hoffmann, Stahr, Kossak, Dohm, Mützelburg, Fischel, Strauss, Kroll, Schreiber, Weitzmann, Hildebrandt, the painter Becker, Roquette, and others. Mitzi sang several of my songs — none but mine, indeed. I regaled the company with my *Étude in D minor* and my *Valse-Caprice*. To close the evening I played Weitzmann's two *Canons énigmes* for piano duet with Hans."

We see what an extensive circle had attached itself to the Bülow family, and it kept on growing. It was joined by Johanna Wagner, Alwine Frommann, and many others. In the year 1859, too, the great artist Devrient, who was now old, made a deep impression on Frau Cosima, both personally and as an artist, by her recitation of Schiller's *Die Glocke*. It is all the more remarkable that the young wife devoted herself with especial eagerness to mathematical and astronomical studies. In this, too, the personal factor played a great part. For it so happened that at this very time the young astronomer Giovanni Antonio Schiaparelli was studying in Berlin. We know that as early as the year 1860 he was appointed second astronomer at the Milan Observatory, of which he became director two years later. He achieved fame by his discovery of the markings on the surface of Mars. In short, he became one of the most famous astronomers, not only in Italy, but also in the whole civilized world. He was also Frau Cosima's master in both these sciences, the latter of which had an especial attraction for her. For all that is great and significant stimulated her to deep and serious efforts to grasp it, at the dictate of an inward compulsion which had its origin in her very genius. It was characteristic of her remarkable nature that she indulged in no mere smattering of *belles lettres* and the arts, but grasped and assimilated everything with her whole heart, soul, and strength.

It is therefore comprehensible that such a remarkable woman, adorned with all the charm of youth, should have increased Bülow's prestige and position, both in his own eyes and in those of others. She had once called her future husband a "venal courtier," and now he had actually become court pianist, for which his father-in-law could not refrain from expressing his deepest personal gratitude to the Princess of Prussia. For it was with full recognition that young Bülow now, too, entered court circles, and the fact that Liszt's daughter was his wife undoubtedly shed a special lustre on him. In a word, she was a social star in the firmament of Berlin, and when, after many long years, she returned to Berlin as the Lady of Bayreuth, all the *salons* opened before her, and she became once more the figure of universal fascination that she had been when, as a young wife, she had held a sort of court in the Anhalter Strasse.

She was also on pleasant terms with the court of the Prince of Hohenzollern-Hechingen, the Mæcenas who led a wonderful life at the Löwenberg, where he had an orchestra of his own, and invited both Liszt and Hans von Bülow to initiate him into the new music. On Bülow's first appearance there, in April 1858, when he conducted the *Faust* Overture, the Prince would not be denied, but insisted upon sending Frau Cosima a valuable bracelet by his hands, at which Liszt was almost more delighted than she was.

Bülow had passed a winter of endless friction and exertion, full of passionate conflict; and he was longing for a rest. But there was one thing which kept him in Berlin — the piano-score of *Tristan*, which came into being during those hard years in Berlin. For Hans von Bülow, too, this was a new world, and none save he, who was a thorough master of technique and had a deep intellectual affinity with his master, could have achieved this piano-score, which was a work of art in itself.

Cosima's attitude towards Richard Wagner was a curious one. After their return from their first visit to Zürich the Master had been greatly worried by the reserve which showed itself in her letters. Thus as early as the year 1858 he wrote to her husband:

" But first I must also tell you that Cosima's reserve towards me really distresses me, since I think I may be sure that the reason she gives — that she had rather tell me everything by word of mouth — is only a pretext, and that, on the contrary, she really feels embarrassed in my presence. Should my manner have been too odd — should an abrupt remark or a little joke have offended her now and then — I should be justified in regretting that in my trustfulness I have let myself go too much, a thing which I always heartily acknowledge and regret when I have thereby alienated a person whom I esteem. In the present instance I am perfectly conscious that there can be no question of anything but a mistake. My unthinking confidence in persons whom I find sympathetic has more than once led to an estrangement before now; may that of your dear young wife be of short duration."

His letters to Hans, like those to Liszt at an earlier date, were now full of his troubles, and the young artist was, if possible, even more self-sacrificing and touching in his devotion than his father-in-law. Frau Cosima, too, took a large-hearted interest in Richard Wagner's position. And when, as the result of a mis-understanding, the young couple were led to suppose that Wagner was preparing to part with *Lohengrin* to an agent for a thousand thalers, she wrote to warn him that he ought not to sacrifice his work in such a way.

At this time Wagner was thinking of bringing his young friend to Bern as conductor, an idea which, though excellent in itself, would have torn Bülow away in the middle of an important stage in his development. For Wagner, too, was of the opinion that he was sure to do great things yet " between Spandau and Moabit." But he longed for the young couple, and all the more so because since the spring of 1858 his position in Zürich, and on the Green Hill, had become rather precarious. As we have seen, he had gone off to Paris in a hurry, but on his return he found matters in no wise improved, and he pinned his hopes on the appearance of the young couple, who had now started out again for Zürich on their summer holiday. Bülow had gone on ahead to give two concerts at Baden-Baden, in order to make good the losses which they had suffered as the result of a burglary at their Berlin resi-dence. Besides, about this time Blandine had sent on to him an idea of Belloni's, by which he was to get a whole series of extremely profitable ("*rentable*") concert engagements. It is most charming to see what an interest his sister-in-law took in the position and success of her sister's husband, with whom she was so friendly. It was a most touching relation which grew up between them, and Hans von Bülow was on terms of close and truly brotherly affection with his wife's brother and sister. Daniel was everything to him, and Blandine was a true friend, who turned to him on all occasions with complete trust.

The young couple met again at Baden-Baden and now continued on their journey by way of Freiburg. They were enchanted with the fine cathedral, as well as with the falls of the Rhine at Schaffhausen. It is charming to read how they arrived by night in the little Swiss town, but found no room in any hotel and so, having with difficulty hunted up a carriage, drove out to the falls of the Rhine, which made a great and overwhelming impression on them as thus seen by moonlight and at break of day.

They next went on to Zürich, where the Countess d'Agoult was waiting for her daughter and son-in-law. He was no longer a stranger to her, but had already come to know her intimately by letter. But now, at this first personal meeting, this glorious woman cast her spell over him. He had too much family feeling not to revere in her the mother of his wife, and to this was added the fact that Daniel Stern was also extraordinarily sympathetic to him as a writer. It was now that he wrote the following fine description of her: "Still wondrously beautiful and noble in form and feature, for all her white hair, she particularly surprised me by her unmistakable and great resemblance to Liszt's profile and expression, so that Siegmund and Sieglinde at once came into my mind. Add to this a dignity and nobility of bearing free from all effort — the elegant, polished ' *laissez-aller* ' which sets those who are exposed to its influence at their ease and sharpens their intellectual faculties, thus making them display their nature to greater advantage. I confess that I am quite bewitched by this experience and can no longer so far restrain my thoughts as not to think with what inexpressible satisfaction I should be filled by the idea of seeing this beautiful and remarkable woman, who in ten years' time will represent the ideal of a matron with a fresh intelligence, side by side with that unique personality, forming the social complement to his Olympian nature. I must not think of it, lest I fly into a rage at the parody and caricature which at present acts as shadow to his light at the Altenburg." It is true that he immediately modifies this harsh judgment by adding: " And yet how unjust it would be to rail against this woman, who had so great a claim to be warmly defended by those who have to some extent learnt to know her! No, it is merely one's natural sense of outward beauty which protests and must protest against her."

The conflict that filled Liszt's life affected him deeply, indeed, and no less so his wife. For the tension which had arisen between Franz Liszt and Richard Wagner on account of the Princess had also reacted upon the Bülow *ménage,* though of course without making the slightest change in their feelings and attitude towards Richard Wagner. But they were naturally oppressed with anxiety about his great, phenomenal being, and it would have been a good idea if, as Richard Wagner too suggested, the young Bülows had brought Franz Liszt with them to Zürich; for he was the only person who could have done any good there. And in the catastrophe which was now approaching, one of those who wished to help did appeal to him, but " to him alone," so that the Princess's feeling of opposition to Richard Wagner was naturally still further embittered, and, in these circumstances, Liszt could not appear at Zürich and so save what might still have been saved.

The events which followed will not be related here: they have been often enough treated in the fullest detail. The brunt of the blame has so far been too much thrown upon Frau Minna, though she could not change her own nature. Furthermore, a construction has been placed upon Wagner's relations with the Wesendonck family that has gone wrong in its conclusions. The moment Bülow entered the Asyl, he found Richard Wagner in the middle of a violent scene with his wife. Had he not been restrained by consideration for his mother-in-law, he would at once have gone on with Frau Cosima to the Lake of Geneva. But he saw, too, that he was bound to stay for his friend's sake, and thus the Bülows played an important part during these last sad days at Zürich.

For Frau Cosima there was something disgusting, nerve-racking, embarrassing, and even repellent about all these incidents, this tension and thunderous atmosphere which hung more and more oppressively over the lively social life at Zürich and the Green Hill. But a great and powerful motive now made itself felt in her, which strongly influenced her feelings towards Richard Wagner in future: an inexpressible pity. The example and proximity of her mother were a strong and material support to her during these days, if, indeed, she needed anything of the sort. But we must bear in mind how the figure of this unique woman shone before her eyes, sunlit and bright, yet surrounded with the glory of a tragic past; how this woman, who had always been a queen of the *salons,* and whom she might proudly call mother, now gathered about her all the great figures of Zürich. Gottfried Keller and Semper were now joined by Feuerbach and Moleschott, and Frau Cosima now became more closely acquainted with them all, and made the deepest impression upon them. It was now that she stood godmother to the son of the poet Herwegh, who is at present engaged in preparing a worthy vindication and monument to his father in the shape of an exhaustive biography. Indeed, thanks to the relations of her mother with the Herwegh family, she felt particularly drawn towards this house, and we know how the poet revered the mother and extended his veneration to the daughter, to whom he remained a devoted friend till the end of his life. Perhaps the Paris atmosphere and memories revived by her mother's influence seemed all the more sympathetic to her amid the far from pleasant and satisfactory happenings at the Green Hill and aroused more agreeable emotions in her. But, little as she suspected it, in the eyes of Richard Wagner she had now become in some sort a predestined guide.

The young couple stayed till the moment when Wagner was preparing to leave the Green Hill. " On August 16," Wagner relates, " the Bülows, too, left me, Hans dissolved in tears, Cosima in a gloomy silence." Meanwhile Wagner felt a sense of liberation, although he was leaving the " Green Hill " behind him and was filled with a new inward discord, for which he was as yet unable to account to himself, save by his sentiment of complete emancipation from what lay behind him. It is naturally most difficult, and indeed futile, to follow up threads which are as fine as cobwebs. The relations between Frau Mathilde and the creator of *Tristan* had been momentous. During its development and formation she had poured out sunshine and light on him; but now a new day was breaking, and the gentle, suffering profile of this wonderful woman already shone before the Master through this fiery glow of dawn.

The young couple returned to Berlin. Everyday cares and the busy rush of Berlin closed round Frau Cosima once again in full force. And now followed a year in which Bülow's creative work and activities really won him fresh scope. It was at this time that a work of his father-in-law's, which he had meant to impose upon the Berlin public willy-nilly, was hissed; though afterwards, when Franz Liszt himself appeared to conduct it in person, it met with complete and glad acceptance by the public. All these experiences were shared by Frau Cosima, and so were all the trials and tribulations involved in the preparation of the piano-score, and the worries about Richard Wagner, who was now in Venice, more than ever tormented by the most grievous financial calamities. Part of this correspondence was now taken over by Frau Cosima in order to make what had to be said tolerable, to some extent at least, though part of it was, indeed, most painful and disappointing. With regard to his wife's feeling for Richard Wagner, Bülow wrote shortly after the catastrophe, with that lovable charm which was all his own: " My wife is very sweet again now, I wish you could ever come to know her otherwise than she has so far been in your house. Hitherto her talkativeness has always been silenced in your presence, and her frank, expansive nature has shrunk back into itself. There was a compliment to you in this, though offered in the wrong way: ' *Ehrfurcht hielt sie in Bann* (Awe held her spellbound).' She is always afraid that you might consider her childish and altogether too insignificant to be able to love and understand you, yet she is one of the very few who are really capable of doing so. But an end to these puffs of her merits (*meritalen Artikelschreiberei*)! " One involuntarily feels how here, all unsuspectingly, he is playing with fire. He was full of thought for Wagner and did him every service of which he could anticipate his need. On his wife's account, too, he was at pains to improve the relations between the Master and his friend in Weimar and writes on one occasion: " After all, Liszt is a splendid fellow, and I think the first act of *Tristan*, about which he is beside himself with rapture, has been a healing balm to him." He closes his letter of January 1 with the words: " Keep a little fondness in the New Year for me and my wife, who embraces you." And a little later he writes: " Here comes my wife with orders that I am to give you her ecstatic greetings, and she adds that you must not take her recent mad letter in bad part, she is quite ashamed of having sent it. The dear child was so happy about *Lohengrin*, you understand, she loves you too. We wept over it together." These were great and noble creatures, who shared each other's emotions; but a great crisis in their destiny was drawing nigh.

The new year brought their visit to Paris, which was to be rich in artistic successes for Bülow, while for Frau Cosima it brought the meeting with her mother and sister, and above all with her splendid old grandmother. They did not accept the old lady's invitation to stay with her, but took up their quarters in the rue de l'Échelle. Her grandmother was overjoyed, however, to make Hans's acquaintance and took the most whole-hearted interest in his concerts, for all her son's pupils and friends could be sure of this wonderful old woman's motherly interest.

But what Frau Cosima enjoyed most was not only showing her husband Paris, but also revelling in the transports into which he was thrown by the capital and its powerful impressions. He had now become an out-and-out adherent of Napoleon III, and his earlier leanings towards Proudhon and the Republic completely disappeared under the influence of the imperial capital. It is interesting to see how in this he also shared the views of his mother-in-law, of whom he said: " Madame d'Agoult is turning away from these bourgeois and becoming more fair to the Emperor, whom I have come to know and admire in Theodor Mundt's admirable book on Paris." He allowed himself to be entirely guided by these impressions, and the extraordinary success of his evening concerts (soirées) could not but confirm him in this. As he himself said: " The terrain of Paris has turned out favourable beyond my hopes, and I intend to exploit it to the utmost of my power in the future."

It was evident that the position of the Countess d'Agoult and, most of all, the prodigious impression made by Franz Liszt had paved the way for him here, so that he was able to gain a real hearing for his consummate art; and in Paris he met with nothing but victories. But in spite of this he had already succeeded in that year in forming a clear impression of musical conditions in Paris, even though in his first intoxication he saw both men and things in too rosy a light. Thus at that time he was in ecstasies over Gounod, not having yet arrived at a true artistic estimate of his conception and travesty of Goethe's *Faust;* whereas even as a child Frau Cosima had estimated Gounod's *Faust* at its true worth and had by this time entirely shaken off the influence of her surroundings in Paris. Now, too, she appeared at his side in a light all her own, both musically and artistically. To this was added the curious emotion aroused in her by noticing how remarkably he was attracted by her mother's position in the literary and political world. It was the exalted social charm of this atmosphere, which he now entered for the first time, and which yet seemed to him quite different from that which the Princess Carolyne diffused round her at the Altenburg. How small and even paltry Weimar seemed to him now! His view of life had become considerably broader, while Frau Cosima found spiritual satisfaction in Paris through closer contact with her mother and above all with her grandmother and sister.

Moreover, it was about this time that Pictet's *Voyage à Chamounix* appeared, throwing a beautiful and absolutely enchanting light on the days which the young couple, Liszt and Madame d'Agoult, had spent in Switzerland in the charming society of George Sand and other friends. Liszt ordered the book at once, both through Blandine and through his mother. It interested him greatly, reminding him of days and hours of the sublimest happiness. About the same time appeared his book *Les Bohémiens,* which he presented to his mother and which his daughter now read. In it she noted, with a curious catch of the breath, the strong and dominating influence exerted over her father by the Princess. But though she herself exerted a similar influence, how different it was — always great in conception and always successful in achievement! This had already shown itself during the time following their return from Zürich.

Bülow had found lying on his table as a Christmas present the libretto of his opera *Merlin*. As early as his Weimar days he had come upon the legend of Merlin in reading Friedrich Schlegel's *Romantische Dichtungen des Mittelalters;* it had attracted him strongly, and seemed fully to satisfy his longing for a subject for an opera. In his delight he wrote about it at the time to his father-in-law and to Wagner, the latter of whom invited him to send him the plan of it, for Bülow had even set to work on one. Amid the unremitting work which had left him no peace since October 1851, the idea had not been dropped, though he had given up preparing the libretto himself. He looked round for a sympathetic poet whose mind should have some affinity with his own. For a time he seems to have had Alfred Meissner under consideration, for Meissner's original lyric vein was musically stimulating to him. After the appearance of Meissner's novel *Sansara*, which also attracted him by reason of its Indian subject-matter, he had quite decided to approach him with his request: " Perhaps I may then venture to bother you with a request which may seem to you burdensome and even overbold, though to me it will be a question vital to my intellectual life." Next Richard Pohl's light and fluent collection of poems came into his hands, and as a matter of fact he did select five poems and set them to music. He entered into negotiations with him, too, about *Merlin*, asking him to make himself acquainted with the literature concerning the subject, which he had already fairly well mastered himself. He seems to have received a favourable answer from Pohl while at Baden-Baden. But Pohl was not the right man to provide him with what he needed. For while occupied with the Master's great works, Bülow had himself arrived at the conviction that nothing more could be expressed by means of symphonies and trios. " In these forms," as he said, " one could have but negative aims." He longed with his whole soul after the music-drama and considered himself capable of producing a great work of this kind. It is curious that in earlier days he had come across the subject of Tristan and had contemplated treating it in the form of a music-drama; but he now turned to that other figure of the Arthur cycle: Merlin. He felt impelled to write an opera in the plenti-tude of his powers! " Figures — men — demigods — a Satan; what delirious bliss! " But he was inevitably disappointed: little Pohl was incapable of creating an opera-libretto out of this subject. But on Christmas Eve 1858 a surprise of the most de-lightful kind fell to his lot. Frau Cosima had noticed her hus-band's longings and strivings with a deep joy; and without say-ing any more to him about it she set to work to sketch out the scenario of this opera-libretto, calling into counsel her friend Dohm, in company with whom she completed the poem. This was only another great and characteristic proof of her wondrous qualities with which she now delighted her husband, who broke into a perfect rapture over the poem and said that in a very short time he would be able to submit the completed first act to his father-in-law, at the same time as the libretto. This marked a climax in the relations between these two, united by so close a bond, yet threatened with a danger of almost the same kind as that which had affected Liszt and the Countess d'Agoult — that is, the great intellectual demands made by the woman, or rather her deep-rooted longing after creative artistic power in the part-ner of her life. The libretto has unfortunately vanished, and so far nothing has come to light of Hans von Bülow's fragmentary setting of it. It is a strange fatality that Bülow thus absorbed him-self in a legendary cycle which undoubtedly pointed towards the same end as that by which Richard Wagner chose to guide his destiny — the Holy Grail. The Merlin legend in itself was by no means adequate to express Hans von Bülow's whole nature. Perhaps it was better suited to the Princess Carolyne, who, like Frau Cosima, had written an operatic libretto — not for Liszt and not for Hans von Bülow, but for Hector Berlioz. It was that of his *Les Troyens*, and there can be no doubt that it was owing to this libretto that even the greatness of Berlioz's art came tragically to grief. At any rate, Richard Wagner thought the text pitiful and Berlioz himself to be pitied.

A singular parallel suggests itself between Frau Cosima and her father's mistress. It was in the fullness of strength and conviction that the former approached the work by which she meant to open up the way for her husband to the heights of Parnassus. Thus it was one of the highest and finest services that a wife could render. How different from that of the Princess Carolyne — working for Berlioz in Franz Liszt's study, while intending to offer her hand to the latter for life!

It is to be regretted that not a trace of this libretto exists. But it can be understood — and in later days the writer herself was well aware of it — that only to a greater and a stronger man was it given to enshrine the Holy Grail in a work of art.

But the effect of this composition upon Bülow's life and work continued to make itself felt for long afterwards. In the year 1860 he was still talking of it, and Liszt, too, never lost sight of *Merlin,* in the unexpressed hope that in this subject his favourite pupil and son-in-law might find himself as a creative musician. For the time being, Bülow was entirely distracted from it by Wagner's *Tristan.* Only slowly did the piano-score take shape, but it was all the more important for the full understanding of this work, which was novel in every respect. Thus the piano-score represents the achievement of a thoroughly kindred genius and, in spite of all opinions to the contrary, must still be reckoned as a sterling work of art today. Bülow suffered during its preparation like a soul in torment. It was like hewing a rock of adamant.

This work also dominates his correspondence with Richard Wagner and is the cause of his attitude towards the estrangement between the Master and Franz Liszt, which, at this period of all others, can only be called tragic. But here Frau Cosima's true and uncompromising power of discrimination showed itself in all its clarity, and from the very first she recognized where the underlying causes of this conflict lay — causes which had had an influence upon her life from of old and even upon her relations with her father. It is attractive to consider the curious superficial similarity between the works of the Princess and of

Frau Cosima. For all her amiability, the Princess was always one of those who approached her friend in rather a dogmatic spirit and forced her literary views, not so much upon his mind as upon his sense of chivalry. This was particularly apparent in his book *Les Bohémiens* (*The Gypsies*), which had just appeared. It is true that, if anybody was in a position to know something about the gypsies, it was she, who ruled, as it were, over a branch of them at Woronince. But it is equally true that she was incapable of saying what Liszt ought to have said on the subject, and what, owing to her influence, he never fully expressed. But how different was Liszt's daughter! Was her husband to write a symphony? She placed the material before him, as it were in program form. Was he looking round for an opera-libretto? All unsuspecting, he found it on his table at Christmas. Richard Wagner was faced with the urgent question of a performance of *Tannhäuser* in Paris, involving the translation of the libretto into French. The most obvious thing was to think of Frau Cosima. But she felt that she could not do justice to the work in French. For a time she pondered over it night and day, but she then announced her firm decision not to do the work. This is not to say that she would not have been the ideal translator; but her modesty and unbounded reverence for this work of art had much to do with the fact that she declined to undertake this great task. Her father was at that time absolutely opposed to any performance of Wagner's works in Paris with French words. Since the year 1849 his ideas on the subject had undergone a great change. He was also right in holding that Richard Wagner, with his German words, belonged to the Germans and could not be rendered in another language. I do not think that it was on these grounds that his daughter declined to make the French version, but rather out of the great and profound diffidence which she experienced before the Master's works.

On the other hand, in this year, 1858, she had already taken up her pen boldly in order to work for the *Revue germanique,* mentioned above. This review could show quite a remarkable group of contributors and would be of interest to us even if Frau Cosima had not sent it some very considerable contributions. Under the editorship of the two publicists Dollfus and

ERRATUM

Page 116 omitted from book

also intellectual power; but it was not so much the latter which turned her into a translator as her delight in the exercise of her knowledge and faculties, and, next to that, the fine, proud aim of contributing, unknown and undetected — for she always wrote anonymously — towards the housekeeping. As this review came out, in which appeared the best work of Cosima's mother, Frau Carolyne followed it with interest and curiosity; but side by side with the mother the daughter was also an unknown, but no less successful, contributor. There is a great and significant charm in this, which seems even greater — indeed, it acquires a graver significance — when we see that at that time Bülow himself turned aside from his opera-libretto and devoted himself to minor compositions. The fact that this took place was due to a sort of self-knowledge, which was, however, erroneous. He once said that he was entirely lacking in the lyric vein in music, and that his true province was " reflective horrors (*reflektives Grausen*)." He came nearer to a true characterization of the tragic phenomenon of his own personality when he once said: " I am a sort of Hamlet, who in the end, however, is unequal to his task and is drowned in the sea of trifles at which he is forced to slave." The beginnings of this mood, certain symptoms of which had already appeared earlier, were depressing and deadening enough. No doubt his later development was already casting its shadow before it. Nobody was more affected by this development and made more efforts to check it than his wife. For in making her translations she was not striking out an independent line for herself, but filling a void which would soon have been bound to make itself felt, in view of her vast inward resources.

And now they were both faced with a task to which they rose with all their spiritual power and greatness of soul. On August 20 young Daniel arrived from Vienna to spend his holidays with his sister. But immediately on arriving he fell very seriously ill, and with the deepest grief and gravest anxiety Bülow watched the germs of a mortal malady develop in him. During his stay in Prague he had formed the closest intimacy with this wonderful young man. At Bülow's great " *Zukunftskonzert* (Concert of the Future)," at which were performed the *Fest-*

116

been impatient. You revolt against the sickness, but you still think sick people weak-willed. I have read to the end of the *Gerusalemme Liberata.* I am a little disturbed by a certain mingling of the sacred with the profane, not only in the character of the work, but also in its sentiment, which I consider a far greater fault. So long as one worships God, so long as one sees Him, so long He is the Almighty and the source of inspiration. But here one is forced to pass so lightly from a love-scene to one of these serious reflections, and the mixture is by no means harmonious. For the rest, I consider that Boileau was most unjust to Tasso. There is more in him than mere *cinquecento.* He shines, above all, in his similes and his description of battles. Erminia is very sympathetic to me and seems to me to be the most consummate figure. As for Rinaldo, he is no Achilles, and, besides, I am a little like Coulon, I do not like privileges. That he should triumph through his valour is good. But through his diamond shield — *halte là!* Long live freedom! I have read *Don Quixote* again. To be really comic a man must have a heart, the source of it is the same in Cervantes as in Molière. Their hero makes one laugh and smile, laugh through one's tears, if the expression goes deep enough. This is high and subtle comedy, the masterly comedy (*comédie de maître*) of which Joubert speaks. Adieu, dear Father. Go on making the finest plans for me, for I love you." These were the last words which he wrote to his father. His tender life was threatened with extinction. It was the Princess herself who made Liszt hasten to Berlin on December 12 to Daniel's bedside. He arrived just in time. Liszt writes characteristically: "You were right, dearest, to send me here, it was, I fear, high time." Thus it was vouchsafed him to spend the last days at his son's bedside, at one with his daughter and her husband as he had never been before. In the letter which he wrote to the Princess about his son's last hours, he has left us a beautiful picture and enabled us to know his daughter in her full self-dedication. Bülow, too, felt this and spoke of these last hours with far more heart: "His malady could not be exorcized, it was a wasting away, a gradual extinction — he had only vital force enough to last twenty years. His last days were brightened in the noblest way by the loving, unaided care of my valiant

Nefftzer are to be found, side by side with Hippolyte Taine and Ernest Renan, Daniel Stern and her friend Ronchaud. The first number had already aroused great interest at the Altenburg, with which the neo-Bohemian group of poets, including Moritz Hartmann and Alfred Meissner in particular, had become very closely connected, besides Hoffmann von Fallersleben and Friedrich Hebbel. Meissner had aroused the Princess Carolyne's especial interest, and through this channel was revived the old connexion with Bülow, dating from his father's time. The year 1858 already brought with it a rendering of Hebbel's *Maria Magdalena,* of which the poet sent a most delighted account to the Princess Magne. It was by Cosima. It is astonishing how quickly this young woman of twenty, who had been educated entirely in Paris, adapted herself to a German literary work which was so completely novel in style, and succeeded in rendering even the most poetical shades of meaning, finding the corresponding French sentiment for them, though they were to a certain extent antagonistic to the French type of feeling. This in itself is an extraordinary achievement. She next translated Gustav Freytag's Roman drama *Die Fabier* and then a piece by Puttlitz, neither of which, however, appeared in the review. On the other hand a whole series of other works were subsequently published in it — not only translations, but also political articles, for politics had a very strong attraction for her. In this, too, there was undoubtedly an intellectual affinity between her and her husband. Since their visit to Paris together, both of them had taken an extraordinary interest in Napoleon III, to whom Hans von Bülow was attached with a positively boyish enthusiasm. He saw in him something out of the ordinary, and amid all the confusion which prevailed in Germany he hailed the Emperor of the French as the predominating figure in Europe. But soon Napoleon had to give place in Bülow's estimation to another: Bismarck.

Once, in a moment of melancholy, Liszt spoke in praise of Cosima's facile pen, and in this he was right. Literature was undoubtedly a distraction for the young wife, and an occupation, too, which was in keeping with the intellectual *milieu* of Berlin. In view of her youth this argued not only innate capacity, but

115

klänge and *Mazeppa*, the *Faust* Overture, and the Prelude to *Tristan and Isolde*, young Liszt had arrived at the deepest comprehension and the greatest admiration for Bülow's commanding ability. He wrote to his father at the time: "Bülow has once again demonstrated the truth of the words spoken at Philippi: 'A lion at the head of fifty deer is better than a deer at the head of fifty lions.'" But it was above all in the *Faust* Overture that the spirits of Bülow and of his young brother-in-law found themselves so remarkably at one. It is worthy of Bülow, and yet quite original, when young Daniel expresses as follows his impression of the *Faust* Overture, which forms the great landmark in Wagner's work: "The *Faust* Overture, that prodigious thunder-roll of suppressed genius, thrilled me to the very marrow of my bones. I cannot get away from the impression that this overture was more a necessity of the heart than an inspiration of genius, and that its strength consists precisely in its truthful impression of suffering. The opening is gloomy and icy cold as a graveyard, but of course there are none of those imbecilities which usually accompany the representation of a graveyard. The inexpressible, that quality that words cannot grasp, which characterizes works that stand and fall by their spiritual intentions and musical form, is so important in this piece that one is involuntarily seized with enthusiasm for a conductor capable of giving such a reading and making one read such things in it for oneself as Bülow." And so he was in the highest degree delighted by the wild enthusiasm with which Bülow was greeted there. And it was with these feelings that he came to Berlin — only to die.

The months between August and October were filled with anxiety about and for this beloved young brother, to whom Cosima clung with every fibre of her being. But Bülow too loved him like a brother, and every free hour belonged to him. Bülow would sit for hours at his bedside, trying to cheer and comfort him and to keep alive within him those hopes which he could no longer cherish himself; and the young wife presided like a good fairy at this sick-bed. She tried to spare Daniel every painful emotion and to promise him every consolation which she could wring from her very soul, shadowed though it was by

117

grave and even hopeless anxiety. She wrote but little of all this
to her grandmother, for she did not want to increase her anxiety,
though by a strong presentiment Frau Anna foresaw the fulfilment of this threatening destiny. Thus on October 18 the old
lady asked her son: " How is poor Daniel? I heard from friends
here who are in correspondence with Vienna that the poor boy
has a nervous fever — I only hope that he is on the way to recovery. It is so long now since his illness began that I think the decisive moment of his sickness must have arrived, and, with the
help of God and the doctor and his devoted nursing, the best is
being done to save his life. I live in this hope. Cosima said nothing about him in her last letter, nor has she ever told me what
is the matter with him, though I have long been asking her about
it. She says that his malady has no name. You spent three days
in Berlin, that may have contributed greatly towards his recovery. Be so good as to write me something about him soon.
How glad I should be to have him with me and nurse him! I
live such a quiet and retired life that I could devote myself to
him entirely."

Cosima's words, that the malady had no name, contained the
whole tragedy. She had spoken more frankly about her brother's
state to her husband's stepmother, the noble and splendid Frau
Luise, and voiced a doubt whether he would be able to return
to Paris. She had no hope, but her care for him was all the more
pathetic, and all the more agonizingly did she enjoy every hour
which was still granted to him. He himself did not give up hope
and even made efforts to occupy his still active mind by reading.
He had his law-books at hand till the last, and shortly before
the end he was still discussing legal points with his father, who
had hurried to the spot. As he lay sick he read Tasso's *Gerusalemme* and *Don Quixote*. He wrote to his father in pencil, but
with a steady hand: " I can still not see you again today. The
tone of my voice is not particularly pleasant. But I should like
to kiss you above both eyebrows and on the brow for the little
note you wrote me. Patience! Today, at least, I have no special
need of it. I have no lack of consolations, it is far more for you
that I fear. You wrote to me so sadly a few days ago. If all
that you were suffering from was your agitation, you would have

been impatient. You revolt against the sickness, but you still think sick people weak-willed. I have read to the end of the *Gerusalemme Liberata.* I am a little disturbed by a certain mingling of the sacred with the profane, not only in the character of the work, but also in its sentiment, which I consider a far greater fault. So long as one worships God, so long as one sees Him, so long He is the Almighty and the source of inspiration. But here one is forced to pass so lightly from a love-scene to one of these serious reflections, and the mixture is by no means harmonious. For the rest, I consider that Boileau was most unjust to Tasso. There is more in him than mere *cinquecento.* He shines, above all, in his similes and his description of battles. Erminia is very sympathetic to me and seems to me to be the most consummate figure. As for Rinaldo, he is no Achilles, and, besides, I am a little like Coulon, I do not like privileges. That he should triumph through his valour is good. But through his diamond shield — *halte là!* Long live freedom! I have read *Don Quixote* again. To be really comic a man must have a heart, the source of it is the same in Cervantes as in Molière. Their hero makes one laugh and smile, laugh through one's tears, if the expression goes deep enough. This is high and subtle comedy, the masterly comedy (*comédie de maître*) of which Joubert speaks. Adieu, dear Father. Go on making the finest plans for me, for I love you." These were the last words which he wrote to his father. His tender life was threatened with extinction. It was the Princess herself who made Liszt hasten to Berlin on December 12 to Daniel's bedside. He arrived just in time. Liszt writes characteristically: " You were right, dearest, to send me here, it was, I fear, high time." Thus it was vouchsafed him to spend the last days at his son's bedside, at one with his daughter and her husband as he had never been before. In the letter which he wrote to the Princess about his son's last hours, he has left us a beautiful picture and enabled us to know his daughter in her full self-dedication. Bülow, too, felt this and spoke of these last hours with far more heart: " His malady could not be exorcized, it was a wasting away, a gradual extinction — he had only vital force enough to last twenty years. His last days were brightened in the noblest way by the loving, unaided care of my valiant wife." For all their tragedy, then, these days marked an inward climax in the life of this extraordinary woman. During the time when this rare being was fading away, she appeared in her full grandeur of soul. This was recognized by her father with deep emotion and admiration. He saw her presiding over the noble invalid, at whose side she watched all night, and whom she shielded from all painful impressions, so as to make his last sleep as easy as possible. Her father has himself described the last moments in a deeply affecting way. He entered Daniel's little room and saw his daughter kneeling by his side. " Silence. Mystery. A few minutes elapse, sands from the shores of eternity. I said softly: 'His breathing can no longer be heard.' She laid her hand on his heart, it beat no more. Then a little later a sigh — he had fallen asleep in the Lord." And she pointed to the beautiful, peaceful features and the still face, which she compared with a head of Christ by Correggio. She alone rendered him the last services; no strange hand touched him. She wrapped him in his shroud and laid him on the bier in her drawing-room, surrounding his coffin with tasteful ornaments fraught with meaning. She announced the passing of her brother to her grandmother in the following beautiful words: " He nestled into the arms of Death as into those of a guardian angel, as though he had long awaited it. He did not strive against it: he was not weary of life, but he had longed with a burning heart for eternity." Grievously as she suffered at the parting, she remained valiant. This is clearly apparent in her letter to Frau Luise: " You are really good, dear Frau Luise, to associate yourself so faithfully with my deep mourning. It is now a fortnight since I closed the eyes of my childhood's companion, my father's only son, the sweetest and purest youth that ever bloomed. I do not think I have been too weak, I know at least that I made effort upon effort, but every minute I feel a growing grief, and I see people and things as through a veil which I am powerless to tear." The relation between Liszt's three children had been a wonderful one, and both sisters above all had cherished a deep and prescient understanding for their brother's genius. Indeed, this wonderful young creature revealed merits and impulses not only of genius, but of a wonderful type of the noblest humanity. And since, compelled by their tragic family relations, the children had clung together from their earliest days, they formed a wonderful community of souls. Blandine's feelings, too, had been the same as those of Cosima. Her letter to her sister, written on December 17, fresh from the impression of Daniel's death, rings like a heart-rending monologue: "Daniel, Daniel, no longer art thou among us! Thou dost leave us, no farther dost thou accompany us, thou who didst lend beauty to our earthly course, whose angelic glance, whose lovely smile, whose goodness, whose tenderness, whose devotion, abnegation, and sweetness caused us to forget life's harshnesses, thou who didst impart to us the noble aspiration of thy soul, thou who didst awake in us faith and love without ceasing. Sweet angel, why dost thou leave us? For a fairer life, wilt thou say, for a nobler activity, that thou mayst be that which I could only hope to be. Yea, thou art in the heart of God, thou dost partake of eternal goodness, eternal greatness, eternal beauty. Thou, the true likeness of Heaven, thou who dost win all hearts, thou who wast naught but goodness, inspiration, and longing, how dost thou now enjoy all these! Thy powers are redoubled, thou dost live, doing the greatest works in God and through God, loving with the love of the Creator. Thou hast died with all the hopes and dreams of youth, without having known evil. But why didst thou leave us so soon? We need thee still; whither shall we find our way without thee? Who shall bring before our eyes as vividly as thou the dreams, the plans, the sacred emotions of our childhood? Who shall remind us of how we loved one another, of how ambitious each was for the other to accomplish great and holy deeds? How proud of us was our grandmother, and especially of thee! 'Do you know,' she said to you one day, 'nowhere are three children like you to be found.' The words are nothing, but Grandmamma believed it with all her heart. Where art thou now to be found, her darling, her Daniel, thou who wast so beautiful, so clever, so good, so simple, so natural, and so tender-hearted? We shall see thee again, shall we not? Thou has gone before us, to prepare a place for us. We shall be united with thee, ah yes, we shall find one another again, and for the sake of this reunion I will grow

121

without ceasing in goodness and intelligence. I will fill my life with works which shall be pleasing to thee. I will think of thee without ceasing, I will long for thee, and then I shall be sure that I am doing what is good. If only my death might be like thine, the crown of a life as pure and noble! " Thus did she apostrophize Daniel, in a letter in which she exhorted her sister to take care of herself, but at the same time begged to be told all the details of Daniel's illness and the last hours of his life, and, most of all, whether he ever pronounced the name of Blandine. And she asked her sister to collect all the papers that could remind them of their brother, for he always wrote down his ideas. But over all there hung like a shadow the gloomy words: " Yes, it was the Princess who sent me the first fateful news. I opened the letter with joy. I had no eyes for the black seal. But farewell, farewell, my angel, I can see thee no more, my tears overflow. Have compassion for me, as I have compassion for you. Write to me, I hunger for these melancholy details; tell me whether Daniel pronounced my name."

Their grandmother received the announcement with remarkable strength of mind. On January 4 of the following year (1860) she wrote to her son: " Thanks, many thanks, for your letter of December 16, so full of tender and deep feeling, which I did not read till today, in order to spare my eyes, which are already getting weak. But when the letter was brought me, I had it read out to me, and I share the grief which you have to endure on account of this bitter loss. God give us strength no longer to *troubler* too much by our tears the spirit of this good child who has fallen asleep, now that he rests in peace. If there is a good place reserved for the dead in the hereafter, then he has earned it here through his diligence and filial love and his gratitude to God and to his father and benefactor. He has a great veneration for you, my dear child, and what a beautiful affection he had for his sisters! "

For a long while to come, their quivering nerves continued to vibrate with grief for their loss, especially those of Frau Cosima, and she never succeeded in recovering from the passing of this wondrous young life. He was barely twenty years of age; but what he consigned to writing in his many letters to his father, his grandmother, and especially to the Princess is profoundly moving and enables us to recognize that in him, as also in his sister Cosima, Liszt's nature met with a wonderful reincarnation.

But life went on and brought with it new burdens and sorrows for Frau Cosima. For in September [1859] news reached Bülow that Richard Wagner had gone off to Paris, in order to carry out his ulterior projects from there. The first impression, on both the husband and the wife, was undoubtedly one of deep alarm. Then they set to work with all their might to help, and during the whole of the first period — which has been called Wagner's concert period — and even more during the preparations for the performance of *Tannhäuser,* which were to end in such a tragi-comedy, we see them both full of the most tireless activity, bringing to bear any influence they possessed which might be of use to Wagner. Bülow himself hastened to Paris, where some of his wife's relatives rallied to his side, though a few of them did not. Among the latter was Émile Ollivier, and from this moment onwards a certain resentment against his brother-in-law begins to be apparent.

Frau Cosima influenced affairs from home gently and clear-sightedly. Even had she so desired, she would not have been able to go to Paris; for she foresaw the approach of a difficult crisis, which weighed as oppressively upon her husband as upon her father. This, indeed, was the time when Franz Liszt began to feel lonely in Germany, for the Princess had already started out on her famous visit to the Vatican; and this loneliness made him weak. On October 12 [1860] Cosima gave birth to a daughter, Daniela Senta. Bülow was overjoyed and felt himself delivered from all the cares which had weighed upon him like a nightmare. Towards the end of November Liszt came to Berlin for the baptism. The ceremony took place at home, where Cosima had arranged a little chapel in her drawing-room. All was peaceful and solemn.

The young wife now attended this precious token of their mutual love with glad hopes and strong and fervent emotion; as a mother too she was very woman, clear-sighted and confident in all hard and troublous days and always filled with a maternal

123

sentiment, which rose to the greatest heights of passion. But it was too much for her strength. She wanted to suckle the child herself and had to be forbidden by her husband, her father, and the doctor; and in the following summer it was necessary for her to go to the Bavarian Alps for the sake of the air. Reichenhall was chosen for the purpose, and at the end of May, Bülow started off with her for the Bavarian highlands. They travelled by way of Weimar, for their father wanted to accompany them as far as Regensburg. They stopped at Bamberg and Nuremberg and, with Liszt as their guide, roamed through the beautiful old cities, Nuremberg in particular making a deep impression on the young wife — that Nuremberg which found its way, as it were, into the libretto of *Die Meistersinger,* in the verses:

> Thy peaceful ways pursuing,
> Serene thou dost abide
> Far from the clash of nations,
> Dear Nuremberg, my pride.[1]

It also found its way into the autobiography, taken down by Frau Cosima from Wagner's dictation. The works of Peter Vischer, Albrecht Dürer's pictures, the mighty buildings, the towering castle — all this aroused a strongly romantic emotion in her. Next they came to Regensburg, and at her father's side they visited the Valhalla, where Liszt especially admired Rauch's Victories, which he called " winged strophes in marble (*geflügelte Strophen in Marmor*)." At Regensburg he took leave of his children. This tour had been of particular significance to him, and he even attached a certain symbolism to it; for he was under a twofold influence at that time: that of his impending departure from Weimar, and that of his marriage with the Princess, who had originally arranged that it was to take place at Loreto, then in Florence, and finally in Rome. But he had also been to Paris, where he had once more seen his elder daughter and her husband, and invited them to the Musicians' Congress (*Tonkünstlerversammlung*) in Weimar. But a meeting

---

[1] *The Mastersingers,* III, i, Newman's translation (Breitkopf edition). — Tr.

with the Countess d'Agoult had also taken place there. We may, indeed, infer that he was impressed by this meeting from the fact that on June 29 — that is, a whole month later — he gave the Princess a full account of this meeting in Paris. This is most curious and is also of importance in connexion with Liszt's relations with his children. He begins his account with the words: " I promised to describe to you my visit to the ' Hôtel Montagne.' Well, the memories which accompanied me on my way there are very sad, and what further happened there was in no way calculated to make them more cheerful. If Nélida saw me again, it was not in the least that she might talk to me about anything which might have interested us, but merely because many people had talked to her about me and my poor success, and also, no doubt, about my kind words. My daughters' names were only mentioned in passing, and that at the end of my last visit, on the day of my departure from Paris. Then she asked me why I had prevented Cosima from following her true vocation, which should have been the career of an artist. According to Nélida, that would have been the best thing which could have happened to her. On this point, as on so many others, I have no choice; I cannot share her opinion. So this entire opposition between our two natures was revealed at once, at our first meeting, when we spoke of none but perfectly general topics, such as the principle of nationalities, Hungary, Poland, the policy of the Tuileries and of Cavour, etc. You know that she has embarked full sail upon the ocean of nationality. Without in any way checking her fine frenzies, I quoted Lamartine's article on Italy, which she considers more than stupid. When I remarked that this article had caused a certain sensation at the Ministry for Foreign Affairs, she answered with her well-known magisterial aplomb: ' It most certainly did not. Nobody who has spent even a week in Italy will share Monsieur Lamartine's opinion. A few months ago, however, I met three persons who had been sent on missions to Italy and who assured me in so many words that Italian liberty was a phantom which must now so far as possible be destroyed.' "

We see how just was the Countess's diagnosis of the political situation, and how unsuspecting Liszt was in view of the great

interview [1] which was then in full swing and was to be used by
Cavour to attain complete achievement. But Liszt's account continues: " At the moment when I wanted to take leave of Nélida,
she asked me whether I could not come some day and dine with
her. ' I should be very glad, but it would be difficult for me to
find a free day.' ' Then perhaps you would come to *déjeuner*
with me? ' ' I accept with thanks.' ' Whom am I to ask? ' ' Whoever may seem good to you, provided I seem worthy to them to
be in your company.' She proposed several persons, naming in
particular Nefftzer, editor of the *Revue germanique,* and many
others." Liszt named Ronchaud, but she refused, on the ground
that he was " boring." In the end he left it all to her. The
déjeuner was admirable and brilliantly served. Nélida naturally declared that neither good taste nor *ton* now existed in
France, that there was no longer any such thing as *causerie* or
conversation, and that all interest in intellectual things was
lost. " You can imagine how much to my taste all these expressions were, and I did not fail to cast a whole series of
stones of stumbling into the beautiful parterre of her flowery
rhetoric, by maintaining firmly and incisively that our time was
superior to any other in this respect, that France was still rich
enough in wit, and that the seven sages together could not rival
the restoration of Paris which had been achieved by the Emperor Napoleon. I then took my leave, and on the day of my departure — that is, a week later — I called upon her again. I
found her alone; we spoke about Madame Sand, whom I had
wanted to visit, but who was still staying in the south near
Toulon. Her last two novels had been a great success. Nélida
told me that Monsieur de Girardin had taken it into his head to
arrange a meeting between her and George Sand again, but
that this meeting had led to no apparent reconciliation. I remarked that they had parted in too bad a fashion to meet again
in a good one. But she retorted: ' You were one of those who
remained faithful to her.' ' Your rupture brought about a slight
coldness in my relations with her, for though at heart I consider
you to have been in the wrong, I none the less acted on your behalf.' ' I had thought the contrary.' ' Without any cause, as of

[1] Between Napoleon III and Cavour at Plombières. — Tr.

old.' In connexion with Goethe and his biographer Lewes, I mentioned Miss Evans, George Eliot. It appears that she has written two novels, the names of which I have forgotten, and that it is being said in many quarters that Miss Evans is the only woman comparable to George Sand. This was a very sore point for Nélida. Fortunately her commanding position as a historian and publicist has remained untouched. From time to time she writes articles for the *Siècle* and the *Temps,* a new paper which has been founded by Nefftzer. After I had discussed various literary and philosophical subjects with her, I began to give the conversation a more personal turn. The question of Wagner and the music of the future, and of the interest which I take in the new musical movement, had already been touched upon at my first visit. I now returned to this with greater emphasis, remarked to her with decision that I stood in no need of friends or of a party, or of the newspapers, in order to complete my career. 'Guermann's frescoes are already painted,' I said, 'and they may paint some more without my troubling myself the least in the world about the nonsense which is said or printed about me.' She was astonished at the voluntary isolation which I continue to maintain, perhaps, too, at the straightforward consistency which is to be found in my artistic life, of which she herself never had much realization, but which shone before her eyes at this moment in a clear light. As she heard me talking of myself, my egoism, and the attitude which I adopt towards the public, with which I am reproached as an artist only, of the absolute similarity between my efforts at that time and my ideas of today, and of the permanency of all that she had found so hateful in me, she suddenly felt an agitation which I could not understand, and her face was covered with tears. I kissed her on the brow, for the first time in many long years, and said to her: 'Marie, let me take leave of you with the peasant saying: " God bless you, and may you wish me no ill." ' She was unable to reply at the moment, but her tears flowed more copiously. Ollivier told me that during her travels in Italy he often saw her weeping in various places which particularly recalled our youth to her. I told her that I had been deeply touched by this reminiscence; and she replied, almost in a whisper: 'I shall always remain true to Italy

— and Hungary.' And on this note I left her, calm and gentle. As I came downstairs, she showed me the picture of my poor Daniel. Nothing at all had been said about him during the three or four hours which I had spent chatting with his mother."

It was a farewell for life that he had just said to the mother of his children, in order that he might offer his hand to another woman, for life too, at the altar in Rome. Such, at least, was his intention. And it was to this latter woman that he wrote this account, in which we are conscious of one thing — that the lady who was talking to him, who, like a well-bred woman, had tried up to the very end to keep back any expression of deep emotion, had none the less showed her heart at the last. Her omission to say a word about their dead son was a sign of the deepest tact on her side. For how could she speak of his dead son to a man who had long since abandoned her and now intended to unite himself entirely with the other?

It was some such thoughts as these that, as it were, hovered about the three as they wandered through the streets of Bamberg and the churches of Nuremberg and trod the marble pavements of the Valhalla.

They next went on to Reichenhall, where at her husband's side Cosima explored the neighbourhood for miles round and became visibly blooming. The holiday did her an extraordinary amount of good, and her husband, too, delighted in being with her among the Bavarian mountains; but only for a short time, for his father-in-law now urgently summoned him back to Weimar for the Musicians' Congress. He could not hesitate, for no less was at stake than the performance of Liszt's most important works; besides which, Liszt was leaving Germany and in all probability would not appear on German soil again for years to come. Thus it was a farewell celebration, which was, however, at the same time to mark the reappearance of the greatest of German artists — Richard Wagner, who was returning to German soil for the first time for this festival, which was to celebrate both his arrival and Liszt's departure.

Meanwhile it was at Reichenhall that Frau Cosima had resumed relations with Alfred Meissner, who was staying in the neighbourhood, and to whom she wrote the following lines:

" Dear Herr Meissner, there is a little lady here who is recalling memories of you and begs you to come and see her during her stay at Reichenhall. Is Tegernsee very far away? Could we not arrange a meeting in Salzburg? So here is a question for you, which is at the same time to bring you thanks for your charming letter and assure you that, if you have preserved the memory of those hours in Berlin, we, too, often look back to them with pleasure and regret." Next she speaks of Reichenhall, which such people as prefer " the establishment of a Christian love of one's neighbour " to other society enjoy after their own fashion, and speaks of the egoism with which they profess to " see." " It's true it's cold, but — it's all right! " This was a favourite catchword of her husband's. " Good-bye, then, till we meet again, amid these mountains and beneath the Bavarian cloud-canopy, or else in Berlin amid sand and utter drought. That is for you to decide.'

This letter at last led Alfred Meissner to send the Bülows his novel about the Jesuits which had just appeared, and which immediately upon her return Frau Cosima began to read and then to translate. She certainly took a great interest in the personality of the author of *Ziska*, as well as in his works, and even in his prose style, about which there was so much controversy in connexion with this very work.

But these impressions were quickly effaced by the appearance of her sister Blandine, accompanied by her husband and another — Richard Wagner. Unlike Bülow, who had spent hardly any time with his brother- and sister-in-law during the whole of the *Tannhäuser* period in Paris, Wagner had found in them good friends. On meeting again at the Musical Festival in Weimar, they therefore determined to continue their travels together and pay Cosima a visit at Bad Reichenhall. Liszt had accompanied them to the station to take leave of them. Bülow himself had already left on the previous day, after being much fêted for his achievements as a conductor, as well as for his compositions, which were received with loud applause. The four of them were talking at the station about Bülow and his brilliant achievements, and Wagner remarked, as a jest among friends: " He need not have married Cosima," upon which Liszt added with a little bow:

" That was luxury." A severe and ominous remark which Liszt ought not, perhaps, to have made. But with what a mass of things he was preoccupied at this time!

On this journey Blandine could once more enjoy life to the full, and, according to the accounts which we have of their stay in Munich, she was in the highest of spirits, which grew higher still when Ollivier, who knew hardly any German, could not understand her merriment. And so they came to Reichenhall, where they were received by Cosima and taken to the house which had been made ready for them. The young wife seemed to have completely recovered, and all of them were relieved of their anxiety about her. Yet it was not so much the whey-cure which had restored her to health as her long rambles and the time which she had spent in the mountain air. But the two sisters now formed a party of their own with the two men and went about together in the greatest gaiety. Generally, indeed, they shut themselves up from the men in their rooms, from which nothing but their merry laughter was audible. It is curious how the two sisters now lived together just as they had done in their childhood, and how easy they found it, while the dark cloud of destiny was already hanging over Blandine's head. Once, when Richard Wagner had compelled them to admit him, he declared that, since their father no longer bothered about them both, he would adopt them, which was received by them with less confidence than mirth. Wagner further relates: " I complained once to Blandine of Cosima's shyness (*Wildheit*), which she could not understand till she made out that what I had said was to be explained as meaning *timidité d'un sauvage*. But after a few days I had at last to think of continuing my journey, which had been so charmingly interrupted till now. I took my leave in the hall, and here I met with an almost shyly questioning gaze from Cosima."

Meanwhile in this sunny valley she found health again. She next returned to Berlin by way of Löwenberg, where she and her father stayed for a time with the hospitable Prince. Shortly after her return she received a very sad letter from Alfred Meissner, informing her in somewhat enigmatic terms of his mother's death. She was deeply shocked and wrote to him in a way which not only must have been consoling to the mourner, but also throws a flood of light on her whole spiritual attitude: " Meanwhile I was far from supposing that such a painful experience had completely engrossed you. Whatever feelings one may have about the loss of one's dear ones, whatever our own particular thoughts about their death may be, they can never compare to the horror of the reality. It is all very well to say that one has been preparing for it for months, or even years on end, that, consoling oneself with philosophy or even religion, one has said to oneself that death is a benefit for those whom it snatches away. At the moment when we return to the earth what comes from the earth, our minds could almost give way, and all the arguments of reason are powerless against the revulsion which takes place in us, the revolt against the ordering of the world, and the fact that in a question which is regarded as natural we feel completely estranged from nature. A void takes possession of us. I know that one lives, thinks, mourns, or loves, but that does not alter the fact that a part of our soul is entirely transformed, and even if one does not lose one's clear insight into things, they are hidden from us, as though seen through a transparent black veil. You are quite right; one has no wish for distraction. To seek a diversion seems to us like an odious action, which in the unmixed consciousness of its anguish the heart feels to be something shameful. One could wish that the inconsolable feelings which one does not put into words might appear upon one's brow, so that the world might recognize them with pity and awe; one would wish the cries which one sends ringing through the city of the dead to be drowned by no intrusive clamour. Above all, one would wish that the visions with which our soul is filled might fill our eyes, so that our senses might share in the constant oppression weighing upon our thoughts. I do not know whether I am right to say such things to you. But I feel that the emotion which death has aroused in me, and about which I hourly examine and search myself, gives me the right to do so. I am always ready to weep with those who weep, so heavy is my heart, and, without having known your mother, I mourn with you and share in the terrible and ineffable moments which you have experienced to the full. And so I can offer you no consolation. All those consolations which were given to me seemed to me like madness, like mere phrases. In my agitation and deepest mourning I reflect that pain is the real content of life, and that all the rest is nothing but its empty and futile adornment. Meanwhile you have found your way back to work. 'Work is victory,' says Emerson, and the little gift which you were so kind as to send me shows that you have attained the composure which usually follows such inward agitation. I have not yet started the *Masken,* for I am still spending all my time among those whom you have unmasked — I mean with the *Révérends Pères,* which, faithful to my promise, I am translating. If the walks at Reichenhall had not distracted me, I should already have finished the book, but the mountains were not so propitious to literature as the 'apples.' It was not till last Sunday that I started upon my little task, and I have just got as far as the 'poisoned apples.' My health is completely restored. Unfortunately my poor husband has returned to Berlin very ill and for a month past has been tormented by the most terrible neuralgic pains, which leave him in a state of sheer perversity and rage. The doctor knows nothing and can do nothing. I have no more to say to you on the subject. You know that all one can do is to recognize the incapacity of the Æsculapiuses through their complete impotence. They always seem to me like certain generals, who await the moment of battle only to prove that they are idiots.

"My father asks me to assure you of his most friendly sentiments. He is just coming here from Löwenberg, where he has been staying for a month after bidding farewell to Weimar. From Berlin he is going to Italy and from there perhaps to Athens. He will not return to Germany for a year. If your feelings and your work permit of a little excursion to Berlin during the week which he is to spend with us here, I need hardly add how glad we should be. Write to him in any case, he has the pleasantest memories of you."

She next adds a very interesting description of Rubinstein: " As for what concerns the movements of the stars and planets, we have Rubinstein here at present, who is again resuming his triumphal progress through the world. He is one of the most strikingly remarkable types in the musical world, which boasts so many at present that that art, which does not belong to the fine arts, succeeds in holding its own. Great originality, but not a trace of genius, an iron will, but absolutely no enthusiasm, a noble character, but without inspiration, a great contempt for mankind, but too great a love of material things, very great assurance, but mingled with too much egotism, refinement, and even charm, but little power of discrimination: there you have a few traits of this personality, which is, I maintain, sympathetic, in spite of his brusquerie and often rough manner. He is hankering after an opera-libretto, and with this aim in view has approached a literary personage here, who, in my opinion, is hardly capable of composing one in the way necessary nowadays. All this between ourselves. And now enough of this. Do not be angry with me for these outbursts of sentiment, do not think that it is a sign of any levity on my part; believe me, I always enter into all your feelings with sympathy. My husband offers you a friendly handshake, and my father sends you a thousand friendly messages, to which I add my most devoted regards."

She wrote this letter in the midst of her work of translation, certain objections to which were raised both on Meissner's side and especially, as we shall see later, on that of the editor of the *Revue germanique*. Meissner had also alluded to Liszt's objections. But Cosima countered this most skilfully by the words: "As for the objections which my father may have had, these are simply null. I have spoken to him on the point, and he was unable to raise the slightest objection." Next she goes on to speak of what was happening in Berlin: "Everything centres on the coronation today, and it may be said that folly has assumed the crown in succession to Their Majesties. For you can have no conception of the jubilation which reigns in Berlin, of the agitation and excitement. For my part, I regard this *mise en scène* as the concentrated essence and symbol of the great masquerade which this world presents. My misanthropic feelings with regard to the general exaltation are bred in the bone, and it is possible that I may stay at home like an old cross-patch."

And now, as we have said, there came a letter from Monsieur

Dollfus, of which she could make nothing, and which she simply
sent on to Alfred Meissner, who told her how to answer it properly. The question concerned the title of Meissner's novel *Zur
Ehre Gottes*, which in her French translation Cosima quite correctly rendered by the Latin *Ad majorem Dei gloriam*. Her energy ultimately gained the victory over Monsieur Dollfus. It is interesting to read her own characterization of her work: " As
regards the usefulness of my work, I do not look at this at all
from the point of view of whether it is printed. I take a pleasure
in becoming intimate with your work, which I find charming.
I have the further pleasure of perfecting myself in both French
and German. That seems to me to be the most important thing.
Whether it is published is a matter of indifference to me, except
that I am anxious to keep the French as well-informed as possible about all that happens this side of the Rhine. Hence there
can be no question of uselessness, and if the folly of the excellent editor had not been infectious, I should not have brought
this unimportant occurrence to your notice. Six volumes of a novel
— that is somewhat alarming for us women, who have only small
ideas. I beg you to tell me nothing about it, though I am extraordinarily curious; for I know that work requires silence,
and I have a saying that it is painful to speak of what one has
done, impossible to speak of what one is doing, and unwise to
speak of what one is going to do. It is extraordinarily wise of
you not to haunt Berlin till your poetic impulse has been stilled.
It seems to me that one can work better in Prague than here:
Hus, Tycho Brahe, St. Nepomuk, the great Jesuit College, the
Jewish burying-ground, and the Premonstratensian Monastery
stimulate one's ideas for work far more than the Great Elector,
Frederick the Great, and our masses of clumsy, deplorable, hol-
low, and bombastic monuments. But we beg you to hurry so that
summer is not over before we see you again.

" I am greatly embarrassed about how to answer you with
regard to this marriage in Rome. For me it is a regular muddle.
I know that it cannot take place. I know that the Hohenlohe
family have intervened to stop it, that the Cardinals were on the
Princess's side, but as for the whole aspect of affairs, the conflicts and developments which are taking place, I know nothing,

and I make it my habit not to understand anything about it, for my only feeling on the subject is one of deep and genuine pain, which fills the depths of my heart with the most passionate vehemence. The word 'heart' has slipped from me. Should you like me to add a few lines in answer to the end of your letter? This is a most delicate matter, and the more careful one is not to hurt people, the more one does so. But I venture to say that you are a truly loving nature, and that you are quite right to marry. I remember our walk in the Tiergarten, when I promised to find you a wife. I can be nothing but happy that you have found one for yourself, and I submit in girlish fashion to the 'trampling.' It all happens of its own accord, without our having anything to do with it, and it is equally beyond our power to revolt against it. I understand taking the loss of a happiness calmly, but not renouncing what one has never achieved or even tried to win. And the more such things as mind and good ideas are worth — all this ballast which weighs us down to our misfortune, and which we hasten to throw overboard if a storm arises — they have nothing to do with love. In any case, for the moment you are happy, in spite of this 'quarrel,' about which I know nothing. He who has not loved utterly has not possessed his life, says Obermann, who is too little known in Germany, and who knew what it means to suffer and to be unable to speak of it. And to possess one's life is the highest, indeed the only true happiness.

"I close, in the fear lest I have already said too much. If your work and your heart leave you time and opportunity, you would give me great pleasure if you were to write to me. Tell me, or do not tell me, about all that occupies your mind. I flatter myself that I can understand it all, and I am a better listener than I am a speaker."

We see what a great interest Frau Cosima took in Alfred Meissner, and how through translating his works she had formed a sort of friendly relation with him, which is certainly original and characteristic. In view of the violent controversy which has gone on up to the present day about Meissner, not so much as a poet — for as such his position is unchallenged — but as a novelist, the attitude of this young and intelligent woman

135

towards him and his work must be of interest. She also favoured him with more detailed descriptions of what was happening in Berlin, which are always an amplification of her short accounts of Dollfus and the *Revue germanique:*

"For the moment Berlin is beside itself. The King's somewhat languid speeches, which there is an attempt at present to interpret as *plaisanteries,* the choice of diplomatists, the cries and threats of the crowd, Varnhagen's book, these are some of the things which are working together to heighten men's hopes and unrest and authorize us to expect from the first the stride of the giant or else his fall. In any case this fall will be necessary, and better than the present state of affairs. The brilliant answer of the Emperor of the French reduces Prussia to her own Lilliputian proportions, and the fable of the frog which tried to blow itself up like the ox involuntarily comes into one's mind. This was a fresh master-stroke of this surest and firmest of all statesmen, who combines in his person the wisdom of the serpent and the boldness of the lion, who is afraid of no difficulty and whose wisdom shrinks from no obstacle.

"You will have read in the papers all the news which I could have given you about my father and the Princess. Fortunately they are in Rome, the city, as Cornelius said to me lately, where grief loses half its force, and where my father will have more opportunity of working than in Weimar. We have but little hope of seeing him in Germany again, and so I am planning to go and see him in that land which so entirely comes up to our enthusiasm — the land of freedom, religion, and beauty. It is all very well for us to crown ourselves with laurels, to imagine that we are progressing, and to sacrifice our time and intelligence in occupations which are considered useful, but we Nordic peoples are exiles, and though we do not say so, we feel that all the developments of the world will take place in that region.

"At the moment my husband and I are hardly ever out of the concert-hall, he as an active principle, I as an amphibious creature, half artist, half passive, a mixed role, to which, however, we women are condemned. On the whole, things are not going badly, and we are well enough prepared for the fray, we have a rich supply of pugnacity and feel strong enough to look forward to the winter with a calm glance. We count very much upon the year '62 bringing you into our part of the world. Do not prolong your stay in Prague for ever, for there you have nothing but beautiful stones before you. That is always something, but it is no compensation to those to whom your coming would give real pleasure, among whom I beg you to reckon us."

From this letter we can quite plainly see the young wife's individual attitude towards affairs in Berlin. It cannot be said that her husband's political views influenced her, but it is certain that, perhaps under the influence of her feelings, he felt the same as she did. It was the peculiar atmosphere of Berlin which was producing its effect upon her, an echo of that which prevailed in the *salons* of Rahel, and also of Bettina, Varnhagen von Ense and his daughter: a certain opposition to all the political phenomena of Berlin, against which there was a feeling of inward revolt; the papers wrote against them, and up to that memorable day[1] in September '62 they undoubtedly produced a serious confusion and impression of weakness in Berlin — more so than the attitude of the King and his trusty henchmen really deserved. But these letters of Frau Cosima's provide better than anything else what information we have about the life of the young Bülow *ménage,* a clear picture of their thoughts and feelings, and of the way in which the young Frenchwoman adapted herself to the life of Berlin. We shall see how this process gradually developed into her complete Germanization. The smallness and pettiness inseparable from life in Berlin in the pre-Bismarckian period were naturally bound to be repellent to this great-hearted woman.

In the mean time she had no lack of successes due to her own activities. Dollfus at last gave way, and in February '62 she wrote to Meissner that the fortress had yielded, though the translation would not appear before July: "I am in no hurry to anticipate the march of events, and, like the *Kreuzzeitung,* I am content with a *moral victory.* I have good news from Rome, to the effect that my father is getting on better than in Weimar, working in greater peace and finding more recreations. As for us

---

[1] That of the "blood and iron" speech of Bismarck. — TR.

here, we make music and bestir ourselves every day. We and every step that we take are attacked. All the same, we are determined to stand our ground. Next Sunday a concert takes place here for the benefit of the Prussian fleet, at which Hans is to conduct. You will have seen that he has been decorated twice, once by the Prince Hohenzollern, and the second time by the King. Auerbach has received the lesser Order of the Eagle after two years of impatience — or of patience that makes a bad impression on the democracy. But since the democracy itself makes a bad impression, that does not signify much."

But life went its way. Frau Cosima heard with painful anxiety of the defeat of the Master's hopes in Vienna. Not so much, indeed, from his letters to her husband; these had a rather animated tone, and it strikes us with a sense of strangeness when he writes to Hans: " I was most delighted with her at Reichenhall. If only the naughty child would take proper care of herself. I hear that she is on another visit to her father, provided only that she does not again let herself be carried away there into these little excesses, which are, however, so harmful to her — she's a wild child, I say it and stick to it! But she has great nobility of nature. You must insist on this, in order to induce her to make every sacrifice, even that of her injurious habits. Out of pride she must remain equable and calm. For the rest, her appearance set my mind at rest greatly. Things will certainly go on well and nicely for her."

A little while later he wrote: " My greetings to Cosima too, who, for all her genius, could not make out the Upper Bavarian dialect. Oh, how easy it was for me! I can already understand Viennese, God knows what they will say to me in it next! The two sisters were so charming, extraordinarily full of genius and charm, that I managed to swallow Ollivier finely along with them! "

But she was not so " childish " as the Master represented her. Shortly after the catastrophe on the Green Hill she had invited Frau Minna to come to see her, and now, at a time when Wagner was faced with new and heavy struggles, he wrote her a letter which set her mind at rest. But he went off full of joy and high hope to his new work in Paris, where he devoted himself entirely to composing the libretto of *The Mastersingers*. It was still, wrote Bülow, a dead secret, which nobody might mention. But he now saw his way quite clearly, and there, on the " Kai Voltaire," he gave himself up to that wonderful poem, which was finished in the shortest possible time. Thus it was in the most miserable surroundings that he produced his most German work, which was imposed upon him by want, and which it was not granted him to bring to full completion till he was under the spell of Cosima's goodness. Never was he so passionately assailed by the longing for "bliss and delight (*Wunne und Waide*) " of his own as during the period when he was writing *The Mastersingers*. It was not splendid household appointments that he required, but loving comprehension, and so his predominant emotion was one of boundless desolation, which cried out within him and was only stilled when his favourite pupil was at hand with his wonderful wife. For so it was that destiny was now developed and fulfilled.

Wagner himself, however, had returned to the Rhine with the completed libretto and had made his well-known contract with the house of Schott, after which, leaving, as it were, all unpleasantnesses behind him in Paris, and renouncing all hopes at Karlsruhe, where Hans von Bülow had for long been trying to prepare the way for him, he settled down at Biebrich. In the midst of his work there, he received a visit at the beginning of July from Hans von Bülow and his wife. Bülow's health had benefited by a drastic cure at Karlsbad, but he knew that Wagner had need of him " both as man and as pianist," and so, after a trying winter, crowded with work, he and his wife started out on their journey. They found the Master in the middle of *The Mastersingers*. As before at Zürich, the early days were by no means gratifying. Frau Cosima wrote a letter on the subject to Luise von Bülow, to whom she also communicated her feelings and attitude towards the great national festival at Frankfurt am Main. But again she gave a similar, though fuller, account of these days at Biebrich to her friend Alfred Meissner. Hence her letter of July 20, 1862 is not without significance:

" At last we have come to rest at Biebrich, a pretty place enough, of which I have become comparatively fond since

coming to know the other bank of the Rhine. I know nothing
more undeserved than the fame of all this neighbourhood,
which has nothing more and nothing less than the *beauté du
diable* — that is to say, a certain freshness and charm, but no
well-defined character. Nothing grand, nothing commanding!
Everything is small, wretched, poverty-stricken, pitiable, and at
the same time as stupid as only things English or ruins can be.
That is my opinion of the Rhine. Do not be angry with me if
it does not agree with your own. I have the same way of looking
at countries as at people — a mad, impossible way, and it
really takes quite an effort to arrive at any sort of balance.
We are only a step or two from Wiesbaden, where we often
go out of sheer idiocy, just as one goes to see disagreeable people because they live in the neighbourhood. I always return in
an even more misanthropical mood than that in which I started.
It is a fearful sight, this accumulation of degraded women,
gamblers, rope-dancers, and Jews, where one looks in vain for
a respectable figure. It is the native land of disreputable people,
who congregate here in the same way as the representatives of
the social hierarchy: here one finds age without dignity, elegance
without attractiveness, aristocracy without nobility, wealth
without brilliance; everything is common, base, vulgar, ignoble,
and if by chance one hears a song of a bird in the park at Wiesbaden, one asks oneself how such a pure warbler can still lift
up its little voice amid this shameless masquerade.

" After these remarks you will ask why I have settled down
in this region. Ah, *voilà!* We are here out of friendship for
Richard Wagner, who has found a nest at Biebrich, and who,
like all mortals, feels the need of exchanging a word with a
friendly being from time to time. He begged us to come, and we
have come and rented a house for two months. I do not much
like it, but I accept it all with a touch of humour, while dreaming
of Tyrol and Italy for next year. We have made a lot of music
since we arrived. The Schnorrs were here for a fortnight, studying *Tristan and Isolde* under Wagner's direction, which they
sang wonderfully, in spite of its alleged unsingableness. Schnorr
is among singers what the Regent is among diamonds — a marvel. He is far more a musician than a tenor, and far more an

artist than a musician. One is forced to respect the theatre when one sees his devotion to what is beautiful, his powers of grasping and interpreting great works, his simplicity and lovableness, combined with real reliability. He is the only tenor who has ventured upon the alarming part of Tristan, and he bears himself wonderfully in it and to the great satisfaction of Wagner, who is accustomed to finding in the theatre nothing but actors and comedians. Wagner's latest libretto, *The Mastersingers* — Hans Sachs — is a masterpiece. Like Shakspere, he has effected a union between lively comedy and the sublime. Greatness hangs like a sun over the plot, which is adorned with the most ludicrous incidents, in which humour is combined with the profoundest emotion, without losing any of its power. Hans Sachs is cast in bronze from head to foot, full of life and strength, as though Peter Vischer had wrought him.

"We felt here the last ripples of the Frankfurt Festival. Much enthusiasm, certainly, much good fellowship — one might almost think that we were becoming Swiss, with the Duke of Coburg as President of the Republic. These festivals seem to me to be directly profitable to the brewers and wine-merchants, and indirectly to the dynasts, who get more excited than is necessary. As for the union of the peoples, it does not seem to me that anything of importance will be achieved in this fashion, and if ever German unity becomes a reality, it will be brought about by other ways than as a work of peace."

This was also in accord with the feelings of Richard Wagner, who thought likewise at that time, though, occupied as he was with *The Mastersingers*, such matters left him quite cold. And essentially these ideas are — those of Bismarck.

This letter to Alfred Meissner was written from Biebrich, where she was now under the spell of Richard Wagner's *The Mastersingers*. Above all, she was suffering very severely from her husband's exhaustion and extreme irritability, for he had never felt his intellectual dependence upon the Master so oppressively as during the early days of their stay at Biebrich. It is clear from his letters, at any rate, that he had by now become fully, if not unjustifiably, convinced that, after all, he possessed no more than second-class ability, and it was only

141

gradually that he once more rallied himself by an effort through contact with Richard Wagner's powerful personality and once more felt at ease among the great and joyous activity of Richard Wagner's house at Biebrich, clouded though this was by anxiety. Here he and his wife met the Schnorrs, who were already working at *Tristan*, which they sang both *con amore* and correctly. But all else fell into the background before *The Mastersingers*, and it was this work which made the deepest impression upon Frau Cosima too. While Schnorr was waking the music of *Tristan* to perfect life, she was able to grasp to the full the deep magic which emanated from *The Mastersingers*. She wrote ecstatically to her father: " *The Mastersingers* is to Wagner's creations what *The Winter's Tale* is to Shakspere's other works. Wagner's imagination has made an excursion into the realms of mischievous gaiety, and by its magic has so conjured up mediæval Nuremberg, with its guilds and corporations, its craftsman-poets, its pedants, and its knights, as to call forth in the sublimest and most noble way the laughter that does most to emancipate the spirit. Quite apart from the intellectual content and import of the work, its artistic execution may be compared with the tabernacle in the Church of St. Lawrence. Like the sculptor of the tabernacle, the musician has here achieved the purest and most graceful form, with the most consummate boldness of conception, and just as, at the base of the tabernacle, Adam Krafft bears up and supports the whole structure with an expression of grave and concentrated reverence, so in *The Mastersingers* it is the figure of *Hans Sachs* that dominates and directs the action with a cheerful and lovable serenity."

These are wonderful words, which show how she had grasped the spirit of the whole work and recognized its deep, profound, and abiding significance. Some time before this she had roamed about Nuremberg with her father and seen and admired it all. She had then not the slightest idea of the plan of *The Mastersingers*, yet she had so thoroughly absorbed the spirit of the place that she was now able to approach the work with the deepest and gladdest comprehension, chiefly owing to her recognition of the fact that here Richard Wagner had begun to create a work which sprang from the profoundest depths of the German genius. But how singular did the contrast contained in these words which she wrote to her father seem to him, living as he then was in Rome, entirely under the influence of the Princess. Thus they fell on his ears like the glad peal of German bells, as a reminder of his friend and his friend's art, as well as of the Fatherland, by which both of them stood and were bound to stand.

Yet this was a strange and restless time. Guests came and went. The news which reached the Master from his anxious publishers at Mainz, near by, was not always encouraging. On top of it all, the painter Willich had appeared, commissioned by Frau Mathilde Wesendonck to paint a portrait of the Master. He had to sit to him, and to his impressionable and excitable nature this was always a most painful moment. Here too Frau Cosima was a help, for while he sat to the painter she read to him. This is a most characteristic picture, a reminiscence, as it were, of the times in Zürich, which had fallen quite into the background of the Master's thoughts, though he preserved the most loyal, faithful memory of the kindly, understanding, and noble woman, regarding her in some sort as the Evchen to his Hans Sachs, while in his Veit Pogner he has left an undying monument to the devoted husband Otto Wesendonck. This scene, in which the Master is being painted for Frau Mathilde, while Frau Cosima reads to him to give him patience, is full of the infinite charm of a subtle comedy. Bülow had of course to make himself uesful both as musician and as amanuensis, by copying out the 145 quarto pages of the libretto for *The Mastersingers* in five days. He was crushed by Wagner's greatness:

"With Wagner as a neighbour, everything else shrivels into insignificance, becomes so puerile, so null and void." He could not so much as read the proofs of his songs, which the publishers had sent him: "The stuff seems to me so lamentable, so paltry, that I simply don't like to look at it." Doubts of his own powers crowded upon him in greater force than ever. He went through all the experiences and sufferings of his *Orchesterphantasie*, which he himself nicknamed the *Selbstmörderphantasie* (*Suicide's Fantasia*): "I wish it was time to fall asleep, and that all was over. I have lost all confidence in myself, and with

143

it all desire to live. What can one so much as begin to do, with nothing but an impotent sense of reverential devotion (*Pietät*)? "

But, as a matter of fact, it was actually from *The Master-singers* that he drew fresh inspiration and strength. He recognized the rare qualities of this work as much as his wife did; and it was a great moment for them both when one evening the Master told them, not without emotion, of his further plans, for *The Victors* (*Die Sieger*) and *Parsifal*. In so doing he gave utterance to a presentiment that *Parsifal* would be his last work. They were all struck by this, especially Frau Cosima, who listened quietly and in silence, while out on the balcony her husband was saying to Wendelin Weissheimer: " You will see, he will attain his end and achieve even *Parsifal* too."

Next followed beautiful excursions on the Rhine. In mid stream off Bingen, Schnorr von Carolsfeld struck up the Steersman's song. Emilie Genast sang Mathilde Wesendonck's five poems, which the Master was forced to offer as a sacrifice to his impatient publisher in order to keep him supplied with works to produce. At Wiesbaden they heard *Lohengrin* together and at Frankfurt a performance of *Tasso,* at which, to Bülow's fierce indignation, Liszt's symphonic poem was presented in the worst possible fashion, as though by way of overture. And now came the parting, which was extraordinarily hard for all of them. They felt that Wagner had no abiding future there, that his work would again have to be broken off, and that he would be forced to start out once more upon his wanderings.

On their return home a gloomy and ominous piece of news arrived from Saint-Tropez. Ollivier wrote to Hans that Blandine was lying hopelessly ill. After her confinement, which had gone off well, a number of symptoms had set in, all of which were alarming: she could not sleep, and had been unable to take any nourishment for a month; she had violent shivering-fits — in fact her condition was most terrible. He had hesitated for a long time to distress Cosima, but now he could no longer keep silence.

And on September 11 what he had dreaded happened. Blandine died suddenly at their property at Saint-Tropez. A wonderful creature, as noble and original as Daniel, had now passed away. During the last few years she had blossomed out in all her charm and sweetness. Spiritually, too, the journey to Reichenhall and the time she had spent there had done her much good, and so had the performance of her father's *Faust Symphony*, the themes of which had accompanied her on her journey. She shared Wagner's enthusiasm for this work. And what a merry time the sisters had spent together! Every hour was like some gracious comedy, and she had herself written at the time to her father how they chattered like magpies and were jealous of each other.

" I am jealous of Cosette, and Cosette is jealous of me out of politeness, for I am good for nothing, since I neither smoke nor play whist." This was a delightfully sprightly allusion to the Princess, who began the day with smoking and ended it with smoking and playing whist. After this she had expected a visit from her father at Saint-Tropez, for he wanted to see his daughter again on his way to Rome. He did not come, and she was deeply upset by his failure to appear. It was in this state of mind that she wrote to him in touching terms of her condition, her love for him, and the relations between his children:

" One of us was taken away at the height of his bloom, when he might have realized so many beautiful dreams. Cosima is in Germany, and I am alone with Grandmamma, as in former days. You are always far away, as before, and we are celebrating April 2 in the sure conviction that Cosima, far away, and Daniel, still farther away, are united with us in our thoughts and join in our prayer — in the prayer that all blessings may be united upon your head."

And she draws a picture of that splendid old lady their grandmother, in all her lovableness, as she went about the room on her two crutches, with her happy expression, her delicate complexion, transparent skin, and eye full of life, so that Blandine often called out: " Grandmamma, how beautiful you are! " And all this centred upon the birth of her son, who was to be called Daniel, like her brother. And she described the little touch of jealousy which she felt for her grandmother, who still treasured her little Franz's baby-clothes. Full of pious

145

emotions and hopes for her child, she had cut some baby's gowns out of the linen which her grandmother had given her, and sewed and adorned them. It was for the child that she lived until her strength failed her, and the fatal day arrived which robbed Cosima of her sister too.

She now hastened to France with her little daughter, Daniela, chiefly so as to console and uphold her grandmother, to whom Blandine's death had been a heavy blow. The old lady received this consolation with all the fine egoism of old age, and now would never let the last of the three children leave her side. And, as a matter of fact, she and Ollivier thought of keeping Cosima in Paris for good, naturally persuading her husband to move there. Cosima herself was at last won over to the plan, nor would Bülow have said her nay. But Liszt thought otherwise and expounded his views at length to his mother: " Poor dear Cosima would gladly have prolonged her stay with you; she clings to you with heart-felt love. But, on the other hand, her husband cannot do without her in the position which he occupies in Berlin and in Germany generally. It would not be a good thing for him to leave his spiritual home in Berlin before being offered an equally secure position elsewhere. Bülow has to pay particular regard to his sovereign, who has appointed him his court pianist and granted him the distinction of an order; his name and antecedents lay binding obligations upon him. He must maintain the bearing of a man who can be relied upon unconditionally. Moreover, the position which he has for years occupied at Stern's Conservatoire necessarily keeps him in Berlin. I have explained all this to Ollivier at length, and he will have written it to Cosima. There is no need to enter into tedious explanations with her. She is quick of apprehension and grasps the essentials of a question. All the same, I share Cosima's regret at not being always near you."

Thus it was Liszt who wanted to keep his son-in-law in Germany, all the more so since it was at this very time that he himself had become homeless. For on October 22 his fate had been decided: his fiftieth birthday was to have been the day of his marriage with the Princess. All was in readiness, the altar in the Church of San Carlo had been decorated, when at eleven o'clock at night there came a messenger from the Vatican forbidding the marriage. It was a great blow to Liszt, but he stayed in Rome and completed his *Saint Elisabeth.*

Cosima returned home and shortly afterwards accompanied her husband to Leipzig, where they met Wagner again. It was a grave and solemn meeting. He too had been deeply affected by Blandine's death, which even filled him with an almost superstitious terror. Together they attended the rehearsal for the concert which Weissheimer had got up on Wagner's behalf, and in which Bülow, too, had promised his collaboration. They were full of an uncanny gaiety. The whole thing appeared to them like some strange adventure, the ghostly character of which was fully revealed when the old hall of the Gewandhaus loomed, unnaturally empty, before them; for, apart from their intimate friends and relatives, only a few visitors from Berlin were present, and Leipzig held entirely aloof. But the Prelude to *The Mastersingers* rose glorious above it all in its grave sublimity and called forth such applause that it had to be repeated.

The whole thing formed an episode quite in the spirit of E. T. A. Hoffmann, and yet with a background of deep sadness; for the Bülows went back to Berlin with fresh anxieties about their friend. In order to be able to contribute something towards the expenses of Wagner's journey, the faithful Hans had already sold the ring presented to him by the Grand Duke of Baden. Wagner accepted it without the slightest scruple, in a spirit that rose far above all superficial considerations. He even wrote to Hans with a recklessness worthy of Renaissance days: "Whoever else still possesses any valuables which he does not care about must cheerfully sacrifice them to me — in all seriousness. As I am now, I have suddenly regained entire confidence that I shall win back and restore all the stuff splendidly and gloriously." And he wrote to his trusty friends about their meeting in Leipzig: "Children, when I saw you both in Leipzig again, my heart leapt within me! Indeed, I love you dearly! Heaven, to be intimate together! To belong to each other! That is, after all, the one thing that matters. Ah, and how hard it is! It is not to be managed by the heart alone, one has to be clever as well! " Then he went on to Vienna by way of Berlin, and when here, too, his fresh hopes were frustrated, he took up his baton in order to win fortune in Russia.

But Cosima mourned in silence for her sister. She shut herself almost entirely off from society, though this was partly due to the fact that she was once more anticipating the joys of motherhood. She revealed to Frau Luise and Alfred Meissner how she mourned, while to the latter she was able to announce that her translation of his novel on the Jesuits had begun to come out. But more than six months after her sister's death she speaks of it as follows in this letter:

" This loss is one of those whose heavy burden extends over one's whole life and casts its shadow upon all one's joys and sorrows for ever. I do not mean to say that one is suffering all the time. What soul could rise to such heights of emotion? But one feels everything differently — that is, as if an enchanted curtain had descended upon everything, as though one's eyes had gained a peculiar faculty of vision. My sister was the most exquisite creature that I ever learnt to know or knew. She was beautiful, gentle, good, heroic. Her soul was such that all emotions found an echo in her and moved her to goodness and tenderness. The extraordinary position created for us by our birth had forged a bond between us three, such as the majority of brothers and sisters can scarcely picture to themselves, and which I now drag about with me like a heavy cumbrous chain. I shall never love again as I loved her, and I often feel as though I had been torn up by the roots, for my heart is always seeking these two beings, who were so young, so original, so truly saintly, so completely mine, and I feel nothing but a void. *Sustine et abstine.* . . . My father is in Rome and, if I am not mistaken, will stay there, and Germany will not see him again. He has turned his way southwards, and I must agree that he has done right. Germany is too much under the sign of Saturn for one to feel happy here."

Amid all this, Frau Cosima had by no means lost her insight into politics. She said about Lassalle, at the time when lawsuits were springing up for him like mushrooms: " He thinks that by this means people will stop leaving him in peace. For my part, I am getting fonder and fonder of peace and the quiet shade and am only half interested in his affairs, in which he always develops an eloquence quite in the spirit of 1793." She speaks of Wagner's journey to St. Petersburg and of his successes, her husband's concert tours, and also, as she was able to describe to Frau Luise, the extraordinary success of his ballade *Des Sängers Fluch,* written for the great Uhland Festival, at which he had himself conducted the great Funeral March from the *Eroica.* She speaks of Berlin politics, expressing the opinion that there was nothing to be done in Prussia at that time save to read the Lamentations of Jeremiah. One did not know, she said, whether one ought to play the part of the weeping or the laughing philosopher — of Heraclitus or of Democritus. She expressed the view that, for the time being, Berlin was a regular jumble of everything: people were for Russia, for Poland, for Bismarck, or for the Chamber. Gounod's *Faust* was more admired than that of Goethe, people fêted the veterans of 1813 and trembled before "our Louis." But in all this there was no grandeur and nothing particularly attractive, for which reason she was withdrawing more and more into family life — the family having meanwhile been swelled by Bülow's mother. For since her sister-in-law had married Victor von Bojanowski, Frau Franziska had joined the young couple, which ultimately made it necessary for them to move.

On March 11 was born her second daughter, who was called Blandine in memory of her sister. Frau Cosima tended the child with touching care, and when in June it fell mortally ill and the doctor had already given it up, it was due to "the miracle of her maternal care," as Bülow put it, that it was saved. During the August holidays he took her for the rest which she needed to Klampenborg, a seaside resort near Copenhagen. The sea air and, above all, the quiet did him and the young mother a great deal of good.

The winter passed away in outward peace and quietness. Bülow had great successes and met with more and more recognition in Berlin, where he was indeed in the front rank of musical life. He developed an extraordinary activity, and Frau Cosima was able to create a secure foundation for it all at home. It may be said that hers was the last of the Berlin *salons* of the old style, which had lasted from the "period of enlightenment" to the days of Bettina von Arnim.

But on his way to and from his concert tours Richard Wagner was their constant guest. With touching devotion and out of the need which they felt to comfort him in his hard and distressful situation, they surrounded him with that gay hospitality of which Frau Cosima possessed the wonderful art. The hours which he passed there were great and fateful ones. And whether he were weighed down with care or momentarily free from anxiety, here alone he met with understanding and deep perception.

For Frau Cosima this had been an incomparable period of formation. This young woman, who had hardly outgrown her girlhood, had developed an intellectual and a spiritual grandeur which are a unique phenomenon. A rare magic emanated from her personality, and whoever came near her felt bound to do homage to her. Even Giacomo Meyerbeer, that much-abused and indubitable opponent of the new tendencies, entered the *salon* of this incomparable woman with a feeling of admiration and a strong impulse to display his best qualities there. And, by a delicious irony, it is her husband who bears witness that he succeeded to the full.

But she rejoiced in the honours won by her husband. She was pleased at being greeted as "*Frau Doktor*" when Hans was granted a doctorate by the University of Jena, and to her father too she was drawn even more closely than before. All his correspondence with Germany went through her hands, and he mentions in his letters that she is the only being in Germany with whom he corresponded at the time. It was she who managed her husband's business. She was in some sort the soul of the newly-founded Tonkünstlerverein and kept up an active correspondence with Richard Wagner — a correspondence which was in the main of a purely business character, yet in which we can read between the lines her great and profound understanding for this unique man, the greatest among artists. If there was ever any question of a misunderstanding or of some fault which he had committed in his attitude towards her or her house, she knew how to admonish him and defend her point of view with womanly dignity.

And so the year 1863 went by, rich in inward suffering, yet rich in the joys of motherhood, for the little Daniela flourished, and so did Blandine, who was most like her mother. They grew into beautiful and lovable children, with whom she played in the way which she describes so delightfully to Frau Luise: " Cosima and Daniela are terribly behindhand, and I am very much afraid that Willi and Heinz will find them both thoroughly badly brought up, but since we are all so full of good thoughts and wishes for the New Year, and joyful thanks for the lovely Christmas presents, they will vouchsafe to be gracious. The surprise, in the shape of the black bears and elephants, enraptured both the little daughter and her mother. I really cannot say which was the more delighted. For the echo aroused in a mother's heart is a powerful one and like no other — a radiance in her child's eye moves her to tears, which she at once restrains and bids to flow. The two of us played in our own fashion with the Christmas presents, and I give thanks in a heart-felt kiss to Willi and Heinz, whom Daniela managed to distinguish in the charming little photograph." She faithfully tended her mother-in-law, who, as a member of the household, was by no means easy to get on with, for all her greatness of soul and amiability. But with the supreme nobility and high-mindedness which Frau Cosima displayed, indeed, in all social relations, she succeeded in ordering her household like a fine, notable, and wonderful wife. Liszt justly regarded her at this time with an admiring eye. And so she stood forth in grandeur and beauty at the moment when the great change in their destiny arrived, and Hans von Bülow was at last really able to lay aside his occupations in Berlin, which had become far too onerous, and which he was already determined to give up. During his concert tour in Russia he was offered a brilliant conductorship in St. Petersburg and only hesitated out of consideration for his wife and children, to whom the harsh climate of St. Petersburg might be, and indeed must have been, injurious. This was a turning-point in his life and also in that of his wife; for all that happened now was big with destiny. On crossing the Russian frontier at the beginning of May, he received word at Königsberg that Richard Wagner had been sent for by the handsome young King Ludwig II of Bavaria, and that after all the want and disquiet and " joyless unrest (*Friede-Freudelosigkeit*) " recently spoken of by Frau Mathilde, by a reminiscence of Walther von der Vogelweide, he was now safe. The " Flying Dutchman " now sailed into the harbour which was to prove so rich in blessing.

CHAPTER IV

THE CALL OF DESTINY

THE LIFE of King Ludwig II of Bavaria has still to be written. There has been no lack of attempts, and even of good attempts, to do so. But the point has not yet been reached from which it might be possible to obtain a perfectly accurate view of this highly original nature. Moreover, very varied hands have made it their task to deal with this copious, though not exhaustive, material. But most of them have been influenced by a medical opinion drawn up shortly before the tragic end of this remarkable King, with a display of pedantic logic and with pretensions to an infallibility which defies all scientific laws. Professor Gudden's diagnosis is in some sense an impediment to an accurate presentment, constructed on sound historical principles, of the King's life and personality. It is true that in recent times exception has been taken to Gudden's judgment in medical quarters too; for he drew it up before he had been in close contact with the person upon whom he had to pronounce an opinion, and, what is more, without thorough observation and examination. This is a serious fault, and history is still suffering from it today, though Gudden has expiated by his death the grave error which he was unable to repair in the light of the scientific and moral progress since made by the study of mental disease. But, dead though he is, there is one crime from which he cannot be exonerated: by his blunder, he drove a king to his death. So far there has been but one of the King's biographers who has brought out this point clearly and precisely, and that is Gottfried Böhm. Even he has not entirely succeeded in shaking off the influence of Dr. Gudden's diagnosis, but he has insisted with justifiable disgust upon the way in which this alienist approached the august person of the King with remedies and treatments worthy of the Middle Ages and allowed his keepers to lay their foul hands upon him. There can be no doubt that from Gudden to Eisner and his accomplices was only a step. Doctrinairism always leads to decadence and even to revolution. For even a doctor may be antimonarchical and through lack of psychological discrimination may point the way towards disloyalty. With the exception of Böhm, nobody but Karl Theodor von Heigel has shown a right feeling towards King Ludwig II and a just appreciation of him, not in writing, but in heart and speech. All others have neglected the very principle of history — that is, that the development of a personality should be traced back to its origins. Thus only two of his contemporaries knew, appreciated, and treated the young King properly: Bismarck and Richard Wagner. Sweeping aside bureaucracy and its emasculated diplomacy, Bismarck took the young King's beautiful hand in his firm grasp and raised it to his lips in reverence for the young man's profound sense of kingship.

History is the study of the past, but also of the forces in it which contain the germ of further development. In this respect Heinrich von Treitschke possessed a certain delicacy of perception enabling him, in spite of his enthusiasm for German unity — which he would have modified, had he lived longer — to do justice to Ludwig I, and in a sense to Max II as well from the political point of view, in spite his hostility to the latter. In spite of all, he too felt that a quite peculiar type of monarchy had developed in Bavaria, appropriate to the position of the dynasty among the German princes and to that of Bavaria among the countries of Europe. The monarchy had a strong and definite bent towards culture which was consistent throughout. Both Ludwig I and his son possessed exceptional gifts in this respect, and, what is more, an exceptional enthusiasm. When the Crown Prince Ludwig, as son of one of the princes of the Confederation of the Rhine, had to accompany Napoleon I on his entry into Berlin in October 1806, he had hardly dismounted before he paid a visit to the studio of the sculptor Schadow, in order to commission him to make a bust of Frederick the Great for his Valhalla, an action which showed that his artistic tendencies had come into being under the ascendant of German nationalism, under which they still continued to develop. He knew no art save one which was high and holy, doing homage at once to the ideal of Christianity and to the German spirit. Fundamentally he required no counsellor to help him find and pursue the right path, and the choice of the artists whom he summoned to Munich was always due ultimately to his own judgment. Such was the genesis of artistic Munich and of Munich as a monument of art. There was no lack of opposition, and in city and Diet alike the development of Munich under the hands of its King was a subject for amusement, jest, and grumbling; for the Münchener as such knows no gratitude. Genuine right feeling is only to be found in individuals, and it is this feeling which gave and still gives the city its fine, harmonious atmosphere. But the King abandoned his throne because he wanted to remain true to himself and make none of the concessions which the spirit of the age demanded of him.

Maximilian II, too, had his own ideal of kingship. Ample satisfaction had been given to the plastic arts. The next thing was fully to acclimatize science and literature in Munich. In this he had only to follow in his father's footsteps, adapting himself to the spirit of the new age. He did so and, as his father had done, pursued his own ideas quite independently. It is true that the persons among whom he had to choose were not up to the same standard as the artists of the first half of the nineteenth century. But science flourished and poetry had found its home in Munich. If we think of Hebbel, Otto Ludwig, and others, they would not, perhaps, have formed such a pleasant symposium about the King as Emanuel Geibel and Paul Heyse, but they would certainly have been of more use to the theatre itself than the prize competitions so generously instituted by Maximilian in order to obtain a flourishing German drama. But all honour to his intentions, and to his achievement too.

It has been said that he died far too prematurely for his son Ludwig II, who came to the throne at the age of nineteen. According to the ideas of average humanity, this is doubtless correct. But there is another question: was the education which he had prescribed for Ludwig the right one, and might it not in the long

155

run have caused even greater harm than it actually did to this young man, who once, in a moment of sombre introspection, remarked, not without justification: " I hate my tutors." But Max II died a sacrifice to his subjects in Munich. During the turmoil of the Schleswig-Holstein question they demanded the return of the King, who was staying in Italy in the hope of curing his serious illness. This demand had the revolutionary character which is typical of Munich, petty and tactless, and for that very reason potent with noble and sensitive souls. " My people have no idea," sighed the King, " what a sacrifice I am making for them." He came home only to die. On his death-bed he summoned his son to his side and made known to him in the deepest confidence his last royal wishes. These have remained a secret for us, for the young King never divulged a word about them. But with head erect he entered upon the government, and from the first he possessed what singles out a prince from among others, and what nobody can teach him: royal tact. This he preserved till his latest breath. His suicide is the best witness to this. But he also possessed his predecessors' instinct and feeling for kingship and for the character of the monarchy which they had so splendidly fostered; but now it was no longer painting and sculpture which predominated, nor science and poetry, but drama and music! And he at once recognized that in Richard Wagner's music-drama their development was at that very time reaching its supreme expression. It is most remarkable to see how Franz Liszt, impressed by the rare transformations that were going on in his friend, expressed this in his own lucid fashion. He did this almost more from the standpoint of a courtier than of an artist. It is true that what he says on the subject was written to the Princess Wittgenstein, which gives his words a somewhat doctrinaire character at that time. But in spite of this he saw the right point: the immortal ideal of kingship, as cherished by this splendid young man, was to reveal German drama in its most comprehensive sense and, above all, in its supreme form: the music-drama, as exemplified by the works of the greatest of composers. But an undercurrent of melancholy runs through the whole of Ludwig II's life. It is to the credit of Gottfried Böhm to have pointed this out and laid stress upon two absolutely tragic manifestations of this melancholy: his longing for abdication and for death. As yet there was not a wrinkle on this youthfully open and beautiful brow, but in the depths of his heart was latent this twofold idea, which could only have been kept under by a vigorous development, not within himself, but in external circumstances, with which his own growth might have kept pace. With the exception of his governess Sibylle Meilhaus, there was nobody in the whole of his entourage who could have understood him; and at the same time nobody who could have regarded the conception of the monarchy from any other point of view than that of the bureaucracy which had been fostered by it and owed it its importance. There are only two who can be excluded from this category: Bomhard, the Minister of Justice, and Riedel, afterwards Minister of Finance. None of the others understood the King, and for this reason they were also incapable of guiding him, for he would always listen to reasonable arguments. Amid the earliest business of state and beyond the signatures which he had to give day by day, there shone before him his conception of kingship, embodied in the works, deeds, and personality of him who had already realized it in artistic form, and who must now be afforded scope for his existence and creative work, in order to reveal him to the world. This was Richard Wagner.

Once at Mariafeld, on the Lake of Zürich, Frau Eliza Wille, with whom Wagner had found a refuge in dire necessity, pointed in a twilight hour to the scores piled before him and bade him look out beyond all prejudices to a great and fair future. It was like a prophecy — but, indeed, every good and kindly word of a noble woman is a kind of prophecy, especially when it culminates in a noble wish; and so it happened now: before the moon had changed, the prophecy was fulfilled. With the greathearted and joyous resolution of youth King Ludwig summoned the artist and he came. It is true that all exaggeration has to be expiated. Yet for this very reason it was a splendid action and redounds to the honour of a king, and especially of this radiant youth who combined with his enthusiasm a strong and uncorrupted will.

And so Richard Wagner came to Bavaria and stayed in the beautiful villa by the Starnberger See. As often before, he had been on the edge of the abyss. He would no doubt have succeeded in saving himself from ruin by his own efforts, but he would have been unable to climb unaided to those serene heights which he required in order to bring his work to perfection. Wagner the man was in the hands of the money-lenders, and in spite of all the applause with which he met, Wagner the artist was in the hands of one who was not prepared to value and honour greatness for its own sake, but wanted to obtain her profit from it. The musical world was divided into two camps: one consisted of open enemies, the other of a handful of uninfluential helpers and devoted friends, poor helpless disciples, accustomed to struggle. What they lacked was the gift of tongues, but no Pentecost ever dawned for them. It was not they who carried their master's gospel out into the world and preached it to the people, but his art itself. It is due to the young King of Bavaria that this was possible amid all the insensate conditions of those days. Thanks to the sleepy routine of habit, the decadence of the theatre escaped detection, and there were but few who felt any impulse towards altering it. Both managers and performers were furious if any attempt was made to introduce changes in the well-oiled machinery of the stage. As an actor, the singer was fully equipped with some six or eight movements of the arms, which constituted what was then called acting. All that was required of him was a voice, but not a trace of inspiration.

In Munich itself things were not so very bad. In his own productions — culminating in the opera *Katharina Cornaro,* which was no more nor less than a reflection of Halévy's *La Reine de Chypre* — Franz Lachner, the court conductor (*Hofkapellmeister*), had certainly brought the institution over which he presided to the highest pitch of artistic development and, perhaps quite in good faith, but at any rate out of unconcealed self-complacency, could not conceive the possibility of any further development. The group of writers brought together by Maximilian II included, above all, two dramatists. Emanuel Geibel's *Brunhild* had been performed and Paul Heyse wrote effective dramas and was certainly not inclined to allow any disturbance of the quiet life of Munich. In the year 1861, however, the young King heard *Lohengrin,* the beauty of which had enraptured his father, but of which his governess, the good Sibylle Meilhaus, already referred to, had alone given him an enthusiastic account. It was an event to him. In this work he recognized the master of the future, and, as Ranke not unjustly observes, the very word "future," which Richard Wagner claimed for his work, made a deep impression upon the King — not for the sake of the mystic word itself, but because he who had uttered it had already translated it into action. All that remained was to send for this man, and the third stage in the grandiose cultural development of Munich and of the Bavarian monarchy would be provided for. And this time it was connected, not with several names, but with one alone.

So Richard Wagner was now in Munich. Once he had shaken off the bewilderment into which this unprecedentedly great and glorious stroke of destiny had thrown him, he began to make himself felt. The King — and this must above all be emphasized — not only wanted the artist and his work, but desired the complete realization of his plans of organization, which had arisen out of the works by a strong process of mutual reaction. And as soon as the two men had poured out their ideas to each other in wondrous communion and recognized the profound affinity of their souls, their minds were at once made up as to the carrying out of their will. This formed the great basis of the Munich period, and in its way it was a wonderful one: a paradise, in which King and poet, the youth and the mature man who had weathered so many storms, roamed together. And after the first effusions they had now to find out where they stood and win a firm foothold, in order to erect this proud new structure of German art on solid ground. They had both to come to themselves.

As Richard Wagner thought it all over and, having once recovered his self-control, took counsel with himself calmly, he felt the loneliness of his personal position, and also his incapacity to bring his work to perfection alone. He needed human society and assistance, but in the first place society. And he could think of nobody but Hans von Bülow and Cosima — of Cosima and her husband. In his very first steps we can see the obstacles which deterred him from simply summoning the young couple to him; for he was fully conscious of his vast love for

159

Cosima, and she was no less so. During recent years it had been the heaviest of burdens upon his life — harder than his outward fate and than all the distress which had overwhelmed him. Not a word had been spoken between them, but he still had a vivid remembrance of what had once been said in that parting glance at Zürich, of the message exchanged by their eyes when they said farewell at Reichenhall, and of the mighty truth which had been revealed to them on that lonely expedition in Berlin — the recognition of a boundless unhappiness which needed no words. In the album of Frau Cosima's faithful friend, to whom she clung more and more closely at this time, he had written Calderón's words: " That which cannot be said and cannot be left unsaid." This friend was Marie von Buch, who was just then being married to the minister Baron Schleinitz. These words are no more nor less than what Tristan says to Isolde:

> " *Des Schweigens Herrin*
> *Heisst mich schweigen:*
> *Fass' ich, was sie verschwieg,*
> *Verschwieg ich, was sie nicht fasst.*

> (The mistress of silence
> Bids me be silent.
> Though I grasp what she conceals,
> I uttered not what she does not grasp.) "

Was he to summon them, and might he do so, now that he had risen from the hopelessness of his great need? In January 1864 he had again written to Hans von Bülow: " I cannot live and I cannot die. I do not know yet in what way my latter end will come." And now that he had become so fortunate, he wrote: " My good fortune and my power are now so great that I am only anxious not to bring upon myself the reproach of lack of faith." It was these considerations which led him to write again from Starnberg on May 18: " I do not invite you both to come to me for a time this year, for I have reached such a pitch that I really shrink now not only from what stimulates me, but even from those who stimulate. Next year I hope to be so far advanced as to be able to propose a nice little plan to you for spending the summer together." He asked Hans only to come, for he must help him to give the young King some idea of his Nibelung music. Then came his birthday, which he spent in solitude, brightened only by the King's wishes and gifts. But, all the same, he felt the need to write to Bülow, and in his words we can notice the mysterious something which was coming between the two friends:

" So this, the strangest May in my life, is really over. A year ago it would have been wonderfully in harmony with the Olympian age (*Jupiteralter*) that I had just then attained. Nothing can compare to what I have experienced during this month. The contrasts in it have been like one of those terrible storms when, at the moment of most extreme oppression, the change suddenly takes place. You will soon hear all this by word of mouth. All I will say now is that in very truth a whole world has vanished behind me, and I really seem as though I were dead, though on the other hand I imagine myself to be as one of the happy dead, who no longer has anything real in common with this world." And once more he summons him, to himself rather than to the King. But a week later he writes again:

"As regards what I now say to you and what I am about to ask you, do not treat it as a sudden idea due to a momentary whim, but as an important clause in the last testament of a dying man. I invite you, with your wife and child and maidservant, to take up your quarters with me this summer for as long as possible — this is the result of long communing with myself. Hans, you find me in prosperity: my life is completely transformed! I am full of the most genuine love, the purest intentions — but my house is desolate, and now, for the first time, I feel this more painfully than ever. Good souls, now do help me over these first days. People my house! A whole storey is ready for you and your dear family: Cosima shall come with the two children. — Ah, how I need the enjoyment of such a noble company of those dear to me — and how I delight in your children! Truly, my good friends, only you are still wanting to my happiness! I went to work in trepidation to think all this out. First I raised this doubt, then that. Now all is clear, we must have one another, and the time is now, now! " And telegram followed telegram till they said yes, and Bülow came with his wife and children.

This summons rang in Bülow's ears like a blast from Roland's horn. It found him in a state of heavy gloom. After the last winter in particular his nerves were in shreds. We can imagine the effect of this on the whole household, and especially on the mistress of the house — all that she suffered in patience and bore with pain, though he felt himself even more to be pitied than she. Yet he pondered for long whether he ought to come; for since the time at Biebrich he shrank from being too near the stars, and the depressing effect of those days had persisted in him for long. What he had written to Raff while fresh from the impression of that visit still held good:

" Slavishly submissive though I feel towards all his works, which remain high and holy in my eyes, I have not yet been able to suppress a certain aspiration towards freedom, as regards myself. Wherever I am able to help him to his rights, there will I go, if I move — which, in any case, will not be to the neighbourhood of any mock Olympus." For he had felt the same dread of the Altenburg too, so long as it had existed. But now another factor was added: his disgust with his existence in Berlin; and the summons to initiate the King into the Wagner scores was highly tempting. Besides, he was not inclined to reject anything which might guarantee him a further existence of not too strenuous a character. And so he started out on the journey to Starnberg, where his family betook themselves at the same time. His health had completely broken down. He arrived a sick man, and it was only thanks to his unprecedented will-power that it was possible for him to accompany Wagner to the castle of Berg and play to the King, who received him with open arms, and with whom on one occasion he even dined alone. The young monarch found equal pleasure in the man and his playing and wanted to keep him on any terms. Liszt was astonished and delighted. It was the very thing which he had always desired for Hans; and he wrote to the Princess that these relations with the King were as extraordinary as they were flattering. " He has advanced further in his favour in a few days than I had done in Weimar at the end of ten years." And he was right. But Bülow was ill, and the damp days by the lake caused his recovery to proceed but slowly. He had to go to the city and took to his bed at the Bayerische Hof.

Meanwhile the Musical Festival at Karlsruhe, of which Bülow was to have been musical director, was drawing near. It was impossible for him to go there in such a state of health, though this meant a disappointment for his father-in-law, which was all the greater because Bülow failed to bring with him Richard Wagner. But the Master declined with some horror to go to Karlsruhe, now that he had attained to fortune and full development without the help of the Allgemeine Tonkünstlerverein, though this had actually been founded in the interest of his own and Liszt's works. But even though Wagner and Bülow were absent, there was one who could not stay away. Leaving her children behind her under the wing of the Wagner household, and her husband under the care of King Max II's former body physician, Frau Cosima betook herself to Karlsruhe. There she met her father, whose experiences of the last few years were written upon his brow, and who had made the journey from Rome at the prompting of the Princess's letters and in accordance with her will. His travels had been very stormy: " The mistral played him a mighty symphony." He had then travelled straight to Strassburg, without carrying out his intention of going to pray at his daughter Blandine's grave. There he had visited the Cathedral, where he was among the crowd which witnessed the brilliant procession on the Feast of the Assumption, which advanced to the strains of the song of *Fra Diavolo*. On the journey he had not been able to resist buying the novel *Manon Lescaut*. And so he came to Karlsruhe. Everything was a disappointment to him. Wagner had declined, Bülow had had to resign, Bronsart and his wife, Ingeborg, were conspicuous by their absence, and he asked himself what he was doing *dans cette galère*. But Cosima made up for everything. He had not written to her again, lest he might influence her in any way; for he was aware of the increasing difficulty of her position owing to the serious illness of her husband and her relations with Wagner. She had telegraphed

to him at Saint-Tropez and Paris about her husband's serious
illness. She was quite equal to the situation, and Liszt wrote
to the Princess: "In this situation Cosima shows very good
sense, and will order things for the best. It is possible that
she will go home as early as tomorrow to nurse her husband;
for I am extraordinarily uneasy about Hans, who wants to return to Berlin; meanwhile the King has offered him in the kindest way an annual salary of 2000 gulden."

Liszt went to mass with Cosima every morning. His description of the Catholic church in Karlsruhe and his comparison of
it with that at Weimar are interesting. Everything in him was
still concentrated upon the "ecclesiastical." It was not until
Cosima's influence made itself felt that he began to thaw. Then
began the rehearsals, and last came the performances, with
which, however, he was highly satisfied. Poor Cosima had to
report to the Princess the complete success of Liszt's works at
the *Tonkünstlerversammlung* (Congress of Musicians). It is
true that he was offended by the absence of the court, though
the Grand Duke made himself responsible for the expenses, and
the Queen of Prussia placed at the disposal of the Musikverein
(Musical Association) what was, in view of her resources, a
considerable sum. He listened to his *Festklänge* in the spirit of
the Princess and was delighted when a young pupil of Bülow's,
Fräulein Topp, played his *Mephistowalzer*, so that he was called
and had to make his bow; and in the end, though there were
many gaps at the congress, he felt quite pleased with it. He
received much homage, and at the various dinners his health
was drunk in state with great enthusiasm. It is interesting that
at the great supper his daughter sat between Eduard Devrient
and Count Theodor Walsh, one of his Geneva friends of the
year 1835 — that is, of the days of his "*pèlerinage* (pilgrimage)." There was at any rate a certain charm for Cosima in
being able to talk to them about her mother; but in order to
efface the impression of this upon the Princess, Liszt added that
the Count was an ardent Catholic and a friend of various very
important ecclesiastics. Cosima passed the time in varied fashion
enough, and it is interesting that she dined at a small party
with Liszt's friend Agnes Street, the lady to whom, as we know,

the whole of the third volume of his letters is addressed, and who had just arrived from Regensburg, where she had intimate knowledge of the affair in which the house of Thurn and Taxis was involved, which in later days also played a certain part at Munich in Richard Wagner's work-room. At last, on Sunday, they moved on to Munich. Liszt had not intended to set foot in the city in which Richard Wagner had found his " glorious " good fortune, and he lays particular stress upon this in his letters. He had meant to arrange a meeting with his son-in-law at Augsburg instead. It was only Bülow's illness, and Cosima's news that Richard Wagner had been summoned to the royal residence on the occasion of the King's birthday, that induced him to continue his journey to Munich:

" For this reason, I had not counted upon seeing him again this time, and only came to Munich to visit Hans." But Cosima had gained her point; for now he could not avoid a meeting with his friend and went to Starnberg. Here all prejudice broke down before his friend's personality and warm welcome, and, thanks in no small measure to the score of *The Mastersingers,* the Princess's influence fell quite into the background for the moment. They talked everything over exhaustively, and Wagner disclosed all his plans to him, even promising to visit him next year in Rome. It was undoubtedly a triumph for Cosima, as well as an absolute necessity, to bring her father and her friend together. It would have been a grave slight and might also have caused a scandal, in view of Wagner's connexion with the King, if this old friend had come to Munich and entirely cut his former favourite.

And so he came to the villa at Starnberg, which had already been so fateful to Frau Cosima. It was from there that she had written to her friend Marie von Buch and, as it were, poured out her whole heart to her. It is significant that almost her last words before leaving Berlin, and her first words on arriving in Starnberg, were addressed to this noble friend, in whose album the Master had written the symbolic words quoted above. From this time onward she was Cosima's faithful confidante, and of all others it was perhaps she who enjoyed her deepest and most beautiful confidence. While still in Berlin, Cosima had written to her: "Dearest, beautiful one, since you could no longer come to me to say farewell, I wish you a splendid journey and a happy return to your Penates. You will believe me when I tell you, with my arms round you, that I am as much convinced of the greatness of your soul as I am delighted with the loveliness of your nature and the fine talents of your mind. Do not forget Cosima Bülow."

And again, on June 17, immediately before her departure, she wrote: "Dearest, beautiful one! Though I had thought of spending the summer at the seaside, I shall in all probability go to Tyrol. I shall then go on to the south of France, Karlsruhe, Weimar, Schleswig, Paris — in short, everywhere but the place which I had intended. Life has always treated me like this, and I have always had to make up my mind to let myself drift, and watch all my plans bursting like soap-bubbles. So make haste, my beautiful one, to visit Berlin again, or I doubt if we shall see each other again very soon." And in the most charming way she goes on to speak of some question of dress, in which little Daniela already took an interest in her sweet childish way. She next wrote from Starnberg:

"I am now thinking, my beautiful one, about what I wrote you in one of my letters with regard to my absence, and I am writing to you under the impression of conditions in the most marked contrast with those lines, far from my home, far from all noise, separated even from the little village of Starnberg by the lake, everything seems remote, so that the whole world forgets me and I forget the whole world. When I have once explained it all to you, you will not misunderstand my words. I have been here three days, and it seems as though it had already been a century and were going to last I do not know how long! And so my spirit is steeped in peace, and I have an infinite longing never to see or hear a town again. We are here with Wagner, whose existence has found peace as though by a miracle. We have talked of you together, and I can assure you that he understood your letter, to which I added a little commentary, in the way upon which we had decided."

Thus it appears that even before Cosima entered the house on the Starnberger See, and destiny ran its course — as, indeed, it was bound to do — Marie von Buch was entirely the confidante of her heart and her love. Her letter goes on: " And what are you doing at Norderney? Mind you grow more and more beautiful! For when I write to you, I feel as if I were the Fairy Cambosse making her bow to the Flower Fairy."

This letter had a fateful significance!

Next came her husband's illness and the journey to join her father, who had stayed on alone with his friend at Starnberg and had left thoroughly impressed by his greatness and importance. " Richard the Glorious " he called him, and with such sentiments, as of a care-worn man who had finished with life, he left him. That evening he wrote to the Princess that her letter had caused an illumination in his heart, finer and brighter than in the chapel of St. Peter's or the Cathedral at Strassburg. " Let me kiss your hands for taking the communion on St. Bernard's day for Hans's intention."

On the following day Liszt went with Wagner to visit Kaulbach and also presented his daughter to the great painter's wife. This was the only visit which he made in Munich, after which he left for Weimar. On the same day Cosima returned with her husband to Berlin, where alone he hoped to find a cure; for he would not hear of Gastein or any other watering-place. It was a strange force that drew him homeward. For once more he was seized with irresolution, especially as offers had been made to him both by the court of Berlin and from Löwenberg, by the Prince of Hohenzollern. Now that the King of Bavaria had interested himself in this great artist, the others felt it incumbent upon them to do their part, so as to dispute him with the art-loving monarch.

It is as though a mysterious hand had tried to arrest Cosima's destiny. While Liszt went off to the deserted Altenburg and became a spectator of the small and petty doings at Weimar — which were in such contrast with the great developments that the young King had carried out or had in view — Cosima returned to Berlin, to wait for an improvement in her husband's condition and do all she could to soothe the terrible state of his nerves and the pangs which tormented him. Gradually he became calmer, and signs of recovery began to appear. But he still hesitated to

strike his tent in Berlin and move to Munich for good. He too
was held back by a curious dread, though he kept repeating to
himself that the King's offer, which had now been communicated
to him in writing in the most amiable terms by Herr von Pfistermeister, Councillor of State (*Staatsrat*), was tempting enough.
Much persuasion was necessary on the part of his father-in-law,
who had appeared upon the scene, before he at last sent an
answer to the court officials at Munich in the affirmative.

As soon as there was an improvement in his condition, Cosima
went off with her father to the Löwenberg, where Liszt was enchanted at the impression made by his beautiful and clever
daughter on the whole of the Prince's court. Her clear laughter
rang through the usually lonely castle, and her father himself
wrote: " Cosette is here. Her splendid good spirits are a delight
to our glorious Prince, who shows in every way how pleased he
is with her." In fact he did not want to part with her and invited
her to go to Paris with him. Immediately before leaving Berlin
she wrote to Frau von Schleinitz:

" At this moment, when I am leaving Berlin provisionally
before returning once more to take the final decision, I cannot
quite collect my wits, my dear, sweet one, and my congratulations will be distraught. But meanwhile I am sufficiently in control of my heart to embrace you tenderly and wish you a beautiful and brilliant life. You know that my disposition is not such
as to fit me for saying the usual amiable commonplaces, but
that all my wishes are serious and unalloyed, such, in fact, as
my nature could alone produce. And so I congratulate Baron
Schleinitz for having chosen you and won as his life's companion
a being possessed of every brilliant quality and excellence, of
every gift of mind and heart. And I congratulate you too, dearest friend, because you are entrusting your life to a man of
whom you have spoken to me in such exalted and animated
terms. I am chary of the word 'happiness.' Those who know life
know how many discords it contains. But I am convinced that
in the conditions which I have mentioned you will have a life
that is brilliant, delightful, and on a lofty plane. And what
wishes could be so ambitious as to desire more than this fine
aim, which I see you have attained to the full. I love you in per-

fect happiness, and embrace you with all tenderness, and strew your path with all the wishes which the fairies lay in the cradle of a king's daughter." And she also adds: " The day after to-morrow I am to meet my father at Eisenach, and we are to travel to Paris together. From Paris he will go on to Rome, and I to Munich, where we are going to settle. Yes, my dear, we are leaving Berlin. I hope it is not necessary to tell you that I regret it more than ever now. Towards the end of October I shall be back here again. See that you stay here till then, it would be splendid if we were to see each other here once more."

The soil of Germany burnt beneath Liszt's feet. " The German atmosphere oppresses me to the last degree," he writes to the Princess. After spending well-filled and momentous days in Weimar and Wilhelmstal he now met his daughter at Eisenach. Once again the Grand Duke had offered to use his influence at the Vatican, in order to effect a marriage between him and the Princess — which now came to grief owing, not to the Pope's ban, but solely to the Princess's own strange and fanatical will — and had tried to persuade him to return to Weimar. But Richard Wagner had also expressed a desire to bring him to Munich and wrote to Bülow that he was out of humour with Liszt because he would not stay there. " Why, why can he not be one of us? "

It was a beautiful meeting at Eisenach. Liszt had celebrated Cosima's name-day with her in Berlin — the Feast of SS. Cosmas and Damian — and had gone to church with her early in the morning. He was deeply affected when, instead of a low mass, they were greeted by the *de profundis* of a requiem mass. Cosima smiled, but he was profoundly moved. At Eisenach they visited the Wartburg with Lassen, who had come to Weimar to take leave of Liszt. Then they went on to Paris, where they took up their quarters in his son-in-law Ollivier's big, roomy house, Liszt occupying the rooms in which Blandine had once kept house. On the third storey lived his mother, who enjoyed perfect health and had also preserved her old freshness of mind and sound judgment. She knew how to say her mind with kindly, healthy humour, not unmingled with a mild and subtle mischief — in short, the old lady remained what she had always

been, a true Frau Aja. On the other hand, Liszt's strange religious bent showed itself in rather a curious form; for the Princess could not leave even the old lady in peace, though she was
on such excellent terms with the Almighty. Liszt writes on the
subject:

"Tenderest thanks, my dearest angel, for your letters and
your beautiful prayer in St. Peter's on September 18, the day
of the canonization [sic] of the Blessed Margaret von Alacque
(Margaret Mary Alacoque). I repeat with my whole soul: may
God grant my mother a holy death, and my daughter a holy
life." The Princess had indeed become a sort of female Conrad
of Marburg.

Cosima had now to visit old Madame de Saint Mars, and her
former confessor, the Abbé Bucquet, who was now supplemented by another, a worthy priest who officiated at Notre Dame.
But the climax of the whole visit was a meeting between her
two parents. Liszt could not avoid accepting an invitation to
déjeuner with Daniel Stern and Cosima, and so the daughter
had the rare happiness of seeing both her parents together and
of at last uniting their image in her own mind. It appears that
the principal object of Liszt's visit to Paris was, at the desire
of the Princess, to induce his mother to receive the sacraments.
But the old lady refused, and, to his deep sorrow, he had to
write that all his efforts had been frustrated by her obstinacy.
He went with Cosima to the Abbé Bucquet in the hope of at
last succeeding in carrying out the Princess's wish through his
influence.

He then returned to Rome, and Cosima went first to Munich
and then from Munich to Berlin, there to make arrangements
for the move with her accustomed thoroughness, while the Master himself had found a house for them and could not resist
sending them a drawing showing them the plan and disposition
of it. But at the same time he offered his friends the garden-
house forming part of the fine property which the King had
induced him to rent on the Briennerstrasse and finally presented to him. But he was extremely anxious about Cosima:

"The poor state of Cosima's health worries me too. Everything which concerns her is out of the ordinary and unusual:

she requires freedom in the noblest sense of the word, she is childlike and profound — the laws of her being will always guide her only to what is sublime. Nor will anybody be able to help her but herself. She belongs to a special order of existence, which we must learn to comprehend through her. — In future you will have the advantage of more leisure and greater and more adequate freedom, so that you can observe this and take your noble place at her side. This too is a consolation to me." But now she herself had proudly and strongly grasped the great and supremely important mission of her life. Once during this time Wagner wrote:

" The neglected state of my household cripples my vital spirits. Oh, poor Beethoven, now I can well understand why he flew into a rage over his housekeeping. And I, who have dedicated more honour and praise to woman than even Frauenlob, I have not so much as a woman's heart which I can call my own." But even as he wrote this, he had won one.

Destiny took its course, and though Richard Wagner shared something of the tragic fate of his Flying Dutchman, yet he might now be certain that the woman who was ready to be faithful to him till death had taken the rudder in her firm but gentle hand and from that moment onwards steered safely through whirlpools, currents, and storms.

The Master had rented the Bülow family a house in the Luitpoldstrasse, into which they moved immediately. Both of them succeeded at once in adapting themselves to the conditions of Munich, and though, as a matter of fact, Frau Cosima assumed the duties of mistress of the house in Richard Wagner's bachelor establishment and to a certain extent entertained for him there, she managed her own house wonderfully at the same time. Her great and lofty intelligence at once grasped the whole situation. She saw perfectly well that Richard Wagner's position in Munich was a perilous one. She knew that the best thing for him would be to leave Munich and live in isolation, so that he might bring his works to completion; for amid the turmoil of Munich none but a mind as great as the Master's and accustomed to the most intense concentration would have found it really possible to pursue his work; and, indeed, before his

171

departure he had completed the instrumentation of the second act of *Siegfried*. But, on the other hand, the King's wishes had also to be carried out, and to her, too, the Master spoke of the exalted duty which kept him in Munich, not to abandon the lonely young man to himself and the monstrous cabals which surrounded him. For now that many decades have gone by since the King's death, it may indeed be said that, in the whole court and among the whole host of his officials, he had scarcely a friend. But the young King wanted to see concrete results too, and Frau Cosima had now to take her full share in this. She did so with great joy, for every event met with extraordinary success. First came the first performance of *The Flying Dutchman* in Munich, conducted by Wagner himself. Bülow was enchanted with this performance, which, indeed, made a great and momentous impression. On December 25 Bülow himself gave a brilliant rendering of Beethoven's E flat major Concerto. This was the only time that Ludwig II appeared in state at a concert at the Odeon. Opposition was already stirring on every side, but it was not necessary to take any notice of it, and fundamentally it was no more than the outcry which has always been raised against strangers in Munich and has at all times been characteristic of the intolerance of certain circles.

But a host of tasks arose for Frau Cosima. She was the Master's secretary, who kept up his relations with the outer world, and managed everything which the much-occupied and high-strung composer was not absolutely obliged to deal with himself. She immediately undertook all negotiations between him and the royal secretariate and even the King. The fact that the King did not want to see him so frequently as before has been interpreted as a sign of diminished confidence. Nothing could be more untrue. It goes without saying that a certain distance had always to be maintained between two such great and introspective natures, if they were not to wear each other out. The King's extravagant enthusiasm became a tormenting anxiety to Wagner; while to the King the grandiose and commandingly superior nature of his friend became a source, if not of discontent, at least of chagrin and disquietude if they met too often. The correspondence between him and the Master was in full

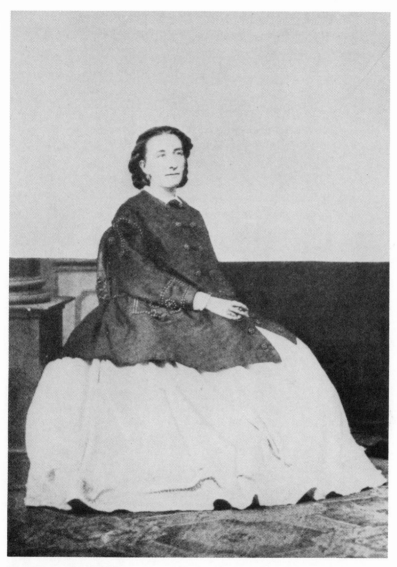

COSIMA WAGNER

About 1865 — *Photograph by Ramme & Ulrich, Bayreuth*

swing; but side by side with it there began another and incomparably more exquisite one, which assumed a particular importance after the catastrophe. For the moment the principal thing was to accede to the King's affectionate desire to acquaint himself fully with Richard Wagner's life-work, and to collect all that he had ever written, so that the King might arrive at a complete insight into his creative work. Harassed by cruel storms, Wagner had changed his residence so often during his life that we may regard it as no less than a miracle that his great works survived all these vicissitudes of fortune undamaged and were never lost, but saved by him, like a second Camoëns salving his *Lusiads* from shipwreck and raging sea. But there was a tender and solicitous hand at Zürich which had collected and faithfully preserved many relics of earlier days that Richard Wagner had handed over to her. One of the great portfolios in which she put away all these gifts of the Master's had now to be opened, and it was Frau Cosima who entered into correspondence with Frau Mathilde Wesendonck on the subject. There is a singular and rather melancholy charm in following these events. On January 13, 1865 Frau Mathilde wrote her last letter to Richard Wagner. It runs as follows: " My friend, Frau von Bülow has made a request to me by letter today about some of your literary manuscripts which are in my possession. I have gone through the portfolio, but it is impossible for me to send anything, even if it were at your own personal desire, for you will hardly remember now what scattered pages and scraps of paper are collected together in my portfolio, so I am sending you a list of all its contents and beg you to tell me whether I am to send anything, and if so, what. I naturally assume that you are aware of the projected publication of your works by His Majesty's command. I was deeply rejoiced to see from this amiable lady's letter that you are well and have gathered your loved ones about you. Receive my heart-felt greetings and think lovingly of your Mathilde Wesendonck." This was the last letter which she wrote the Master, and she wrote it in order to avoid answering Frau Cosima. The Master was therefore bound to take up the pen himself and enlightened her about his whole destiny, with reference not only to outward changes, but also to those which were going on within him. He wrote about this whole episode:

" He [the King] knows that he must not give me much trouble over it and always contrives to appeal to my friends. And this is what he did on the present occasion. In response to his repeated request, that is, I had been forced to state what I had written and what had become of it. And so I had to give information about the big portfolio on the Green Hill — there was no getting out of it. That is all the harm there is in it. What he wants is to have it all got together in order to put it in safe keeping and to know that he is in quite complete possession of me. Yes, children, he loves me, he really does! " And now came some deeply significant words, in which we still catch an echo of the impression made on him by her attitude at the moment of his dire need at Mariafeld: " If in spite of everything things will not yet go well with me, there may well be reasons for this. The lighter my cargo of faith becomes, the higher I rate myself. I have now hardly any faith left in anything, and if this void is to be filled up, there will be need of a tremendous ballast of royal favour. Once I was to be had cheaper; now my perceptions are horribly acute, and it will hardly be possible for me again to be disappointed at the appalling weakness which shrank back from me on all sides as though from a madman. But I still do what I can, and am glad to expect anything of mankind. My young King helps me in this, for he knows all and has a will! So I must have a will too, though this often gives me very strange sensations." This was in some sort his retaliation for recent events in which Frau Mathilde had played a certain part, and that owing to her doubts of him and her failure to understand the greatness of his sentiments and, not least, of his sensitiveness. For, in spite of all, Wagner was a kingly nature. This, too, is what determined the relations between the two. But clearsighted as he was, it was precisely in these January days of 1865 that his whole feelings were overshadowed by a grave anxiety about the King, which had far more effect upon himself than any attacks from without. Beginning imperceptibly, these attacks gradually gathered strength, and though they were doubtless stimulated by little diplomatic negligences and jars, they were on the whole inspired by the object of getting rid of one who had become a burden and more than a burden. But Wagner saw yet more: he saw into the depths of this royal boy's heart, and his conception of him reminds us of C. F. Meyer's wonderful picture of two contrasting temperaments: in these verses the gardeners dig up a figure of a marble boy in the vineyard of the Capulets at Verona and show it to the learned Master Simon. Juliet falls on her knees beside it and says with characteristic sweetness:

" What is thy name, sweet boy? Now tell me, pray!
Out of the grave rise to the light of day!
Dost bear a torch, and wings to fly withal?
Amor art thou, that dost all hearts enthral! "

But Master Simon heeded not the maid
And, gazing on the figure, sternly said:
" The torch he quencheth, and it flickereth,
The boy is lovely, but his name is Death."

Indeed, it seemed to him that either life and development to a supreme degree or else black ruin would be the fate of this solitary King; and he felt it his duty not to abandon him, but to carry out his will both intellectually and spiritually and endeavour to fulfil his desires. He was no courtier, and Frau Cosima had no occasion to twit him, as she had once done her future husband, with being a " *vil courtisan.*" On the contrary, we may here refer to the pretty business into which Wagner was nearly drawn by the father of that M. Street[1] whom Frau Cosima had met shortly before. This lady's father, Klindworth, was a diplomatist in Brussels, who was planning great enterprises on the strength of small means, and in one way or another had his finger in the pie at every court. He now came to Richard Wagner one day, to persuade him to co-operate in his scheme on behalf of the house of Thurn and Taxis at Regensburg, which was vastly rich and disposed of equally great — indeed inexhaustible — resources from another quarter, sufficient

[1] Mrs. Agnes Street. — Tr.

to justify plans for founding a new state comparable to the mediæval dreams of a Kingdom of Burgundy. And since Liszt's daughter was presumably also a friend of her father's friend, she too was called into counsel. She was as shrewd and elusive as the Master, and as his partner played her cards as brilliantly as he did. The Privy Councillor (*Geheimrat*) had to retire without gaining his object, and Wagner's account of the affair consisted of one remark: " I continued to be dense (*Ich blieb dumm*)."

But meanwhile their great projects were ripening, or seemed to ripen. The King pressed more than ever to have them carried into effect. For the more clearly he came to apprehend them, the more he lost that wise calm which he had still displayed in a letter to the Master in September: " It is very true that nothing appreciable has been achieved in our day as regards institutions for the promotion of art, and that the whole lot of them need thoroughly remodelling. I freely admit that it will be difficult to bring about an improvement in this sphere. For nowadays, when people are for the most part selfish and bent upon nothing but money-making, the feeling for true and glorious art has already sunk very low. And so I urgently advise you, dear friend, in carrying out your new purpose, to go to work in the way which you mentioned to me in your letter — that is, in the most circumspect way. I am firmly convinced that we shall succeed in effecting a thorough reform in the sphere of organizations for the promotion of art, *for a steadfast will and incessant perseverance can do much.* At any rate, a training-school will have to be founded for the performers of music-drama. I consider such an establishment absolutely indispensable." The King wrote this at a time when Liszt was staying in Munich. In the spring of the new year he was still more eager to be of assistance to his artist friend in carrying out his plans — more eager, even, than Wagner. But his chief wish was now to secure the production of *Tristan*, though from Karlsruhe as well as from Vienna — on all sides, in fact — it was whispered that such a thing was impossible. He gave the command, and work was begun. The conductor and, above all, the performers for *Tristan and Isolde* had already been found. It is true that Wagner would rather have seen another Isolde than the wife of his friend Schnorr, who was ten years older than her husband, but since she had quitted her retirement and returned to the stage on purpose to make the performance possible, there was no other choice. There had been no lack of negotiations, and the question of a conductor, in particular, had been a difficult administrative problem to solve, on account of Franz Lachner, the court conductor. But the King's word was final. On March 20 he wrote to the Master: " I joyfully accede to the wish expressed in your last letter by entrusting Herr von Bülow with the directorship of the orchestra in your work *Tristan and Isolde*. I cherish a firm conviction that I could confide this task to no worthier person (after you)." Next followed the rather anxious question: " Do you think the performance of this work will be entirely successful? What about the singers? I am looking forward to it with a joy which no words can express; to me too it is all like a dream."

Bülow was absent on a concert tour and returned to Munich on April 2, when rehearsals at once began. It was none too soon, if the task was to be performed in time, and if he was to bring it to a happy issue, as Wagner's " second self," to use the Master's own words; and he threw himself into it heart and soul. On April 12 he fixed the first orchestral rehearsal for ten o'clock. Scarcely two hours previously Cosima had borne him her third daughter, Isolde. This was a fateful day, and one is involuntarily reminded of the words in the first act of *Tristan:*

> *Wonne voller Tücke*
> *Truggeweihtes Glücke!*

> (Guileful rapture,
> Treacherous joy!) [1]

But now opened a period which Wagner himself has characterized as the greatest and happiest of his life. It should not be forgotten that from his *Lohengrin* onwards he had been precluded from testing the musical effect of his works, as a whole at least, otherwise than on the piano. And now all at once the

[1] *Tristan and Isolde*, I, v, Jameson's translation (Schott edition). — TR.

whole great prodigious structure of his *Tristan* rose up before him. The impression produced upon Frau Cosima was perhaps quite different from that which was produced upon himself, for it was he who had discovered and experienced these unprecedented new potentialities of music, and only the strong consciousness of his genius could warrant his certainty that, though departing from the beaten track, he had proceeded surely and unerringly.

I shall not describe the progress of these rehearsals nor go into details about the incidents connected with them. All that need concern us here are the feelings and attitude of little Isolde's mother towards the whole work. It was her prodigious spiritual power that lifted her above the divided allegiance in her life and upheld her during this time. For her, like some Isolde, the whole of this Munich period was but the " empty day," in the sense of that of *Tristan and Isolde,* that great song of day and night. She sacrificed everything to it and found complete peace in an extraordinary display of activity. She had acted as the Master's secretary and continued to do so. She wrote to the King what Wagner himself had neither the time nor, what is more, the inclination to tell him. She was initiated into all his plans and made them her own. We may safely speak of a collaboration between these three: the King, Cosima, and Richard Wagner; and there can be no doubt that, though from a distance, the King felt no ordinary respect for his friend's friend, and that it was almost easier for him to carry on a correspondence with her than with Wagner. For in spite of the writer's reverence — awe, indeed — even in his letters Wagner's mighty intellect had overpowered him. For whatever may and will be said when they are published, Wagner's letters are not inspired by that unbounded self-interest with which he was then being reproached in the newspapers, but by an uncompromising sincerity. No prince had ever a confessor who told him the truth so directly, clearly, and affectionately, but at the same time so inexorably. This was perhaps [a novel experience for] the young prince, who, if we wish to draw a historical parallel, appears to have been like the young Athalaric, grandson of Theodoric, the great King of the Goths. Both now and even more so in later days the Master felt that the King lacked one thing — the right man. Could he, an artist, replace such a person, who would have had to be at the centre of political life in Bavaria and in Germany, if he were to be the young King's faithful Eckart? No. And so there was only one agency which could prevent too abrupt a clash between their ideas and enable the artist to react upon the King only as a creator of works of art — which had indeed been his original wish; and that was the clear-sighted, level-headed nature of Frau Cosima. She was only eight years older than the King, but as a matter of fact her influence over him was that of an experienced friend, and never did he find a more faithful or understanding helper. It was not granted to him to see her, but he felt the rare magic which emanated from her; and the more strongly life reacted upon him, the more deeply he felt the need to exchange ideas with her. There is a great, remarkable, and unalloyed fascination in their relations, which reveal Frau Cosima to us in all her greatness as a woman, but at the same time in her deep and steadfast devotion to the Master. His art, his position, had to be upheld, and so she ventured out of her own exalted and wondrous atmosphere into the harsh light of day — and perhaps there was something rash in this. If she had confined herself to being the intellectual intermediary between King and the artist, then, though no doubt none of the bitter conflict would have been avoided, she would have remained unaffected personally. But that was not her way. And so through all this time she stood firmly and confidently at the Master's side.

Long before the rehearsals of *Tristan* began, the storm had broken over him. It is quite untrue to say that it was only the gutter press of Munich which raised its croaking voices against him like a raucous chorus of ravens. They were quite other persons who employed this chorus; they had been working against Wagner since December 1864, and with the full intention of driving him out of Munich. He was accused of egoism; but the leaders of this chorus were acting out of wounded vanity and a perfectly definite hatred for all that was great. They were petty in tone, language, and style. Recent research has revealed the fact that the well-known article: "*Richard Wagner und die*

öffentliche Meinung (Richard Wagner and Public Opinion) "
was written by none other than Oskar von Redwitz. The veil of
anonymity which the poet author of the sugary and insipid epic
Amaranth had thrown over his biting and mendacious invective
was torn down, revealing the face of the writer, and Hans von
Bülow erected a monument to " Amaranthus " in the *Kladderadatsch* which may perhaps outlast the memory of his poem. But
it was a monstrous piece of hypocrisy that was thus brought to
light, and it should not be forgotten that on December 4 old
von der Pfordten had become minister, and so the ominous
crescent rose over Munich which the newly-ennobled minister,
harking back to the old days of the crusades, had placed on his
coat of arms. The minister led the opposition to Wagner, whose
enemy he had been ever since his days in Dresden. In the so-
called cultured and artistic circles of Munich it was easy for him
not so much to enlist confederates as to unite them under his
wing. Frau Cosima saw and felt this, and though at first she conducted affairs courteously, yet later, when everything hung in
the balance, and things had either to change for the better or end
in a catastrophe, she attacked this wasps' nest firmly and un-
flinchingly. It is quite at variance with the truth to try to shield
her in any way and to say that she dissuaded Wagner or ought
to have dissuaded him. We may now recognize that she pursued
the right way at this time, and if harsh and vigorous language
sometimes passed her lips, it was an expression of genuine feeling, and as such justifiable. But it always hit the right mark
and the right people.

At first, however, the disturbance raged outside the enchanted
circle which Richard Wagner had drawn about him. The rehearsals of *Tristan* started and went on, filling everybody with
enthusiasm and delight. Wagner himself saw more and more
clearly how prodigious and yet how true his work was, while
Bülow acted as its interpreter, and Schnorr was by now fully
conversant with it and absorbed in it. After the celebrated performance of *Tannhäuser* which took place by royal command
shortly before the rehearsals began, he described his stay in
Munich to Frau Cosima as the finest moment of his artistic life,
and what he said to her was exactly what he felt: " I know quite

well how much is due to myself, what a small part of the achievement springs from me, how compellingly Wagner's inspiration surged and strove within me, and yet I am proud this evening: from this day onwards I feel that I have received my consecration as an artist. I possess the certainty that I am not unworthy to receive the inspiration of Wagner." And yet at this very time Wagner himself was deeply agitated. He wrote just now to Eliza Wille: "My longing for ultimate rest is unspeakable"; and another letter runs: "I long for nothing but rest, for I can bear it no longer." As early as February the King had written to him: "I must confess that I was pained to read your letter today. Whatever the matter may be, whatever the cause of your grief, reveal it to me. Whatever uneasiness you feel about me, I beg you, dear friend, to hide nothing from me." It was precisely during this *Tristan* period that Wagner was going through two experiences: the grave and fateful question of Cosima, and his no less ominous anxiety about the King. In April the King again laments to the Master: "Oh, do not long for death. I am prepared for everything, everything, but to know that you are afflicted, that is hard! . . . Once more I implore you, hide nothing from me." These were no superficial trifles, but point to the grievous spiritual struggle amid which this song of songs from the wondrous realms of night was to reach its full development. And so Wagner says to the King: "Fidelity to you (*Dir*) till death! You (*Sie*) are beginning to have doubts of humanity; let it be my task to reinstate it in your esteem. *Per aspera ad astra!* Like Isolde, so Brünhilde too shall be united in death with her beloved, the purest love shall be made manifest in *The Victors,* Parsifal[1] shall behold the crown of the Grail."

And while the Master was completely absorbed in *Tristan,* the King came to take an ever greater joy in his art-work as a whole, with which he wanted to become familiar down to the minutest details. Indeed, it is evidence of this young and highly gifted man's delicacy of feeling that he should now have searched out all the Master's writings and works, for which purpose he continued, as before, to make use of Frau Cosima.

[1] This spelling was not finally decided upon till February 1877. — TR.

He writes: "When last winter you sent me a list in your handwriting, I found among other things a scheme (*Programm*) for the Overture to the *Flying Dutchman,* for *Tannhäuser,* and for the Prelude to *Lohengrin,* and the draft of a drama, *Jesus of Nazareth.* How glad I should be if I might soon receive these writings!" And so the performance of *Tristan* drew nearer and nearer. All the gossip, which was chiefly connected with some hasty words which her husband was said to have used in the theatre, and had as its object to deprive the Master of his best helper, ended in nothing. *Tristan* came round, and public invitations now went out into the world. Frau Cosima thought of her friend and summoned her in cordial terms: "Dearest Excellency, have your boxes packed and come quickly, quickly. *Tristan* is to be next Monday. It will be a wonderful performance, worthy of the work. I will tell you everything you like, dearest friend, when I see you. I hope that you will not hesitate, and that we shall be able to talk together of you and your life. At the moment I have no time at my disposal for another line, for I do not know which way to turn, and it is not yet a month since my confinement. All my family commiserate me, and I submit, in the belief that they are to some extent in the right. I embrace you with all my heart, my dearest Excellency." And she adds by way of postscript: "Herr von Bülow kisses your hands, and Wagner, with whom we are staying at the moment, sends you his respectful greetings."

The general rehearsal arrived, which was like a first performance. Then followed a period of disappointment, due to the illness of Frau Schnorr von Carolsfeld, her delays and hesitations, and those of her husband; and last came that series of performances which is engraved as in bronze, not only in the artistic history of Munich, but also in that of German art as a whole. For Frau Cosima, too, it was the fulfilment of her supreme desire and, as it were, an affirmative answer to the question which she had put to fate. For with *Tristan* and with this really wonderful performance Richard Wagner's art-work was revealed to her eyes in its full grandeur and momentousness. She discharged her duties towards Bülow, and as hostess in Richard Wagner's enchanting little palace, gaily and with ease. During the long pause between the general rehearsal and the first performance she succeeded in providing brilliantly for the comfort and entertainment of the guests. Everybody was struck with enthusiasm by the fascination of this woman. An echo of this is to be found in all the reports and could be read of alike in Paris and in Königsberg, where Köhler sang the praises of Frau von Bülow's amiability; while in Munich itself everybody who approached her was enchanted.

After the third performance she next went with Richard Wagner and the Schnorrs to Tegernsee, where they spent a few days full of sunshine and light. Then the King summoned them back for the last performance. There was also the wonderful concert in the Residenztheater, which marked the real climax of Wagner's first period in Munich. The Schnorrs then took their leave, and a few weeks later, news reached them from Dresden that Schnorr von Carolsfeld was dead. This news came as an overwhelming shock to the Master. He hurried to Dresden to the funeral of the singer, whom he loved, accompanied by the faithful Bülow. They arrived too late. The earth already covered the remains of this wonderful man, who had in a sense given Wagner his work. He belonged to the circle consisting of Bülow, Cosima, the King, and Schnorr. For to Wagner he was an incarnation of one portion of his art — that is, so to speak, all his ideas on scenic and dramatic production. Wagner returned home shattered and only regained his composure by an effort. In this he exactly resembled Frau Cosima: he felt the loss of a loved one more deeply than anyone else. Just as Frau Cosima had mourned for Daniel and Blandine, just as in later years she nearly died over the Master's bier, so a real gloom descended on his spirit after this death.

The King was unable to console him, for all his sympathy, and in spite of the fact that he himself had death in some sort always before his eyes. Yet the words he wrote him are wonderful ones. He felt the death of Schnorr quite in the spirit of *Tristan,* and if Wagner wished to find consolation, he had it in these two beings, the King and Frau Cosima. " The purely human element which is dormant in us all, for which reason we all feel ourselves to be brothers, as it is immortally revealed in you, must blaze into a purifying flame in the breast of one dead. The people will not allow itself to be led astray by anything in its thoughts and feelings, but happy are they who lead it aright. Glorious victory will fall to their share. How strange is the vision of that wondrous lady, your friend, the content of which you communicate to me! One word on this point! She perceived, indeed, in the depths the eternal darkness that I wrote to you lately it was your mission to illuminate. Above in the clouds you were enthroned like a true Parzival. Your spirit shall subdue the darkness of evil and unbelief by its kindling rays. And that night too will be led into eternal brightness, and light and truth alone shall obtain dominion. This is your work; so courage! No shrinking! Brilliant victory! I write this at a remote hut among the glorious mountains; night reigns in the deep valley. Tomorrow I shall admire the mounting of the first rays of the victorious light, a symbol of your coming victory." And he went on to say: " We shall never part, we mean to become more and more firmly united, otherwise I shall leave the world for good, which I think of doing in any case hereafter, when my only one is no more." But, in response to an invitation from the King, Wagner went off to a quiet mountain hut on the Hochkopf, where in solitude he recovered once more and plunged deep into the Indian poem the *Ramayana* — in some sense a poetical anticipation of Schopenhauer's philosophy, which now, too, brought him consolation, so that on his return he produced the wonderful plan for *Parsifal,* his sacred stage-festival (*Bühnenweihfestspiel*), in writing which he found health again. The King, too, was enthusiastic about it to the highest degree, and in his youthful ardour kept urging the Master in almost every letter to continue working at it.

Meanwhile Frau Cosima had hastened to Budapest with her husband to meet her father. She felt this to be an absolute necessity, and, besides, she was impelled by a childlike feeling that she did not want to miss the production of her father's new work. Liszt had arrived from Rome, where, under the heavy compulsion of destiny, he had at last resolved to take the minor orders. It is significant that he writes to Bülow to break the news to his daughter, to whom, when it came to the point, he felt unable to write that he had been ordained: " On April 25 I received the minor orders in Monsignor Hohenlohe's chapel in the Vatican, where I am now living. It is superfluous to add that neither lack of reflection nor sentimentality led to this step, of which only three persons have known since April 2, Monsignor Hohenlohe, the Pope, and the Princess Wittgenstein. The significance that may be attached to it is rather that of a logical outcome of my life — as it has developed, at least, during recent years — than of a change in it. We will talk of this at our next meeting." And this took place at Budapest, where he now met with extraordinary triumphs. The performance of his *Saint Elisabeth* was a complete success. This charming and delicate work impressed the Hungarians, and Bülow too at the time, so that he wrote a very fine article on it: " *Franz Liszt und die Heilige Elisabeth* (Franz Liszt and St. Elisabeth)." In this he placed Liszt in his true light as a " Hungarian," while still recognizing his German qualities, and said very justly: " He who has satisfied the best elements in his own nation has lived for all nations." But Frau Cosima's analysis of her father's work is still finer and more original. Liszt was highly delighted and astonished when he read this remarkable criticism. At first he had no idea who had written it, and never suspected that his own daughter had taken up her pen in his cause.

For the rest, those were beautiful days that they spent together, both at Gran, where he and his children were the guests of the Cardinal Primate, and at the old castle of his friend Baron Augusz, then president of the deputy-governor's office (*Vizestatthalterei*) at Budapest. In short, he was highly delighted with his successes and, above all, too, by his son-in-law's playing and his daughter's wonderful bearing. It may indeed be said that, at this festival offered to her father by the whole of Hungary, Frau Cosima shone her brightest between her father and her husband.

The Bülows returned to Munich, but Liszt could not make up his mind to carry out his previous intention of accompanying them there. He had not been to *Tristan,* and he still avoided the Master. He was dominated by a strange state of mind, which found its issue in renunciation and was in some sense a concrete illustration of the words which Wagner put into the mouth of Parsifal in his draft libretto: " *Stark ist der Zauber des Begehrenden, doch stärker der des Entsagenden* (Strong is the spell of him who desires, but stronger still that of him who renounces)."

But into this world Wagner did not follow him, and pursued his way in defiance of his fate. He had now recovered his balance, and as soon as the young couple returned, they set to work, at the urgent instance of the King, to carry the Master's projects into effect. In honour of August 25 Richard Wagner had presented the King with the score of the *Rhinegold,* which he had written at Zürich with a golden pen. Frau Cosima had also remembered the King's birthday. The King writes to Wagner on this subject: " I also received from your friend Frau von Bülow a charming and significant gift, which conjures up before me at the moment every one of your sublime works." This was a birthday cushion, which the Master himself had undertaken to present to the King. The King was greatly delighted with it, as also with the other pieces of work which Frau Cosima did for him. She arranged a " Wagner Book," in which she collected everything that might interest him. She copied extracts from the Master's diaries, in order to submit them for the King's inspection, and, above all, she collected everything that the Master had ever written, grudging no effort and undaunted even by the refusals which she had to face from many of those in possession of the Master's manuscripts. It was a touching occupation, and now the King pressed for more still. He wanted an autobiography of the Master, for now, since *Tristan,* he was insatiable in his demands. What he wanted was a picture of the development of his art in general. He also wished to hear the Master's views on German affairs. Thus it was to some extent he himself who turned him, if not towards politics, at any rate towards subjects and connexions very closely associated with them, which were also given a political colour by his enemies. But what he had most at heart was the biography. Shortly before the catastrophe he wrote to him again: " My beloved friend, how is your biography getting on? I should be very much interested to have news of it." We may see from this that fundamentally the idea of

Richard Wagner's autobiography, which he afterwards dictated to Frau Cosima during the days at Triebschen, is to be ascribed to the King's initiative. His interest embraced the whole of Wagner's creative work. There is a certain grandeur of conception in this. It was not isolated works which interested him, nor was it the man alone, but the artistic and spiritual development of this unique and commanding artist. He wanted to know how he had come to begin *The Ring of the Nibelung,* and to write *Tristan and Isolde.* All these wishes were communicated to Frau Cosima. Even if her own heart had not impelled her to do so, the King's will and, so to speak, the King's invitation led her to make herself thoroughly familiar with this life and all that surrounded it. There is a fate in everything!

It was perhaps owing to the King's own initiative that during these September days the various projects of organization fell rather into the background, and this was a good thing, most welcome above all to the Master himself. To him all these questions were but means to an end. To take only one instance, his memorial on a school of music for Munich was in no way written with any egotistical purpose, but only in the cause of art. Inwardly he was already to a certain extent tired of all this. All he wanted was to give the King satisfaction in artistic matters, and also to secure a sphere of activity for Hans von Bülow, for he destined him for the directorship of the school of music. But here they were soon faced by the greatest and most unexpected difficulties. For no sooner did financial questions come into consideration than the head of the royal secretariate raised doubts, and, for the moment at least, succeeded in winning the King over to himself and his views; otherwise the King could not have written: "I am consumed with a burning desire to see your works performed again at last. The music of your works is my vital force, I can no longer do without them"; and then continued immediately afterwards, in direct juxtaposition: "How glad I should have been to send you an answer at last with regard to Herr von Bülow's appointment. Unfortunately I can say nothing definite as yet. This year there have been extraordinary calls upon the privy purse, so that I am forced to be very prudent. But I will never give up hope: everything will be brought to a crowning consummation." No doubt a certain hesitation can be observed in him in this connexion, but he soon inclined once more towards the minister's ideas. During these very days he had received another packet from Frau Cosima's hands: " How fascinated, how enchanted I am with the contents of all the pages from the diaries, which I thank Frau von Bülow with all my heart for kindly copying! " She had also sent him the essay " *Was ist deutsch?* (What is meant by German?)," about which the King writes: " How true it is when you say that the German princes have forgotten how to understand the spirit of the German nation! We ought to lead the way, to show what it means to comprehend the spirit of the German people and guide it to its full development! I too indulge in dreams of this, and enjoy the supreme moment by anticipation. Now I know surely and definitely that we shall be victorious! I have not the slightest doubt of that." And a few days later he writes with reference to the school of music: " I mean it, I mean it! My resolution stands firm. Bülow shall have the sphere of activity upon which we have agreed. I request you to inform him of this. Now we must act." And he canvasses all their plans, and promises to economize in things which do not serve their great aims. It was during these days that Frau von Bülow must have discussed these matters with the officials of the royal household. On this occasion the total sums which the King had spent for artistic purposes in general during the year were specified. It was she who conducted the negotiations for the Master, and so it was a monstrous proceeding on the part of the Cabinet when the amounts mentioned to her as inclusive of everything were represented in inspired articles in the newspapers as having been paid to the Master.

It was no light task for a young woman to keep watch over all these things while at the same time gratifying the King's demands for various pieces of work. But it was she who always succeeded in keeping the King's interest alive in this way, and an echo of this is to be found in all the letters, so far as we know them. He even says once in reference to the Bülows: " Leave me and your faithful friends the Bülows the responsibility for

trying to keep the suffering of the world at a distance from you.
We shall certainly succeed."

And so October came round, when the King appeared in
Munich for the opening of the October festival. It was on this
occasion that the King sanctioned the loan of forty thousand
gulden, long solicited by Wagner, which was naturally to be
paid back. Pfistermeister had uttered urgent warnings against
the fulfilment of this request, and it is said that matters even
came to an open breach between him and Wagner. At any rate,
the cashier refused to deliver the sum by the hands of an em-
ployé of his department, so Frau von Bülow undertook to call
for it in person at the offices of the royal household as Wagner's
representative. The Master wrote a very forcible letter to the
King, describing how this lady had been treated at the offices
of his household. At first, at any rate, she was herself compelled, with the assistance of her servant, to carry the sum, for
the most part consisting of heaps of silver, down to the cab
waiting below. It was not till afterwards that a junior official,
with rather less abject sentiments than the gentlemen at the
head of the department, offered to help her. They already felt
quite sure of success and believed themselves to be quite near
their goal. Every possible intrigue was resorted to.

In spite of this, the relations between King and artist remained unaffected. Once again a meeting between them took
place, at which all their feelings found expression, though a
shadow already hung over this meeting at Hohenschwangau. It
is interesting to read how the *Volksbote* writes on November 12:
"Yesterday Wagner arrived at Schwangau. Pfistermeister has
gone on a hunting expedition in the same neighbourhood." So
the latter was holding himself in readiness to intervene at once
should the decisive moment come. In the mean time negotiations
were also carried on not only for the new school of music and
dramatic art, but also for a musical review, to be edited by the
well-known Dr. Grandaur, with the assistance of Heinrich
Porges. Grandaur was by no means an avowed opponent of
Wagner's, but he none the less declined to "embark upon an
unpopular enterprise, without at least having some security that
it would be possible to carry it out honourably." Wagner was

189

astonished at these words of Grandaur's, but Frau Cosima was "indignant," and gave unreserved expression to her indignation. Moreover, the political newspaper for which Fröbel had been designated as editor caused much bad blood. The King himself discussed it with the minister and Pfistermeister and was forced to declare: "I want to think over the Fröbel affair again in detail. In spite of all the difficulties, I shall clear it up; but you see that they are great. Nothing is done to make it easy for me to gain an insight into these affairs. I should, indeed, have done better not to mention your name in the Fröbel affair; who could have thought that those people were so false and perfidious?" Thus wrote the King on November 15, when he still seemed perfectly firm and confident. It was this fidelity to the Master that led him into a slight mistrust of Bülow at this time. "What is this I hear about Bülow? How the news has distressed me! It fills me with the deepest concern. I must confess that I had not thought Bülow the man to let himself be blinded by merely apparent triumphs (*Scheintriumphe*), as I may call them. The men whom we need for our great purposes must have confidence in themselves, they must lead the way assured of victory, they must stake everything on the attainment of our ideals and allow themselves to be deterred by no obstacles. God grant that he do not desert our standard. . . . I still hope much from his wife's influence and heartening encouragement." This was naturally a misunderstanding, which it only took a word from the Master to dispel, so that shortly afterwards the King writes: "My mind is now quite at rest about Bülow." At the same time he expressed his most cordial thanks to Frau von Bülow for sending him "*Kunst und Klima* (Art and Climate)," and added: "I would gladly go on writing to you; unfortunately there are many claims on my time at present; many greetings to the lady your friend (*die Freundin*)." This was the same letter of December 3 in which he criticized the article which had meanwhile appeared in the *Neueste Nachrichten,* as follows: "That article in the *Münchner Neueste Nachrichten* did no little to embitter the closing days of my stay here. It was no doubt written by one of your friends who wished to do you a service; unfortunately he has done you more harm than good."

190

This article of November 29 has a history of its own. It is signed with the letters "fr." — that is, the abbreviation of Richard Wagner's pseudonym *"Frei Gedank"* (i.e., Free Thought; a pun on that of the minnesinger Freidank), and it is surprising that the King was not pleased with it, for there is nothing at all in it save such ideas as constantly recur in the most explicit form in the King's letters to Wagner. As early as November 16 he had written: " But who would have thought that those people were so false and perfidious? " — and " those people " neither were nor could have been any other than those of whom this brilliant article says: " I venture to assure you that by the removal of one or two persons who do not enjoy the slightest esteem among the Bavarian people the King and people of Bavaria would be delivered at one blow from these trouble-some mischief-makers." Much has been written about the author of the article. At first it was thought that it should be ascribed to the worthy Pecht. Next Peter Cornelius gave it as his opinion that undoubtedly this final blow at the royal secretariate, against which Wagner's sensible friends, and even Bülow himself, had advised him, and from which they had tried to dissuade him, had been dealt by Wagner himself, in collaboration with Bülow's wife alone and at her instigation. Others thought that they could detect in it the hand of the eminent Heinrich Porges. Nothing of the sort. According to Richard Wagner's own statements, the article was written by Frau Cosima, who took it in person to the office of the *Münchner Neueste Nachrichten,* thereby showing that she lent it the full weight of her personality. This was in keeping with her spirited character and her grasp of the fact that, in view of the attacks from all quarters, which were becoming intensified, they must now act; and that in one way only could a catastrophe be avoided: by the fall of their opponents. She was fully informed about the whole situation and saw no possibility of arriving at any result by any other means. She would cer-tainly have approached the King directly, as she did so often both before and afterwards in the Master's interests, had it not been necessary to deal with these questions quite independently of the King himself. Things had now reached breaking-point, both as regards von Pfistermeister, head of the royal secretariate, and the minister himself, and the point at issue was not the expenditure on art and the theatre, but the fact that, now as later, Richard Wagner had not consented to become a mere instrument of the minister.

Among the men of learning who have been transferred to the service of the State in Germany, this minister, von der Pfordten, is a figure apart. In 1843 he had been professor of Roman law at the University of Leipzig and had endeared himself to King Frederick Augustus by the part which he had played in politics, so that in March 1848 he had become a member of the Saxon Ministry. But he was and remained a professor, and never really developed into a statesman. Robert von Mohl, the old professor of jurisprudence, who was himself by no means an amiable character, has left the following description of him: " The small personal regard which he inspired was due to the whole way in which he bore himself. Though his exterior was far from aristocratic, Herr von der Pfordten's bearing was extremely self-important, and his demeanour was that of an official superior rather than of a colleague. One was conscious that he had risen rapidly to a position of command, without previous experience of the great world, and had occupied it for a long time." He had been prime minister again in the days of Maximilian II and had been forced to resign by the violent and powerful attacks of the Opposition in the Chamber. It was then that he coined a phrase for the King — one of the few which he had in his repertory — " I intend to have peace with my people (*Ich will Frieden haben mit meinem volke*)." At that time he had made use of it towards the Chamber, and now he brought it into play against Wagner; and the son of Max II repeated it after him as dutifully as his father had done. Thus did von der Pfordten gain the victory over both the King and the artist, whom he absolutely hated. Devrient had written about him earlier: " In Pfordten personal antipathy for Wagner is mixed up with his judgment of his work, and the statesman has armed the critic with violent and narrow principles." One saying of his was: " The exaggeration of individual personality (*Überhebung der Persönlichkeit*), which is apparent in Richard Wagner, is the destructive principle in our social and political life at the present day, and if princes would only hang together a little, as the democrats do, it would never be permissible to perform Wagner's music anywhere."

Yet it was this very Pfordten who had approached Wagner shortly before the Munich catastrophe and, before allowing matters to reach the point of an open breach, had even consented to an offer of alliance from the Cabinet to the Master. This had happened late that very autumn, and it was none other than the then chief clerk in the royal secretariate, Appellrat Lutz (an official of the Court of Appeal), afterwards a minister, who, with the undisguised intention of winning the Master's collaboration, had explained to Wagner the Ministry's line of procedure, which was at that time entirely prompted by Bismarck's policy. The Bavarian officials would have tolerated Wagner's political activities if he had fallen in with their views; but now, since he had rejected their proposals, they did all they could to compass his downfall, and that by methods which were neither the purest nor the most noble. Frau Cosima was aware of it all, and it was with this in mind that, adopting Richard Wagner's ideas as her own, she wrote the article, which was in a certain sense no more than a fresh repudiation of the Bavarian Government and its at that time decidedly democratic tendencies.

And so the alarm began to be raised and Munich was in a turmoil. It would, however, be false to suppose that it was the actual citizens of Munich who were concerned; on the contrary, it was the newspapers — inspired by those elements of which we know — and the literary world, which felt itself injured and slighted by the King; and, as so often before, the members of the municipality played their part, too. They could not be content till they had collected signatures to a memorial against Wagner. Quite eight hundred were got together, but the King was given mendacious reports of thousands. The minister, too, worked on the King's feelings with his old adage, which the King once more took down word for word after von der Pfordten had expressly declared to him, in defiance both of truth and of the real conditions: "Your Majesty has to choose between the love and happiness of your people, and the friendship of Wagner, who is despised by all good people." These were not the words of a skilful and experienced statesman, but of a professor inspired by the deepest malice and the most violent jealousy. Such, in general, is the part which he played in the whole of this conflict. However that may be, the King yielded and now begged Wagner to leave Munich for a time. Wagner did so in his own noble fashion, for at such moments he always displayed a wonderful and truly princely dignity. Towards the King he bore himself, not as a humble servant, but as a devoted friend, who wrote to his King calmly and solicitously: "My King, it pains me that you should suffer, when a mere exertion of your royal power would procure you peace." But it should not be forgotten that the Queen-mother, who was so short-sighted in these matters, as well as Prince Karl and the whole court — in fact, everybody — was pressing the King to let Wagner go and holding out prospects of a revolution of the most serious kind. All this was an illusion, though it was believed in by these persons, whose credulity had been worked upon in the same way as that of the King. To this was added the outcry of a depraved journalism, which felt very grand because for once it was made use of by Government circles. A direct parallel with the Lola Montez catastrophe suggested itself. It cannot be said that this incident, which had occurred such a short time before, would have occurred to the Müncheners again of its own accord had it not been for the incitement which came from the old and embittered Grillparzer in Vienna:

" Die Agnes Bernauer, eine Baderstochter,
Warfen die Bayern in die Donau,
Weil sie ihren Fürsten bezaubert.
Ein neuer Salbader
Bezaubert Euren König:
Werft ihn, ein zürnender Landsturm,
Nicht in die Isar, doch in den Schuldturm.

(Agnes Bernauer, a barber's daughter, was thrown into the Danube by the Bavarians for having bewitched a prince. A new twaddler bewitches your King: rise in your wrath and cast him, not into the Isar, but into a debtor's prison.)"

We can imagine the sour face of this great poet, but small-minded man, as he wrote these venomous words, which were now echoed in every conceivable form in the Munich papers. Yet shortly before this the students' corps Suevia had given an entertainment in the King's honour, and preparations for the performance of *The Love-feast of the Apostles* (*Das Liebesmahl der Apostel*) by the Akademische Gesangverein (university choral society) were going on in the midst of the catastrophe.

But Richard Wagner departed. "Sad but composed," he bade farewell at the station to Frau Cosima, Peter Cornelius, Porges and his wife on December 10, at a quarter to six in the morning. Accompanied by none but his servant Franz and his sick old dog Pol, he travelled to Switzerland. Nothing had power to humiliate him, and the young woman, too, returned home proud and erect. Her husband was on a concert tour and could not be expected back till the 15th. Wagner, indeed, had felt the need of him, but on the other hand he was glad that Hans von Bülow had not been personally involved in the catastrophe, which nobody deplored more than the King himself or felt more bitterly. As a matter of fact, an ambitious, spiteful, and self-seeking bureaucracy had robbed him of the man who might perhaps have had the greatest influence in leading and directing him in the right way. Fröbel tells another strange story in his reminiscences, about an old woman who is said to have appeared to Richard Wagner and declared to him that he was the sole protector of the young monarch against the corruption of his court entourage. She also spoke, it was said, of the King and his high mission and said that she had previously appeared to Ludwig I and Max II, but that they had not followed her advice. It was, however, written in the stars that this young King was destined for great things. "Do you believe in the stars?" asked Wagner. "It is written in the stars that this young King has been singled out for great deeds, and you, Herr Wagner, must protect him and warn him against the evil thing by means of which ill-disposed persons are seeking to ruin him." This was doubtless a romantic story, yet there was a trace of truth to be found in these predictions — which were truly prophetic words; besides, there was another, a young and beautiful woman, who, without any prophecy, but rendered clairvoyant by her powers of intuition, tried calmly and confidently, with all the subtlety of her nature and all the superior qualities due to her education, to influence the King in the same direction, and, for a time at least, succeeded in many respects in doing so. This was Frau Cosima.

At first, indeed, she gazed after the Master with anxious care and deep and wistful emotion, as he wended his way towards Vevey on the Lake of Geneva, from whence he went on to Geneva, there to find a refuge, for a time at least, at the villa known as the "*Campagne aux Artichauts.*" Her heart and her thoughts went with him. But she was firmly resolved to act as his representative in Munich, at all events to the best of her ability. She saw things clearly, and so did Wagner himself. As early as December 23 he wrote to Bülow: " My program with regard to the King is this: A year's leave for you, if you wish it. No sort of performances. Myself either here or there — quietly finishing *The Mastersingers.* In May 1867 a performance of it at Nuremberg under royal protection. Then??? He would have to maintain his position as ruler, make himself master, clear the rabble out of the way. Slowly and alone, supported by nothing save a fortunate concatenation of circumstances, he must himself work out his own way and find the right men. I — as far away as possible from all this, you and Cosima certainly not near. For this reason — let us retire into the background."

So we see that scarcely had one world collapsed about him before he was building himself another. And the King gazed after him, with lamentations summoning him as often as he could manage to do so, both by telegram and by letter. Yet we see how at this time Frau Cosima began to acquire quite a strong influence over the King. She writes to him: " I lay my most heart-felt thanks at the feet of the royal friend who graciously puts his trust in me. I too had a letter and yesterday a telegram,

which I venture to communicate to Your Majesty. The letter
says that our Friend wants to remain quiet for a week and close
his eyes: ' After a week of complete inaction I will communicate
with you again. I am, indeed, recovering and beginning to find
rest. At present I can do no more, I can do no more, and the
slightest contact causes me pain. I want to see nothing more, to
know nothing more. For a long time I must remain deaf and
blind. Only take care of yourself, do as I am doing, we shall
collapse and go mad if things go on like this. If only our nerves
would grow calm once more! Then indeed we shall manage to
live by artificial, quite artificial, means. I have finished with
nature. You understand me, and that is my consolation; if complete appeasement is possible, I have hope.' How the page about
Roland moved me. O celestial powers, grant that all our experiences may be lies, all knowledge vain and nothing worth, that
our love alone may abide true and mighty. How I thank my
sovereign lord (*meinem Herrn*) for having graciously understood how humbly I expressed my petition, my desire. I have to
add, by way of explanation and apology, that I was glad to see
how the people crowded round the King's august person on all
sides, counting upon him, appealing to him alone. I know quite
well that in politics things are not done like this, that every
Tom, Dick, and Harry is asked his good pleasure, and so it did
not occur to me that any attention could be paid to the so-called
program, it only seemed to me as though your gracious reception could mean nothing but this: You belong to my people, you
have come to me here in ignorance of the possibilities and im-
possibilities of a ruler's life. As a father I receive you graciously
and affably. As King I order you to calm yourselves and not
to interfere in matters of which you know nothing and which
belong to my sacred office. This was the significance of your reception in my eyes, it seemed to me that it must be calming in
its effect. But what Your Majesty does is good, and if I revert
to it, it is in order to lay my excuses at my dear sovereign's
(*meinem teuren Herrn*) feet." This has as subtle a ring as Mark
Antony's speech in Shakspere's *Julius Cæsar*: " For Brutus is an
honourable man; so are they all, all honourable men." And she
manages again at once to inform the King of incidents which

197

have occurred: for instance, the postponement of her father's work *Saint Elisabeth,* announced to her by Baron Perfall. And she quietly adds: " Will Your Majesty be so very gracious as to have the order communicated to the management, so that the performance may take place at the time graciously appointed by Your Majesty? " For not only was the performance of this oratorio, which Liszt had himself conducted at Budapest in August, a courtesy towards his father-in-law on Bülow's past, but since the catastrophe of December 10 it had become a point of honour and had, at the same time, a diplomatic significance. An attempt was now being made to eliminate Wagner's music, though this was already an impossibility with the music-loving public of Munich, which had become more and more sympathetically disposed towards his works; but his enemies had been deprived of their rallying-cry, and though the " Abbé Liszt's " *Saint Elisabeth* might excite the opponents of the " Prussian " Richard Wagner, this excitement had to be silenced. And, as a matter of fact, Bülow had staked everything on securing a performance of the work in due form.

But the best diplomatist was undoubtedly Frau Cosima, and she knew how to conduct the Master's affairs clearly and firmly. As early as January 3 she received a letter from Intendanzrat Lutz (an official attached to the management of the court theatre), in which she was informed that seats at the theatre had been reserved and placed at her disposal just as they had been for Herr Wagner in his time. The question of the Master's salary was also settled, and she next received word that " His Majesty the King has declared that it would not be displeasing to His Highness if you would kindly give some intimation to Herr Wagner about the communications which I had the honour to make to you yesterday with reference to his return to Munich." But this wonderful official style conceals something very significant. The King had his official decisions made known to the Master, as it were, through her. He went even further. On January 15 Lutz writes: " Today His Majesty the King commands me to inform you that for important reasons, with which I am not myself acquainted, His Majesty cannot think of Genelli, the painter at Weimar, for the Nibelung cartoons. I am therefore to request you to communicate to His Majesty in writing any remarks which you may have to make with reference to the above-mentioned cartoons. If I have understood our Sovereign Lord (*den Allerhöchsten Herrn*) aright, this last utterance has reference to an observation of which you yourself seem to have held out a prospect to His Majesty. Finally, I have been directed to ask you whether the biography of the singer Schnorr has already appeared, and where it is to be obtained." There is something touching, and at the same time rather diverting, in finding in these communications of the councillor an echo of the King's deep feelings with regard to the Master's works. And it is interesting to see how this lady deals with the question about Genelli. " How kind and gracious of Your Majesty to state the reason for which Genelli is certainly impossible! How well I recognized you in this trait! The arrogance of these painters, who, relying upon a brilliant past, regard themselves as the patricians of art and look down upon poor musicians from the height of their position, which has been a distinguished one for centuries past, though at times, too, a miserable one! The days are over when the glorious Leonardo da Vinci was at once poet, musician, and painter. Incidentally, it may be that Genelli has felt some doubt as to his ' ability (*Können*).' When Your Majesty's late lamented father commissioned him to paint a subject out of the history of Bavaria, he declared himself incapable of doing so. He had become so thoroughly imbued with the antique that other subjects had become almost entirely strange (*wildfremd*) to him. I had wanted to add this when I recommended him. Would Your Majesty have any objection to Wislicenus, also in Weimar? He has none of Genelli's mastery, but displays vigour and poetry in his compositions. And if Your Majesty could spare the time for it, I should like to speak of a young French artist of talent, whom I do not know personally, but whom I know that Wagner admires and esteems. Kaulbach has twice petitioned me with regard to the *Nibelungenring*. Can it be true that he has so little sense of the beautiful? Would it be acceptable to Your Majesty if I were to inquire of Frau von Kaulbach quite unofficially whether her husband would like to make pictures for the poem?

" But how well Your Majesty sees through the narrow-minded and brainless specialists! "

We see how clearly and confidently she was able to suit her subtle and cleverly calculated answers to the King's questions; while at the same time she always furthers the Master's cause: " The letter which I received from our Friend today bears witness to the same state of mind — courage and hope. ' What am I to do? ' he writes among other things. ' I am cut off. Where I am at Easter, there I must be able to stay. A summer in Geneva is out of my reach in the circumstances, so I must once more take counsel with myself in order to arrive at a final resolution, heart-rending though it may ultimately be. It must come from within myself. Nobody can advise me, I feel it; there is only one man who could help me.' " And she adds: " What I think of doing is to go off without saying anything, per- haps on Monday, not even announcing my arrival to our Friend; what message ought I, and may I, give him from my King? "

Meanwhile a sad event had occurred which brought about a violent change in his destiny. During his journey to the south of France, where he had looked in vain for a permanent abode in which to continue his work, his wife Minna had suddenly died in Dresden. It must be said that up to the very end he had stood by his unfortunate and suffering wife in the most chivalrous way, and in this respect had maintained relations with her in spite of all his own distress. As late as June 1863 he had writ- ten to Hans von Bülow: " You would not believe what anguish of heart this still causes me with regard to my wife. She writes to me very little, but when this does happen, I always feel as though a crushing calamity had fallen upon me. The slightest contact tells me how wickedly foolish it is not to break with her altogether, but still to leave a loop-hole by which hope may pass in and out and torture the poor creature. That is the stage which I have reached now: and once more I am tortured and fretted by a thousand imaginings. God, what a creature one is, with one's over-sensitive feelings for a wretched being! . . . Nothing on earth could decide me to subject my wife to the abominations of a civil divorce. And so the wretched state of affairs continues,

KLINDWORTH, TAUSIG, *and* BÜLOW

The three men who made the piano-scores of Richard Wagner's music. *Tristan*-period, Munich, 1865

and, believe me, I live in misery. . . ." Amid all the monstrous attacks which a diabolical journalism systematically made on him by order of those in high places, the *Münchner Volksbote* even alleged that he was leaving the wife from whom he was separated to starve; upon which she issued a public declaration on January 9 in which, " out of fidelity to the truth," she established the fact that she had hitherto received an allowance from her absent husband, which assured her an existence free from anxiety. She concluded her declaration with the words: " It gives me particular satisfaction to be able to silence by this my declaration one at least of the manifold calumnies uttered against my husband." But this was not enough, and the same paper alleged that Wagner had called forth this declaration by a temporary allowance. An official contradiction was necessary from the Dresden poor-relief authorities to force the paper to retract its statement.

With her death a great barrier between Richard Wagner and Frau Cosima was now removed. Yet she found it hard to leave Munich; for in the Master's absence she had a high task to discharge there in keeping alive the relations between him and the King, in the interest not only of her friend, but above all of the King himself, who was accompanied throughout his whole life by two gloomy trains of thought: the idea of abdication, and that longing for death which he actually satisfied in his hour of supreme trial.

Meanwhile, on February 24, the *Legend of Saint Elisabeth* had been performed with unexampled success under the conductorship of Hans von Bülow, and greatly delighted the King, as did a second performance, at which he was present in person. Next Frau Cosima started out on her pilgrimage to the " *Campagne des Artichauts*," in order to bring consolation to her lonely friend, in accordance with her husband's expressed wish. While Bülow went off on a concert tour, she and her eldest daughter, Daniela, stayed with Wagner; for nearly a month she kept house for him, and restored this agitated creature, who was so violently at war with the outer world, to inward peace and the calm which was such an absolute necessity to him in his lonely state. She was his confidante and helper, but in the spirit

of a lofty discharge of duty, which she assumed out of a supreme capacity for sacrifice and delight in it. In spite of all
obstacles from within and from without, she had grasped perfectly clearly the aim towards which this unspeakably exalted
sentiment ought and must be directed. She knew that none but
she could give him peace and strength to fulfil his great German
mission. But, in womanly fashion, she also attended to practical
matters. She saw at the first glance that, quite apart from the
fact that his lease expired on April 1, Geneva was no place for
him to stay in for good. He must find a permanent abode, not in
French, but in German Switzerland. They searched everywhere,
but in vain. Then, on the last day of March, while taking a trip
in a steamer on the Lake of Lucerne, they saw " a simple little
two-storeyed house " rising " on a projecting tongue of land, in
peaceful park-like surroundings, among venerable trees." They
made inquiries about it, but received a discouraging reply. None
the less they visited it on the next day; it was Easter Sunday,
and Wagner saw with delight that he had found what he wanted.
He at once rented it for a year, and this was a fortunate step.
Before long he was able to say: " Nobody will get me out
of here again."

Frau Cosima now returned to Munich, and on the 4th the
King wrote to her: " The news that you are here, my friend (*die
Freundin sei hier*), has filled me with ecstatic rapture! I implore
you to tell me in the mean time all you have heard from our
beloved Friend. How is the dear fellow's health? Oh, what glorious days you must have spent with him! " And now, as in
almost all his letters, he poured out questions about the Master's
work, about *The Mastersingers, Siegfried,* and *Parsifal.* And
then he added with charming tact: " How I delight in the compositions which I am to hear today for the first time by your
great father, who has become so dear to me! I hope with all my
heart that you found Herr von Bülow and your children well on
your return." He was correspondingly depressed when he heard
of the Master's firm resolution to stay at Triebschen. He was in
consternation and placed his own hunting-boxes at Wagner's
disposal as a residence. He awaited the Master's decision with
an impatience which is evident in his beautiful and warm-hearted

letter of April 6 to Frau Cosima: " Forgive my impatience, but the longing of my soul is too intense. I should be so glad to hear whether you have any news from our beloved Friend today. Oh, may all angels hover round him and make him decide to accept my offer! I have a presentiment that it will be for his good! Echter is just painting the slaying of Mime by Siegfried; in that too I recognize a fateful sign. There is still time! We must set about the great work prudently, but surely; the powers of darkness must perish, they will be thwarted by a resolute will, an impregnable fidelity and an ardent love." And he openly states that on the day of Wagner's death he too must go hence. " It would be madness to live if he were once gone." And he concludes: " How dear you are to me for the sake of the love that you show him in such tenderly intimate ways! He has but few who sincerely love him, but they are true to him till death, they are all his own." He begs her to turn to him in all matters concerning his friend, in all his cares; he has heard, in particular, that she has met with every kind of oppressive and vexatious treatment at the hands of his subordinate officials. But she was able to send a wonderful answer to this letter: " As I start these lines, my heart is so torn by the most contradictory feelings that I ask myself what state of mind they can possibly reveal to you. In the first place I thank you for your readiness to afford our Friend the peace of which his weary soul stands in such need — ah, he is ill and exhausted! The little house in the Briennerstrasse, which I supposed he would never leave, will be vacated by his servants on September 1 and placed at the disposal of the administration of the privy purse, and so those who grudged him this snug shelter will no doubt be content. And he is resting in the thought that he may regard Triebschen as his ultimate refuge. I can hardly tell you how I thank you, our only friend (*einziger Freund*), for understanding and sympathizing in this. You know what love means — you know in what it has trusted. I rejoice unutterably that you are still full of hope, that you still preserve your fine faith in our plans. As for me — I do not despair, but I live only in the minute. Once again I am faced by a separation from our Friend, we shall have to let him lead his lonely existence for yet another winter — I do

not know how he will bear it. If our enemies meant to annihilate
us — they have succeeded. They have wounded us in the very
fibre of our inner life, in the depths of our souls — may God
forgive them! My husband and I had meant to go back to Munich
last Thursday, when I received the letter from Frau Schnorr,
imploring me to postpone our return: the last rumour which our
enemies had put about was that Hans is a Prussian spy, who has
betrayed the secrets of Bavarian policy to Bismarck's Government. This is just stupid enough to seem credible to the excited
populace. She writes to me that she has heard on all hands
that we could not return to Munich now without danger. Yesterday evening we received a telegram from Berlin. My husband had written there to the good Bechstein to send him some
piece of information to Munich because everything had calmed
down there by now. The telegram ran as follows: ' Your information is incorrect. You cannot start without danger.' Since
Bechstein is an incredibly calm, almost phlegmatic person, he
must have received information about things of which we have
no idea, since we, and you too, most noble friend, always think
people better than they are, and ascribe to incapacity what had
its origin in the deepest malice. We decided on the spot to stay
here indefinitely, going back to Munich later for a few days, to
pack our things and leave a city where we have dreamed the
finest dreams and passed the most splendid hours. May I beg
you, then, my gracious friend, to send one of the gentlemen of
the secretariate to us in Munich to arrange the conditions of our
leave in business-like fashion? I think they will fulfil this behest
gladly, for, apart from our ruin, the one thing at which they
aim is to separate us from you. My husband is going to Basel
today to see whether he can possibly find employment there.
After Munich he does not want to stay in Germany, for all our
hopes were set upon this aim. There is no place for our art in
Germany. People would receive us with derision for having believed in its triumph. But God's will be done — I have resigned
myself." And she referred to a letter from the King's aide-de-
camp, Prince Thurn and Taxis, who had been instructed by the
King to suggest a meeting. But she utters the following warning:
" And yet, my most glorious friend, I admit that I tremble and

quake. Those in power are capable of anything. The city is in a great turmoil at present; the people are obscurely conscious that their affairs and those of the King have been badly managed. I hear that risings are in preparation. How convenient it would be for our enemies, who are in difficulties, if some extraneous matter were to create a diversion! How gladly they would throw a friend of the King's to the dogs a second time! Everything gives me cause for fear. The newspapers will be authorized to discuss such a meeting, as well as any visit here on your part, my dear friend (*mein theurer Freund*). Their malice will be directed either against you or against your Friend. I am in the most terrible anxiety and dare say nothing. I do not want to upset our Friend. He would be so glad to go; the low spirits to which he has been a prey for a few days past would be dissipated by this prospect; but, for my part, I am afraid he may be murdered. Nothing is sacred to those who are persecuting us; they have attacked our honour and peace, they have played with our lives as though they were balls; they know that we have seen through them, and I believe that H.v.d. Pf. is still revenging himself on us for the letter which I wrote to K. Lutz about him from Geneva at the time. I knew when I did it that I should pay dearly for it, but I did it none the less, because I recognized that truth to my most exalted friend (*den höchsten Freund*) was my first duty, and that even if I had to accuse my own child, I would do so freely for the Only one (*dem Einzigen*). Oh, let us endure what we cannot cure! It was not granted us to triumph over our enemies. They are more powerful than ever, we do not want to provoke them, this conflict is too much for us. Our hearts are broken, our lives have been forcibly wrenched out of their course, let us seek and find peace in humility and patience and renounce where we cannot conquer. But a thousand blessings upon you for your affection, and God grant that our sufferings may one day turn out for your good. Even if the envious gods will not allow the supreme task to be accomplished, everlasting praise and glory be yours for having intended it." And she changes the subject beautifully to himself: " For a day past we have had sunshine. I think it was your dear letter that brought it. But now it is clouding over again, and nature is beginning all

too soon to lower again. What a singular destiny it is that has
united us here by force, only before long to separate us with
equal violence! We stand here, if not without courage, yet utterly
devoid of will, and can only call our own souls to witness that
we desired nothing but what is good. You see, my exalted friend
(*mein hoher Freund*), how I pour out my whole soul to you —
may I beg you ever and always to tell me what is in your heart?
I will no longer communicate it to our Friend, lest I move him
too deeply. Yet I should like you to tell me without hesitation
or scruple the motives which stir your great soul, if the impulse
to impart it comes upon you. For that is the only thing I can
offer you — my understanding." She next speaks of *The Mastersingers*. " *The Mastersingers* has now advanced successfully as
far as Beckmesser's song; this second act is simply heavenly.
It is impossible for me to hear Sachs's monologue: '*Wie duftet
doch der Flieder* (How fragrant is the elder),' without my eyes
filling with tears. Every single word seems to be at once transfigured and made clear by the divine music, till it seems to me
that now for the first time I am really understanding the poem.
God grant that this work may look forward to a speedy completion. How it lifts one up to think that at this moment, when
Germany is a prey to the greatest distraction, this German
work is unfolding its pinions as none has done before! This
alone gives one courage and hope. Perhaps it is so great and
momentous that we must needs suffer persecution for its
sake!"

But they returned to Munich, where Bülow at once conducted
the *Eroica*. She writes to the King on the subject: " How utterly
I lost myself in the *Eroica*! Never did it strike me with such
massive power! Of course I thought, too, of him who is afar, and
felt that he is the hero hymned by Beethoven. How beautiful
that in this feeling I was at one with your august self (*mit dem
Hehren*)! " She next gives him extracts from a letter of Richard
Wagner's: " Today, Tuesday, a glorious morning — market
day — boat upon boat, from Uri, Schwyz, and Unterwalden to
the market at Lucerne: An exquisite sight, quite ineffably beautiful — against this background, this lovely smooth surface of
the lake, where every boat is surrounded by a radiant aureole of

silver. Such a morning is not too dearly purchased by a trying month of winter. Now I understand my choice and the winter which I am approaching: Walther has already sung of it, '*am stillen Herd zur Winterszeit, wenn Hof und Haus mir einge-schneit* (By silent hearth one winter's day, when locked in snow the castle lay),'[1] there will I dream of the dawn of spring; how I mean to love the winter here! Let sincerity, the high-est sincerity, be our dogma! See, there is but one other whom I can draw into this union, into this faith! None but Parzi-val. And so may he be our guardian angel! Once again, let no-body disturb us here, let holy tranquillity prevail. These are the last years of a hard and tortured life, which are now to find their goal, their crown. Nothing has moved me so much for some time past as renewing my acquaintance with the Melusine legend. Oh, God — the departing Melusine, returning in ghostly fashion in times of fear! I was shaken as by a fever: I could have dis-solved into atoms for grief and pity. God! what poetic con-ceptions men have found for all things, in order to bring them-selves to a consciousness of the riddle of existence! And it is no good, they play with their prodigious poems like silly chil-dren. What have I to do with this world? — This mystery of the spell! Raymond by misadventure slays his uncle by night in the woods — moonlight — the flight through the woods; a wondrous voice calls to him: Melusine, longing to be freed from the spell, woos him, gives him infinite delight, and is betrayed by him. On moonlight nights she still tends the youngest of the children, then no more is heard of her. Night — the elements. Guilt — magic: unbelief, doubt, the breaking of the spell. Long wailings through the night and on the breeze. Moonlight. The birds are merry and sing bravely." Then suddenly he returns to the country-side. " Have you heard the starlings' strident chatter yet? The meadows round about are covered with magnificent cows. By day and night you hear the tinkling of their bells. This tinkle is lovelier than any sound that I know. The caprice of the changing tones, the glorious bells, the pride of the owner, are indescribably magical. I would give all the bells of Rome for

[1] *The Mastersingers*, I, iii, Newman's translation (Breitkopf and Härtel edition). — Tr.

them." He next wrote to her on April 7: " Can you not imagine what a fine and heartening stimulus Parzival's offer and his letters afford me? But I have been true to myself and have crushed down all weakness. Today I wrote to him, once again I was able to write as it is always in my heart to do, and it has done me good. I recognize more and more the wonder of his love, I revere it, yes, I revere it in amazement, like a holy revelation! " Thus she managed to raise the King's spirits by the vivid pictures which she selected from Wagner's letters, thereby conveying to him her own impression of the new abode, about which she says: " The house there is being put into thoroughly good order by the kindly owner. We propose to go there after the model performances (*Musteraufführungen*). First I shall take the three children there in May and make all necessary arrangements, and I shall also take our Friend his peacocks and many other things as well, so that he may be a little more comfortable. Then I shall return here for the model performances." Next she frankly discusses the situation with regard to the rehearsals of *Lohengrin*, gossips about the scenery for the first act of *Tannhäuser*, the pictures which the King was commissioning Kaulbach to paint, and the military band which was to perform the various arrangements of *Rienzi*, *Tristan*, and *The Mastersingers*. And she adds: " And since I am on the subject of military music, I venture to inform my most gracious sovereign that yesterday I wrote to Herr Lutz on the subject of the military band of the Guards (*Leibregiment*), which has been forbidden to perform Wagner's music, and he is quite inconsolable about it. I hope it is not displeasing to my dear lord that I should speak to Herr Lutz about it." We see that the intrigue against Wagner raised its head everywhere. But though she appealed to Lutz on behalf of others, with regard to Lutz himself she had to say: " I venture to send the *Melusine*, since I have been told to do so. I was almost afraid that my sending it might incommode my good lord. Herr Lutz returned the manuscript of the biography to me, saying that there are still many books lying on Your Majesty's table. I hope that the most benevolent of princes (*der Huldreichste*) will graciously accept the gift." It is rather typical that a manuscript of Wagner's which the King had not read should have been sent back, in order to make it appear as if it bored him.

Frau Cosima next went with her husband and father to Amsterdam to the performance of the " *Graner Messe* " and wrote the King a gossipy letter about it: " I have now been back from Holland for two days. My father was in good health and the best of spirits there. All the messages I gave him from Munich caused him such deep pleasure that he felt simply bound to write a few grateful lines to our protector, which I venture to enclose. We spent beautiful days there, filled with art; the ' *Graner Messe* ' was performed for the first time, and the applause with which the eighth Psalm was greeted was warm, genuine, and unmixed. The splendid people there welcomed my father with the most simple affection and solid enthusiasm, and he felt happy among them. But may I venture to say that I was almost home-sick? Happy though I felt, I am perfectly sensible of the fact that my whole being has its roots here under the guardianship of our dear protector. I hope that my father will come to Munich within the year, as he longs to do, in order to thank his gracious lord. Today was the general rehearsal of the Ninth Symphony! God, what a work! I felt a real unhappiness when its strains died away, it makes me feel the weight of life doubly; it bears one aloft, it exalts one to the stars and plunges one in the uttermost depths of the fathomless abyss, and smiles away all the woes of earth from one's soul." And how finely she says of one of Schubert's works: "My father has devised a program for Schubert's *Phantasie,* which Hans plays tomorrow. The work as written for the piano pleased him quite exceptionally, but when he came to play it, all its qualities were not sufficiently brought out. So then he arranged it for orchestra and gave it a title for his own benefit, ' *Die Wanderschaft* (Wandering).' For the first movement he thought of a young man starting out bravely and boldly, who goes his way through life innocent and ignorant, wandering fresh and free. Lovely pictures rise before him, sweet melancholy laps him round, and laughing inconstancy. The first stanza of one of Goethe's wanderers' songs might almost have been composed for this movement:

'*Von den Bergen zu den Hügeln wiederum das Tal entlang,*
Da erklingt es wie von Flügeln und da neigt sich's wie Gesang.
Und dem unbedingten Triebe folget Friede, folget Rat,
Und Dein Streben sei die Liebe und Dein Leben sei die Tat.

> (From the mountains to the hillocks
> Then again the vale along,
> There a sound of beating pinions,
> Here a reverence as of song.
>
> And on this unfettered impulse
> Follows peace, and follows rede,
> And let love be all thy striving,
> And thy living be a deed.) '

Now is heard the wondrous theme of one of Schubert's most beautiful songs: '*Da, wo Du nicht bist, da ist das Glück* (There, where thou art not, there is happiness),' runs the song, and the notes fall darkly on the soul; the bright scenes have faded away, the man no longer observes, he feels.

'*Denn die Bände sind zerrissen, das Vertrauen ist verletzt.*
Kann ich sagen, kann ich wissen, welchem Zufall ausgesetzt.

> (For the bonds are torn asunder,
> Trust is left disconsolate,
> Can I know, or can I utter,
> Cheated by what tricks of fate.) '

But the man is to endure, not to succumb, and Schubert will have him endure freshly and courageously, even lightly and joyfully; and, once again, the last stanza of Goethe's poem is suited to the last section of the musical work:

'*Bleibe nicht am Boden haften, frisch gewagt und frisch hinaus!*
Kopf und Arm mit heitern Kräften, überall sind sie zu Haus!
Wo wir uns der Sonne freuen, sind wir jede Sorge los.
Dass wir uns in ihr zerstreuen, darum ist die Welt so gross!

(Rooted to the ground remain not,
　　Bravely venture, bravely roam!
Head and arm with cheery purpose,
　　Everywhere are they at home!

Whereso'er we joy in sunshine
　　Every care is cast aside.
For it was for our amusement
　　That the world was made so wide!) '

And with a mighty radiance the music surges past." It sounds like a beautiful lesson that she imparts to her royal friend's artistic sensibilities, afterwards begging him to pardon her for her excess of enthusiasm. " But," she continues, " I am again feeling at home here, and today's performance brought you, Benevolent one (*den Gütigen*), so near my soul once more! " The King received all this in the right spirit and replied: " Your dear letter and that of your father delighted me greatly and filled me with enthusiasm. My warmest, most heart-felt thanks! How proud your trust makes me, dear friend. I too believe in a golden age, for which we shall not have to wait much longer. The very thought of being allowed to love and reverence such souls as yours and his is celestial bliss, as is also the thought that I am dear to you both." They exchanged the Master's letters to either of them. And this now led to a slight and yet highly characteristic conflict. On May 8 Frau Cosima wrote to the King: " The accompanying lines were broken off by our Friend, he sent them for me, for he knows that I am glad to know and keep everything of his. I send them in my unbounded trust, and ask, ' will he invite the Dear one to the third performance of *Saint Elisabeth*? ' I say ' we,' for my fidelity and affection give me the right to consult with my lord. Can we? May we? If there is any possibility of it, I beg for a word of consent; if not, I shall understand your silence. The Gracious one (*der Huldreiche*) need never give me his reasons. What would our Friend say to my having told you? But it seems to me that in our alliance everything may and must be open, and I shall

211

write him what I have done." But the King now replied very dejectedly, but decidedly, too: " I must admit that I was greatly surprised at the tone in which the letter which you were so good as to send me from our Friend was written. In accordance with your wish, I am sending it back to you. You know the depth and significance of our love, and will see that it is terrible for me still to have to be parted from the Only one. If circumstances were in the least propitious, how gladly would I invite him! But if he were to come now, all hope of our ever being able to welcome him here again permanently would vanish. For the sake of his own peace and happiness it is not possible now. He used to show such confidence in me, and wanted to leave every-thing in my hands, and he was right; for he can build upon his friend as upon a rock. And now he seems to be nervous, and utters complaints. Is not that bound to sadden me? I beg you, dearest friend, to tell him that he may leave everything to me with an easy mind. Yet even when he misunderstands me and is unjust to me, I love him deeply and truly, and this love will never depart from me. In this matter, alas! he has no clear vision. That is certain. Ah, why, once more I must exclaim with pain, why does he not count upon me unconditionally? " And now Frau Cosima at once threw herself into the breach: " Yes-terday I committed a great wrong! Assuming that my good lord would see from the breaking off of the letter which I communi-cated to him how it was at once blotted out from our Friend's mind, I omitted to add a passage from the continuation of the letter to myself which would have provided a full explanation. ' How sad! ' begins our Friend to me. ' You see what dismal thoughts are taking possession of me in my loneliness! It is the Ninth Symphony that has cast a spell over me! You know how this work still rings in my ears. To miss hearing it was a depriva-tion to me, and *Saint Elisabeth* too! I almost went with you to Amsterdam just to hear some music. I send you the above non-sense, since you insist once and for all upon having everything. You will see from it in what a miserable state of mind I often am. I build on Parzival as on a rock — he must decide, he must act for us, let him be our steersman and guide us towards our end.' I felt but one thing, that he was deprived of music, and

I wanted to consult with the Only one. I felt, too, that it was impossible for any misunderstanding to arise between us. Besides, time pressed, if the invitation had proved possible. And so I omitted to add this and committed a grave error, for I caused an anxious moment to him to whom I wish the greatest happiness, even at the price of my own tranquillity and peace. My imprudent zeal led me astray, and instead of abiding by our Friend's real state of mind, or at least supplying what was lacking in a passing mood of no importance, so as to give my lord a complete picture, I offended against both him and our distant Friend. Kindly forgive me, my august friend (*mein hoher Freund*), that for which I find it so hard to forgive myself!"

But on the very next day she was able to inform the King that she was going to Lucerne with the children and would stay there for a few weeks. "Am I to give our Friend any message from our protector? May I venture to write from Lucerne?" Next she speaks of Kaulbach's *Tristan* sketches, which she had seen: "The first hasty sketch seemed to me very successful." And she also reverts to Semper: "Has Semper's inquiry been conveyed to my gracious friend? Without in any way desiring to give an opinion on the point, it seems to me that he might nevertheless construct the model. As for when it will be carried out, that is another question, which, however, will be less important when once the plan and model are in existence. Then let other generations complete it, if our own times are too grievous and serious for us to revel in joyous art." And she concludes her letter with the words: "I am always dreaming one dream; will it ever be fulfilled? Like Paul, I hope against hope and I believe. We have seen a wonder and can bear witness to it." But on the next day the King sent her a cordial answer, saying that the letter had been celestial consolation and healing balm to him. He goes on: "I request you to express my most heartfelt thanks to Herr von Bülow for all the glorious pleasures with which he has refreshed and enraptured me during the past winter and spring. I shall be grateful to him as long as I live. Oh, what a successful performance that was of *Saint Elisabeth* yesterday! The divine strains still echo within me. Now I am back again at my beloved Berg. Ah, what blissful hours I passed here with our beloved Friend! How happy I am to be here again! A year ago at this time we were still at the general rehearsal of *Tristan and Isolde*! Let me know quickly when you think that *The Mastersingers* will be finished, and whether our Friend is now working at it. Promise me to induce the dear fellow to take up *The Nibelungs* again. I beg you always to let me know if he is in need of anything. Ah, how gladly do I fulfil his every wish. I shall write to your esteemed father shortly. How I rejoice at the prospect of seeing him in Munich next year! Then at last we shall all be together, we who were created for one another. Yes, we belong to one another. Do you hear anything from our Friend now and then, dear friend, about his plan for *Parsifal*? " He next inquires about the new school, and praises his friend's plan as glorious and grandiose, though he does not underestimate the difficulties. But he concludes: " In the autumn let our Friend draw near; help me to move him." We see that it was really the King who was insisting upon these organizations. So soon as he had any sort of rest from his officials, he felt bound to take up this plan, which was only remotely connected with Richard Wagner and his life and work, in order to bind him more firmly to himself. Fundamentally Frau Cosima, too, shared the Master's views, and now, when she was once more going to Triebschen, her first concern was to secure his tranquillity there. On May 18 she wrote the King a beautiful and characteristic letter: " When I took my leave, I hoped to be able to send a peaceful and pleasing report from Triebschen. I thought that the resting-place so long desired had been found, and rejoiced at being able to send the Benevolent, August one (*dem Gütigen, Erhabenen*) simple descriptions of a quiet life. But now everything has become serious again, very serious. I tremble for the well-being of our dear one here. Ah, Generous one, protecting friend, if only it were possible for our poor Friend, who has been so harassed by life, to live for a time in peace, how grateful I should be to Heaven and Heaven's emissary! When I saw him at Romanshorn I was shocked, and we both burst into tears, but I soon recovered when I saw Triebschen. It is beautiful here, my dear friend. The simple but large

214

garden runs down to the lake, before us rises the Rigi in its massive splendour, with Pilatus like a mighty dragon to one side. His name and his legend live on in the mouths of the people, to the eternal shame of the indifferent, who allow dreadful things to happen and are content not to have combated them. In fine weather it is quite intoxicating here, and on the first morning, as I settled the little ones in the garden and the strains of *The Mastersingers* floated down to me from above, I thought my heart must leap for joy. My thoughts turned towards our guardian angel, and I recalled the dear one at Berg. Though I had gone farther away, I seemed to be nearer to our kind friend. How contentedly I communed with our Friend who was creating there, and with the friend who makes such creation possible! In the evening came the message from Monsalvat, and I really thought that I had nothing left to wish for. On the second day I received your kind letter. I was preparing to write about the school of art exhaustively and in detail, and about how I think the plan can best be carried out, and I meant to describe all our quiet life to our Glorious one (*dem Herrlichen*), when the telegram arrived for our Friend, and then the letter, and I saw our Friend's terrible distress and anxiety! Ah, could I but find words to express the anguish which I endured! It was as though I saw our benevolent protector in desperate danger, in desperate suffering and pain, and yet I had to set our Friend's mind at rest. My dear and gracious friend, may God spare your heart the distress that I then suffered! I have the feeling that our Friend would be ruined for ever if he were now to be torn from his peaceful life here. How do things look now in Bavaria? How powerful do his enemies remain? What is to become of his — of our art, if his mind cannot be at rest? And our Gracious and Loyal one, what awaits him? Are not the conflicts upon which he is embarking inopportunely alarming? As we talked it all over together yesterday, our Friend said that he would beg our sovereign to send him somebody with whom he could discuss the whole situation, with whom he would come to an understanding about everything. . . . He wanted to go to Berg himself, but I dissuaded him. Who knows what difficulties he would bring upon our protector by such a step? Patience and calm!

For we are secure — ' our lord is a strong tower of defence
(*eine feste Burg ist unser Herr*) '; that is our text. And now
today comes your gracious proposal. I could have shouted for
joy at our unanimity; though so far away, we are so near to one
another! Who could possibly hurt us? Yesterday we resumed
the biography. In the mornings I copy it out, in the evenings our
Friend dictates to me. Yesterday arrived the big new photograph. I have it in safe keeping, so as to put it up on the 22nd
surrounded with flowers. The little one delighted me beyond
words; I had seen it at Albert's and — may I confess my au-
dacity? — wished that our kind friend would give it to me! I
wrote to my father that our gracious sovereign had become
fond of *Saint Elisabeth*. On arriving in Rome he intends to
make a fair copy of the Prelude and send it to the Gracious one.
My husband is now holding his rehearsals. What is the position
now with regard to these performances? War seems more
threatening and inevitable than ever. I do not care to think
about the future, but try to content myself with one day at a
time. Today it is fine and glorious. Oh, if I but knew that the
soul of the Wonderful one is suffering no more! When once
salvation has come, when Parzival has found consolation, then
will I close mine eyes. Then shall I have seen that for which
my soul was longing, then shall I enter, singing and giving
praise, into that world beyond, upon which I have sometimes
called in my bitter need." Frau Cosima's anxiety about the King
was well justified. The newspapers were already looking ahead
and talking of a mobilization of the Bavarian Army and the
summoning of the Diet for the 22nd. And now, thanks to Niemann's refusal, the performance of *Lohengrin* fixed for that
day had become impossible, whereupon the King resolved upon
a flying visit to Triebschen. Accompanied by nobody but his
aide-de-camp, Prince Thurn and Taxis, and one groom, he started
out on his journey and succeeded in reaching Lindau and Romanshorn unrecognized. The surprise at Triebschen was complete. The servant would not even admit him, but the visitor
insisted on sending in his visiting-card, and now Wagner rushed
downstairs in jubilation to lead his royal friend into the house.
He spent two beautiful days there, when many things were dis-

cussed and the King reaffirmed his oft-repeated resolution to extirpate evil influences root and branch.

But his visit had not remained a secret. As early as the 23rd a report was spread about that the King had departed, nobody knew where; and on the 24th the papers were already full of information about this adventure, and once again the attacks began. People were particularly exasperated because a group of Munich art-lovers had got up a collection for presenting a silver laurel-wreath to the Master. This present to the " infamous instigator of these disorders " was exhibited for a fortnight, which was regarded as a slap in the face to the dignity of the city of Munich! In short, the *Neue bayerische Kurier* opened the attack with a regular roll of drums and now no longer against Wagner and Bülow only, but against the " carrier-pigeon Madame Dr. Hans de Bülow." She was abused in the vilest way, and these attacks were also to some extent directed against the King, false and alarming reports being put into circulation with a view to shaking his position. There can be no question that these attacks were well calculated to undermine monarchist sentiment in the country. The King had promised to attend the opening of the Diet; he was ready to hold the great review of the troops and to be present at the great Corpus Christi procession. But all this was fruitless. The attacks became more and more violent, and Bülow, as we know, found himself compelled to take steps to protect his wife's honour by means of public statements, as well as by calling out the editor, Dr. Zander. Such was the immediate result of the King's visit to Triebschen. We can see how low journalism had sunk in Munich, and how it tried to attain its ends by every method of calumny and vilification. The position was a terrible one for Frau Cosima. She now gave vehement and absolutely despairing expression to her feelings in a letter to the King: " For the first and last time I implore you on my own behalf. I fall on my knees before my King, and in humility and distress I beg for the letter to my husband, that we may not leave in shame and disgrace the country in which we have desired nothing but what is good — and, I may also say, done nothing but good. My dear and exalted friend, if you make this public statement, then all is well; then we can stay here; then we shall be ready to build once more upon the ruins, full of courage and consolation, as though nothing had happened — otherwise we must go hence, insulted and abandoned, depriving our distant Friend of the only friends who could give him no more than their own existence, with their fame and reputation, and who must now build this all up again somewhere else, in order to be able to offer him a sanctuary. My most august friend, who entered into our lives like a divine apparition, oh, do not consent that we, the innocent, should be driven out. Your royal word alone can restore our honour, which has been impugned; it can do so completely, everything will go down before it. My dear lord, I venture to say what the hero said to the King who was conferring an honour upon him: ' *Sire, vous faîtes bien* (Sir, you are acting rightly) '; you will do right to protect us, and the people will understand it. And should there be those in the immediate entourage of our Dear one (*des Theuren Menschen*) who see any harm in not allowing one's friends to go away in disgrace, then, O dear lord, it is not for these people to speak on this occasion. In a grave and sacred hour you spoke to me of your deep sense of the nothingness of the highest earthly possessions in comparison with the obligations of affection. You know those mysteriously decisive hours in which the truth stands forth as bright as daylight. In the name of these consecrated hours I say it: write my husband the royal letter!

"I cannot describe how I left our Friend and met my husband. I hurried there for one night to make the final arrangements. With what feelings did I enter the rooms in which our Friend's face, carved in marble, received me with a pallid greeting! As I left Triebschen, my very soul broke forth in bitter tears! Heaven grant that these tears may not be the herald of tearful days. Tomorrow I return to my husband in Zürich. From thence we journey on, we know not whither. Perhaps we shall leave Germany for good. If there is a possibility of your gracious letter, then I will persuade my husband that we should return home — otherwise — how could we stay in a city in which we might be treated as malefactors? How could my husband manage to carry on his work in a city where the honour of his wife has been called in question? My royal lord, I have three children, to whom it is my duty that I should preserve their father's honourable name unstained; for the sake of these children, that they may never cast aspersions on my love for our Friend, I beg you, my most exalted friend, write the letter. If the letter is possible, I will gladly bear all earthly trials in return for this happiness. If it is not possible, then I herewith take my leave of our kind friend, I kiss his royal hand in humility and gratitude, I call down the blessing of God on his exalted head and withdraw with my noble husband, who has perhaps received his death-blow, to a place where peace and respect await him, the weary and innocent one. If I could but say that our ruined lives would satisfy the dæmon, and that good would come of it for our King, then perhaps the deeply wounded heart of a wife and mother would once more be able to rise superior to it and attain happiness; but I do not believe it. It is not at us alone that the wicked are aiming."

The King wrote the letter, which, to the extreme resentment of their enemies in Munich, again appeared in the newspaper, and, as chance would have it, in the very number containing the news of the declaration of war. And the paper added the following abusive comment: " Those who at this fateful moment would wish to count upon the respect, hope, and trust of millions of Germans for the head of the greatest of the middle states cannot really be gratified at finding the Austrian manifesto and the King of Saxony's proclamation side by side in the self-same number with this letter to Hans von Bülow." Yet it is precisely the political aspect of Richard Wagner's influence at this time that is misunderstood. It had been he who had advised the King to remain neutral. The King had not followed his advice, though in his inmost heart he did not want to have anything to do with this war and was, indeed, absolutely indifferent to it — to the war, that is, not to his people. For Bavaria the war was nothing but what is called a " ministerial war," brought upon her by von der Pfordten through his dubious and vacillating policy, which had deceived even Bismarck himself up to the last moment. Meanwhile it was actually at the Master's prompting that the King went off to Bamberg to the Army headquarters, and

219

the unexampled jubilation with which he was received there obviously pleased him.

But the war ended as it was bound to end — in a complete victory for Prussia. The Bavarian troops broke down, as Bavarian politics had done, under bad leadership. And it was this which hurt the King most! He wrote to Wagner on the subject: " God be praised that the independence of Bavaria can be preserved. If not, if our representation abroad is lost, if we fall under the hegemony of Prussia, then away! I will be no shadow king bereft of all power." Yet it was not from the political point of view that he had first grasped this idea, but from quite a different one. It is important for him and for the judgment that will ultimately be passed upon him that we should look rather closely into this precise phase of his development. On July 21 he wrote to his friend Frau Cosima: " I earnestly beg you not to be alarmed at the contents of my letter. I do not write to you in a mood of desperation and melancholy, as you might perhaps think, oh, no; I am serious, yet at the same time cheerful again. In your last letter from Munich you reminded me of the fact that once, in a very grave hour, I had told you that I held the duty of love, of sacred, god-born love, to be the supreme one! Dear friend, this is my faith, by which I will live and die. And now I feel bound to tell you that it is quite impossible for me to have to be parted any longer from him who is my all. I cannot stand it. Fate has destined us for each other, it is for his sake alone that I am on earth, I see it and feel it clearly every day. But he cannot be with me, O dear friend. I assure you that I am not understood here and shall not be understood. All hope is lost here, and in this respect times will not change. Nothing will be effected by removing the members of my secretariate and the ministers. As King I cannot be united with him, the stars are not propitious to us. Things cannot go on like this — no, for without him all my vital force evaporates. Where he is not, I am alone, abandoned. We must be united for ever. The world does not understand us! But what does the world matter? Dearest friend, I beg you to prepare the beloved one for my decision to lay aside the crown. Let him be merciful, let him not demand that I should bear these torments of hell any longer.

My true and divine mission is this: to remain at his side as a true, loving friend and never leave him. Tell him this, I beg you. Represent to him that by this means all our plans can be carried into effect, that I shall die if I must live without him. Love works miracles. Then I shall be able to do more than I can now as King. Then we shall have power to work and live for coming generations. My brother is of age, I will hand over the government to him. . . . We do not mean to be idle, I hope to be able to be of use to him and serve him. I implore you, write to me very soon to say that the Only one sees that there are loftier crowns, more august kingdoms, than these luckless earthly ones; that he is in agreement with my plans, that he understands the might of my love, that he knows I can live with him alone. O my friend, then shall I live for the first time. Deliver me from this illusory existence (*Scheinexistenz*). . . . Do not call my intention extravagant or wildly romantic. By God, it is not, and men shall at last learn to understand the might of this love and predestined fate. I implore you, place all this before him, implore him on my behalf. He will not condemn to separation him who is on earth for him alone. He will not try to represent to me that kingship is my real vocation. If he does, my mind, my heart, might give way. But now my heart is broken, I force myself to live, and I know that this is no momentary mood, which might pass over; oh, no. United we are capable of much, there is nothing to be done here, this is not and never will be the right place for our great plans. . . . It is not the difficult political situation which drives me to this resolution, that would be cowardice. But the thought that my true mission is only to be achieved in this way, that is what induces me to take the step which we have discussed; here and in these circumstances I can be nothing to my Dear one, I see that clearly. There is my place! Thither it is, to him and to his side, that Fate is calling me."

We know Richard Wagner's state of mind, which he now unburdened in grave, one might almost say fatherly, expostulation with the young King. Nobody could have written with more truth and sincerity, in a graver and more admonitory tone, than he did. And we may here add the reply of the woman to whom the King had addressed the fateful information that for his friend's sake he was ready to renounce his throne and country. Naturally she, too, was most profoundly affected. But she was not the woman to meet the King in a spirit of falsehood, and so she wrote to him in her own characteristic style, from the depths of her rich, limpid, and yet almost elfin soul:

" Could I but send you the tears, the wishes, the apprehension, and the cares of these recent times, that would be the only possible answer to your letter of yesterday! I cannot tell you what I have suffered on your account and in sympathy with you since you left Triebschen, and to me, too, the idea and the intention to which you give expression rose up suddenly before my soul in a night of anguish. Ah, I know, my dear friend, that the removal of a few miserable creatures will not do everything. Since coming to know the various classes of society in Munich, which either lead or allow themselves to be led, or else shrink timidly in dread of an unknown power which makes itself felt everywhere, I have a real horror of the place, and in my eyes you are a martyr to the crown, just as our Friend appeared to me as a martyr for art. It seemed to me as though this supreme and sacred rank were the cross laid upon you. How can I fail to understand you now, when your great, profound soul pours itself out to me and tells me what I already knew by intuition? And yet, and yet, my wonderful friend, I recoil shuddering from the thought, and, just as in the poem the rider anxiously interrupted the melancholy monarch who wanted to reveal to him the nature of the world, exclaiming: ' Stop, stop! ' so I can hesitate where you move so bold and free, the ground reels beneath my feet, soul and senses fail me. For, dearest friend, in this dreary age, when on all sides faith is but a thing to chaffer with, I have verily believed in monarchy by the grace of God, it has been an article of faith to me. Yes, in you alone have I believed as King. Now I stand in the midst of an earthquake; I have to admit that you are right in everything, yet I cannot soar to the same heights. Our Friend is writing to you. He is naturally far calmer than I am and received my information gravely, but quietly. He seemed to be prepared for it in advance, and his powerful intelligence exempted him from the anxiety and alarm to which I am a prey. He can look with a steady glance into the future, and in spirit erect the edifice of art on the ruins of the present. But at the moment I can still see nothing but the ruins, and scarcely dare to hope. . . . I have for long past noticed with inexpressible misgivings, august friend, that you are not understood there, that people do not know you, that scarcely anybody can learn to know you. I had always hoped that some decisive act would impose silence, obedience, and awe upon many, if not all. But what is all this if you are suffering and pining, if your inner voice summons you from one vocation to another? How much remains to be said and discussed in this connexion! And so I look up to you, great and dear friend, and comprehend you in every fibre of your being, and I know too that in your place I should feel as you do, yet I dare not exhort you: ' Cast off the disastrous burden, let illusion be far from your heart.' . . . If I cherished a wish, it would be this: that our dearest friend should leave his throne, the last among kings, that good angels should bear his crown up to heaven, and that humanity, bereft of its godlike qualities, should drag out its miserable existence on a dead level of utter vulgarity. But these are dreams."

But it seems as though the young woman were speaking to the King like some good spirit, in order to soothe him and, for the very reason that she did not abruptly contradict him, to give him calm — calm, and clear ideas. And so she concludes in her characteristic way with a reference to German affairs: " I hardly know how it happens that the events which have broken over us like a storm have not worried me much on behalf of Germany. I have an unshakable belief in the continued existence of Germany, and it seems to me that it may be all to the good that much that is rotten and bad should be brought to light. This is how we have interpreted the significance of events, which are, indeed, no more than a prologue. But what have noble and lofty natures to do in this confusion? That is indeed another question, and a hard and gloomy one. Nowhere does one perceive a spark to warm the heart, nowhere an effort or a deed to fill the soul with enthusiasm! On all sides are spectres that walk by day." And she concludes: " My noble, dear friend, I have answered you by revealing to you the feelings of my soul. Our

Friend will send you the word for which you long, and confirm you both in the grandeur of your intention and in the patience with which to await the holy hour of its realization. But I pray God, from whom kings receive their might and rank, to raise you up and console you, that He may send you His angel, as it appeared to the Redeemer on the Mount of Olives, and that you, the dispenser of happiness, may attain happiness and peace. Ever faithful, both in the anguish of death and in the joy of salvation! " And in fact the King allowed himself to be calmed and dissuaded from his idea by the young woman's subtlety as much as by the Master's grave words. He then said that he repented of many letters by which he had made Wagner uneasy, and begged Frau Cosima for forgiveness like a boy: " Ah, dear friend, you know that I have often so much that is painful to go through, and so you will not think the worse of me if in my painful agitation I do not always succeed in controlling my feelings, but cannot but say outright what is in my heart." And once again he allows himself to find his greatest consolation in Wagner's works. " I do not want to complain, far be it from me. Rest assured that our Friend's tranquillity and peace take precedence of everything else in my eyes. How happy it makes me to think that he is working at *The Mastersingers*! How noble is his plan with regard to the performance of this work! Oh, could it but be realized! I hope and will not falter. Oh, had I but been able to spend an hour with him lately! He is the centre of all things for me, nothing has any meaning or significance apart from him. It is now my firm and definite hope that I may succeed in breaking the hostile, evil powers and bringing them into entire subjection. The wicked will receive their well-merited punishment, and the pure will rise to the top. Then will come the time when we may be united in life as well, without being torn apart again." He speaks hopefully of the school of art and of all their plans, of the building of the theatre and how it is to acquire the necessary independence and firm consistency in all its parts. He adds, to be sure, that it is impossible to hurl all the vipers swollen with venom into the abyss at a single blow. It should not be forgotten that at that time the King was suffering from the shock of an unsuccessful war, that he had advisers who did not themselves know what they wanted, and that in this feeling of isolation he turned to the noble pair who told him their opinion with full comprehension and candour, though still with noble consideration for his deep feelings. This was indeed inevitable. It must be said that at no time was the King more sinned against and injured than during this year.

And now the King's birthday came round again, and Frau Cosima wrote to him: " A threefold welcome to the day which gave you to us. It shines like a star in a succession of gloomy days." And she sent him the portrait of the Master as he was at the age of twenty-six, when he was writing *Rienzi.* She had sent for the portrait from Paris. And now followed a period of some enervation and exhaustion for the King. Bavarian independence had been saved, and the peace had been brought to a happy issue by Bismarck's wonderful intervention, so that the political situation in Bavaria was now better than it had ever been before. But on the other hand it was clear that a minister who had brought the State into such danger — who, for instance, during the war had even sent word to the Army commander that a battle must be fought, thus occasioning the disastrous and unnecessary bloodshed at Kissingen — must go at all costs. In these circumstances the very last thing that was wanted was a Wagner controversy. We know that in political questions the King's great tact always caused him to do the correct thing in decisive moments. He was, of course, not free from a certain vacillation. He himself uttered a warning against a meeting, especially with the Bülows, though he had proposed one earlier. " But the thought that fresh suffering and harm might come of it bids me renounce what I long for. Hitherto, when I have been here in the country, I have granted no audiences, except to the ministers, if they had something particularly urgent to report. This is known in the city, and I cannot help being anxious lest the wretched creatures might take it in the wrong way if I made an exception and received you, dear friend, and your husband, and lest fresh mischief to you might be the result. . . . Would it not be possible, then, for you to remain in Munich? Ah, must I live joyless in a foreign land? Perhaps next spring, after finishing *The Mastersingers,* our Friend might visit

Nymphenburg, and there write *The Nibelungs* and *Parsifal.*
Then all would be well again. I will give Neumayer's proposal
due consideration and then slaughter the idiotic Mime. Oh, stay!
I urgently beg you to tell me exactly what our Friend said
about Neumayer's proposal. In his last letter he confesses to
me that the idea was already dawning upon his soul that I did not
love him. O dear friend, could this be possible, could he have
such thoughts about ' Parzival ' ? That is not like him. I have not
deserved it. Oh, stay! With courage and perseverance the enemy
will be vanquished. Our enemies are vile, it is true, but stupid,
very stupid. I will not be cheated of this. We mean to prove to
them that we will not be turned aside from our true course, we
are far too noble, too great, for that. We may say this of ourselves boldly and proudly. Oh, Nymphenburg, could he but come
there! If this too is impossible, then I shall be seized with despair. For I must repeat, the thought of having to be separated
from him any longer is killing me." We see what his opponents
were doing by keeping Wagner away from the King.

But Frau Cosima always finds something wonderful to say
in response to all his plans and insistence: " Thanks be to you
for all that you have decided! Let us quietly submit. Long, hard
habit had made deprivation almost easier to me than enjoyment! My gracious lord, you say that we are to stay, and if the
word of any being on earth could decide us, it is your kind word.
And yet I answer: We are not going, we are withdrawing. For
we are now getting out of the way of those powerful enemies
who have brought things to such a pass that our protector in
distress cannot speak to us without danger, that the Friend who
withdrew for a few months can no longer contemplate returning,
that all our artistic plans are shattered, and that we are treated
like hapless adventurers. Our decision has not been arrived at
in a hurry. Yesterday my husband had another conversation,
lasting for an hour and a half, with the director of police. He
was very pleased with this man, who seems to be very noble and
well-meaning, but he came home confirmed in his intentions.
Everybody knows — it is an open secret — that the entourage
of our august friend cannot forgive me and the Dear one far
away for having associated openly and freely with the King.

All the evil reports that have been shamefully circulated with regard to myself can be traced — as everybody says and knows — to one person here, with whom I was actually on friendly terms so long as there was any intercourse between us, but who meant to make things here impossible for the friends of our Friend. This powerful hostility makes itself felt in all our relations. The orchestra is unwilling to obey a person who is unpopular locally, the journalists are becoming impudent, they are allowed to say absolutely anything, in fact they are encouraged to do so, the public is becoming scared, it does not know what to believe, for we have to keep silence. And so we are, as it were, surrounded by a wall, and the star which shines upon us and to which we address our songs has so far been unable to change anything in our outward circumstances. We are going away. We mean to stay where we are master in our own house, and there wait upon your wishes, my dear friend. My husband is and remains your servant, and your most willing, devoted, and enthusiastic servant — if you want music, he will hasten to you. This is why he has chosen the insignificant city of Basel, so that he may be near you, and because he desires no other master than you, my dear friend! We are going — pray be so good as to understand me — so as to be possible in Munich, in order to make your work easier! All is yet possible, but the personal scandal in which the vulgar are indulging with such confidence and energy must cease. When you, Dear (*Theurer*), have reached the point at which people obey, or, if they do not obey, are removed, then the decree will be promulgated for the school of art, my husband will be created court conductor, and artistic life will be in progress; then the wretches will have been silenced, or, if they still talk, they will be harmless. For we shall meet their impure words with pure action. Then will our golden age have begun. — I had thought that our Friend's withdrawal would have sufficed to make this high and difficult task easier for you. But I see that we must go too! How hard this will be for me! All my acquaintances, both here and elsewhere, remind me that I have always said: ' I mean to die here, I shall never go away.' Things were to be ordered otherwise. But you see that I still hope, and how strongly I hope — our presence now seems to me to be an obstacle to our artistic plans. For we cannot help you, Benevolent one, so long as the men are there who are trampling us underfoot, or, rather, so long as they are allowed to trample us underfoot. We are withdrawing, and seeking a refuge, so that when the right hour has struck, we may be at your service. Above all, my husband remains in your service. I do not want to spend another winter far from our Friend, in constant anxiety about his condition. For that reason I am going too. Let me say nothing, my dear friend, of the fact that my heart is nearly breaking — you know how happy I have been here, weaving a tissue of art — and hopes. The bonds forged by *Tristan* will not be loosed. We need a little more time than we had thought, and instead of being happy at once, we have suffered much. But this very thing is a sign to me that we are not ruined. People have tormented us, they have poured contempt on our most sacred feelings; let me believe that all our distress will be for the good of our art, and that while, confident, though much tried, we withdraw into the shadow, you are carrying our cause into the light. Everything is in your hands; let us go in peace, we shall return when we are to return, when we may return, when our banner is set up." In this she was advocating more or less the idea which her father had suggested to his son-in-law in his well-known letter of July 11. Perhaps she proceeded rather more diplomatically than her father's letter. At any rate, she managed so to modify his ideas that they were in full harmony with her own nature. Not that she shilly-shallied. She went straight to the point, as in her article of November 1865, and now writes: " Yes, people are stupid, and until its head shall be trodden underfoot, stupidity alone reigns over this world. What, indeed, can these paltry creatures understand of our aims? They think that they are threatened, simply because they are incapable of understanding it all, and always assume that there is nothing but personal interest concerned. They are stupid with regard to the ideal world because they do not understand us. We are stupid with regard to the real world because we cannot conceive how far vulgarity can go, how cowardice suddenly turns insolent, and how worthless people can swagger. And so two stupidities stand face to face:

the sublime stupidity of the martyr, the godlike folly of Siegfried and Parzival, and the stupidity of Mime, the material and
vulgar cunning. And here Nothung must come to the rescue."
She next describes the impression made on the Master by
Neumayer's work and above all by the King's letter: " About
your letter, or, rather, with regard to your letter, my august
friend, he wrote to me with reference to you: ' He is poetry
itself.' " She next speaks in quite a business-like tone, but with
shrewd judgment, about Kaulbach's cartoon of Isolde's ecstasy
(*Verklärung*), which she considered the best he had done,
" though I had pictured the situation quite differently. Our
Friend did not consider Isolde transfigured, he wanted to have
her represented as smiling and enraptured, not so mournful
as when she really thought she had lost her beloved. I shall be
delighted to look at Echter's sketches, and the Nibelungen series
too, and I offer you my most heart-felt thanks for your kind
permission.

" I have no further news of Semper, but I was glad to hear
that you, dear, noble friend, had a favourable opinion of him.
He is and remains a genius, his plans are wonderful. May I
inquire whether the small model of the festival theatre has been
ordered of him? I will also ask our Friend about the prelimi-
nary studies. But I do not think that he has made anything of
the sort except for *The Nibelungs.* . . . *Jesus of Nazareth* is
locked up in the Altenburg at Weimar. It belongs to the Princess
Wittgenstein, who has always been intending to come back to
Germany from Rome to set her papers in order, when she would
hand over this manuscript to me for you, Dear one (*Theurer*).
But she has not yet done so. My father is working at his *Christus*.
He is sad at our decision and would be glad to know that we
were in Munich — that is, near you, my august protector. Well,
we remain at your side. We are leaving the people who are separating us from you, Exalted and Noble one, so that we may
serve you the better. We seem to be going away, but we are
really drawing nearer. . . . My husband wanted to be in Basel
on the 15th, in order to make a few very modest musical arrangements for the winter. Stuttgart and Berlin have been proposed to him, but he avoided both cities on account of the court,

in order to be able to remain in your service, dear lord! So make use of him as you wish. The distance is not great. Your orders can never create any disturbance in his life, for he arranges it with a view to them. He is now only waiting for the confirmation of the leave which you have graciously consented to grant him, before withdrawing — I am staying here a little while longer. The children are staying at Triebschen, for our Friend is glad to have them about him, and they afford him a little innocent distraction. It was the last thing which I could still do for him."

We know that it was precisely owing to Bülow's attitude that Ludwig was confirmed in his plans. And Frau Cosima's letter also influenced him to the same purpose. As to this the King writes: "What you say about Herr von Bülow has touched me deeply. How well I know the value of the faithful and affectionate sentiments towards me which fill his heart! I see that we must now act if everything is not to be lost. I mean to prove worthy of my great Friend. So here is my plan, in brief: I shall write an autograph letter to Herr von Neumayer, appointing him head of my secretariate. This will do a great deal of good, for Mime will be powerless when he receives his dismissal, and morally as good as dead, and the other vulgar souls too; Fafner will be gone, and on the first of January the faithful Friedrich will become director of the theatre (*Theaterintendant*), while simultaneously I shall appoint Herr von Bülow as my conductor; we will also remove the incompetent Perfall. Now what do you say to this plan, my dear friend? I must act; an end must be made of the aims of these miserable wretches. I implore you to inform our Friend of this and beg him to come back. Why should he not be able to come in the spring, but then stay, stay! Semper is at work on the plastic model." This was more than could have been expected at the time; and Frau Cosima accordingly writes: "I really do not know what to say to you. I have been a stranger to joy for so long that it is almost death to me! I have not stopped crying since I read your dear letter, and I feel as though I must die, for I see the opening of the golden age, for you, for the Friend, for holy art. Now could I close my eyes, when I once more behold a happiness such as I experienced once through

230

you alone and could only feel again through you. . . . All that you propose to do seems to me splendid. God grant that you do not meet with too much trouble and annoyance in connexion with it. God grant that everything may be settled at one blow. My husband will go to Basel, so that nothing will be changed in appearance." And all that comes from her is an outburst of " tears and prayers." " A fervent prayer such, perhaps, as no other woman's soul ever offered up! May God strengthen you, you will now have to go through critical and unpleasant hours. Would that I could bear them for you! If you will allow me humbly to offer a modest piece of advice, it is this: to go through with your bold and boldly determined policy; I believe that the hardest task that can be imposed upon your beautiful soul is imposed upon it now; the pitilessness of justice. Unhappily none of us can help you now, the King alone can rule. But so soon as the royal act is accomplished, we mean to stand by you, as we can do with our whole souls. And if but one step has been taken, all is already accomplished. If you but knew how the country is waiting upon you! When I heard recently of the postponement that had taken place, I thought that now it was no longer possible and that we must submit. Resolved now to go, I drafted a letter to you in the silence of a sleepless night, in which, with the lucidity and calm of deep renunciation, I laid the whole situa-tion before you as it appeared to me, bereft as I now am of all desires, and as it will appear to subsequent generations. I told you how these pitiful, wicked persons were trying to rob you of the trust and love of your people. I said: let us now go forth, to wander, to work, and to perish. Abandon us; we shall under-stand and not murmur. But let one thing be the price of this sacrifice: do not give yourself up; oh, do not let the wretches exult in the fact that they have come between King and people in order to secure their own position, laying sacrilegious hands upon this highest bond, forged by the will of God! Now all this has become superfluous, now I call down blessing and happi-ness upon you! Whenever you have any disagreeable impression, think of the blessings of those who have been so sorely tried. I confess, my dear friend, I fear for you now. The work which you have in hand is so utterly unfitted to your idealistic nature: to

tread on toads and sweep away spiders is no task for an angel. —
But the angel dwells among men. He had to be put to this, the
hardest of tests, if he was to fulfil his true mission. Besides, I
am comforted by the circumstance that everything can be done
quickly, indeed it must be done almost in a hurry." In later
days she herself made an observation upon this sort of style,
from which we gather that she was obliged to adopt this uplifted
tone in order that the young King should understand her aright.
It was all in keeping with his nature, and, besides, it should not
be forgotten that the state of affairs in Bavaria had become more
and more gloomy. For long past, the attack on Wagner had not
been aimed at him alone, but the whole campaign was directed
against the person of the King. The agitation had spread to the
masses, and the foreign papers, too, now began writing in a tone
which was hardly equalled even shortly before the King's final
catastrophe. They reported details about the state of the King's
health and about consultations for which doctors with a smattering of so-called psychiatry had been called in. One newspaper
had the effrontery to say that these doctors' opinions had been
by no means flattering to the King. We can see from this how
low was the level of those who influenced these papers, and what
construction it was considered legitimate to put upon a scientific diagnosis in those days. This hostile tendency accompanied
the whole of King Ludwig's life, and, as we know, after many
years these desires and ideas were actually fulfilled, though at
a time when the court, in particular, would have nothing to do
with such machinations. Frau Cosima was undoubtedly aware
of these things, of which, indeed, Richard Wagner afterwards
informed the King, who then braced himself for vigorous action:
not only did he deal with the wasps' nest in his entourage, but
he also showed himself to the people, thereby gratifying the
Master's heart-felt wish, as well as that of Frau Cosima. But
once again she was able to exert a calming influence in her
characteristic fashion, and so she continued: ". . . and now I
am also to assure you that our Friend is coming. I will answer
for this, my dear lord. If all is accomplished here and *The
Mastersingers* is finished at Triebschen, then we will once more
build up the life which ought never to have been disturbed and

against which not a soul in the country had anything to say. I hear this daily and on all sides. My husband will perfect and develop your orchestra, the trusty Friedrich will turn the theatre into an artistic institution, our Friend will do creative work, we shall produce our effect and bring profit and peaceful greatness to the country. You will see, we shall not remain isolated, we are the sole rejoinder to the dominion of brute force. God grant that you may see all this as I do, now that I have experienced and heard so much." She next sent him a volume of Schopenhauer: "One of the profoundest and most acute thinkers in Germany, whose writings have an influence and importance for our Friend comparable to that of no others. I may say, indeed, that they have had a decisive effect upon his spiritual nature. For thirty years Schopenhauer has been ignored; now people are beginning to take an interest in him for the first time, while all the other academic bigwigs, who crowded out the true philosopher, have gradually faded away and vanished. Nobody has had such a profound grasp of the Christian religion as our Friend, nobody has placed it so high, or so reverenced the Holy One, the Crucified."

It is not without interest to see how she submitted the plan of Peter Cornelius's opera *Gunlöd* to the King: "I enclose a sketch for a musical drama by Cornelius, which I like very much, and which I imagine would not be displeasing to our august friend. Peter Cornelius was of opinion that Wagner's *Nibelungen* must be given first, so that such subjects might become possible. I replied that, on the contrary, such gigantic things make everything of the same *genre* impossible. He ought to be quick and finish his work, I said, and I was quite convinced that he would find a public. The public demands an ideal only when it is given one. If it could demand the ideal before being given it, it would create it for itself." This sounds very different from the way in which Peter Cornelius judged Frau Cosima in one of his ill-tempered moods.

But the King replied: "Yes, I am resolute and firm, our dear Friend must not doubt that for a moment. I hope that my people will next begin to understand me. I read a great deal lately among the mountains about Athens at its prime and Themistocles.

With what enthusiasm it filled me! It would be hard to turn our Müncheners, with their minds clouded with beer, into art-loving Greeks. But we must not flag; great things will yet happen. In October Semper's model will be finished. After the foundation of our school I will start, at any rate, on the festival theatre. It will be a worthy temple of Wagner." And he concludes: "The beasts shall fall to the right and to the left, I will hurl thunderbolts into the crowd. Yes, those who imagine themselves to be so firmly established are hastening towards their end, thus I cry with Loge! "[1] And she replies in the utmost delight: "Your happy determination becomes you so splendidly, Beneficent one (*Gütiger*), that yesterday, all alone as I was, I absolutely shouted for joy. And so I go about in an uplifted frame of mind, thinking joyfully of you. For if you meet annoyances so gaily and with such spirit, like a very Siegfried, how can we fail to attune ourselves to your mood? Yes, my friend, thanks to you, I go my way full of hope. In writing to my father, who was so sorry to see us leave Munich, I have just said: 'I cannot tell you why, and it sounds rash at the moment of our departure; but I know that we shall soon return, and that for good, full of honour and joy — we shall soon attract our public to us.' You saw, dear friend, how in spite of all the cabals *Tristan* was well received, and if the performances last year were not better attended, that was because such anxiety prevailed that people would not venture out to them. They thought that it was all no more than a display of fireworks, soon over and completely forgotten, and for this reason they did not want to compromise themselves with those in power. Matters were far worse here when Ludwig I carried out his splendid building schemes, and the worthy Germans grumbled and growled enough. But there the buildings stand, and the people are glad, and these works, the sense of which the people could not grasp at first, now redound to the great honour of the King, the city, and the whole of Germany. Oh surely, my friend, even if the people do not understand you, they will divine your intentions and love you. I am intensely delighted that Semper will shortly have finished the model, and when that is in existence, and Semper thus hon-

[1] *Rhinegold*, Scene IV. — TR.

oured and satisfied, we can wait till our work has taken root, and the trust of his people enables the King to have it executed in stone."

Frau Cosima had now once more betaken herself to Triebschen and now sent further reports on the course of life there: "The *Wahn* monologue is finished, and unspeakably beautiful. Need I tell you that, Dear one?" She went on to describe the troubles which again threatened about the arrangement of the house, as was inevitable in view of Wagner's nature, so unlike her own:

"We smiled at once gaily and sadly as we were recalling yesterday how I have always found him in trouble about the arrangement of his house. It will be quite comfortable and cheerful at Triebschen now. If this tiresome upset does not last too long, I hope that the composition of the third act will be finished by Christmas. The remaining part of the winter our Friend will devote to the instrumentation of these two acts, and so the performance will be possible by the spring. How much, what great things do we not promise ourselves from this performance, and it is all due to you alone, exalted protector.

"In the evening after tea our Friend dictates to me his biography. We have got as far as Paris, at the time when the *Faust* Overture was written (1839–40). I simply cannot tell you how terribly the detailed knowledge of these bitter times affects me, and how touched I am by the gentleness with which our Friend judges everybody's abominable behaviour towards him. So as not to disturb his beautiful and edifying state of mind, I say that all these experiences were quite easy to bear, though at times I can hardly write for indignation and emotion. O unique and beyond all words exalted friend, what a contrast you are in this respect to the rest of the world! It is really as though God had assigned you as your vocation to set all things to rights. Although we work at it daily, the biography advances slowly, on account of my strength, which at times entirely fails me. Yet I hope that before very long I shall have got the biography into order too. We really live here as though in a fairy-tale and see and hear nothing of the world. About midday our Friend tells me what he has done during the morning. In the afternoon he roams about the pastures and meadows, and I usually go to meet him. He then spends a little time with me and the children, who are very happy here. In the evening he narrates his hard life, and the story always turns into a hymn to ' Parzival.' Our Friend is just hailing me in the distance; am I not right in saying that we are living in a fairy-tale and have found sweet forgetfulness of life? We hear nothing but the tinkle of bells as the herds of cattle descend from the high pastures and wander in the meadows which have been cleared among the woods, gazing at us every day in friendly curiosity with their great eyes. . . . During the next few days I think of visiting Herr von Bülow again at Basel, where he has settled down as well as he can and begun his musical activities. Such an obscure town has this advantage at least, that he need explain nothing or say nothing to anybody. But what a nest of Philistines! Music as carried on there is an honest, straightforward, and dull business affair. But he will not hear of any capital but Munich, nor in general of any big affairs, and has just refused rather a brilliant offer from America, not even reading the letter containing the proposal, but asking me to deal with it."

She continued to work at the biography and now gave the King a description of the new arrangements at Triebschen: " Now the disturbers of our peace have gone and it looks quite cosy and comfortable here. The drawing-room has gained a big wall by the blocking up of two windows. On it hang the *Tannhäuser* picture and the *Rheingold* cartoons in all their glory, and the busts of the guardian spirit of this home and of the Spirit whom he protects lend it a finish. A stove has been conjured up here by Loge, and on it stands the clock with the minnesingers, the first Christmas present. Opposite the long wall, in a well-lighted position between the two doors, hangs the portrait in oils, the first birthday present, beneath which are amassed all the gorgeous things that our Friend has received in the course of his life, silver goblets and wreaths, in the midst of which stand out splendidly the two statues of Tannhäuser and Lohengrin. Between the two windows stands the piano, over which hang the medallions of Liszt and Bülow. The little room next the drawing-room has become the library. Hohenschwangau and the photograph of our lord and protector lend it a charming animation.

It is extraordinarily quiet and comfortable downstairs here; we call it ' Stolzing,' and have not driven in a nail or set a chair in place without exchanging a glance and imagining ' Parzival ' to be here. A strangely happy dream. Upstairs is the work-room. Today Beckmesser received his musical introduction after the incredibly beautiful scene between Walther and Sachs. When our Friend played me the setting of the words which he had just written, and sang: ' *Das waren hochbedürft 'ge Meister, von Lebensmüh' bedrängte Geister* (Those Masters whom the world had wasted, Who life's embittered draught had tasted),' [1] we both burst into tears. Could I but send you, dearest friend, the music which our Friend has found for these words. He is just coming to table, to dine and seek recreation among the children. Russ, the gigantic dog, who is impossible to train, and Kos, the badly trained terrier, also add to the snug atmosphere, and the two peacocks, Wotan and Frigga, strut proudly and tranquilly about the garden."

Meanwhile Hans Richter had arrived and made himself at home. Frau Cosima writes: " He is modest and industrious. He tells us all sorts of things about the far-reaching intrigues with which he has himself come in contact in Vienna. Proposals have been made to Löwi, the singing-master there, for the establishment of a *conservatoire* in Munich under the direction of Herr Rheinberger. We let him go on with his story undisturbed, since we are fortunate enough to be able to laugh at these pitiable affairs. But I am saying all this and have not told our dear friend that my heart was tormented by such gnawing anxiety about our Friend's health that I wrote to Dr. Standhartner at Vienna and have asked him to come here. . . . Our Friend felt no anxiety, but looked wretched and had constant attacks of oppression over the heart, I was almost out of my mind with anxiety and spent half the night on my knees. Standhartner telegraphed to me today that he cannot get away from Vienna before the 7th. But now our Friend seems to me a little better, and I do not know what I ought to do. I naturally do not want to trouble such a busy doctor unnecessarily, but I am still very uneasy and should

[1] *The Mastersingers*, III, ii, Newman's translation (Breitkopf and Härtel). —TR.

be glad if he could prescribe to our Friend what he ought to do. I think I shall let him come, though he may be annoyed with me if he finds my anxiety groundless. I should be very glad to hear from you, my dear friend, whether you approve of my action."

These were the symptoms of the malady which continued to torment the Master for years to come, till it put an end to his life, in Venice.

" I have one message from our Friend in connexion with Prince Hohenlohe; he asks me to request our august protector not to give his gracious attention to any proposal from him, for he does not know this gentleman at all and would have cause to blame himself severely if he were to recommend anyone to our Dear one about whom he knows nothing directly. When he mentioned the Prince before, it was only in order to see his beloved King delivered from a person who had the insolence to set himself up against his master's inclinations. He had nothing political in mind. But he is happy that the Dear one reposes entire confidence in Herr von Neumayer, and asks me to request him, in his unbounded affection and inexhaustible goodness, not to give his kind consideration to the name which was mentioned, but to act or not to act according to his own judgment and opinion, without any reference to the proposal that had been made, and, since Herr von Neumayer has won the royal confidence, to listen solely and wholly to his proposals. He wanted to write himself and put all this before you. But since I know how easily he is upset by everything, I begged him to let me humbly convey it to you. Tomorrow I am going to Basel for a few days to visit Herr von Bülow. He was informed that a certain Count Platen (a determined enemy of our cause) was going to be chosen as intendant of the theatre. He smiled and said nothing. We have also been questioned on all sides about our loss of favour, for people are curious and always will be, so that it is a pleasure to tell them nothing." And to conclude her letter she describes a dream which had brought the King to Triebschen on the Master's birthday. " Nobody had been present but worrying and unwelcome people. But at the end, as though conjured up by magic, our guardian spirit appeared. My annoyance at the stupid company was so great that I pretended to be unwell, so as to scare them away. And we were left, our tutelary spirit, the Spirit, and I. And our hearty laughter over my successful stratagem woke me up."

Now came the time when, energetically prompted by the Master, the King made that progress through the Franconian provinces which he undertook with such fine enthusiasm. He describes it to Frau Cosima as follows:

" At last I find a moment of grateful peace amid the tumultuous festivities. I take advantage of it to write you a few lines, my dearly beloved friend. I need hardly say that I constantly think of you and the Only one, and that I often feel myself drawn, with a mighty and unquenchable longing which I cannot endure much longer, to the cosy retirement of Triebschen and the inspiring intercourse with him, my dearest one (*dem Teuersten*), which is the one and only thing that affords me happiness and bliss. You know me, you understand the essence of true friendship and the depths of my love. It enchants me and fills me with sincere delight that our Friend is better again. Thanks, heart-felt thanks for every piece of news that you send me. Oh, do not cease to give me news of yourself and him very often! . . . I am receiving numerous proofs on all sides of sincere, unfeigned affection, of the fidelity and attachment of the people to their hereditary prince. You are right, perfectly right, when you say that we alone are capable of grasping the true and deep significance of this journey. By means of it I mean to lay the firm foundation-stone upon which we intend in the near future to establish what is glorious and eternally imperishable. Every day I become more and more convinced that Neumayer is the very man we need. And how pleasant it is, too, to work with him! What a contrast between him and the slow-moving intelligence of a Pfi and his associates! How I thank you from the depths of my soul for the pages of the biography which you so kindly sent me! I long for some quiet hours, in which I may absorb myself in this world which is so sacred to me. You give me your word, do you not, that immediately after finishing *The Mastersingers of Nuremberg* our dear one will at once resume the Nibelung cycle. My time is very much taken up on this tour, and I have never done with torchlight processions, balls, and illuminations; I frequently give banquets with from fifty to eighty covers. In the long run this is really rather tiring. I recently gave more than two hundred audiences on a single day, standing all the time. But in such a connexion one cannot speak of trouble. I think of arriving in Würzburg on the 23rd, and on the 27th shall certainly be in Nuremberg, where I mean to spend four or five days. Next year I shall stay there still longer. But very many things will have happened before then, if God will."

It is touching to read with what anxiety Frau Cosima watched the King's progress:

"These journeys — we all know what they mean, we know what sacrifices our Dear one is making in connexion with them, we know for whom and for what. We follow your every step. I am very glad that the people should revel in the sight of their King. He is and ought to be and represent to them what is highest. Yet when I hear of all these splendid rejoicings, the only thing which I really ask myself is in what state of mind our friend is, whether he is pleasantly animated or inwardly melancholy, that is all that concerns me. You see that I cannot rid myself of my anxious care. I may say, indeed, that my feeling is one of constant trembling, wonderfully supported by the most unshakable confidence in you and your mission and in its inevitable fulfilment. My love for you and for him is like the flight of a swan — sure, powerful, yet tremulous. Please be indulgent towards this feeling." And now follows a picture of the atmosphere at Triebschen:

"Just now Stolzing was turned into a nursery. Our Friend first played with the children, then sat down at the piano and went through the Ninth Symphony. While at one and the same time I was drawing into my soul the glorious strains, enjoying the quiet merriment of the children, and sharing our Friend's sense of well-being, I could not help thinking of you with tears of emotion. It is you who have conjured up this rich world of peace amid one of agony, it is you who have made it possible for us to be together, it is you who have given peace to the head which never knew it before; you entered this tortured life like a redeeming angel, and there was peace."

Meanwhile the choice of Neumayer as head of the royal

secretariate turned out better for Triebschen than had been expected, and satisfaction was felt at his first activities. But these hopes were short-lived, and the King had scarcely returned from his journey when he dismissed him. There was a variety of other incidents, and in particular that little drama caused by the widow of Schnorr von Carolsfeld, to which she managed to impart a fanatical and mystical tinge. There was also the removal of the King's friend Friedrich. All these things are reflected in the correspondence: " Intentions (*Absichten*) everywhere, insight (*Einsichten*) nowhere," sighs Frau Cosima. But she is able to send news of the Master: " He has resumed his work, which these ghost-stories had made impossible for him for a whole week, all but a day. Beckmesser is raging against Sachs: ' *O Schuster voller Ränke* (O cobbler full of cunning)!' I simply had to laugh out loud when he played me the beginning of this outburst of rage yesterday. If God will, the peace of Triebschen will be spared for a time, and things will make rapid progress. I promise you with all my soul that so soon as *The Mastersingers* is finished, *The Nibelungs*, the life-work, which was not to be finished before you appeared, will be taken up, and then *Parsifal*! I know that all this will happen. If I am sad and anxious at times, that is the result of long sympathy with his sufferings, which had reduced my heart to an almost perpetual state of quivering. But in my inmost soul I cherish the certainty which bears me high above all earthly sorrows. I know that our Friend will yet complete it all. His health, too, is getting on tolerably, so that I was able to stay for some time at Basel without uneasiness. I found my husband well and full of vigour, and inclined for music. People there all told me that they no longer knew themselves since he had been there, he had kindled such life among both musicians and the public. No circle is too narrow for his activity, and so wherever he goes and stays, he sows the good seed according to his powers."

The King's progress through the Franconian provinces decidedly did him good. He dealt with situations in a way that was very much to the credit of a young man aged twenty-one. We see how easy and simple it had been to guide and direct him and to maintain the relation between him and the people, which had really been established by him alone, and thus to create the right basis for his outlook on life and his sense of duty. His nature was an exaltedly emotional one, but for the very reason that he was in direct communion with nature, far from disinclined for physical exertion, and could rise to the severest emergencies, all this might have been taken advantage of quietly. He describes his position with a certain humour: " The day before yesterday the presentations lasted uninterruptedly for four hours on end. I received four hundred people, then there was a great banquet. On top of that a ball. I am promising myself great things from my stay at Nuremberg. That is the place where I shall devote particular care to winning men's hearts, which I never succeeded in doing in Munich. That is, the opening of men's eyes on the subject of our great and immortal Friend must come about here gradually, but all the more surely." Next indeed he complains of Neumayer's attitude towards the Master and expresses the feeling that he in no wise deserves the trust reposed in him. Yet the King is also conscious of the superficiality of these ceremonial duties: " How insignificant and insipid all men seem to me by comparison with you and him! What pitiable, grovelling insect souls! Mediocrity and narrowness almost everywhere, wherever I turn my eyes. The people are good, the innermost core is sound, but they have no judgment and are easily led. I see from the papers that there will be no respite in Munich from the agitation and Wagner-baiting. I firmly believe that in Nuremberg the populace is more intelligent and well-meaning than here. *The Mastersingers* will kindle its enthusiasm. I should like to hear it in Munich too one day, for in spite of the fact that that city and its inhabitants do not stand very high in my estimation, yet I am fond of the place where I spent my earliest youth. Besides, the stage on which Tristan suffered and died is dear to me. If I am to have even more cause to lose my patience with the inhabitants of what has hitherto been my capital, nothing shall prevent me from taking up my abode in Nuremberg and transferring my Government there." In this connexion he felt some perturbation at the provision in the peace treaty which secured the King of Prussia joint possession of the fortress at Nuremberg. But he genuinely intended it, and this found full expression in these very letters to Frau Cosima. She tried, however, as it were, to combat his antipathy for Munich by a description of the city, intended to dispose him favourably towards it: " I may perhaps be allowed to greet you in Munich, the city where I once declared that I meant to die, where I knew inexpressible joy and unspeakable suffering. I remember how, when I visited this place as a stranger, I liked it extraordinarily. The noble architecture, the churches with their fine style, the theatre, where, as it so happens, I saw *Tannhäuser*, with Schnorr as visiting singer (*Gast*), the absence of factories, stock exchanges, the faces of rich financiers, and noisy traffic — all this made such a pleasing impression upon me that I said to Hans how glad I should be to live in the city. ' How should we get here? ' he asked; and then he enlightened me about its musical condition, and my wish was silenced. But the beautiful impression could not be effaced."

About Wagner she writes: " Now that he is undisturbed, our Friend is quietly going on with his work. He is just playing me Walther's visit to Sachs, where he is trying on Evchen's shoe. This flower blossomed early this morning. Yesterday our Friend told me that, in the pause which would occur after the completion and performance of *The Mastersingers* and the resumption of the *Nibelungen*, he intended to revise *The Flying Dutchman*, so that it might be worthy to stand beside *Tannhäuser* and *Lohengrin*. I was immensely delighted at this, especially as I know that it has been a long-cherished wish of the Dear one and was discussed last year at Hohenschwangau."

Meanwhile she had taken pains to obtain the manuscript of *The Death of Siegfried* (*Siegfrieds Tod*), which was in the hands of Councillor Sulzer at Zürich, in order to supply the King with a copy. During his visit to Darmstadt the King had himself found out that W. Weissheimer, the conductor there, possessed the manuscript of the sketch for *Wayland the Smith* (*Wieland der Schmidt*), and had taken steps to obtain it. For the rest, the dictating of the biography went on. Wagner found it hard to go on with it, in view of the impression likely to be made on the King by his miserable annoyances and experiences. But she said: " Had I not begged him most importunately to tell me everything, however painful it might be to relate, he would have passed over many things unnoticed. I was so bold as to maintain, in opposition to him, that it was for this very reason that you had asked him to do it, and so he plunged into a sea of unedifying reminiscences. I hope that your sympathies will not be unpleasantly affected in consequence. To me it seems that his greatness and incredible good-heartedness shine with an even brighter light through all these mean afflictions."

In spite of the joyful welcome given him by the citizens, the King found much in Munich that could not but dash his spirits. The Schnorr incident, too, was calculated to sober him, and yet it must be said that in this affair he proceeded calmly and clear-sightedly and settled it in truly kingly fashion. The situation brought about by this woman and her excitable and fantastic character was perhaps one of the most difficult which Wagner, and Cosima, too, had to face. But she speaks of it very acutely:

"In connexion with this incident, I remember a saying of Alexander von Humboldt's, which I did not understand at the time. I was deploring in his presence an episode occasioned by the wretched evil entourage of the King of Prussia, Frederick William IV. 'It is I who have to suffer from it most,' he replied, ' but, believe me, even the worst entourage has its value and importance. It preserves what matters most — the King's inaccessibility. Since the King honours me with his friendship, everyone feels justified in aspiring to it, and if it were not for the host of courtiers — ignoble though they unfortunately often are — the King would be simply unable to defend himself against intrusion, and everybody would have a right to push in.' Conditions of that sort were quite new to me at the time, and I did not understand what he said at all. But my father told me that he was perfectly right. Now I understand their significance. I hope that you are taking the matter lightly; that is, that you are not so much annoyed about it as our Friend was."

Very dextrous, too, is the way in which she warns the King against working at night: "I feel indescribably foolish to mention this, but cannot help it. I have nothing further to say about this, nor have I even any request to make; all that your painfully anxious friend will allow herself to say is to express a fervent wish that you would take great care of yourself." Very beautiful, too, is her reply when the King told her that he had visited the grave of Hans Sachs. " When I was in Nuremberg, I unfortunately did not visit the grave of Hans Sachs. *The Mastersingers* was not yet in existence, and what I had read about the shoemaker-poet had left me rather cold. Now, of course, I would gladly make the pilgrimage there. My spirit stands in pious joy before this visit of yours. Ah, let others crumble Germany to bits and crush her into a pulp, let them work their wicked will by the right of might, let them fetter her and mould her until one is sick and sorry, in my eyes you have saved Germany. For you and you alone have recognized the Only one, and by so doing you have accomplished what all the others, God knows where, are trying to do — or are perhaps not even trying to do — for who thinks of Germany? O God, what we went through a year ago! Earth and heaven collapsed before me, and I felt sure that I could not face such extremities a second time. The month of December is unusually sad for me. Seven years ago, on the 15th, I lost my brother, whom I may indeed call a saint; at the age of twenty he was filled with disgust for the world. But hallowed night brings consolation for all mourning; what prayers and supplications will I then make for the being who brings salvation."

It is very remarkable how decidedly and really commandingly the King now expressed himself on all questions; for instance, on the subject of the head of his secretariate: " He is not frank and truthful, he is a charlatan. Many people allowed themselves to be corrupted by his intellect, wit, and eloquence; but, God be thanked, my eyes were opened in time. His health is really very much impaired. His vanity is unbounded, and he is full of pretensions. He is far too constitutional and follows that line to an exaggerated extent. As monarch I cannot and may not like this. Do not be alarmed at all this, dearest friend, we are true to one another, we belong to one another till death. We shall be victorious. We are sufficient unto ourselves and shall conquer by our own strength, courage, and endurance. I am now seriously thinking of putting Prince Hohenlohe into Pfordten's place. The Prince is a man very free from prejudice and with a firm character, and will serve us better than Neumayer ever succeeded in doing! Now a few remarks about my intentions with regard to the performance of *The Mastersingers*. Place of performance: Nuremberg. If this cannot be managed, then at any rate in Bavaria, above all on no account abroad. I should sink into the ground if this were to happen. I think the best thing would be for Herr von Bülow to go to Nuremberg this winter and sound opinion there thoroughly, getting to know the most enthusiastic and prominent citizens, instructing them in the most important of our plans, and enlightening them about the spirit necessary for the first performance of such a wonderful and unprecedented work as *The Mastersingers*. Hans will be a warm advocate of our cause, the Nurembergers will enter into our plan with ardour, recognizing what an honour is being done them, and filled with enthusiasm at the thought of being allowed to contribute towards fulfilling their King's greatest wish. The director will not be able to raise any opposition. Hans will act as conductor and in the mean time will be good enough to look round in person for suitable singers and performers. Why should not all this be successful? So what is to prevent the performance from taking place in the summer — say about Midsummer? Our Friend seems to have thought that *Wieland der Schmid*[*t*] (*Wayland the Smith*) had not come into my hands. Count Holstein handed the manuscript over to me at once. He is faithful and attached, he always takes charge most conscientiously of my letters to you, dear friend, he is a really loyal servant, straightforwardly devoted to his King. Our Friend also expressed his opinion that the credit for initiating my journey to Franconia belonged to Neumayer. Oh, no, that is not so. However, people thought so and tricked him out in borrowed plumes." A rare energy had taken possession of the King. Thus on December 20 he writes again: "Yesterday I accepted Pfordten's offered resignation. So the miserable creature who behaved so badly in our affairs is gone now, and Pfi. and Pfo. are now powerless, and if I approach you with a friendly request, I may say that my life's happiness depends upon its being granted. I would not make this urgent request if it were possible to grant it only at the cost of our Friend's peace and rest; that would be most unjust.

246

But it is not so. How does our cause stand now! For me this year has been the most terrible through which I have ever had to live. People think that our plans are frustrated, and even the appearance of this may do great harm. Now to the point. I implore you, dear friend, to induce the Dear one to come here after the completion of *The Mastersingers* — that is, in the spring. He will see that prejudices will disappear. He ought to make the attempt to please me. Only see, dear friend, I cannot endure this separation. I may say this for myself, for a long time I have persevered bravely in my disconsolate loneliness, I have had to endure atrocious things. I have not a single soul here who understands me. Oh, sympathize with me, and beg him to come. In my abandoned state I feel so utterly forlorn, letters are no substitute for speech. Ah, everything had begun so ecstatically, I was so overjoyed, that I scarcely dared to believe it was all true, and now I am cruelly cast out of this bliss, parted from all that I hold dear, condemned to drag out my life in grief among more or less mean-minded people (with a few exceptions) — oh, it is hard! You, dear friend, know this state of affairs which makes me so unmeasurably wretched, you know the only physician who could help me, but will not take me out of this misery, and means to let me spend another year like the last. A few more years like this, and my life will be at an end. In the spring, no later. Write to me quite soon and at length. How happy I should have been to see the Dear one often with me, to draw inspiration and refreshment from his words, to share in his life, to be initiated into the mysteries of art! Now I have to receive tiresome people, give boring banquets, be patient, and give myself trouble, and I have nobody who understands me, I am alone, alone. So Pfordten is going and Hohenlohe is becoming minister. In the winter come tiresome visits; the period of court festivities, which I hate, is approaching, everything is in confusion in the theatre, these excellent, block-headed people imagine in their infinite blindness that their power has been victorious and that they have succeeded in parting us. Nothing but facts can speak here; our Friend is coming near, to live close to his friend. In spite of everything I see that we have to make a fresh start in Munich. My cousin Sophie (youngest sister of the Austrian Empress), who is full of enthusiasm for our Friend, asked me to send him her most friendly greetings. Will you be so good as to convey them to him? "

Thus he leads up to the first news of his relations with this clever and original Princess — relations which were, however, to bring him no happiness and were, indeed, to prove of evil omen.

Next came Christmas, and Frau Cosima describes how she arranged the tree; she next enters into her friend's complaints of his loneliness, which had moved her most deeply. With regard to the resignation of Neumayer she writes:

" I was startled by the fact that yet another had failed to maintain his position, and because I was in indescribable anxiety the whole time, and burdened you with it too, my exalted friend. One man — only one, who should understand you as well as the people do, who should lighten your heavy task — what would I not give to know that such a one had been found! That is why I was as delighted as a child when I heard that Prince Otto had gone to Nuremberg; perhaps, then, I said to myself, he is the one worthy of the highest confidence. But, setting aside this feminine sentimentality, I say firmly and with conviction that with you, my exalted friend (*mein hoher Freund*), we need nobody. You, my King, will surely discover what the country needs by the light of your own consciousness. I only regret that you had this unpleasant experience."

She was, however, herself a prey to gloomy inward thoughts at that time, owing to the fantastic intrigues of Schnorr's widow, and she pours out her feelings to the King with wonderful confidence: " I have been crying all the morning; for I am a mother, and it cannot be a matter of indifference to me to see my honour smirched. But time will come to the aid of me and my children, and one thing I know, and I alone know it: that in this ruin of all that is good and true, the four beings for whom alone I care, you, my sovereign and friend, my father, my husband, and our Friend, will never, never, misjudge me. This is a consolation, my gracious sovereign, which has raised me up in the hardest hours of my life. Last night, when I could not sleep for sorrow, I turned over in my mind my whole life, with its anxieties, distresses, and hopes, and I had to admit that a deep and inviolable peace has taken possession of my heart, and that this peace has been raised to a pitch of utter ecstasy since *The Mastersingers* has been resumed. I should like to compare my soul to the sea, whose surface alone is disturbed by storms, but whose depths remain calm and untroubled. And today the peace which I experienced in the night must continue. I said it, I wept long and violently, I felt that I had not deserved such a thing and from such a quarter, I felt utterly defenceless against the fathomless malice of the world. I was full of pity for my children, my husband, my father, our dear one, and you, my noblest of friends. But I find the consolation for which I long in contemplating the good which has come to me. What happiness must be mine, that I must thus expiate it! Soon my soul rose exultant to meet the fresh trial. This is the price which I pay for the happiness of having stood by our Friend. May I pay it triumphantly! "

This was a reaction caused by the importunities of the unfortunate Frau Schnorr von Carolsfeld, who persecuted both the Master and the King incessantly and was trying to destroy the tranquillity of Triebschen. And so the Christmas holidays went by. Her husband had not been present, it is true, but he arrived during the last days of the year. She writes with regard to this: " Hans, the true and faithful, is here. All four of us are going to Zürich to see Semper's model. How splendid that it is finished! — the time will soon arrive for the performance." She had sent the King the new version of Walther's Prize Song to celebrate the New Year. Meanwhile Bülow, Wagner, and the King had all been deeply concerned about the condition to which Frau Cosima had been reduced by the agitation caused by Frau Schnorr. But it passed over, and she looked forward to new conditions with a certain pleasure. The relations between the King and Triebschen had never been better than at this moment, and we feel in every word of the King's how it was in particular his veneration for this wonderful woman that inspired him, as well as his love for the Master. Thus he writes to her: "Yes, dear friend, this year must be a year of happiness and blessing. How pleased I am at your visit to Zürich, how enchanted with your description of the model! I am sure that I have not made a mistake in the choice of Prince Hohenlohe. I regard Pfo.'s stupid outcry as the last throes of the contemptible dragon now trampled in the dust. It is impossible for me to describe the joy which now fills my soul. I am in rapture at the news of the Dear and Only one's arrival; I shout for joy."

Indeed, the news that Wagner was willing to come to Munich had delighted the King deeply. Wagner was the only friend whom he believed himself to possess and really did possess. This is sufficiently clear from his words: " During our recent correspondence from Nuremberg, you expressed the opinion that my brother might be an understanding, sympathetic friend to me. Oh, no, beloved friend, he is quite an ordinary person, without the slightest feeling for the exalted and beautiful. He is often hunting all day and is much in the company of my shallow, brainless cousins, and his evenings are largely spent at the Aktientheater, where he is in ecstasies chiefly over the ballet. I will shortly send word to Sophie that our Friend was delighted with her greetings. This will make her perfectly happy. I hardly ever have occasion to see her, but write from time to time. My faithful and devoted Count Holstein is the bearer of these letters. Sophie is a loyal, sympathetic soul, full of intelligence. Her fate has a certain similarity to mine. We both live amid an entourage in which we are not understood, we exist, as it were, in an oasis amid the sandy ocean of the desert."

At the beginning of the year he again began to enter into more detail about his artistic plans and writes: " Now to business: Very soon after my first interview with the Only one I contemplate charging Herr von Bülow with the establishment and direction of the new school. I quite see that the building of the new festival theatre is meaningless unless the school is founded, and yet I think it would be best to entrust Semper with the building at once. It will be some years yet before it is finished. Meanwhile the school will be flourishing and blooming, and the German nation, whose spirit has sunk so low, will at last recover confidence in itself, and the other peoples of the earth will pay homage to ours and bow before its spirit. We will bid the age of Pericles arise once more; we will not sit, like others, with our hands folded and sigh: ' If only we were the ancients! ' Thus

Bülow and Semper, those noble and eminent men who have so often been misjudged by the world, would have an honourable and worthy task, which they will never regret having undertaken. Would our Friend write to Semper in my name? I am so happy and confident of victory. Great things must happen this year. *The Mastersingers* will be performed, the school of music will be established, the foundation-stone of the great festival theatre will be laid. I am at one with my faithful friends in the cosy intimacy of Triebschen, I listen to the words of him whom I truly love, I listen in spirit to the new music from *The Mastersingers*. How splendid it is to become so intimate in thought! But when I awake from these golden dreams I feel this isolation most terribly."

The way in which Frau Cosima answers this letter, in which the King lays bare at once the depths of his great heart and the boldness and joyousness of his ideas, is characteristic. We see that he wants to create, to do something positive, and to introduce what he has created into an age to which he is for the time unable to contribute anything else. But Frau Cosima replies in her characteristically acute and sensible way: " When I hear your voice, I feel at once that I am in the land of fairy-tale and miracles, and as though, in spite of the gloomy winter clouds and the snow which covers everything, the weary earth must suddenly become verdant once more. You make endurance possible, and when I think of you, my whole store of worldly wisdom and experience suddenly seems to me to be worthless. The immemorial, miserable order of this world seems to me to be overthrown, my painfully won resignation seems all nonsense, and I feel as though our planet were still sending its message of light to the other stars and radiating consolation to them as they have so often done to me. I simply cannot tell you, dear lord, how delighted I was at the opinion of Prince Hohenlohe which you kindly communicated to me. His attitude with regard to the interview entirely justifies your exalted opinion, in the first place because he frankly consented to it, and in the second place because he asked for a postponement, though only a short one. This last request shows that his intentions are sincere and that he knows that serious relations are in question here, not mere

251

capricious, passing inclinations. Though I well know that the nobility has sunk low and that the present kind are decadent and unworthy of their forbears, yet I have always been of the opinion that a man of lofty ideas and independence of thought is more readily to be found among them than among the bureaucratic, quill-driving bourgeoisie, which at best produces only parvenus. May Heaven grant that Prince Hohenlohe prove a real aristocrat, such as German history has produced in plenty: an upright man of unbiassed judgment, honouring and loving his King. — Testimony is now pouring in on every side against the unfortunate Grand Vizier Pfo. He has managed his affairs so well that he has not a soul on his side."

In contrast with all these political questions she goes on to speak of *The Mastersingers*: " If only, dearest friend, I could send you the wondrous strains, if only I could tell you, too, how blissfully this morning dream is unfolding itself! It is like a soft musical radiance. In this soft, sunlit transport one does not know whether one is listening to light or seeing sound. As the curtain falls (just as in the third act of *Lohengrin*), the whole of old Nuremberg is astir amid the pealing of bells, it is as though the old houses themselves were moving off in solemn procession. I think that on hearing this the heart of every German must leap and quiver in his breast for proud joy and splendid consciousness of his heritage. And then, the delicacy of the musical detail is so subtle that I can only compare it with the wondrously dainty arabesques of the tabernacle in the Church of St. Sebald, which Master Adam Krafft supports with such calm confidence, just as here Master Sachs supports a far greater wealth and adornment of music and poetry."

Then once again she becomes a true woman and describes her journey to Basel: " It was my husband's birthday on the 8th, and I seized this occasion to convince myself of the state of his health. Thank God, it has improved, the fever has abated and he can attend to his work. During the next few days he is playing at Freiburg im Breisgau and then at Baden-Baden, at the desire of Princess William of Hesse, who is said to have complained bitterly that she never heard good music there, whereupon Hans was written to. I am always a little scared by the manners and customs here, and in order to make myself feel a little more at home I go to see the Holbein drawings: I feel better among their austere yet cheerful German faces. Since *The Mastersingers* that type has become so familiar to me, I might almost say that I feel a kinship for it. God! How grateful I am to our Friend for all this! I can say, like Eva to Sachs: ' *Was wäre ich ohne Dich* (What should I be without thee)? ' It seems to me as though, without him, I should never have come to life at all, or that I should have had no more than an insignificant existence. It is he whom I have to thank for all the emotions which elevate and console. I know no distress for which I have not found alleviation in his mind. There is only one thing which could cloud this happiness — his own fate. But now that you have appeared, I know no real sorrow. How gladly I send him to you, august friend! Otherwise the thought that he is leaving Triebschen would be horrible to me, I never want to think of him again as out in the world. He must remain in the woods, at his loom. But when he goes to you, he is soaring upwards to his star."

Next she goes on to speak of Prince Otto. " What you are so good as to confide to me about Prince Otto, beneficent friend, is entirely in harmony with the impression made by his face. I remember, too, that when our Friend returned from Hohenschwangau, what he told me was not very edifying. My wish was father to the thought; I had imagined that in order to please his royal brother he would end by collaborating with him, not from any right impulse or enthusiasm, but out of sincere good intentions. This was expecting altogether too much, and so I have to think of you as quite alone. I have a lively recollection of your appearance at the concert at the Odeon, which you attended out of kindness to Hans and at which I was able to observe, from not too far away, with what patience and long-suffering you were endeavouring to convey some impression to the cousin who accompanied you. It seemed to me to be a labour of Hercules."

In short, this correspondence forms, as it were, a running commentary on the Master's doings, and touches upon all that concerns the King himself. But at this moment the latter had entered upon a fresh stage in his life, which aroused general excitement and in uninitiated circles general delight. This was his betrothal

253

to the Princess Sophie, daughter of Duke Maximilian of Bavaria. On hearing the news Frau Cosima wrote briefly: " So you have found the thing for which I have so long been praying on your behalf from the depths of my soul: the woman who should understand you, love you, and be loved by you! A three-fold blessing on this year! " The King replied: " Your affectionate letter, assuring me of your sympathy in my happiness, touched me deeply. I believe firmly that you and our Friend will one day be delighted to make the acquaintance of my future wife. I love her truly and ardently, but our great Friend will never cease to be dear to me above all, all. This must be a year of good fortune. It has begun so well, it will bring us nearer to the great goal, and soon will the glorious work, begun amid so much affliction, be crowned with success. Oh, write to me soon about your life at Triebschen. Sophie charges me with her most cordial greetings to him and is deeply rejoiced at the thought of making his personal acquaintance. I will shortly send a photograph of my dear affianced bride."

The correspondence went on quietly. Frau Cosima reports as follows about the life at Triebschen: " As always, sunshine and your letter arrived together, a radiant pair, at Triebschen's quiet abode. Today it is overcast again. The *Föhn* blows eerily and the lake looks like the one in the story of the fisherman and his wife, who could not be satisfied, but must needs be empress. And so I summon up my yesterday's sunshine from within me, by telling our friend a little about the life at Triebschen, as he graciously requests. Our Friend is well, in spite of the dreadful storm which turned us into a regular swamp here yesterday, while one reads in the papers that there is skating everywhere! Apart from Düfflipp, with whom our friend reported that he was much pleased, we see and hear nothing at Triebschen. In the afternoon our Friend regularly takes his walk with the giant Russ, equipped in his horrible red waterproof boots, exactly like his ' Dutchman.' This is the only event of the day. *The Mastersingers* and the biography are accordingly making splendid progress. I venture to enclose a copy of Walther's dream, as he describes it in the scene of the competition. Our Friend lately came to the conclusion that it was absolutely impossible to let the same poem be recited twice in the same act. But it has got to be the same, and yet different, clear and concise; besides, it would have been repugnant to Walther to repeat the intimate happenings in Sachs's room in such a fashion, before the people and the Mastersingers. This difficult problem, which has been giving our Friend unusual trouble during the last few days, has, in my opinion, been solved with wonderful success. The second poem is the interpretation of the dream and a more vivid impression of it. It is the dream become the master-song. It is what he can and will tell the world about it, the way in which it has worked itself out in him between the blissful morning in the room and the festal day in the meadow. It is wonderful, too, how our Friend has varied the music; one does not know whether it is the same or different, and as one listens, one dreams. I have also enclosed Beckmesser's nonsense. Our friend will be astonished to find Hans Sachs's new strophe on this page. It was composed on the night of January 28, between two and three in the morning, after I had been talking to him for a whole day about the conclusion of the work. For, in his opinion, the drama was completed by Walther's poem, and Hans Sachs's great speech was not pertinent to the subject, being rather an address of the poet to the public, and he considered that he would do well to omit it. I made such a piteous face at this, adding that the words *Will ohne Meister selig sein* (I mean to be happy, Master or no) ' are an essential part of the characterization of Walther, that he thought it over, though he naturally remained of his own way of thinking. It gave him no rest all night, he wrote out the strophe, crossed out what I had suggested, and also added the sketch of the music in pencil. Such are our events at Triebschen, which are only interrupted and thrust aside by one thing — I mean, by the great news. A week ago, when, contrary to all his habits, our Friend left his study during the morning and came downstairs to me, I was thoroughly alarmed, because I know how important a quiet morning is to him; for it means concentration on his work. But I soon regained my calm when our Friend remarked, with a smiling glance: ' I have received a splendid message.' ' From Monsalvat? ' I asked. ' Yes, only guess what ' — and he read me the delightful words of the telegram. And now we joyously rummaged among our reminiscences. Our Friend remembered quite well having seen and noticed your august affianced bride (*die hohe Braut*). He described how Duke Maximilian had been enthusiastic about his *Lohengrin* — at least, so he had been told at the time in Zürich by a musical director from Würzburg. A host of pleasing impressions of every possible kind now gathered about the news, which visibly delighted him, and at last he said to me gravely, yet with a smile: ' I am certainly no stranger to this union.'

"We are now working at the biography every evening as busily as ants. ' Why, you write as though the Holy Ghost were dictating to you,' he said to me lately. ' Well,' I replied, ' there is something very like a Holy Ghost concerned in it.' We have come to where he finished *Tannhäuser*, and various meetings have been put on record, notably that with Spontini. The day simply vanishes, one does not know how. In the morning at the loom till midday, in the afternoon the Flying Dutchman's career through mist, night, and swamp, on his return the necessary letters, in the evening he dictates: this is how our Friend's day is divided up. I do not make so bold as to lay my sentiments at the feet of your future queen, adding that the happy woman who brings you happiness is sacred and dear to me, that I bless and praise the exalted being whom you have chosen, and that in this noble and touching union I see a pledge for the welfare and good of us all."

It is wonderful how in these letters Frau Cosima says nothing about what weighed so heavily upon her spirits, or about the grievous inner conflicts which agitated her both now and for years to come. Once more she saw the approach of a difficult moment, on which Hans von Bülow throws light in his characteristic fashion in his letters from Basel. He had soon come to feel at home there, and even the small society of the little patrician city was highly sympathetic to him now, especially owing to his friendship with Joachim Raff's brother-in-law, Dr. Merian, and his amiable wife; and when the negotiations with Munich seemed finally to have broken down, he had quite made up his mind to move to Basel with his family. But a move could not be contemplated at the moment, for, as he wrote at this time to

Bechstein: " Early tomorrow I am starting for Lucerne to join my wife. I am rather anxious about her: she is on the eve of her confinement and is in bed with a fever. A pretty state of affairs. For six months past I have been living *en garçon,* without family, hearth, or home. All my belongings are still in Munich, where I am paying rent up to the end of April. Long live King Ludwig II, who is responsible for all this *misère!* " He hurried to Triebschen, from whence on February 20 he was able to announce to Dräseke: " On Sunday morning (the 17th) at ten o'clock my wife was happily delivered of a healthy girl. Her condition is quite normal and causes me no anxiety up to date; but though I am hard pressed for time, I shall not return to Basel till there is absolutely no sign of danger left." At the baptism, which followed shortly afterwards, the child received the names Eva Maria, Émile Merian and her grandmother Marie d'Agoult acting as sponsors.

Meanwhile the King was pressing for a meeting with Richard Wagner, and in spite of his work on *The Mastersingers* the latter decided upon a short visit of a week to Munich, where he had a beautiful, moving, and momentous meeting with the King. This was the first-fruit of the new regime established by the Minister-President, Prince Hohenlohe. Frau Cosima sends the King the following account of Wagner's return: " I think you would like to hear how dear Sachs returned home to his work-room, and, since he is still very tired himself, I venture to make my little report, at the same time begging your kind indulgence, for I am still very weak myself. I travelled the short distance without the doctor's knowledge and went as far as Zürich to meet our Friend. I confess that I was extremely anxious. He has become so unaccustomed to seeing people that, when I heard of the crowd in his room at the Bayerische Hof, I was quite beside myself and thought that he was sure to fall ill there. Need I tell you what it was that kept him up? I met him in Zürich, when he was not a little surprised at my exploit, for I ought by rights to be confined to the house for another fortnight. It had been my intention not to talk at all, for I certainly found him fatigued; but it was no use. He had to tell me how he had found you and how you were in both health and spirits. He had to repeat your gracious greetings, to please me, and he wanted to tell me another fine and confidential piece of news, and so we talked a great deal, till I peremptorily called a halt and refused to answer any more; whereupon, to my delight, he fell asleep, and we reached Lucerne by moonlight. He laughed when he woke up, and found himself refreshed, and so we came to Triebschen, where we again talked a great, great deal. Today his first word was: ' I have a beautiful letter to write to Parzival.' I begged him to leave it alone for today and promised to write a few words. Now he is resting. He had a good night and is glad at heart. At peaceful Triebschen he will soon recover from his agitation, and nothing will remain but the beautiful memory of having seen his Parzival again. I had been through so much unexpected worry lately that I had looked forward to this visit to Munich with some apprehension. I had to say to myself that the measure of suffering is never full. Now that everything has turned out so well, the tears which I did not shed during the time of trial overflow, at once expressing and obliterating the deep pain which I endured. It has done our Friend good to see the Gracious one again. He said to me repeatedly: ' I am quite encouraged.' He also gave me a detailed account of a meeting about which he had been unwilling to write. How happy I am that it was possible, that it was ventured upon! This meeting made our Friend happy to the depths of his heart and filled him with the fairest hopes.

" In her first letter to our Friend, the ' *hohe Braut,*' [1] your august affianced bride, was so gracious as to think of me. May I venture to say to you, my dear lord, that I kiss in fervent affection the hand which she, the chosen one, so sweetly extended to our Friend?

" *Lohengrin* in June, how splendid! I said to our Friend that I should go raving mad shortly if I did not soon see and hear one of his works! But now it will all happen! Our Friend is well satisfied with his conversation with Prince Hohenlohe and sees in him a real support. I simply cannot say how this sets my mind at rest, and he had to laugh aloud when I exclaimed: ' And, after all, it has all happened so quickly! ' He said I must have quite forgot-

---

[1] The title of an opera planned by Wagner in his early days, the libretto of which was used by his friend Kittl for his *Bianca und Giuseppe, oder Die Franzosen vor Nizza.* — TR.

ten all our distress and sufferings, as he had almost done too, and, he hoped, his dear Parzival as well.

" So *The Mastersingers* could not be dealt with! It is heavenly, and I had rejoiced so much in anticipation of our exalted friend's delight. Well, summer will soon be here. Winter takes its leave tomorrow; it has been long, but it has borne splendid fruits, so there is more magic! "

The appointment of Herr von Putlitz as director of the theatre (*Intendant*) had also been discussed at Munich between the King and the Master, and he had declared his readiness to accept the position. Wagner entrusted Frau Cosima with the task of reporting upon him, for " our Friend wanted to start working at the score today, on the first day of spring, and accordingly asked me to take his place, adding the comment: ' I know Parzival had rather see me engaged in creative than in practical work.' " And she proceeds to speak of Putlitz, one of whose works, as we know, she had translated into French during the days in Berlin: " I really have no more to say about him than that he is a straight-forward, high-minded, and thoroughly cultured man, that he is passionately devoted to theatrical management, and that, for the drama especially, his appointment would be of advantage. He understands absolutely nothing about music, so far as I know; but he does not set up to be a judge of it, and indeed we have no need of a man who will favour our art. There is an old French proverb which says that, if one has God on one's side, one has no need of the saints. There is another and higher protector who sees to it that our art shall flourish and increase. It would there-fore be quite sufficient for the director to have in general a feeling for what is noble and great and a respect for the artists. I naturally cannot rate Putlitz so very high as a poet; yet his pieces are certainly not among the most insignificant produced today, and certainly they are not among the vulgar ones. I venture to hope that he will not make too unprepossessing an impression personally, for he is amiable and possesses delicacy of feeling. May God but grant that our little crew may be increased by an efficient person, so that we may start out more securely than ever on our voyage to the Promised Land. But how few are worth anything! In this connexion we may indeed say that ' Many

259

are called, but few are chosen!' I have nothing more to report today, except that he has just started the scoring and that the spring has given it its blessing — a gentle, light, warm rain has fallen, bringing fruitfulness to the earth, which is now putting forth blossoms, while *The Mastersingers* grows. The biography is also to be taken up again this evening. It is the lovely season of ardent growth and germination, all things are calling and beckoning to one another. During the next few days we intend to visit the Grütli. It was there that we went a year ago, when we drank of the spring and took our oath. It was there that we met 'Graf Arnold' and knew what it signified that we should meet him there."

The King's answer was full of rapture and enthusiasm at the meeting:

"Oh, my dear friend, those were unforgettable days that I spent while the Sublime one was here. To see him again, to talk to him again at last, after enduring the torments of a long separation, was a happiness such as can only be compared to the more than earthly bliss of the spirits of the blest. Though I could only hear a little of *The Mastersingers,* even this little was like dew from heaven. This is indeed a year of happiness, blessing, and redemption: the hostile powers of our crafty enemies are banished to their caverns, and men now begin to suspect that what we are doing is no common thing, and that the weapons turned against us and our work are shivered in fragments against the armour of our will and strength.

"The words spoken by Posa to his Queen in the solemn and transfiguring moment of his death, as his supreme legacy to his Carlos, for whom he had lived and died, have always affected me deeply: 'Tell him that when he comes to manhood he is to respect the dreams of his youth, that he is not to open the heart of the tender flower of the gods to that deadly insect which vaunts itself to be superior reason, that he shall not be led astray if the wisdom of the dust blaspheme against inspiration, the daughter of heaven.' I vowed to follow them faithfully. I may say proudly and with a pure conscience that I have kept my oath, neither shall I, nor can I, ever break it! How glorious will May and summer be. My Sophie sends me her most fervent wishes for

260

my truly beloved one from the depths of her heart. All happiness to you, dear ones! May God's angel spread his wings in benediction and protection over dear, cosy Triebschen and those who dwell in it. In a lucky year has Evchen been born! "

Meanwhile the King pressed onwards with his plans. After much confusion and many vicissitudes his arrangements with Bülow were settled, and on this account Frau Cosima had to return to Munich. And so she wrote the King another farewell letter from Triebschen, in which she described to him a lovely excursion on Palm Sunday: "We were in the most glorious spirits this Palm Sunday. At midday on Saturday we drove out from Triebschen and wandered along towards Beckenried by the same road as we had taken with our friend on May 23, recalling those beautiful hours. At Beckenried we missed the steamboat, so took a boat to Brunnen instead. The sun withdrew behind the clouds. This threw us into rather a melancholy mood. It was real weather for a farewell! That same evening we drove from Brunnen along the newly-constructed road to Fluelen, where we arrived in complete darkness. Soon afterwards the moon came out. I went to the window and cried aloud at the enchanting sight. The glittering giants stood like sublime, imperturbable spirits; it was as though they awaited my farewell greeting. You will hardly be surprised if I tell you that we talked of nothing but you, always saying the same, yet always different things. Anything else would have seemed to us a profanation. At Fluelen we heard a very curious night-watchman, who sang quite a different song from the usual one, and became a perfect *Meistersinger* nightmare to me all night long. In the morning our Friend, who was in the gayest of spirits, told me that he had dreamt of Beethoven, who had grown old and feeble and no longer composed; our Friend played him some things out of his works, and Beethoven was endlessly good to him. The sun was now shining; it was almost hot; we got into a little carriage and drove to Bürklen. How beautiful the road was! The meadows were gay with trees in the full glory of their blossom, the mountains looked down, good-humoured and splendid, into this lovely little world, we soon fell silent, and only at one point, where the living brook flowed across the meadow, the trees appeared

261

to stream with light, the mountains seemed transparent, and a little church showed itself on an eminence, its bells ringing out in alternation with the cow-bells, we cried: ' Oh, how beautiful! ' ' It is Palm Sunday today,' I said to our Friend. Last year we made our excursion on the day of the Passion. This year we are making it on the day of triumph, today the green branches are being distributed, today the people are acclaiming Him who was misunderstood! We were at Bürklen. The people, in their Sunday best, were on their way to church, I entered with them and prayed with all my heart for you, beneficent friend; my prayer was for the chosen of your heart and for our Friend. In Church I took the emblem of peace, the consecrated branches, and went out filled with thoughts of love. We drove back to Fluelen by the same lovely road. On the way we met a number of strange figures: they were Italians, poor, wretched *pifferari*. We were greatly struck by their bronzed faces and lean limbs, muffled in cloaks of a curious cut and patched together. They did not beg, but when our Friend beckoned to them and gave a few francs to one of the four, they thanked him with much emotion. The strange spectacle passed by us like a dream; the wonderful, eternally inarticulate resignation of these men devoid of everything is almost like the calm, sad gaze that one notices in animals from the most distant parts. ' God! And these too are men! ' said our Friend, with tears in his eyes. And I thought to myself: ' God grant them too a happy Palm Sunday! ' From Fluelen we took a boat to the Grütli; it became finer and more brilliant every moment, the Uri-Rotstock, the Priesterstock, the Mythen, and whatever all their names are seemed to have donned their most festal raiment. We came to the flower-bed where bloom the Parzival flowers, then to the three springs, of which we drank, renewing our sacred oath. For a long, long time we remained plunged in contemplation. ' It is at such moments as these,' said our Friend at last, gazing down from the height into the dark, blue water, as through a veil of flowers, ' that one creates and lives.' We left this holy world. The boat carried us to Brunnen. At Brunnen we embarked, and in five hours were back at Triebschen. Today the *Föhn* is blowing, and it is overcast — my last day here! Yet I return to Munich with hope in my heart. If you but knew, my King, how the sight of you this last time has strengthened and rejoiced our Friend! Surely we can have no more real difficulties, no real enemies. All the annoyances which are necessarily bound to confront us will be calmly brushed aside, like little thorny sprays on a glorious road."

She next comments on the forthcoming performance of *Lohengrin* and speaks with some decision about the choice of the singers. She makes one interesting remark which throws a singular light on the intrigues at the court theatre at the time: " This morning we heard that, in spite of the fact that Fräulein Mallinger was chosen as Elsa by our sovereign lord, in spite of the fact that our Friend wants her and that my husband has allotted her the part, Intendanzrat Schmitt cannot let her have it because, on the renewal of his contract, Herr Possart has stipulated that no parts are to be taken away from his fiancée, Fräulein Deinet! ! ! And so when the King has expressed a wish, this august wish is to be thwarted by a piece of clumsiness on the part of the Herr Intendanzrat, and this piece of clumsiness is to be binding upon us! I write this in jest, for I know that a saving word from our sovereign will set the matter to rights." But at the end of her letter she again spoke seriously about the questions of the day: " Once again there is talk everywhere of war. I have long since laid aside any views on the subject and have only continued through thick and thin to cherish the wish that our protector may be defended from annoyance. The whole of my politics and of my patriotism amounts to this. How finely you quote Schiller's words! Long live the dreams of youth! In them the most daring dreams have already found their realization."

Next followed the move to Munich and the beginning of work and rehearsals. It fell to Frau Cosima to arrange their new abode, which was also to provide the Master with a lodging. And in the middle of her work she writes to the King: " Ever since I have been here, I have been longing to tell you that here, within the walls of your city, I feel happy, and all painful memories are swept away by the thought that here, my beneficent lord, we are near you. Since the middle of April I have been playing Martha so exclusively that there could be no thought of settling down for a quiet moment, and to you I may not, will not, and cannot write in a hurry. While I was looking forward with real impatience to the moment when I could once more be mistress of my time, the dear tokens of your gracious favour were accumulating: the *Saint Elisabeth*, the beautiful picture of the Flying Dutchman, and today the flowers. You know, my exalted friend (*mein hoher Freund*), that I can thank you no more; I can only lay at your feet my heart-felt joy and my fairest hopes, together with my sentiments of loyalty. I have already ventured to send word to the Gracious one through Councillor Düfflipp that all is well here and promises to go on better. I think we are going to go through a beautiful and sublime experience; according to all appearances, things are rather more peaceful in this world of wolves. May joy and happiness but be yours! I simply cannot tell you how indifferent I feel to all other things, such as are generally called important. I have good news of our Friend. He is extremely busy, the instrumentation of the second act will soon be finished, and he writes that he will make it possible to be here by the 10th to hear *Saint Elisabeth*. I mean to finish and crown my hard work and arrange rooms for him in our house. There is something wonderful about our Friend. Anyone who has grown accustomed to his society, whose soul has become knit up with his, finds everything else so indifferent; the cleverest people seem to me as flat as a water-meadow since I have been intimate with his pure nature, which belongs to the heights where the glaciers are. I cannot read or think over anything without asking myself: What would he say to this? Or without recalling what he has told me about it. I tell you this, my beneficent friend, and yet it is to you alone that I can say it, because to you I do not need to say it."

Next she begins to gossip, especially about Peter Cornelius:

"Yesterday Peter Cornelius read us the libretto of his *Gunlöd*. In this work one can see plainly that, had it not been for the *Nibelungen*, it would never have existed. But this is not to censure it. If I wanted to find a fault in it, it would be that the characters are lay figures rather than flesh and blood. But the whole plan is noble, the songs are full of go, and the whole produces a fine impression, quite distinct from the usual run of operas. I have advised Peter Cornelius to make a copy of the libretto, and if my beneficent friend will allow me, I will venture to send it in a few days. I have been quite delighted with Fräulein Mallinger lately. She will be a beautiful Elsa and Elisabeth for us. God grant that the men turn out tolerably. On the whole, women are always more satisfactory, they work harder and are more easily inspired. My two eldest children have just come back from Berlin, where they have been spending some time with their grandmamma. The first thing they saw in my room was " the King " of Bavaria, whom they now regard absolutely as the god of our household. Our Friend will soon bring me Isolde, Evchen will continue to stay at Triebschen, as the long journey might do her harm. Hans Richter will take care of Isolde on the journey. Soon the whole household will be complete and in order. My life in Munich has received its dedication by this letter of today to our friend! I know, my dear lord, that everything will turn out in accordance with our dreams, hopes, and struggles."

In this, however, she seems to have been a little disappointed. But it cannot be said that the responsibility for this rested upon the King. He was extraordinarily kind to everybody, and to Frau Cosima too:

" My most heart-felt thanks to you for your letter, which delighted me greatly. How glad I am to know that you are here again, how happy it makes me to say that all that we have longed for so ardently and struggled for so hard is at last approaching its brilliant fulfilment! It is indescribable. Next Friday will afford us glorious hours. Oh, what a pleasure to hear your father's wonderful work again! How I rejoiced yesterday evening to see you at the theatre, dear friend. You, too, I am sure were not particularly edified by the superficial, trivial melodies, worthy of a street-singer."

He expresses himself clearly and firmly with regard to the allotment of the parts in *Lohengrin,* though he was unable to settle the matter quite so decisively as he had intended. But what he says about his longing for the country is significant: " It will be a real benefit to me to be able to leave the city at last. For the world, the spirit of the age which prevails at present, is horrible. People are so perverted and cankered with the pestilential ideas of modern times. This can lead to no good. And now another thing, quite in confidence. I recently heard of a remark of Herr von Bülow's which did not particularly please me: namely, that nothing was left to Bavaria but to belong to Prussia in the end. But let this remain quite between ourselves. I count upon him in the firm confidence that he will think of nothing but the furthering of our artistic interest. I recall with delight the opinion which you expressed in your last letter to me about royalty and its importance. Alas, that such views are so seldom to be met with! I am not in general inclined to harbour grudges, am not of an irreconcilable disposition, but I must confess that it goes against the grain to forgive the Müncheners their behaviour and to forget all the things of which they were guilty towards me, their lord and King, especially last summer. Their guilt is so great that neither repentance nor remorse can purge it. But let there be an end of it! I exclaim with Schiller: ' *Der Dinge Göttlichstes ist vergeben* (Forgiveness is the divinest of things).'" And he also speaks of the commissions which he has given to artists: "Yesterday I again received a fine cartoon from Kaulbach, representing Lohengrin's farewell. I am thinking, my friend, of sending you a photographic reproduction of this picture shortly. I am delighted that you are pleased with the 'Flying Dutchman' after Spiess. Echter is busy painting at his Tristan pictures, Ille at that realm of sagas the Edda. I am sure that if you had been present at the festival of the order which has just taken place on St. George's Day, you would not have regretted it. This antiquated and apparently out-of-date festival has none the less a deep significance. It is capable of arousing enthusiasm. All that is required is to infuse fresh life into it and ennoble it by the consecration of poetry." This has quite a different ring from what so many people have said about the King's conception of this celebration.

But Frau Cosima hastened to give the lie to the intrigues and calumnies hatched with regard to her husband's alleged Prussian sympathies: " The kind lines which I received today seemed sad to me and at the same time depressed me so much that I cannot help speaking a word of inexpressible gratitude and happy hope. Graciously permit me, my beneficent lord, to say what I must say: that Herr von Bülow *never* used the words of which you graciously informed us. When I say that Herr von Bülow has taken steps to sever his connexion with the Prussian State, thereby almost coming into conflict with his family, my august sovereign will graciously see that once again the favourite method of calumny has been resorted to. I have always told you the whole truth about everything — that is no merit, for I cannot do otherwise, and our Friend too, has certainly intimated to what an extreme decision he was prepared to proceed at one time. So when I tell you that these words were not used, I know that the Beneficent one will believe me. I shall say nothing to my husband. For he would not rest till he had found out the slanderer and punished him. The best punishment for these contemptible persons is always to ignore them. But how can such people exist, who can have the effrontery to repeat such things to our dear friend? Is all reverence lost? Does intrigue no longer know any bounds? Is it enough that they should enjoy doing harm to anybody for them to be at their low tricks again at once? But no more of this. Ah, the malice of this wicked world! But I cannot thank you enough for having informed me of this with such kind confidence, and the best way in which I can express my gratitude is to swear by all that is sacred to me, by our Friend, by my father, by my children, that he did not say it.

"I did not know that I could have been present at the celebration of St. George's Day, and so I refrained from expressing my wish. Now I deeply regret that I was not there. My beneficent lord, how I understand the mood reflected in your letter of today! My heart turns cold when I think of last year. I know that these feelings have nothing to do with forgiveness. God! The wickedest people are really only to be pitied, and my wise motto is: 'Blessing to the good, pity for the wicked.' But there are certain experiences which cloud the whole soul's horizon. God grant that you have not reached the same pass as I unfortunately have. For you, my King, were able to help, and you have helped. 'The King before all,' as the old Spanish poem says. It has always been my lot to look on and see to what grief people come in the end in spite of all their submissiveness and forgiving spirit; may our dear lord's holy angel preserve him from this. Men have no reverence for anything; indeed, all feelings of honour have become so foreign to them that they no longer understand the poets who have given the highest poetic expression to these sentiments. Thus, for example, the works of Calderón have simply perplexed people here. They gape at them and would smile were it not for the weight of centuries that lies upon them and will not allow them to be turned to ridicule. People comfort themselves by saying that they are not suited to our age! No indeed! Soon they will have advanced so far as to say with Falstaff: ' What is honour? Can it set to a leg? ' God-forsaken world! But this is only the surface. It was in our day that our Friend was born and you, Glorious one! Is not that a fine consolation? What do we care whether these two stars hang over a hapless world? They shine, for all that! "

Meanwhile Wagner too had arrived in Munich again, and the King was bent upon speaking to him, at least on his birthday. It is touching to read how modestly he mentions his wish: " I should be very sorry if I could not see him on his birthday and express to him in person my ardent wishes for his good fortune and happiness. I quite understand that he does not like his quiet to be disturbed. But if he really has it so much at heart, he could retire to the friendly seclusion of peaceful Triebschen again immediately after his birthday. Ah, it would be hard not to be able to greet him on his birthday: but so be it, in God's name, if it is really for his good! But the renunciation would be a terribly heavy blow for me. Yet once again let his will be done." And he adds: " I look back with joy and pride on May 22 of last year. Oh, could I but see you again at last! "

This birthday of Wagner's was particularly fateful, and it is charming to see how Frau Cosima celebrated it. " For about an hour past I have been in the little cottage, and mean to inaugurate it today by telling you, Exalted one, that our Friend has arrived. I am setting out the presents here which I am giving our Friend, first the piano and then the little trifles. Early tomorrow morning Senta and Elisabeth go to the Bayerische Hof. The former will recite the first three stanzas of a poem by Walther

von der Vogelweide: *Maienwonnen (The Raptures of May)*;
Elisabeth will carry a little basket of roses. I shall wait for our
Friend here, and if our gracious sovereign does not command
him to wait upon him before about one o'clock, I shall be able
to show him the little display that we have made here, and give
him my birthday greetings. I only venture to say this because
Councillor Düfflipp told me that the time of his visit to Berg
had not yet been fixed.

" My dear friend, you were so gracious as to think of me
today. How happy this has made me, how I thank you — your
friend, faithful till death! May I here bitterly bewail to your
sympathetic soul the reason why I am not coming. Since the
spiteful gossip of which I was the subject, and the malicious reports disseminated about me by that wicked woman, I have become nervous and hesitating. I know that not a soul believed in it,
but it has made me feel embarrassed. I was conscious of this
when I sobbed so bitterly that morning at Triebschen. I owe it
to you, above all, my gracious friend, to renounce anything
which might give rise to the slightest talk. To you I complain
bitterly of how hard the sacrifice will be for me today. Yesterday,
when Councillor Düfflipp mentioned the audience that had been
arranged, great tears rolled from my eyes. Forgive me in your
pity, my gracious friend! A year ago I had the good fortune to
see you. Today I must be content to be present in thought between the two beings to whom I joyfully make any sacrifice of
my own pleasure. At one o'clock I shall return to Munich; if
you will leave me our Friend till then — for he arrives at eleven
o'clock — I kiss your dear hands in gratitude.

" Our Friend looks well, but I think he can and may stay
here a little while. The utter loneliness of Triebschen is not
good for him; he becomes soured, and I am firmly convinced that
he will be able to work here. At any rate, you will see him
and settle everything in the best and most splendid way.

" Councillor Düfflipp brought me some rhododendrons and
lilies of the valley from my exalted friend. They are still blooming beautifully in my room, which is entirely filled with gifts
from the Gracious one. As I look at the sweet, fragrant things,
I cannot help thinking of the meadows near Triebschen, and how

full they were of glorious flowers last year: they knew that
Parzival was approaching! Today it is gloomy, but there are days
when one does not need sunshine. The exalted lady (*die hohe
Frau*) was so good as to send me her friendly greetings. But I
entrust my cause to you, my dear lord; you will find the most
beautiful things to say to the sweet Princess from me, so that
she may know how sacred and how dear she is to me."

Meanwhile, however, a difference of opinion arose between
the King and the Master about who was to take the part of
Lohengrin in the forthcoming performance. The latter had proposed his old friend Tichatschek, who was one of his faithful
friends, but of the older generation; and it must be admitted
that there was some justification for the King's dislike of this
singer's external qualities and rendering of Lohengrin, whom
Ludwig represented to himself as an absolutely seraphic being.
Even Wagner himself had been absolutely horrified at the acting of this *tenore robusto* at the first performance of his *Tannhäuser*; for at the contest of song, where Tannhäuser shakes off
his abstraction and breaks into the melody "*Dir, Göttin der
Liebe, soll mein Lied ertönen* (Thee, goddess of love, my song
shall hymn for ever),"[1] Tichatschek considered it a brilliant
inspiration to advance towards Elisabeth's throne, and, so to
speak, roar his hymn to the goddess of love into the unfortunate
lady's face. But though in this matter the King was justified in
giving expression to his æsthetic scruples, the Master was true
to the sentiments of loyalty and the obligation by which he
imagined himself to be bound in memory of the days at Dresden.
Frau Cosima was highly alarmed at this conflict and tried, so far
as she could, to act as mediator.

"The Master is going, Sachs is returning to his workshop;
may all the good gods accompany him, the dearest among dear
ones! May I now lift up my voice as though from far, far away,
may I be allowed to find in my exalted friend's graciousness to
me an excuse for approaching him invisibly and speaking to
the Gracious one as though I were a spirit? I want nothing, my
King, I am striving to obtain nothing, I wish for nothing. With
our friend's departure the die is cast, and all that you decide is

[1] *Tannhäuser*, I, ii.—TR.

sacred to me and will always be so. In this inward consciousness I venture to place the situation before the King: Hitherto you have been our protector, not only against the enemy, but also against fate itself. It was our sweet pride that we were allowed to endure so much in common with our royal defender, that we found in his heavenly patience and indulgence the power of endurance and the duty of perseverance. It is a hard fate for our Friend, my dear lord, a hard thing for him that he has no performers for his works. Perhaps in the whole history of art there is no other example of such a gulf between creator and creatures; he growing constantly more godlike, they constantly more bestial. But how is he to bear his fate if we do not help him, we who love him? If you lose patience, Only one (*Einziger*), how is he to keep any, how is he to continue to hope? Certainly, my gracious lord, you are right. He [Tichatschek] is wooden and stiff in his gestures, I admit, perhaps even repellent to those who are not ready to abstract themselves from the rendering in order to give themselves up entirely to the musical impression. Ah, my King, we suffered with you. None the less we have ventured upon it. There is nobody better in existence. Niemann horrified me when I saw him in the part. Nachbauer does not sing any of our Friend's music. So there remained Vogl. Very well, he will not run away, we can always fall back upon him. It was perhaps expecting too much of your exalted benevolence, my gracious friend, charitably to endure with us the great faults of Tichatschek's rendering, in a passage which one ought and wants to enjoy. But, dear lord, it is to yourself, to your own indescribable goodness, that you owe it, that, without speaking a word, our Friend and I have felt ourselves at one with you, the Beneficent one. Your friends might surely be forgiven for being conscious of your mingled pleasure and pain. But now the sheep are without a shepherd, the King does not favour the performance of *Lohengrin* with his presence! How sad, how dreary, how meaningless it will be to get up this performance for the benefit of the Müncheners, which was not what was intended! Had I heard that we were to submit, I would have ventured, dear lord, to beg you to come here, in order to attend the first performance. But since, alas, alas, it has so happened that there had to be a

sacrifice on your side for our cause, I would have said: Make
the sacrifice. I would go further, and say, a sacrifice for our royal
master himself; for he could not censure and punish his Friend
— so sorely tried, so highly honoured — for the choice of but
one singer, that the obtrusive crowd might look on uncompre-
hending, astonished, and alarmed. But God forbid that in this
matter I should offend, even with the best intentions. Our Friend
is still away; my husband, as is his duty and obligation, will still
conduct the work, in case the management commands a performance with Tichatschek. I will witness this strange proceeding
alone and try to understand the reason for this trial. I know,
my dear friend, that, whatever it may be, it can only be accompanied with eternal gratefulness to you. How could I listen
to the strains of *Lohengrin* without my heart going out in exultation to you, beneficent guardian spirit, whether you be near
or far. It remains the saddest thing in my eyes that the recent
rehearsal made an unpleasant impression on my dear friend.
I myself was touched and delighted. I had got over the singer's
gestures, his voice gave me pleasure, and then the whole thing
overwhelmed me. The character of the individual performer was
lost. Perhaps while listening to such things I see too little, and I
would give all my pleasure for you, dear lord, not to have had
this disappointment. It is sad, noble protector, the divine work
will now be distorted, all the Master's hopes are as good as
destroyed, this performance of *Lohengrin* is like a drooping,
withered bud in our lives. For what is it to us that the people
are enchanted with it — as, I hear, they are — if you have suffered? But what is the use of these lamentations? Ah, graciously forgive a sorrowful heart. When I read Councillor Düfflipp's letter and saw our Friend's quiet, kindly resignation, I
felt as though I should never know joy again! As though this
were the first separation between us and our lord, as if we could
have desired anything that was not pleasing to the Dear one!
The trouble to which our Friend had so cheerfully put himself, out of consideration for his only prop and stay, thrown
away, lost, squandered! How cruel are the gods! They have
robbed you of a long-desired pleasure, and us of our sole reward after trials so long endured. In such a frame of mind as

this, what am I to say about the glorious bouquet? The roses of wonder were equal to the wonder of the roses! I received them, all blooming, as fragrant bearers of a lovely message, they spoke to me of the joy which awaited us all; but now I look at them sadly. They are still the same, as beautiful and fragrant, they still bear sweet witness to my lord's graciousness, and yet it is a melancholy glance that falls on them — where you, my King, strew roses for us, fate lavishes thorns! And as I looked on them in their beauty, I thought of the long pain of parting, and then of our struggles, our joy at the imagined victory, the happiness of performing the divine work before our lord, and involuntarily the words of the Greek poet came into my head: 'But when the godhead meditates treachery, who shall escape that is born of mortals? Who so fleet-footed as to evade it with fortunate haste?'

"My gracious friend will take these lines in good part. Yesterday I dedicated to him all the emotions aroused in me by the glorious work. Now I send you, the Exalted one, the greetings of a sad heart, loyalty makes joy and sorrow sisters."

The King was in an equally melting mood. But it must be said that his antipathy for Tichatschek was quite as well justified as was Richard Wagner's chivalrous intervention on behalf of his friend of past days. It is touching to see how the King pours out his heart to Frau Cosima about this episode, which was in itself so insignificant:

"The night is already far advanced, but it is impossible for me to retire to rest without pouring out my heart to you today. I triumph and exult in ecstasy, once again I adore the mind that created this work. I feel today as I always do after enjoying a work of our great Friend's. It is hard that I must go on living, for I feel as though I had beheld the bliss of God. Several years ago I said to myself that I should like to live to see the completion of the *Nibelungen* and then die in ecstasy after the performance. Now, since I have known our Friend, I feel differently. Now I want to go on living as long as he does. All the more did I take this last sad catastrophe to heart. O beloved friend, about five years ago I heard our ever memorable Schnorr as Lohengrin. His singing, his acting, instinct with intelligence

273

—which, God knows, is certainly essential to music-drama — made a deep and powerful impression upon me. No wonder that I simply could not bear Tichatschek, not to speak of Bertram Maier's croaking voice and his acting. The punishment with which our Friend threatens me by his departure is too severe. I may say that I have not deserved it. For I may boldly assert that it is my steadfast love and loyalty, my enthusiasm for his works, that, as he himself admits, has saved him. No, dear friend, nothing must or shall estrange us. So many things are often distorted by subordinates, with the best intentions. Now I beg you urgently and pressingly to try to persuade our Friend to come back again at once. Oh, if he only knew how I am suffering from his absence! It is too much, too hard, to be borne with equanimity. Oh, do write quite soon. If you only knew how deeply each one of your letters delights me! And now yet one more wish. I understand, to my joy, that you want to move into the little house on the lake. It is ages since I spoke to you; I long to do so. Tell me whether you, too, do not think it would be a good thing for me to pay you a visit there. I consider this very necessary, in order to make such unhappy misunderstandings as have just occurred impossible in future. A real estrangement between you and me, or our Friend, can surely never happen, the world would fall to pieces sooner. But people are so glad to sow discord. Once again I beg you to call our Friend back again for me and to write to me soon. Forgive my haste and bad writing, it is almost two o'clock in the morning. The holy strains are still ringing in my ears. I cannot describe how the end affected me. The rapture of being able to hear a work of our Friend's cannot be compared with any earthly happiness. One simply cannot describe it."

Frau Cosima had been seriously perturbed, as much by her friend's departure as by the King's state of mind. She was well aware that if this mood were not dissipated, a separation between the two was indeed bound to occur. But it was also self-evident that she must defend the Master's departure to the King, for she and she alone understood it, because she knew his whole nature. She did so in her most characteristic way:

" Today for the first time I ask myself what I am to say and how I am to say it. Usually when I write to you, my emotion flows in an even stream, which has a source and a destination. Today my soul is torn by feelings of the most varied description, as it was yesterday at the performance. The work itself seemed to me finer, more glorious, more incomparable, than I could ever have imagined. I was unspeakably delighted at the success of the performance, at my husband's fine conducting, and, above all, at your joy, my dear lord. But then once more a bitter pang of pain shot through me. Our Friend was far away in the distance, sad, though composed. This clouds all my joy, and I feel in my soul how calamity never ceases to prevail over the happiness which our Friend reveals to us in so wonderful a way! Now comes your beautiful letter, and I sit sadly musing, a picture of helplessness. For this is how the matter stands, my beneficent friend. When our Friend was so ill and wrote to his sovereign that he wanted to stay at Triebschen, I wrote and telegraphed to him that he must not do so. Contrary to my usual practice with him, I said that he must do violence to himself and come to you, for you were longing for him. And so he came, feeling not at all well, but inspired solely by the wish that his presence might give you pleasure. As circumstances would have it, he scarcely had the good fortune to see you at all, my King. It was only through his interest in the performance of *Lohengrin* that he could show the Exalted one how he loves him. For in his state of health not even for a god himself would our Friend have undergone the annoyance of having any dealings with the authorities at the theatre. For your sake he did so with pleasure and enthusiasm. The general rehearsal arrived. Had our exalted friend seen fit to summon our Friend to him and kindly inform him that Tichatschek had produced an antipathetic impression upon him, our Friend would certainly have managed to enter into the feelings of his royal protector; he would willingly have acquiesced in everything, and his wounded heart would have felt no injury. But we had scarcely left the rehearsal when the Councillor's letter arrived. Our Friend had started on his journey, I wanted to go to Starnberg myself to carry him the discouraging message that his august friend had rather give up the performance of *Lohengrin* than go to it if

275

Tichatschek took part in it. I was unable to go, but sent a friend, who reported to me that Wagner was well and calm. On Wednesday our Friend came to see us. My first question was: 'Where is Parzival?' 'Parzival is gone, and I am going away.' We begged him to stay another day, and he consented. We spent the Thursday with him at Starnberg at a farewell dinner, at which the children were also present. I wrote my letter to you, my dearest lord. We packed up our things and took our friend back to Munich. In the evening we received Councillor Düfflipp's letter, conveying the royal command that Vogl and Fräulein Thoma were to take over the parts. You know, my dear friend, what a royal command means to me. My husband made his arrangements on the spot for the performance to take place in two days' time all the same. Our Friend was silent. I asked him not to start on Friday, as it was an unlucky day. With the kindness which I know so well, he complied with my request, and while my husband spent the whole day at the theatre, I tried to distract and cheer our Friend. . . . He was deeply depressed, and asked himself why these intimations, which came in the form of a royal command, had not been made to him personally, in a kind and friendly way. He felt himself to be superfluous — to some extent, indeed, a nuisance — he wanted to go, and I could say nothing, for I understood him. He was sincerely cheered by my husband's resourcefulness, and when, later in the evening, the latter reported that the opera would go quite well with the altered cast, a load was removed from his heart, and from mine too. He left early on Saturday in dull weather, and I always watch his departure with a heavy heart. He resigned himself to his fate. He wrote a few appreciative words to the orchestra and chorus, refused the satisfaction of a letter from him which Tichatschek had demanded and in which he was to have expressed his satisfaction with the performance, but commissioned Councillor Düfflipp, who had borne himself discreetly and with the utmost consideration during the whole of this delicate episode, to say a few kind words to him on his behalf. My husband soothed the feelings of the two singers whose services had not been required, and went on with his business as though nothing had happened. And, as a matter of fact,

KING LUDWIG II OF BAVARIA

nothing had happened. The royal will had been fulfilled, as in duty bound, the Master had been present at the rehearsals and had then withdrawn to his refuge to work. Tichatschek and B. Maier gave it out that they were suffering from hoarseness, and so all was well, and nobody was sad but I! And so I am still. I know why you acted as you did. You need not explain any· thing to me, even if, in your boundless goodness towards me, you wished to do so. I will only beg you graciously to put yourself in my place — in our place. While all that we were desiring was merely to carry out our glorious friend's will, suddenly, like a thunderbolt out of a fair sky, comes a royal command conveyed by the secretary. It was hard, my gracious lord, for it was undeserved. Tichatschek had given us great pleasure by his splendid voice and the characteristic quality of his singing. But a word from you to our Friend would have sufficed, and our Friend would happily have stayed here. He bowed to the fate which dogs him. In my opinion, beneficent friend, we should leave him in peace; but I will do what is pleasing to you. If I am fortunate enough to see you again, you will permit me to ask the Exalted one in what form I am to tell our Friend that he is to return. With regard to a meeting with you, my gracious lord and friend, I think that we could come together as follows: I cannot retire to Starnberg altogether, for the rehearsals for *Tannhäuser* do not permit my husband to be entirely absent; but I would stay there for a time. If it were possible for me to be presented on that occasion to the exalted lady who is to be your bride (*Ihrer hohen Braut*), I should esteem myself happy. You know very well that I ask for nothing and willingly renounce everything. I only fear lest a meeting between our exalted friend and me — simple and natural though it seems to me — might excite ill-natured· comment. Not for the highest happiness in the world would I cause you, my dearest friend, even a shadow of uneasiness. I had rather wait till our hour comes. But it goes without saying, gracious friend, that if you find an expedient, I shall respond to your kind summons. Alas, I know very well that people would gladly sow discord. As early as March certain people were saying quite brazenly that Wagner might come if he liked, but he would not see the King."

277

This letter shows this remarkable woman's full elevation of mind. We can feel between the lines of it a slight trace of the most subtle humour — the same humour which prompted her to say, in the words of Evchen: "*Was ich mit den Männern für Müh' doch hab'* (Ah, what trouble I have with men)!" But her chief object was to defend the Master and to justify him, without doing so in so many words. And she succeeded to the full. Amid the critical conditions of Munich, subject on all sides to the scrutiny of unfavourable eyes, she knew how to go her way firmly and confidently, at the same time showing the King that she ought not to pay her respects to him anywhere but in the presence of his affianced bride. And she did indeed succeed in smoothing over the painful incident and re-establishing the connexion between King and artist. She did so by communicating a letter of Wagner's to the King: "Today I received a letter from our Friend. He says: ' On my arrival everything produced on me a peculiarly strange impression of silence and tranquillity. A silence that can be felt lies over foolish Triebschen. Only Russ was quite beside himself with joy at seeing me, and Koss. The beasts tumbled frantically over and over each other, quite crazy with affection. Now everything is going on quietly again, and on Sunday I enjoyed a deep and solemn silence, which really affected me, and prompts me to deep, mild introspection. Nothing has happened here, nothing at all. The peahen is sitting, and suffering sorely. She had laid her eggs in a remote corner of the garden, so that she is wet through with the everlasting rain. She only comes once a day and demands a hasty meal, then off she goes again to her sitting. So today, since it is raining so pitilessly. I have had an old table put over the creature, which serves as a roof. The doves are getting on well, there is much that is already recognizable, and at any rate all of it will soon be reduced to a little form and reason. Today to work again. Tomorrow, with God's help, I think I may get back to the poor score again. It is a queer thing: this very scene of the thrashing had already got so fearfully long that it seemed as though it would never end. Now it is behaving in exactly the same way again. They have got to stop thrashing! . . . Early this morning came the King's letter. I hope and believe it all and, especially, desire it all. During my rainy journey my imagination was still busy with *Lohengrin*. And so I have let it go, it no longer concerns me. The swan which once led me on to my hard life-and-death struggle has disappeared, as by a miracle, below the surface. It now comes into *Parsifal*. All that flutters before me now is the dove. No telegram arrived. I am almost afraid that something may have happened to upset things. Why do I hear nothing yet? All is so silent, so silent; how strange! I cannot really say that I am melancholy; on the contrary, my heart is warmed by a fine confidence; side by side with much that is sad, I am conscious, on the whole, of much that is good, and, what is more, that at the decisive moments I have acted rightly, whatever the cost. Farewell.' Thus writes our Friend. I like this mood of his very much. I think that for the present we will leave him to himself. After the silence will come the time of revival, and then we will celebrate it splendidly and well, shall we not, my gracious friend? " The King understood this letter and answered with equal delicacy: " This morning I received your dear letter shortly after waking. I had just been dreaming about an interview with Herr von Bülow, who advised me to have *Lohengrin* performed in a hall without any public, since the latter had behaved most tactlessly on the previous day, by hissing and shouting to such an extent that it had hardly been possible to play the Prelude through to the end, and a lady had made so bold as to sing to the public from her box offensive and satirical verses about me, set to waltz tunes, for having allowed such a work to be performed. Such was my strange dream. What you tell me about our beloved Friend's state of mind at present makes me sad. I wrote to him lately from the Hochkopf, where he once spent a few days in quiet seclusion and abandoned himself to the first painful impression caused by the death of our Tristan." He next proceeded to discuss the resources of the theatre with great technical knowledge and fine discrimination and, above all, to sing the praises of Hans von Bülow: " I am grateful to Herr von Bülow from the depths of my heart for his tireless energy, industry, and zeal in following out my most passionate desire, and for all the rest of my life my memory of the performances of *Tristan*, and of this last one of *Lohengrin,* will remain with me indelibly. I know how much I have to thank Herr von Bülow for this and will never forget all that he has achieved. He has for ever won a right to my most heart-felt gratitude. I request you kindly to inform him of this. Cornelius's intention to write something about *Lohengrin* has given me great pleasure. I think he would succeed better with this than if he were to attempt any creative work. For these experiments of his seem, after all, to be nothing but weak imitations of Wagner's works." We see that she succeeded in overcoming the King's depression sooner than that of the Master, who continued to feel the after effects of this affair for a long time to come, and it was no easy task for Frau Cosima to make the King see this, still less to make him understand it. But in the attempt to do so she achieved one thing, in that his confidence in her found more and more marked expression, and his esteem for her delicacy of feeling greatly increased. Thus a few days later she wrote:

"Today I have received the second letter from our Friend, and I consider it my duty to convey the news to the Gracious one. It still has a plaintive note. Our Friend entrusts his peace to my keeping after the recent inward storm. If only I can, I will preserve it with pious fidelity, even as I love him. 'I cannot yet write to my Parzival,' he writes, 'for every word which might look like a reproach would be senselessly provocative; yet any complaint must appear in this light, and to write to him without complaint, after scarcely seeing him and yet losing so much time from my score, would again be senseless. You and you only can tell him all. I need tell you nothing; you know all and sympathize in everything. As for love, ah, it is certainly no longer any good. Consider my life, and how, each time I have avoided it, nothing comes of it but an increase of the deep-lying, disturbing influences which destroy all peace of mind. I am so despondent that now I no longer desire anything but that I may succeed in bringing the poor *Mastersingers* to its full consummation. That is all. Oh, I should have done better to spare myself this last sad journey.'" All he aspired towards now was peace, and he laid particular stress upon his anxiety about Hans von Bülow's health saying that, come what may, he must go and take a cure. On his way to St. Moritz he must pass through Triebschen, where everything could then be settled about *The Mastersingers.*

Frau Cosima next casts a glance towards Munich and the rehearsals of *Tannhäuser*, notes with her flashing and commanding eye what had been done so far, and then continues: " But if you only knew, dear friend, what disorder and lack of discipline prevail here. A whole week has been wasted for the *Tannhäuser* rehearsals because the Intendanzrat has given Herr Betz and Herr Bausewein leave, so that the general rehearsal cannot take place. My husband came home yesterday in despair. He is straining every nerve to carry out this difficult enterprise to his sovereign's satisfaction; but he is obstructed at every step. Whether from ill will, as many maintain, or from narrowmindedness, there is, at any rate, a lack of really serious application. He writes out everything with the greatest accuracy. And now, among other things, an incorrect score has been introduced, yesterday he had the whole chorus about his ears, and in the middle of it all the Intendanzrat was heard to boast that he had the King behind him, and that when the betrothal festivities came round, he was going to be made intendant of the theatre and raised to the nobility; while, as a pendant to this, it was said that Wagner is in disgrace. I only tell our glorious friend this so that he may know how matters stand here, and that, if delays and postponements arise, they are certainly not to be ascribed to us. My husband makes light of it all, but the days are going by, and he is not supported by the smallest zeal or the slightest sense of duty on the part of the Intendanzrat."

Here those brilliant gifts which were able to manifest them-selves at Bayreuth in the form of such positive achievement were already clearly and surely in evidence. Not only, however, was she able to indulge in negative criticism, but, amid all the intrigue and mismanagement, she also insisted upon the positive results that could be arrived at through the King's will:

" Still, we have made a good step in advance. Yes, my dear lord, it is hard going, but we are on the upward grade. For instance, I am quite firmly convinced that my father's Mass would not have received such favourable notices from the press had not our cause found a refuge and sanctuary here. The whole tone has changed, and once the handful of vulgar intriguers here is got rid of, our art will come into its own. I had quite a shock today when I heard some inveterate Philistines talking of Semper's theatre with enthusiasm. I could hardly believe my ears.

"And so I call down fortune and blessing upon you. Do not weary of fighting at our side, for we have truth in our favour." And she concludes with a charming picture: "My Senta has just had the good fortune to see the King in the procession. She told us a great deal about it and maintained that she at once recognized the visitor to Triebschen." She says of Wagner: "He has many, many friends here, as everywhere. God bless both him and you, my dearest lord. I cannot separate you both in my heart, it seems to me as though the soul would be extinguished in you and him alike if I were to think of the two of you in isolation."

In her next letter she went on to speak of the King's dream of *Lohengrin* in the concert-hall: "Your horrid dream, which you so kindly described to me, drew a good, hearty laugh from me. The experiences in connexion with *Tannhäuser* in Paris, and much that we have gone through at the hands of the public here, became wildly confused in your fancy, and so that extraordinary vision arose, which must certainly have been a perfect nightmare, though it cheered my spirits. For the popular saying that, when one dreams of a wedding, a death takes place, and vice versa, is certainly connected with the primeval wisdom of the early seers. And does not life teach us daily that laughter brings forth tears, and tears laughter; and does not what takes place in dreams happen just as truly as what comes to us in the dream of life? And now that you have already borne the suffering of this horrid scene, dear friend, we ought to be able to assume, with the people and the wise men alike, that our performance of *Lohengrin* today will be beautiful and full of solemnity."

And in fact, thanks to Bülow's brilliant conducting, the performance was a fine and gratifying one. She gives the King an exact report of it, as well as of a whole number of theatrical questions. She takes Perfall's part and expresses the opinion that there must be one official to take the responsibility and introduce uniformity into the whole. She shares the King's interest in the theatre and manages to lay her finger on the weak place. She was indeed his adviser in this sphere, and in this connexion the King makes much the same impression, in many ways, as Duke George of Meiningen. " I was uncommonly glad when I heard that our dear lord had ordered several pieces of Calderón's. If only people here would play the roles even tolerably."

Next she goes on to speak of the King's projected visit to Paris:

" The rumours that you are going to Paris for the Exhibition are becoming more and more persistent. Though I do not know whether you have decided upon it, I should quite understand it and admire you for making this sacrifice to certain considera-tions. And in the end the sacrifice will have its reward, for in Paris one sees most clearly what the world is and what it wants. I do not mean to say that humanity is better elsewhere, but it does not make so obvious and brilliant a display of its desires and capacities; there everything finds frank and daring ex-pression: sensual pleasure, money, comfort, amusement, that is what people want and what they know how to provide as no others can. It is an instructive spectacle for the wise, but no atmosphere for idealists. Since I am on the subject of rumours, I will also add that I heard lately from a very well-informed source that Semper was to be invited to Berlin. It would really surprise me if people up there were suddenly to find out what is meant by art and take such a bold step. But I do not believe it, for I know Berlin conditions only too well." Thus in this letter she manages to draw the King's attention to all that she con-siders necessary, and above all to Triebschen, where once more Wagner was living entirely for his score, and rejoicing in the thought of his loved ones:

" There are only a few of these. Only a few have understood him, but these — we may proudly say it, my exalted friend — make up to him by their loyalty for the whole world. He knows it too. In his last letter he said to me that he would devote this

283

winter to the biography, the publication of his works, and *Siegfried*. Today he speaks of *Parsifal* (*"Parzival"*). We shall see it all yet, my noble friend. I wrote to him lately that it would happen to him as it did to Titian, who painted his finest work in his ninetieth year."

Besides this she was the best assistant to her husband and his works. She knew how to set forth his merits and services and also how to draw attention to his opponents, who were constantly hampering his work by their intrigues. But she is particularly concerned with the King's journey:

" Be so good as to allow me to send you a farewell greeting and to wish you with my whole soul what is best, fairest, and most happy. Naïve as it may sound, I thank you for undertaking this journey. I knew, without being told, how the Exalted one was feeling about it, and for the very reason that I am so far removed from all splendour or politics, obviously far from you, I feel myself justified in doing so, because I am perhaps the only person who can measure the sacrifice that you are making. I do not hide the fact, my King, that since this journey was spoken of, I have been uneasy. I can never get my anxiety out of my head. I had to do violence to myself to avoid mentioning it in my last letter. Though, strictly speaking, it is no business of mine, yet I feel justified in taking the most intense interest in it. Once again, my lord and King, thanks be to you for winning this victory over yourself. Ah, all the gay show there is so utterly indifferent to me that when people talk of the pleasure that awaits the King there, I can only say to myself: I know better. Only, as the King says, it is important, and perhaps even necessary; and since all the monarchs of the world are appearing there, any abstention would be interpreted as a demonstration."

During the interval the arrangements for *Tannhäuser* in Munich were to be perfected, and she gives a clear account of this too. She concludes her letter most exquisitely:

" Once again, a thousand times, a happy journey and a happy return to you. Although I shall not see you, I shall be waiting for you, my good lord. The heart has its own ways, it cares little about the senses, still less about time and space, while, on the other hand, it is troubled by things which it alone perceives, as though they belonged to its own special province. This is a mystery, but a blessed one. It lends me wings and enables me to soar above everything, and in the lowest depths it brings me peace. If it were not for the beauty of fidelity, how would one be able almost to smile at all partings, all limitations, all difficulties? Yesterday I wrote something of this to our Friend, whose society I none the less miss so much. Hail to you, my exalted friend, and hail to fair wisdom! Would that fate might give me occasion to prove what the being whom our Parzival loves is to me."

The King sent a beautiful reply to this beautiful letter:

"Though I am very much taken up at present with the preparations for my journey to Paris, I cannot help sending you before my departure, dear friend, a cordial greeting in return for your kind letter, which I received on the heights of my beloved Herzogstand, to give you my warmest and most heart-felt thanks. I am deeply touched by all the affectionate things which you say about my dear betrothed. Sophie charges me to give you her cordial greetings. Rest assured that you will find in her a true and sincere friend. I do not doubt that the World Exhibition will afford me much interest, but I think that after about six days one will be glad to come home again. Napoleon's acquaintance will be of value, and I am also curious about the Empress, about whom I have already heard so much. I scarcely think that she will be ' comparable to my Empresses of Austria and Russia.' "

But after his return from Paris he writes from Soiern:

"At last bright and beautiful days of peace and quiet reflection have come round for me again, such as I have never sought in vain on the mountain tops, with heaven's balmy, health-giving breezes blowing round me. What grateful peace, after such days of rush and world-wide bustle as I have just spent in the modern Babylon. And yet I do not regret the time I spent there. For amid much that was unpleasant, and even highly repellent, I have seen much that was interesting and beautiful. It was a real comfort to me when before my departure I received your and our Friend's last letters. These tokens of affection did me a world of good, for I only decided very reluctantly to leave my dear home and go out into that loveless

285

foreign land, which, though offering me much that was interesting, had no lasting attraction for me. I was filled with absolute horror by the bad pieces, corrupting to the morals and devoid of all intelligence, which I saw at the theatres. I find the French people, their language, and, above all, Napoleon's parvenu regime if possible more antipathetic than ever. The Exhibition has glorious things to offer, there is no denying that, it borders on the miraculous. I strongly advise you, my dear friend, not to miss it. I passed from six to seven hours in the Exhibition without feeling tired, and I inspected it very thoroughly. But what a comfort when once again I beheld the oak-trees of Germany, when the breezes of home blew about me, and the blessed mountain water refreshed me, after I had been forced to breathe bad air for a whole week and to drink lukewarm water, while the world of pleasure, with its atrocious language and infernal, senseless din, had disgusted me with Paris, which I should otherwise have found so beautiful and interesting! It saddened me to catch a distant echo of *Lohengrin* from the Bavarian band, and to be forced to hear it desecrated by being performed before that people. How I longed to be back in Germany! Yet I think with delight of an excursion to a castle called Pierre Fond [Pierrefonds], which quite reminded me of Mark's royal castle, as seen at the end of the first act of *Tristan and Isolde*." The King next praises the performance of *Tannhäuser*, criticizes what he had disliked in it, and affirms with deep fervour his loyalty and veneration for the Master. He concludes: " I read with interest Cornelius's essay on *Lohengrin*. But I find Porges's style far more attractive and shall look forward anxiously to his next article." There is something touching in the way in which he was able to estimate the faithful Porges's works at their true value and refused to be in the least dazzled by witty writings.

Frau Cosima's description of a church performance of the Palestrina mass is very fine: " I felt greatly comforted upon hearing that Your Majesty was in the church which I attended today, being for once unfaithful to the Basilica for Palestrina's sake. It was a most welcome proof to me that Your Majesty is restored to health, for which I thank God from the depths of my soul. I ought indeed to feel uplifted by this alleviation of my anxiety, as well as by the impression of peace in Palestrina's noble mass, not to speak of two cheerful letters from our Friend bearing witness to the best of spirits. He has found a quiet house with a garden, very quiet and retired; he has hired a piano and now means to set to work again. Yesterday he wrote to my husband about *The Mastersingers* and a performance of it at Nuremberg in the year 1867 under the conductorship of my husband, if that is agreeable to Your Majesty. He advised doing nothing about the art-school or any other enterprise. Nothing could be undertaken with any prospect of success in present conditions. Deeply as this grieves me, I cannot say that he is wrong."

And as a matter of fact fresh difficulties seemed to be offering themselves and fresh opposition to be arising. Perhaps these were connected with the foundation of the new paper which was now to appear upon the scene, and about which she writes: "During the last days of my stay in Munich I spent much time with Dr. Fröbel and convinced myself that he is worthy of all our Friend's sympathy and high esteem. Among many other things, he told me one that gave me particular pleasure: namely, that Prince Hohenlohe always speaks with such warm affection and devotion of his royal master, not merely saying what duty and necessity demand, but saying it with fire and fervour. It did me good to hear this, and it has raised the Prince higher in my estimation than if he had succeeded in uniting all Germany! I was careful not to speak to Dr. Fröbel about the tendency of the paper and did not even read his program, in order to obviate troublesome misunderstandings, but I informed myself as to the progress of affairs and was highly delighted that they were proceeding so flourishingly; I think our cause can go hand in hand with it: Fröbel is a straightforward and open-minded man. He was in my box at the first performance of *Tannhäuser* and I was delighted to see him so carried away. 'Now I understand,' he said, 'why these works require a royal protector.' This meant a great deal — the sublimity of the work, the wretched state of the nation, but, above all, the greatness of our protector.

"But I have not said a word about Triebschen. I greeted it

again as if it had been my home (' *In dir erwachten seine Lieder:* In thee his songs did once awaken ').[1] Our Friend had come as far as Winterthur to meet me. Unfortunately he was looking very ill. He again had to interrupt his work for a few days. I am now counting upon the continuation of the fine weather to restore him completely."

From Triebschen she now casts a glance at the King's life, especially at Hohenschwangau, where he was with his mother and her household. Life there was always pervaded by an inoffensive but very prosaic atmosphere. And so she says:

" I admit that it often makes my head reel to behold the creatures who are called to a royal station nowadays. It seems to me that there is only one thing that can sustain you, my exalted lord: the idea, the consciousness of the sacrifice which you are making. And why are you making this great sacrifice? In order to forward a great cause. Slight as the connexion may seem to be, yet this is so, and your great, noble, free spirit can find refreshment in the thought. If the King fulfils the duties which seem to him so painful and worthless, how much more are the people bound to stand in awe before his ideal life! I should like to say that our Friend is now sacrificing himself likewise; by contributing to Fröbel's paper, and meaning to contribute still more, he is descending from his royal elevation. He is doing this in order to teach people and attract them to him, so that we may find it easier to carry out our whole undertaking. Just so, beneficent lord, when you sacrifice yourself, you are opening up and smoothing the way. If we are to win through, we must enlist unlimited affection and be supported by enthusiasm. This calls for sacrifice, and that not only in the form of great, daring deeds, but in that of the most painful hourly self-sacrifice — an agony. Yet all men are condemned to it, and we have the strength to say to ourselves of our own free will: I will endure this and that for the sake of the one cause. I say this to you for your comfort, truly beloved lord, out of my deepest sympathy. There is a saying of Savonarola's which I have imprinted deeply upon my mind: ' He who is not willing to bear his cross with Christ will be forced to carry it with Simon of Cyrene. And the

---

[1] *Tannhäuser*, II, ii.—Tr.

cross consists of needle-points and accompanies every moment of our way. We fall beneath its weight, until we have the courage to clasp it to our hearts. Then our way turns heavenwards.' " It was a correspondence of quite a special kind that went on between this young and yet so experienced woman and the enthusiastic young man. She always knew how to guide him upwards and then to lead him back with a sure hand to practical things. But at the same time she succeeded in bringing to his notice in the right way all the needs arising out of Wagner's works and actions. She checked him where checks were necessary, and urged him on when it was necessary to expedite matters.

And now, at the beginning of September, Councillor Düfflipp appeared at Triebschen by the King's command, to discuss all outstanding questions with the Master. The meeting was a highly auspicious one, and the Master felt a deep confidence in him. But Wagner, too, would not hear of any undue haste: " Our Friend begged him to set nothing on foot, but again to think over all the reasons which he had given him, to consider the situation now that it had been accurately placed before him, and then to draw his conclusions. We parted on friendly terms, and I hope he will have nothing but what is good and beautiful to report from Triebschen." The most important thing was the foundation of the *Süddeutsche Presse,* which also met with the Councillor's entire approval. On this subject Frau Cosima writes:

" Fröbel's program has made a great sensation. I think that in the foundation of this paper is contained the possibility of a renaissance of the German spirit, and I therefore hail it with sincerely uplifted joy." But she could not rid herself of her anxiety for the King. " I am in constant anxiety, my exalted sovereign, because the great do not love you and are for ever conspiring against you. But the people love the King and put their confidence in him. May those who seek to loose the bond uniting the King and his people be for ever accursed! Oh, have faith in your people, my exalted friend, as we believe in the German people as a whole, and faith will be the seed of miracle." And she concludes: " When I consider that the betrothal of our sovereign coincides with the completion of *The Mastersingers,* that the school of music and the newspaper are also being founded, and that many popular misunderstandings have been cleared up, I feel all at once as though we might look forward to a splendid period of creative activity. Many sacrifices will of course be demanded of all parties. But how fine, how consoling is the bare possibility of such a blossoming-time! Be patient, dear King, for everything rests in your consecrated hands. Already I am floating away to the remotest spheres, delivered from the present, which at times weighs on me so heavily." The King thanked her most cordially for her letters: " Of all the letters of good wishes which I received on the occasion of my double celebration, yours and that of our Friend were the dearest. For they came from the two hearts which alone truly understand me (with the exception of Sophie) and by reason of this understanding love me truly and deeply. And the power of this love is unconquerable and eternal! " He spoke hopefully of the impending performances of *Lohengrin* and *Tannhäuser,* and above all, too, of the negotiations with Fröbel and Porges, who had been in view from the first as his artistic colleague. The King's interest in Wagner's works extended to the ways and means of making them comprehensible to the people. In this connexion even the minor contributors had also to be considered. He writes: " How I thank you for having conveyed to Cornelius the advice to write about *Tannhäuser* too. Porges will shortly send in an article on the first act of *Tristan.* I think I am not mistaken in asserting that Porges's work is the best and most competent which has yet appeared about our great Friend. What pure gold is to be found in his articles, by comparison with so much washy stuff, the bombastic spate of words of so many modern *literati!* And already he is triumphantly hailing *The Mastersingers* by anticipation."

Next came the performance of *Tannhäuser,* under the impression of which Frau Cosima wrote: " The Feast of St. Michael (Siegfried), the Slaying of the Dragon. The last letter which you so kindly sent me bears witness to such magnificent spirits that I felt completely reassured about many of the anxieties which nearly always have their origin in my heart. Once more

I felt with ineffable certainty that you have your own star, which overrules things for you, and which you follow. I understood and honoured you in all things! At the beginning of the *Tannhäuser* music I felt as if I were in a fairy-tale. You alone in your box, my father — the first who recognized this work and acted as its champion — at my side, my husband below in the orchestra, our Friend absent, yet near me in spirit, and at last living in peace and comfort, thanks to his protector's love; and, added to all this, the heavenly strains — I thought I was dreaming, yet I saw and heard it all! The performance was a fine one. I have just mentioned my father. He has been here for a week and is staying till next Wednesday evening. I cannot omit to mention that his highest wish is to be allowed to pay his most humble respects to his noble protector, who is so dear to us. I begged him not to have recourse to the official channels usual at courts, for I would venture to obtain this joy for him. I know that the King will approve of my feeling in this. My poor husband, who kisses the King's hand most humbly, is very unwell. But he is most happy to have the honour of being allowed to conduct the opera on the occasion of the performance in celebration of your betrothal. He will make a selection of suitable works. *The Mastersingers* will certainly need a good three months. But first it is necessary that the parts which have already been written out should be distributed to the singers appointed by our Friend, so that they may make themselves familiar with their difficult task in advance. Yesterday I was present with my father at the performance of *Lohengrin.* He is enchanted with the orchestra and says it is the best he has ever heard. Nachbauer is better than Vogl, but his unevenness makes me rather afraid. In the second act his voice comes out very brilliantly and effectively.— He is so good-tempered that when I made a few comments to him — as, for instance, that the ' *Heil, Elsa,*' ought not to be bellowed out, and that in these works the point is not to show off whether one has a high C or A or X and Z — he took it quite quietly. Things went splendidly yesterday, and again I was as much overcome as if I had never heard a note of our Friend's. After the first act I sobbed like a child, at the end of the second I was trembling, and by the end I was unable to say a word. You can imagine, my exalted friend, what a satisfaction it was to my father to see our Friend's works — which he succeeded by desperate efforts in getting performed amid obstacles of the most contemptible description and in the teeth of the whole press — now, under royal protection, and conducted by his own son-in-law, come out into the light in all their glory, amid triumphant applause."

Liszt was, indeed, in a singular frame of mind. We know that he was at Triebschen, that he was paying a visit to his friend after a long interval and discussing with him at length those deep and vital questions which affected him, as a father, quite as deeply as they did his daughter and the Master — and yet, like the consummate artist that he was, delighting in the " performance " of *The Mastersingers* — for he played right through the score, while the Master sang the vocal parts. The third act in particular affected him most deeply. At Munich he had celebrated his daughter's name-day at the house of his old friend Wilhelm Kaulbach. The great painter's daughter also succeeds in giving a most cordial and enthusiastic account of this beautiful and festal morning. It was in honour of Cosima and aimed, in the first place, at disarming all rumours that he was not on his daughter's side. She was most deeply delighted and encouraged; but her glance wandered back once more to the Lake of Lucerne. " Yes, Triebschen is beautiful, so calm, so grand, so varied, and the rooms are so nice and comfortable now. I have again spent a little time hanging, arranging, and grouping. Our Friend takes a daily pleasure in all the pretty things. By your love, if I may say so, you have made him a present of a whole past. He is now surrounded with tangible things which are so entirely his that one would think he had spent his life with them. Not once have I strolled through the rooms without belauding this miracle from the depths of my heart. Who was there to love him then? Yesterday, among the many friends who are here now, the Wesendoncks, too, were announced from Zürich. I advanced eagerly towards Frau Wesendonck, since everybody who has ever shown friendship to Wagner is precious to me. But I cannot describe the dismay which I felt. Such coldness, such an inherent indifference for all that is beautiful! As I went away, I thanked Heaven that our Friend is delivered from all those connexions and now lives for the one real person, his Parzival. I have heard nothing from Semper for a long time; but what Councillor Düfflipp told me about his forthcoming appointment gave me unspeakable pleasure. It is both profitable and honourable to a country to possess such a man. There is not a building in Munich, rich as it is in outward adornments, that can hold a candle to the festival theatre. — Cornelius! Ah, God! If only people would not try to teach Wagner his business! I was quite indignant at his article and mean to tell him that that sort of thing must stop. Let him work for the *Süddeutsche Presse*, but there we ask for a little more colour! " She concludes: " I heard something about a visit to Nuremberg, and wish the Exalted one good fortune and patience for this purpose. I suppose it has to be so. I find that one comes more and more to regard one's everyday life as a daily adjustment. I, at least, do everything that has to be done at the time when it has to be done. But all the time my soul is going its own way. And so I endure antipathetic contacts with equanimity. For my heart always feels far removed from the compulsion of common things. May you have the same experience, Benevolent one (*Huldreicher*)! " It is interesting to see how it came about that she recommended to the King Dr. Karl Heigel, afterwards his biographer: " He is a Bavarian. He came to Berlin with special recommendations from Geibel. We made his acquaintance and tried to the best of our power to be useful to him. He has talent, some poetical tales of his quite pleased me. But I have no idea what his capabilities are now, for since leaving Berlin we have heard nothing at all about him. Personally I am not at all pleased that he should have used my name, but I cannot prevent it. The report that Dr. Heigel imagines my husband to be 'a friend of the King's' is just a piece of gossip." At the same time she describes the growing effects of their propaganda among the Müncheners, and the conversion of the latter by means of Wagner's works. The last performance of *Lohengrin* had enchanted her father, and a few Berliners and Viennese whom she had seen had sat with their eyes and mouths wide open. " They may show off their needle-guns up there and their discipline, too, which is indeed admirable.

293

But we can point to the 'German spirit,' for the revelations of which we are securing an existence here. Zumbusch, who is just making a bust of my father, told me that Redwitz had come to him and said, apropos of *Lohengrin,* that he had never been so much affected at the theatre; it was the most beautiful, poetic, and sublime thing he knew. And so one after the other they are all coming round — slowly, but they are coming. How grateful I am to our exalted friend for having allowed Father and me to see Semper's model. It enchanted my father and filled me with fresh enthusiasm. Ah, what a splendid artistic life will begin when this building is started upon — and the improvement in trade! Such an enterprise brings into being what a hundred academies are powerless to achieve. And now I must really allow myself to relate a little incident: My father was calling upon Count P., an old acquaintance, and the Count introduced his daughter-in-law to him. My father had just come from inspecting the model, and expressed all his admiration for it. Upon this the good lady jumped up as if she had been bitten by the tarantula, and said: 'What is the use of this building and this expenditure? They haven't any idea what they are going to act in it.' My father laughed and said: 'Count A. flew into just such a rage when it was mentioned in Rome. Allow me to repeat to you what I said to him: They know very well what they are going to perform in it. But even if nothing were ever going to be performed in it, such a monument is of the greatest importance for a city. It brings in ten times what it cost, and a city in which there are great works of art never comes to ruin. In the second place, as regards the cost: In Paris they spend forty millions on a theatre and do not get a masterpiece. Semper does not ask even for two millions and produces a building to which there is nothing comparable in the modern world.' To which the Countess, who was already somewhat crest-fallen, replied: 'It is making us a laughing-stock abroad.' — My father: 'Countess, thank God that for a long time past you have already had the good fortune to be a "laughing-stock."' She stared at him in amazement, and he went on to say: 'When King Ludwig put up all his fine buildings, nobody here saw the object of it. People abroad were funny about it too and turned them into ridicule — until they all began imitating the fine initiative displayed by the King of Bavaria; and you will agree with me that Munich now has cause to praise the audacities of King Ludwig I, which it once combated and opposed.' Whereupon the good lady gave in."

But the King, for his part, was in a gloomy frame of mind, for he had resolved to break off his engagement to his cousin Sophie. This incident created a terrible scandal in certain circles, as was indeed comprehensible; but it must be said that in this matter the King proceeded firmly and with composure, and what he confided to Frau Cosima in this connexion reveals him in a really splendid light. " My heart positively exulted when I read the last letters from you both. It made me intensely happy to know that you were in such a cheerfully animated and uplifted mood, which was imparted to me too and made me happy, though I have recently had to live through grave, very grave days. The matter which was tormenting me is now settled, and it is better so. I am calm and cheerful again, the peace which had flown from me has once more entered into my soul and, I confidently hope and firmly believe, will never leave it again. Since I know, my friend, that you take the warmest interest in all that affects me, in my happiness and in my sorrows alike, this time, too, I will follow the promptings of my soul and pour out my heart to you, for you have always received this so affectionately. During the summer of last year I frequently wrote to my cousin Sophie, telling her about my enthusiasm, which she shared, for the Master, our great Friend, for whom she, too, felt an enthusiastic love and veneration; I also sent her books, letters, etc.; her mother heard of the correspondence which was going on between me and her daughter and thought, as she naturally would, that these were ordinary love-letters. She was incapable of imagining that it was a question of purely intellectual relations. People are like this, and measure all that is sublime with their little yard-rule. Sophie, whose feeling for me was really one of love, felt unspeakably unhappy when she heard that this was not so on my side, and, out of tender-heartedness and a really sincere pity for her unhappy state, I let myself be carried away into the rash step of the betrothal. I had known her from youth up and had always loved her like a true kinsman — truly and deeply as a sister; I had given her my confidence and friendship, but not love! You can imagine what a terrible thought it was for me to see the day of the marriage drawing nearer and nearer, and to have to recognize that this union could bring happiness neither to her nor to me. And yet it was hard for me to know whether I ought to withdraw. It is for freedom alone that I long, for freedom, freedom do I thirst. Now I have wrenched myself free. Why should I be compelled in my unhappiness to rush blindly forward, when I am still so young and have time enough before me to find the being who is destined for me by God? Why fetter myself, why forge my own bonds, why marry a being whom I have always loved as a near relative, but not in such a fashion as to desire to raise her to the position of my queen and wife? The future lay concealed before me, black and sombre. Why should I for ever cut myself off from the possibility of finding happiness? Supposing that, even within a year, the being had appeared whom I should have known to be the one destined for me by God! Supposing that true love had drawn me towards her whom I should have been forced to follow! How indescribably wretched I should have been! I should have had to go on, to sacrifice myself to Sophie, who would then have been my wife. Oh, it must be a hard fate to be sacrificed! And now the question was how to dissipate the threatening storm which I myself had conjured up. I thought it better to forestall the unpleasantness and explained the whole situation in an exhaustive letter to Sophie. Now her hand is free, she may still be happy, and I too. What would have become of all our plans if this unhappy marriage had been concluded; if I had been driven to despair by inward suffering, grief, and mourning; where should I have found the inspiration which would have given me enthusiasm for our ideals? My very soul would have been crushed, my golden dreams would have had to evaporate like idle fancies. No school of art would have been established, no festival theatre would have arisen. *The Mastersingers* would not have existed for me, the *Nibelungs* and *Parsifal* would not have brought me beatitude. Only a shadow of myself would have dragged out a gloomy existence, devoid of peace and joy, and a tenfold death would have brought me a longed-for happiness. Now all, all will come to pass. I have awakened from an agonizing, torturing dream, and feel the old unbending strength, which may not be untrue to its high mission. Need I tell you how happy the last performance of *Lohengrin* made me? I drew from it the strength to break by force the oppressive bonds which irked me. This work, divine in its origin, never fails to exert its magic power. Now I revive again:

> ' *Ja, nun erkenne ich sie wieder,*
> *Die schöne Welt, der ich entrückt,*
> *Der Himmel blickt auf mich hernieder,*
> *Die Fluren prangen reich geschmückt.*

> (Once more I see the world before me,
> The beauteous world from which I fled,
> The heavens graciously bend o'er me,
> The meadows with rich flowers are spread.) ' [1]

My inward peace, the triumphant, exultant delight of my soul, will allow no care to arise. Now flowers spring up before my mind's eye, where there is really nothing but cold ice and snow-fields, such as are to be seen here now. Poetry hovers round Hohenschwangau, though this evening my mother makes her entry, and prose with her."

This letter is remarkably clear and mature for a young man of twenty-two. But it also shows his chivalrous cast of mind, and how much he was misunderstood, even in the royal family itself. He had no need to fear misunderstanding from Frau Cosima; and she writes: " What can your friend do but congratulate you? You know, my gracious friend, that what I had desired for you was a companion who should share with you the joys and distresses of life, and how happy I was when I thought you had found such a one. And since you tell me today that she was not this, I cannot but congratulate you upon having taken a step which was certainly excessively hard. I confess that when I heard about the interference on the occasion of the betrothal, I

---

[1] *Tannhäuser*, I, iv, Newman's translation (Breitkopf and Härtel edition).—Tr.

felt inexpressibly uneasy. But I know how little importance is generally to be attached to what people say, and the overwhelming desire to know that you had about you a true and lovingly understanding soul caused me to shrug my shoulders at my own situation. Now I am anxious again (though in a different way). I fear her (*Jene*), I fear her very much. People will be furious at your decision. Her powerful connexions are capable of stirring up much trouble. It is a difficult time. Oh, might I but beg you humbly, my friend and King, to abandon your isolation for a little, so that the people may know their sovereign better. I beg you to do it for the sake of the good cause. I believe, dear Lord, that if you can bring yourself to do this, your important decision can produce no impression whatever. This is my only anxiety; otherwise, my exalted lord, how can I fail to understand and sympathize in the feeling of deliverance with which you are filled? Ah, these people who want to arrange and settle everything for the best cause the most grievous misunderstandings. And, this being so, since she (*jene*) would have tried to harbour illusions, it was certainly best that, even at the last moment, you should have explained things truthfully. I am only sorry for the Princess Sophie in all this, but if she loves, she will soon resign herself, and if she does not love you, then she, too, must be feeling a sense of deliverance. Thank you, my exalted friend, for telling me this. These must have been difficult days! What is easy for a private person becomes almost insuperable for a king, and even apart from the public bearing of this proceeding, your fine, noble heart must have felt it quite hard enough to cause the Princess this pain. I should like to think, my King, that she loves you either not at all, or infinitely. In the latter case she would be thankful to her ' brother ' for having been truthful and frank with her, and not worry about the painful situation at the moment. Time, which ' puts an end to all things ' (*die ' Allenderin '*), will act as a balm here too. I admit that I wish the next few months were over. I dread the intrigues which will be hatched, I dread them greatly! Oh, my King, forgive your friend's anxiety! "

Upon this the King sent Frau Cosima a very fine medallion. She thanked him warmly:

"If it is to be the dearest thing in the world to me, she shall only show me happy hours in your life. The noble symbol of the Saviour's Mother, who followed Him faithfully even unto the cross — the highest example of motherly love, grasped and reproduced by the great artist: I feel a double pleasure in wearing it and in looking at it, for it has become the symbol of your kindness to me.

"For the whole of this long week I have had no news from our Friend. Instead of this I have been edifying myself with '*Deutsche Kunst und deutsche Politik* (German Art and German Politics),' which I consider incomparably fine. So far nobody in Munich has found our Friend out, but after No. 4 [of the *Süddeutsche Presse*] I think nobody will be left in doubt. Much as has been written about King Max, nobody to my knowledge has grasped the idea of the Maximilianeum as our Friend has done, though he is apparently so remote from these things. I think our dear lord will have been pleased with the articles. At the house of Zumbusch, who is doing a bust of my father, I met Oskar von Redwitz, whom I liked far better than I had expected, for his dramatic and lyric poems had not edified me much. I look at all men from the point of view of possible intendants for the theatre. What has surprised me very much is the general reception given to the great news. I had expected a little sympathy for one side. But great was my astonishment when I heard on all sides nothing but: 'That is a good thing.' I have kept my father with me for a few more days — 'from five to six.' I am loath to let him return to Rome now, though he is not in the least perturbed and, even if he were, would only go off there all the more quickly. I am shortly expecting my mamma-in-law, whom I have asked to come to Munich, for she is alone and advanced in years. The good lady does not share a single one of my views. But I am in such towering spirits about the way in which our cause is advancing, so confident about the further development of artistic life here, that I would readily take upon myself the burdens of the whole world in order to expiate that one happiness. So long as I know that you, my King, are cheerful, and our Friend contented and in a creative mood, so long as I see us here advancing slowly but surely, then I really do not know what I should find hard. May all good spirits be with you, my exalted friend."

Meanwhile the King had given fresh proofs of decided personal initiative in face of the attacks which had been directed against him and his Government in the Reichsrat. She writes on this subject:

"May I say it? Joy prevails throughout the whole city at the King's action with regard to the Reichsrat, and this rejoices my soul so much that I am happy — though still rather sad."

Frau Cosima next speaks with glad hope of the developments in Munich. She praises Baron Perfall, who, she says, will serve the cause, and reports that *The Mastersingers* is completed and their friend on his way to Paris. In short, everything seemed to be turning out for the best. And this hope was also shared by the King, who now even came forward with a plan, which shows how deeply he sympathized with and understood all the new tendencies in music. He writes: " I cannot deny myself the pleasure of sending you a few lines today, the very day of my arrival. A thousand thanks for two such charming letters. I received the first as I stepped into the carriage at Unterpeissenberg on my way here from Hohenschwangau. It filled me with heart-felt joy and real exaltation. It did much towards making it easier for me to come here. For you, my friend, will find it comprehensible that it is always hard for me and costs me an inward struggle to return to the city, where I have been through so many sad experiences and suffered so painfully in the past. Today, too, I was in the gloomiest and most melancholy frame of mind the whole day long. God be praised, our own affairs are going well, people are getting more and more reasonable. Yet it is hard to forget all the sufferings that my dear friends and I had to go through owing to these very people. I request you, my friend, to tell our beloved Friend in my name that very shortly indeed I shall send an invitation to your father to take up his abode here permanently, and that I mean to entrust him with the directorship of church-music; also that I am going to send for Semper. I further request you to do all that lies in your power to induce your dear father to comply with my most ardent desire.

" I rejoice anew every day at having regained my freedom. Union with Sophie would have meant spiritual death to me. Now my old enthusiastic delight is awakening with renewed force, and, by God, I mean to see to it that never again shall it run the risk of becoming chilled."

As a matter of fact, the greater part of Munich sympathized with the King on this occasion. Furthermore, he was not to be blamed for his longing for nature, which never met with any understanding throughout the whole of his life. What is regarded nowadays as a matter of course, that a man should spend all his free time in the mountains, was at that time imputed to the King for a fault and almost used as a basis for conclusions as to his mental condition. But Frau Cosima writes as follows: " I am delighted to send my greetings to Hohenschwangau, where you love staying! Amid your innumerable burdens, distractions, obligations, and all the rest of it, how could you fail to be drawn towards the place where you feel happy? I contented myself with a glimpse of you here at the recent performance of *Don Giovanni* and with seeing, to my delight, that you are well, and with greeting our gracious protector from afar. Everything is happy and cheerful again here: the people can now tell one another that they have seen their King; they attach great importance to this, for which you cannot blame them! I hope my noble friend will not take these words amiss about not blaming them! Yesterday morning I already heard a great deal of talk, and among it much nonsense. It was said that the King had made it up with the Princess Sophie again. I made no more sign than if I had been dead, and, as is my custom, let the good people chatter their fill. I was recently granted the honour of being received by the Grand Duchess Helena. She seemed to be very happy at seeing the King, and if I am not very much mistaken, she is thoroughly capable of appreciating what is great, in both heart and mind. She was very kind to me and made the most pleasant impression on me. In her lady-in-waiting, Fräulein von Rahden, I made the acquaintance of a rarely gifted being, serious and good. We soon got upon the subject of Wagner and understood one another. Circumstances may have been responsible, God knows, for the fact that at the time the Grand

301

Duchess did not do for our Friend what it was apparently so easy and at the same time so important to do. She herself was extremely amiable and kind to him. One cannot find fault with her for not doing as you have done, my incomparable friend." And she goes on to say:

"Your summons to my father touches me deeply! Whether he will be able to respond to it at once, I do not know. At any rate, it is a splendid pearl in the long, golden chain of favours which binds us to you for ever. Quite unintentionally I find myself in the sphere of adornment, and now I must pause once more and thank you. I will wear the cross of forget-me-nots until I hang it round Senta's neck, when I shall tell her that the fairest flowers of affection have bloomed in the crown of our life. The large ornament is lovely and bears your colour! Today I received the first letter from our Friend since his return from Paris. He is glad to be at Triebschen and is now correcting the biography. People are gradually becoming reasonable here, and I believe that the great changes which are pending will go through without the slightest friction. My husband is announcing his Beethoven evenings for the benefit of a fund in aid of poor musicians. He is bent upon at last silencing the nonsense about classical and non-classical. Porges recently said very justly: 'I know no such thing as classical music, there is good music and bad music, and what we make is good. If by " classical " is meant unity of style, which is the correct interpretation, then *Tristan and Isolde* is more classical than *Don Giovanni.*' I was much pleased at that."

She congratulates the King on the tactful visit to Possenhofen which he had made with his Russian guests. But he replied: " I return the letter which you so kindly sent me, with my warmest thanks. It was really a pleasure to me to read it. How just and pungently characteristic are our Friend's remarks on affairs and personalities in Paris! I really delighted in them. I am very glad and happy to be at last staying among my beautiful mountains again and able to take the invigorating exercise in the open air which does me so much good. It is a real agony to have to be mewed up for long indoors. During my week's residence in the capital I only rarely managed to get any walking or to enjoy the fresh air. For the rest, I do not regret having been there. After all, the bandy-legged members of the Reichsrat recanted at the last minute. Not till now have I found enough time to read our dear Friend's most interesting article on 'German Art and Politics,' If only our Friend would make his views public in this way oftener and if only the other German princes would pay attention to this article! Oh, what our Friend says about the estrangement between the German princes and their people is only too true: that the latter are so often rewarded by blank ingratitude, that vigorous and beneficent action is to be expected of the princes as an expiation. The way people go on gossiping in Munich is really too absurd. How can they believe such stuff? I am very glad to have no more to do with Possenhofen and its inhabitants. I think I may certainly take it that Sophie too is now quite calm, for she has known for a long time that I do not love her, so that she could not possibly have found happiness through me. We should never, never have been any good together. God be praised that I am rid of her!

"I should deeply deplore it if your father, whom I esteem so highly, were unable to accept my invitation to come to Munich for good. In his last letter our Friend expressed his confidence in decided terms that your dear father would comply with my wish." He next discusses the production of works by Gluck and goes on to say:

"I have a longing desire that a few new dramas should be rehearsed in the course of the coming winter. Our Friend certainly agrees with my opinion that the time has at last come to present such works to the public, and to open its eyes to the false ideas that are always rife with regard to the theatre and its deep importance. There is still time; before it goes down and is entirely corrupted in the conflict with vulgarity, in the bottomless pit of materialism, now shall a saving hand be stretched out to the people." And he concludes: "Our activities will be of abiding and indestructible benefit to the German people, and their fruits will be handed down to future generations in centuries to come, and fire them with a new enthusiasm for what is eternally pure, eternally true and beautiful; while the superficial French civilization, with its veneer of brilliancy, will fall

303

into ruin; its reign is at an end; the German spirit will put it to shame."

But there were considerable obstacles to his hopes of awakening German drama to fresh bloom as well on the stage of Munich. And Frau Cosima's commentary on his ideas is as follows: " It seems to me that we have gradually to bring into existence quite another public and a different art. I can scarcely wait for the moment when the question of the theatre will be regulated. The way in which things are going on here is indescribable. It would, of course, be splendid, and worthy of you, my exalted lord, to produce the Greek tragedies. But with what actors? The few people who could have been made use of, and that only by great industry and study, have been scandalously removed. But by a new organization of the theatre such performances might certainly be made possible. I am most firmly convinced that Baron Perfall would share in these exalted intentions. His straightforward character and open mind are a sure guarantee that he would have a due reverence for the exalted will of our royal master. I shall never forget Intendanzrat Schmitt's words: ' The King is fond of classical works; very well, he can pay for them.' I was horrified at such insolent cynicism and departed in silence. If only the theatre is in good and proper order, then I have no fear for anything else, for I also know that the efforts of the school of music will bear the most splendid fruit, after which a consistent spirit will progressively enhance artistic conditions till we have Semper's festival theatre and the performances in it. Then we shall have done our part and set an example. But so long as the theatre is not permeated by your spirit and will, so long all is lost: our Friend's golden words, the experiment of the school of music, the isolated model performances — let us but have the theatre, and the whole battle will be won. I have faith in your magic wand. The Glyptothek was powerless to turn the Müncheners into Greeks; perhaps we may make real, genuine Germans of them! I think that of Calderón's works the comedies, such as *La Dama duende* and *El Segreto a voces* might possibly lend themselves to a proper production here first, if only we had a stage manager who could bring it home to the actors that they are not the poet's masters, but his most obedient servants."

The King, however, in close collaboration with Düfflipp, was eagerly endeavouring to find a dramatic director for the theatre too. Frau Cosima warned him against this: " I think it would be better for us not to be too hasty in finding an artistic director, in the first place because we shall not want a man who puts on airs and comes here with a great reputation and great self-assertiveness, but all practical questions will have to be settled first, in order to put an end to the abominable perfidy that prevails here. What I consider practicable is to choose Herr Schmied as an ordinary stage manager; that is, a man whom one hardly knows and to whom the public pays no attention personally. He will occupy a subordinate position and come here with no pretensions, he has had practical experience and has proved by his articles on the theatre that he understands something about it and has a reverence for the great writers. Paul Heyse would naturally be prepared to act only as literary adviser. My objections to him are as follows: In the first place, his Jewish origin — in which I most humbly beg my exalted friend to see no caste prejudice — but a deeply grounded fear of a race which has caused great harm to the Germans. Secondly, his lack of experience of stage conditions; thirdly, his own productivity. For him the dramas of Paul Heyse will always come before the works of Schiller, Goethe, and Shakspere. Fourthly, the inability and inward reluctance to enter into others' views on art of a man who naturally considers himself a writer of quite a superior stamp. Fifthly, the trouble there would be in getting rid of Paul Heyse should the experiment not turn out to your satisfaction. There would be a regular scandal, the newspapers, all Jewry, both secret and avowed, would take his part as one man. I consider it decidedly better for things to be managed by simple, competent, and modest persons who are not in evidence. Later, when the need of a well-known name makes itself felt and the bulk of the work is done, there will still be time enough to indulge in the luxury of Paul Heyse. But, in my opinion, the institution ought first to have acquired quite a definite character of its own, so that Paul Heyse, too, may know what obligations he is assuming and to what arrangements he has to adapt himself if he means to direct this artistic institution. The completed

305

program must first be clearly and definitely before the public. If a man like Paul Heyse were to be brought in at once, he might assume, from the present anarchical state of affairs, that it is he who is to apply the motive force according to his own ideas, the result being clashes, if not friction, which cannot be for the good of the institution."

Frau Cosima spoke with extreme frankness, but it must be admitted that to a certain extent time justified her severe strictures. It is clear that it was not out of sheer anti-Semitism that she cherished a prejudice against Paul Heyse — who on his father's side, moreover, was descended from an old German family of scholars — for she always championed Porges's cause most warmly and maintained a true and lifelong friendship for him.

The King entered into the question with equal decision in his next letter: "I fully approve of what you say about Paul Heyse and am ready and willing to make the experiment with Hermann Schmied in all confidence. But I must admit that it is a mystery to me how such a cultivated and experienced man as Herr Schmied undoubtedly is can seek his salvation, if only for a short time, in managing the despised Aktientheater. In his place I should have turned in disgust from such a suggestion, which would have seemed to me derogatory. It is to be hoped that Schmied will justify the hopes reposed in him. I have heard nothing but good of his literary works, especially his novels." He then goes on to say: "I was heartily delighted at the success achieved by Herr von Bülow at his recent Beethoven evenings. Will you have the goodness to congratulate him most heartily on my behalf? You were certainly present, were you not, my friend, at the performance of *King Richard*? It must have been a most enjoyable evening.

"For the last ten days absolute winter has prevailed here. But today the sun is shining again in all its glory, so I am indulging a hope that the snow may now completely disappear, and that I may at last be able to ride again. As a substitute for this, it is at present my habit to make short sleighing excursions in the Tyrol near by. I am sure that you, my friend, would be enchanted with this neighbourhood. It is an earthly paradise, and it does me such good to be able to breathe freely here once more, before having to bury myself alive in the city for some months.

"Yet there is one thing more that I must tell you, dear friend, though I must always conceal it from our Friend at Triebschen, for the remembrance of it always renews his grief, and tears open the wounds which have scarcely healed. It is that I have a consuming desire to hear the strains of *Tristan and Isolde* again. If only, my friend, you could advise me in this matter, which I have so much at heart! I am better and happier than I have been for a long time past. Yesterday, as on November 29, I celebrated in my heart my own feast of the resurrection, in that the terrible thing — marriage with one whom I did not love — has been avoided. I ought never to have let things go so far. If it had proved impossible to break my engagement by good means, I was firmly resolved to put an end to my life by means of cyanide. How happy I am now that this was not necessary, that I shall live to see the fulfilment and crowning of our work, that the heavenly strains are blooming in me once again, that all my youthful dreams are to be fulfilled! Oh, to attain the highest aim of existence, the sight of the ideal which one cherished in one's heart, descending from the golden spheres of heaven into the earthly world to impart its beneficent fruits to all who joyfully believe in this Messiah and faithfully await him, with the hope that nothing can shake, with the love that overcomes all things!"

Meanwhile another press campaign had broken out in Munich in connexion with the Fröbel case and was taken advantage of by Fröbel himself, in the usual fashion of Munich journalism at the time. He was indeed quite at home amid all these proceedings. But we should be all the more on our guard against judging Munich and its affairs by the intrigues, gossip, and chatter of the journalists. They kept receiving fresh instructions from a certain quarter, consisting not so much of a party as of a group of pushing persons. Frau Cosima's opinion of these noisy demonstrations was extraordinarily accurate, when she declared that the whole thing belonged to the domain of gossip, and that the situation in general and the public ferment had been terribly exaggerated. "Nobody is really influenced by these things. On the very morning when this nonsense appeared in the *Neueste Nachrichten,* my husband conducted *Die Jüdin* in perfect peace and tranquillity, and people in the audience were saying: 'It is nice to have Bülow conducting again.' Thus there is not the slightest cause for alarm or ill humour. And so, my exalted friend, do not let these insignificant, unimportant things, which are so petty and provincial, destroy your pleasure in our work. If you have taken any notice of them, even for a moment, it would be well to forget them. I know that people are reckoning upon the King's getting sick of this everlasting talk. But if these low people find themselves disappointed by the King's imperturbable calm, they will make an end of their incessant harassing. And so my advice to our dear friend is patience, patience. It is almost harder than courage, but here it is indispensable. I once wrote in jest to our Friend that Ulysses stuffed his ears with wax and cotton-wool so as not to hear the sirens' song, and that we needed to do the same so as to hear nothing of this croaking, yelling, and screeching." The King took such words as these in perfectly good part, and with great understanding. In his answers he expressed his agreement with this clever woman's letters in a fine, boyish way.

And now came Christmas with its rich presents and a wordless greeting, to which Frau Cosima replied as follows: " But my friend sent me loving words in the silent night. I think that his friend will not trouble or vex him if she says that they gave her deep pleasure. The beautiful presents, the bracelet with the stone of hope, the pictures of legend and fairy-tale, and the carpet were set out on my table, and spoke to me of the graciousness of my sovereign. I have presented our Friend with the figure of Siegfried and the pictures for his room, which they now adorn. How good it is of my lord graciously to accept the portrait of the Master from my hand! " And she goes on: " God grant that our dear lord's mood may grow brighter and his dislike of Munich less. I have grown fond of the city because it is yours and have at last got to the point of no longer hearing any more about inessential things that are annoying."

But she also managed to represent Heinrich Porges's position with regard to Fröbel's paper to the King in the right light, as well as making sure that Düfflipp should use him in accordance with the views of the Master and his mission. Wagner himself had hastened to Munich for the holidays, with regard to which she writes: " Our Friend has just arrived for the Christmas festivities. He had promised my children to come, for he had bought them all kinds of toys in Paris and was bent upon keeping his word. I had previously resigned myself to not seeing him till later. But now he is here, and may all good spirits protect him! I mean to shield him and look after him in my house as well as I can. Besides, he wants to hurry on with *The Mastersingers*. But what is to be done? The Intendanzrat has made no preparations, absolutely none. On the contrary, he has given everybody leave for the time during which it was to have been worked at. But I mean to urge on Baron Perfall to the best of my ability." And she concludes with a reference to Schiller's biography, which she was reading with that inexpressible melancholy which always takes possession of one when one follows the life of one divinely endowed among men.

Meanwhile the year was not out before the King became convinced that, essentially, Fröbel was no more nor less than a bad journalist and a vulgar person. He therefore wrote very briefly, but decidedly: "I consider it urgently necessary that Fröbel should depart from here for ever, for I know his black soul only too well." In fact, all that was needed was to put things before him clearly and firmly, without coming into conflict with his peculiar idiosyncrasies, and then one might be sure of a good and confident decision. Frau Cosima naturally exulted when the King himself spoke his mind so decidedly as to the removal of the mischief-maker, who by ceasing to print " *Deutsche Kunst und deutsche Politik* " had not only offended Wagner deeply, but also done him serious harm in the eyes of the public. She now suggested that Fröbel should print the concluding article and then go. It had not escaped her knowledge that the editor-in-chief of the official organ, though appointed through her agency, had complained of her direct to the royal secretariate and even to the King.

Meanwhile the King, too, had come to the right decision with regard to Wagner, and sent for him on the evening of December

28. Thus the whole affair was cleared up, and the Master's former wonderful influence on his young friend made itself felt in the most beneficial way. But Frau Cosima knew her power of working upon the King's mind by timely proposals, even when he received them unfavourably at first. She was not afraid of him and often told him home truths, though in a most charming way — as, for instance, with regard to receiving deputations, and again with regard to the tenor Niemann. It is interesting to see how she quite justifiably raked up memories of Paris against the latter:

"There was one thing that made me doubtful about Niemann, and that was his bad behaviour in Paris: he was cowardly at the critical moment of the negotiations, and lazy and obstinate while at work. For instance, he was unwilling to learn a couple more bars than he had been used to singing. But, as Your Majesty justly remarks, if he can sing *Lohengrin,* then he must be able to act *Tannhäuser* for us too. In this case it would be a good thing to write to the singer that the object here was not a role for Niemann, but a faithful and perfect rendering of *Tannhäuser.* Perhaps it would then be possible to surmount his laziness and lack of artistic conscience." Here we already see signs of the energy with which she directed affairs at Bayreuth in later days, after the death of the Master, settling all personal questions, in particular, according to her own point of view and convictions. On the other hand, the picture which she draws of her husband's activity is a beautiful one. "Now, as in the days of *Tristan,* he is in his element — that is, musical work. He can never have too much of it — in fact, he can never have enough, and I am delighted at the cheerful temper which always upholds him during these splendid tasks, serious though he is in general, and at times, too, embittered by the course of events."

And so the memorable year 1867 had drawn to a close and that of *The Mastersingers* now began. The main thing, however, was to prepare the way for this work. The King's command was far from sufficient for this, for at first absolutely no consideration was shown for him on the part of the recalcitrant elements in the Cabinet and the theatre. Vigorous hands were forced to intervene; and the gentlest, while at the same time the most vigorous, were those of Frau Cosima. She knew the King and his wishes, the most urgent and vehement of which was for a repetition of *Tristan*. It should not be forgotten that the performance of the works played a leading part in the subsequent relations between the King and Richard Wagner, the King wanting them to be performed at all costs, and even ceasing to pay any further attention to Wagner's justifiable requests when the Master was far away. And so she reverted to the desire which he had uttered shortly before this with regard to *Tristan:* "My husband, our Friend, and I were discussing the possibility of the performance of *Tristan*, and we agreed that, with time and goodwill, it might certainly be managed. Fräulein Mallinger took alarm when Hans recently spoke to her about Isolde. But I believe that when once the heavy incubus of the musical world has been thrown off, people will be inspired by another, more courageous and active spirit. I have heard of a tenor, Bachmann, who will shortly come here as a visiting singer. Our Friend had already thought of him before; he is said to be musical. In the last resort *Tristan* might be produced with him. Kindermann would be very good as Kurwenal, so far as voice is concerned, and Bausewein could do King Mark without difficulty." But then follows a very severe criticism of the state of the theatre in Munich: "I was not much edified by my recent visit to the Hoftheater (Court Theatre). *The Magic Flute* went off wretchedly, and *The Two Marksmen* (*Die beiden Schützen*), an old novelty by Lortzing, enraged me by its insipidity and crudeness. Perfall has a hard task before him in this institution, which has gone to the dogs; but it is absolutely necessary that he should proceed on some principle; otherwise there can be no thought of educating the public. Iffland's *Huntsman* (*Jäger*) gave me great pleasure. Though it naturally cannot hold a candle to the works of the great German writers, yet it gives evidence of direct observation of the conditions and affairs of the time, and on that account I like it far better than any *Governor of Bengal* (*Statthalter von Bengalen*), or *Hans Lange*, or whatever the names of all these hashed-up productions may be. Yet I had to recognize, to my sorrow, that our actors are no longer capable even of playing well and with natural warmth. My husband wants to produce

Byron's *Manfred* with Schumann's music, an experiment in which my father was extraordinarily successful at Weimar. Possart is coming tomorrow to discuss taking the principal role. If he is not too much infatuated with himself, I shall say something to him about the fact that I was not particularly pleased with his Richard II. He had none of the beauty, ardour, and enthusiasm of a king who believes in the justice of his cause. All that was left was a distorted picture of incomprehensible bitterness and heedless presumption." She next goes on to speak of the impending performance of Gluck's *Armide*, which she deplores on practical grounds. But her opinion is very fine and just: " Gluck is a problem: profound as a musician, full of feeling as a dramatist, he must be understood and reproduced by an intelligent mind." And so she chatters on, all in the interest of the performance of *The Mastersingers* and of the Master himself, whom, though distant, she always brings, as it were, before the King's mind: " Our Friend is present at all our work from a distance. He has accompanied me to the theatre a few times, where I was pleased with the Müncheners at least for taking no particular notice of him." She next tells a delicious story of how she had invited a number of ladies to tea, among them the wife of Professor Windscheid, when suddenly Wagner entered. " They were all seized with embarrassment, and almost with apprehension, as though the Dutchman had come into the room where Senta was spinning. The angels of Hohenschwangau followed one after the other as though on Jacob's ladder. At last the good souls disappeared, and I explained to our Friend that he must not imagine that he can show himself like an ordinary mortal." She even goes further and suggests to the King that it might be useful if she were to be brought into contact with the Queen-mother, either as reader or in some other capacity. " I do not know why, but I have got it into my head that she might be won over to our side, by which means much distress and torment might be obviated for our sovereign. You will easily understand, my friend, that, in spite of everything and everybody, I am bound to love and honour your mother. Besides, there is much that comes within the Queen's influence. It may be foolish, but I have got it into my head that I could make very many things comprehensible to her." And she concludes: "And so, having made my confession, I hope for absolution." The idea was an obvious one, and those who have known the Queen-mother will not feel disposed to deny that Frau Cosima's rare qualities might have inspired her with a certain sympathy. To this, of course, was added yet another consideration, which might have exerted a strong influence over the Queen at that time: that is, Frau Cosima's deep piety, based on a strictly Catholic upbringing. There is a certain fascination in following up this train of thought. In fact she tried every expedient, not out of personal ambition, but out of the feeling that it was her mission to help.

At this very time the state of things at the theatre was causing her great anxiety on account of the performance of *The Master-singers*. She managed, so to speak, to bring pressure to bear on the King by declaring that there could be no thought of Wagner's returning to the score of *Siegfried* before the performance of *The Mastersingers*. The latter must first receive a worthy production, and then, and not till then, would the other be possible. In this connexion she next drew attention to the grave errors in the production of *Armide* and to the incessant delays in starting the rehearsals of *The Mastersingers*, and concludes as follows: "God grant that the time of waiting will come to an end with *Jessonda*. I do not think our artistic conscience will tolerate that we should any longer look on at the way in which, for example, the rehearsals for *The Mastersingers* are constantly being rendered impossible and every superior mind forcibly held back. My husband has gladly and proudly renounced all activities elsewhere. He has given up the flattering invitation to conduct *Lohengrin* in Paris, solely in order to devote himself entirely to his task here, which is so dear to him. What must be his feelings if he is forced to regard himself as entirely superfluous? What am I to say to him to exhort him to patience and hopefulness, when I realize with a sort of despair that everywhere in Germany *Lohengrin, Tannhäuser,* and *The Flying Dutchman* are included in the repertory, that everybody is taking trouble over *The Mastersingers,* and that here, in the very spot where our Friend has alone met with ineffable affection and a divine understanding of his creative ideas, everything is always paralysed as

313

though by malevolent powers. Yes, my dear lord, *Armide* made
me unspeakably sad, and it was certainly not Meister Gluck who
was responsible for this. Forgive me if I seem one-idea'd. I
cannot lose sight of our cause for a single instant. It is an exalted
personage who is responsible for this — a responsibility which
is his sublimest merit in my eyes." And it must indeed be admitted that the principles governing the theatre, and the tendency — almost pathological in its intensity — to shelve as far
as possible all important dramatic works, in so far as they had
no financial backing, had reached an incredible pitch in Munich
at that time, in spite of the changes which had taken place on
the appointment of Perfall. It was all the more to the credit of
Bülow and his wife — but also of Richter and, above all, of the
work itself — that in such conditions it was carried out so brilliantly.

But there was yet another factor which contributed towards
this: namely, the appointment of Semper as rector of the new
Polytechnic (*Polytechnikum*) that was about to be founded. It
was Councillor Düfflipp himself who persuaded Frau Cosima to
intervene in this matter. She writes: " Councillor Düfflipp said
to me recently that if Prince Hohenlohe would take this in hand,
it could easily be achieved, and Semper in the service of the
State would not meet with anything like the same opposition as
Semper in the service of the court. I wrote to our Friend that,
since he was on such good terms with the Prince, he might enter
into correspondence with him on the subject. Our Friend was
afraid that if he took steps in the matter, he might give rise to
misunderstandings, and begged me to speak to the Prince. But
since I do not know the minister at all, I felt scruples about
approaching him, for, after all, he might not be willing to treat
of a matter of such importance with someone unknown to him,
and, what is more, a woman. I asked a confidential friend of the
Prince to come and see me, a thoroughly trustworthy man, and
discussed with him the state of affairs at the moment, the present
position of the Prince and his influence over the other ministries,
especially over Herr von Schlör, who will have the decisive say
in the matter if, as arranged, Semper is to become president or
rector of the Polytechnic. He assured me that the Prince would

espouse Semper's cause warmly. In view of the difficult position occupied by Schlör at present with regard to the clerical party, the only thing that would carry weight would be that, at one of the ministerial councils, the King's Majesty should deign to make known his august views on the importance of Semper directly and with decision, and most graciously recommend to the minister, Herr von Schlör, that he should choose the leading architect in Germany as president or rector. If Semper is appointed by the Ministry, then spiteful tongues will be silenced; and in time, if the King considers it advisable, the building could be begun — though the wisest thing of all would certainly be to say nothing at all about this."

The King was the less averse from this because he was firmly resolved to proceed with the laying of the foundation-stone of the new theatre as early as the following March. This aroused great alarm in the Master, and Frau Cosima brought her whole influence to bear to delay the foundation of the theatre, which had once been so vehemently desired, and regarded as their ultimate goal. She wrote to the King clearly and definitely on the subject: "Councillor Düfflipp was with me today and discussed the King's proposal to lay the foundation-stone of the festival theatre. Hard and indescribably painful though it is to me, I think I ought to tell the August and Gracious one (*dem hohen Gnädigen*) that, in view of the feeling prevalent in the country this year, it does not seem to me advisable to attempt anything of the kind. It is true, dear and beloved lord, that nothing could lend such noble lustre to your reign as this building. It will be the finest and most important which Germany, or even Europe, will have to show during this century. Kaulbach remarked recently that it would be ' a pendant to the Cologne Cathedral, a proud emblem of what German art can do.' But in the times in which we live, and especially, perhaps, in Bavaria, a prince must start upon such a work at harmony with his people. Such a great idea ought not to seem a momentary whim of one in high places. This would paralyse the enterprise from the outset and paralyse the good which might result from it. The King, my lord and kindest friend, is not yet understood, he is unknown. His people know nothing of him but the reports which

315

his miserable servants have thought fit to disseminate about him for some time past; consequently, no faith is felt in his enterprises. Oh, if only the King would resolve to give up his retirement for a time! If he would deign to make himself known to his people by displaying a great and visible interest in public events, soon, very soon, the festival building would be possible. At present everybody is against it, the aristocracy, the middle classes, and the people. At present they do not say to themselves what such a building would mean to art in general, and to trade and industry in particular; for they are incapable of saying anything in its favour and see no more in this grand purpose than a fantastical chimera, through which capital which might be used to better purpose is squandered. Once the King is known — and, in his case, to be known is the same as to be loved — everything will be different. The material conditions exist, the political constellations point towards peace. The only thing still necessary is the temporary surmounting of antipathies, which unfortunately seem to me only too easy to explain. But, my dearest lord, what we are concerned with here is something great and peerless. The day on which the King should lay the foundation-stone of the festival building amid the loving acclamations of his people would indeed repay the self-control which the tiresome fulfilment of his royal duties in their outward aspect has cost him. But as matters stand at present, I must beg you — and our Friend joins in my request — not to insist on laying the foundation-stone. The King is still too isolated. My highest consolation is that all things are possible for him. I know the intrigues of the infamous people who count upon the fact that the King shuts himself up so much, and rejoice that he is growing more and more strange to his people. I divine these machinations and know what danger they portend. Many, many nights have I spent in grief and anxiety about them, but I know with equal certitude that a firm resolution on the part of the King will suffice to put an end to this, if he will but show himself, and then our ship would be able to spread its sails on a calm sea. I do not believe that the King can undertake any grand and sublime enterprise at present, because no faith in it prevails. But if my exalted friend can do violence to himself and turn towards mankind and let the royal sunshine fall full and warm upon them, in spite of their shocking and revolting vulgarity, then, O my dear prince, our golden age will have come." She once more appeals to the King on the subject of Semper's appointment, which had become problematical, and concludes with the words: " Much as has been accomplished, the radiance of joy is still lacking. The task is to maintain the crown in its sacred prestige and bring art to its supreme consummation. The warmth of my language is prompted by the abominable thought that the King is unable to perform such a noble work as the laying of the foundation-stone. Yet, impossible as it seems to me at present, I hold it correspondingly possible in the time which is drawing nigh — a time to be hallowed by the royal sacrifice." None of the King's royal officials has drawn attention more plainly than Frau Cosima or Richard Wagner, who did so repeatedly, to this stage in the King's development, which, though concerned essentially with what was a mere matter of form, was, as history has shown, so fraught with destiny. It was no small matter for them so to exhort the King at such a moment, when the performance of *The Mastersingers* was pending, the rehearsals were now in full swing, and the King was hoping by this very performance to prove his loyalty to his friend.

A powerful spirit was indeed stirring in the theatre at Munich, as it had been in the year 1865, at the time of the performance of *Tristan*. Not only did all men feel the musical greatness of this unique work, but they felt that in it the German spirit was being revealed, and that there was an intimate and wonderful connexion between the song of songs of German citizen honour and the song of songs of the German *Reich*, of " *Siegefried*," as Wagner later expressed it.[1] The rehearsals proceeded with unprecedented vigour, and an ardent enthusiasm was felt on all sides, both by those directing them and by those who took part in them. On the evening of June 18 — that is, immediately after the general rehearsal — Frau Cosima reports to the King in her beautiful and amiable way: " These lines are to greet our exalted sovereign and bid him welcome to

[1] In *Das deutsche Heer vor Paris.* — TR.

the hall where we have so often before been blissfully united by the wondrous strains of the Only one. It is you, the generous dispenser of favours, whom we have to thank for the genesis and, if I may say so, the incarnation of the divine work. To you be our eternal, inexpressible, unceasing thanks! Now, as I have been listening to the sound of the well-known strains, I recall the days when I was able to report to our exalted friend the progress of *The Mastersingers.* Our Friend was also thinking about those days, and today he asked me to whom else in the wide world, often though it hears his name, he could have breathed a single word about all this wonderful time of growth and blossoming. And this is saying nothing against the world, to which, as it were, he pours out such a sweet farewell in *The Mastersingers,* but it is saying much for our compact. May God bless you, my exalted lord; the performance, even regarded merely as such, will give great joy to our gracious friend. What the Spirit has succeeded in effecting here is incredible. Performers whom one could not previously have characterized as anything but insignificant have blossomed out in real warmth and beauty. Yesterday we had a glorious day: in the morning the first two acts, and in the evening the third. They were taken through without a pause, and we were all overcome by them. At the end, in his own fashion, which it is simply impossible to reproduce, our Friend expressed his thanks, or rather his delight, to all who had taken part. He threw a most momentous light on the significance of such a performance and uplifted and ennobled all those who took part in it, by declaring that to artists was reserved the mission of elevating decadent art. Porges and I can remember the words well enough for him to have managed to write them down and sent them to a newspaper, the editor of which, strange to say, seems to have felt the full import of the speech, short though it was. It is, indeed, impossible to calculate the influence which such a work may have. To me it seems that the true school begins with it and that it is quite impossible to foresee in what direction this tree will put forth branches. The immediate gain which our Friend saw in it — that of arousing and uplifting lifeless or somnolent natures — is in itself of inestimable value. To you, my King and friend, there remains the splendid vocation of prolonging this instant into something permanent. All hail to you for desiring to do so! *The Mastersingers* is a great work, and due entirely to Triebschen." But she was already trying to forestall the King's restless ulterior wishes, which were shortly to have a somewhat tragic issue: " It is almost impossible for me to think of *The Rhinegold*. I can only dream of *The Ring of the Nibelung* as the outcome of a flourishing condition of all outward affairs, in which it is hard to believe now, as well as in connexion with the festival theatre — but whither do I wander? *The Mastersingers* is here — ' *Glückauf zum Meistersinger* (God speed to the Mastersinger)! ' "

And there, indeed, was *The Mastersingers*. Never before or since has the Hoftheater at Munich seen such a wonderful performance, in which all the performers discharged their duty joyfully in the true spirit of the composer, and at which the public recognized all at once that the controversy raging in Munich centred on the greatest of German masters: that it was Richard Wagner, persecuted, hated, and exiled though he was, who in this song, having for its subject the duty of honouring the German masters, had expressed this quality with a perfection achieved by nobody before him. A mighty enthusiasm swept through the house, and all agreed that here was a work than which nothing more wondrous could have been conceived. All the knaves, in or out of office, who had hitherto opposed the Master were unmasked in all their baseness, ignominy, and dishonour by this, his artistic achievement. Such was the great effect produced by *The Mastersingers*. Richard Wagner himself found the greatest satisfaction in it, and we should never forget that the King allowed him to listen to the performance at his own side from the royal box, which has been so shamelessly desecrated since the Revolution, its historic past being trampled underfoot. It was a scene worthy of the age of the Renaissance when the Master sat by the side of his young friend and protector and, in defiance of all court etiquette, was then invited by the King to step to the front of the royal box and acknowledge the applause. It is true that aged court marshals and equally venerable court ladies almost fainted at the sight, but the people recognized the greatness of this noble, kingly heart and rejoiced that the artist, who had been abused and jeered at as no other had been, should thus receive a satisfaction which compensated for all the sins committed by inferior minds.

With appropriate tact, but also a fitting *amour propre,* the Master retired to Triebschen immediately after the first performance. What further happened in Munich could only be accomplished by his faithful friends. For him the climax there was over. Under the influence of this prodigious success, it was now his intention, having forged this work of art, to strike the mighty blows which should complete the cycle of his destiny in *The Ring.* This is echoed to some extent in Frau Cosima's next letter, but also in that of the King. She writes on July 5, while still in Munich: " My exalted friend will have entered into the feelings which prompted me to keep silence till today! I am like the good Sachs, ' *Ich gebe mich den höchsten Empfindungen nur in der tiefsten Seele hin* (I abandon myself to the highest emotions only in the depths of my soul).' It is impossible for me to express any of them, I feel as if a word would be my death, or, worse, the death of my rapture. I think that the only speech to render such impressions is glorious creation, such as belongs to our Friend. Since seeing our Friend at your side listening to *The Mastersingers,* my beloved King and master, I have found no words to send you. Our friend's portrait arrived, followed by a wonderful wreath of rhododendrons — I was utterly at a loss what to do. As in duty bound, I expressed, as it were, my official thanks to the good Councillor, and my soul trusted to the soul of my exalted lord alone to understand my mute speech, which never ceases to bless and praise him. And in saying this, my kingly friend, I am almost at an end of my words. What more could I say, how could I describe my state at that moment:

' *Im Traum war ich und thöriger als ein Kind,*
   Machtlos der Macht der Wunder preisgegeben!

(In dreams [I was] lost and foolish as a child,
   Powerless before the might of this great wonder.) ' [1]

[1] *Tannhäuser,* II, ii, Newman's translation (Breitkopf and Härtel edition).—Tr.

" Heaven grant that you may be allowed to preserve, as I do, the exalted mood which you have yourself conjured up, and that no annoyances have occurred to dim it. The portrait is now the *genius loci* of my house, which greets and welcomes me when I return, and blesses me when I go out, at once the ornament and pillar of the hearth. Our Friend described to me how once in Munich there was a fire in his house; he quickly thought what he should save first, and took nothing but the score of *Siegfried*. If Loge were to play a prank in our house, I know what I should save: the ' bright and lasting souvenir of the beautiful days of *The Mastersingers*.'

" But the performance of *The Mastersingers* was wonderfully beautiful. Betz seems to me quite incomparable, Fräulein Mallinger fascinating, Nachbauer sings his part brilliantly, and nowhere could I hope to find a better David than Schlosser. And the chorus, how true to nature and full of life! One completely forgot that one was in a theatre. How it hovers in the distance — yet it is as though one were still living through it. All the foreigners, especially the French, were beside themselves and maintained that they had never seen anything more perfect. All the staging, the whole of the scenery, was magnificent. It was a joy to have experienced such harmonious collaboration of powers, such zeal and inspired will! Now the time is past, but not done with. Under your most exalted and dearest protection it will be repeated. Praise and blessing to our sovereign! "

This was the last letter that she wrote to the King for a long time to come, and it was a worthy and beautiful close. But destiny went its way, and we see how it now laid its hand upon the relations between the King and this wonderful woman. The signs of this are already perceptible in his answer: " Most deeply loved friend, you are an angel. Your letter proved this to me anew. Accept my warmest thanks for it, and the assurance that it afforded me a most great and heart-felt joy. After each performance I was more enraptured, and the fire of enthusiasm for this divinely inspired work blazed up in me more mightily! The hours which I spent at the side of our dear Friend, the great and immortal Master, during the first performance of his glorious work I number among the most beautiful that I have ever

321

experienced. They will always remain unforgettable to me, like that visit to Triebschen, of which I always think with the most intense delight.

" Two years ago I felt it my duty as a true friend to show you that letter of Frau von Schnorr's, in which she had the insolence to indulge in the most shameless calumnies against you and our Friend. And now, too, as a true friend, I think I ought not to conceal from you what I have learnt from a thoroughly trustworthy source: that a man who till now had always been regarded as a true and sincere friend of Wagner's has raked up the same contemptible calumnies against you and our Friend. That man is Röckl. You will understand how hard it has been for me to tell you this, but my intentions towards you have always been so good that I should always have felt bound to blame myself if I had not revealed this to you. I beg you to beware of this man, and also to warn our Friend against him. Oh, this base calumny! You can imagine how it hurts the faithful Parzival that his faithful friends are always the object of cunning and spite. Oh, humanity! False friends! The world loves to blacken what is radiant and to drag the sublime in the dust. But do not fear; there are still beautiful hearts which are afire for what is exalted and glorious. How true are Schiller's words: ' Fear not your enemies: their might is crippled, their weapons are shattered ' — against the firm and impregnable faith of the King, your friend! Accept my most cordial greetings and the assurance that my love for you and our Friend knows no bounds. No calumny can impair it."

This too was a last word. The King had no thought of parting and wrote these words in the deepest and most fervent loyalty. But destiny went its way, and it was characteristic of the Master's nature, as well as of her own, to clear the situation up completely. The time for a new conflict had come.

CHAPTER V

STRUGGLE AND VICTORY

MUCH has been said about the reasons why Richard Wagner and this wonderful woman did not extricate themselves earlier, with a firm and unerring hand, from the entanglement in which they had become involved — an entanglement as inevitable as the way in which it found a solution. Experienced persons, well acquainted with the circumstances, have not unjustifiably asked why the Master did not simply explain to Bülow that separation from Cosima was a matter affecting his very being, and that she was his destiny. It could safely have been expected of a man of Hans von Bülow's chivalrous disposition that, though cut to the quick and wounded to the depths of his heart, he would none the less have yielded to this frank confession, and at once consented to the divorce. The opinion has been expressed that the great love of these two was dominated by a crass selfishness which, even in the midst of their great passion, did not lose sight of the fact that they needed Hans von Bülow, and that it would have been impossible to produce *The Mastersingers* while the scandal of a great divorce suit was fresh in people's minds. In view of the sufferings which for long years were the most important element in the life of Frau Cosima, and of the Master too, how petty and paltry these arguments are! — not to mention her absolute consciousness that she alone could save the Master and his works. In later days Liszt coined a wonderful and tender phrase in speaking of his daughter's second marriage: " *C'était une mission* (It was a mission)." This, however, was only a phrase, which he adopted, so to speak, as a useful catchword. His judgment was at first by no means so simple, fatherly, and priestly. As late as September 1868 he wrote to his friend Mrs. Agnes Street, to whom he told everything which he could not confide to the Princess: " It would be very hard to explain the vagaries of the great man of Lucerne. Attribute them to the frequent storms on the lake and let us leave it at that. The rules of conduct followed by grown-up and honourable men are only binding upon mediocrities. Wagner's head is a smithy of a very different order. He forges masterpieces, mountains of adamant." He was always mindful of the Master's greatness, but since he had been under the influence of the Princess, he was no longer altogether just to him as a man. This was not without importance at this precise moment, and in the circumstances it was, indeed, fateful. For, if the Princess refused to give up the manuscript of *Jesus of Nazareth* on the ground that it was anti-religious, she may well have been capable of influencing Liszt as a father, too, through her dominance over him, causing him, kind though he usually was, to use his paternal authority in opposition to Wagner's union with his feminine genius. For she succeeded in making him hold aloof from his unique friend, as well as in setting up a barrier between himself and his daughter, which, however, was in the long run powerless to hold out against the deep feelings on the part of both of them. The father's eyes gazed longingly after his daughter, the only child who was left to him, while his friend's wondrous music, written under her ægis, fell upon his ear with tones even more sacred and sublime than the bells of St. Peter's, which summoned him to divine service. There is perhaps no episode in the history of mankind which, on close consideration, has power to produce such a moving impression as the relations between Liszt and Wagner, and Liszt and his daughter, on the one hand; and between Wagner and Cosima, and Wagner, through her, and Liszt, on the other. It is with a touch of irony that we hear the voice of fate in certain words once spoken by the Princess, who had warned Liszt against Wagner, because, in comparison with the latter, he would appear as a mere follower — a fate to which Liszt afterwards bowed: the great man who towered above him became his son-in-law. The Princess was mother-in-law to Prince Hohenlohe; but Franz Liszt, from whom she was parted, so to speak, at the very altar, became the father-in-law of the greatest artist of his day. In this lies the great difference between the ultimate destinies of Carolyne Wittgenstein and Franz Liszt, which, for all the tragedy associated with it, was a wonderful one.

But the real reason which induced the Master and Frau Cosima to cast a veil of mystery over their great love — thereby, as a matter of fact, laying a heavy burden upon both their conscience and their feelings — was to be found in the deep affection of them both for Hans von Bülow. How often did each breathe to the other the word " renunciation " ! They too suffered what is expressed in the verses:

> *Die Vorsicht sprach, " Das wird nicht frommen,"*
> *Die Sitte sprach, " Vernimm mein Wort ":*
> *Da ist der Strom der Liebe kommen*
> *Und ohne Wahl riss er uns fort.*

(Prudence whispered: " Have a care! "
Morals said: " Hark to what I say! "
Then came the flood of love, and bare
Us helpless on its flood away.)

But this was not all. It is a mistake to say that Frau Cosima did not in the first place give her hand to Hans von Bülow out of love, and that this ill-starred marriage was due to Franz Liszt's influence. This view is false and at variance with the truth. Frau Cosima did love Hans von Bülow, and never, during her whole life, did a word of depreciation pass her lips, even in speaking of him to the Master. The letters which she wrote him, both during her betrothal and as his wife, are so warm-hearted, and permeated with such a noble and even ardent passion, that a breath of warmth and happiness must have gone out from them to her husband. There were moments, certainly, when she could be hard and domineering; for every great feminine emotion was present in her: her nature possessed the qualities of a Semiramis, in the grandest sense of the word, quite as much as those of a Brünhilde, and, to a far greater extent than the gentle, kindly lady of the Green Hill, those of an Isolde.

She knew that Hans von Bülow was a man in no way suited for marriage and having no comprehension of it. The artist's creative work and will were his whole life. But he had loved her brother Daniel, and Cosima, too, was very near his heart, especially since, with her wonderful, many-sided nature, she always stood by him as a true comrade in his artistic work. There can be no question that, as a pianist, Hans von Bülow received his highest education from his master's daughter, and in all artistic questions she was his best adviser. And so she remained even when the mighty transformation came, and it was her essential magnanimity, and the feeling, which continued to make itself felt in her for many years, that he would suffer from this deprivation, that held her back from the revelation of her great love and of the overmastering necessity for a separation. The same was true of Richard Wagner. For if Liszt saw in Bülow his best pupil and artistic heir, Wagner in many respects rated Hans far higher. He was a friend to him in the highest sense of the word, and, regardless of the profound deference shown him by Bülow even in external things, the Master, more than anybody else, hailed in him a superior nature and, in some sense, a comrade. It was precisely those who claimed to be his most faithful friends who misunderstood him most. Frau Cosima knew this, and that is what guided her judgment and her attitude towards the Master's disciples. Thus during these very days of tension and rupture she writes to Klindworth, by whom she set more store than by any of the Master's friends, with the exception of her husband: " I am very glad that you have carried away a friendly memory of the house in the Arcostrasse, and I earnestly beg you to regard it as your own, for you will always be sure of a joyful and affectionate welcome there. It is to be hoped that your deliverance from London will be the beginning of a new and happy period of your artistic life, and that you will soon have a tolerable report to give us of Moscow. I say nothing of your good friend, for all things have their limits. You will have heard from Hans that I found our Master very fatigued. I like to think that he is better, and that the break in his solitude, which has been far too complete, is good for him in both heart and mind, but especially in health. It was not nice of you — if I may be allowed to scold you — not to go and see him. In your place I would have given up even *Lohengrin* to see him again. He has all too few devoted friends, all too few who are willing to bear the yoke of admiration and lighten it by affection. These few ought not to be negligent of such rare meetings as are scattered through life. But I will not make your heart too heavy, though you have made mine heavy in this way. For after assuring Wagner that you attached great importance to coming and paying your respects to him, I had to bear being laughed at a little. I am to tell you from the Master that it would be a pretty business, after all, if the artist were to disappear behind his works. He would feel that he was being altogether too Olympian, and he had rather be treated like a man. ' *Doch alles in Liebe und Güte* (But all this in love and charity),' as they say in *Der Freischütz.*"

These words, written in August 1868, were highly characteristic of the attitude adopted by the Master towards his disciples, and by Frau Cosima too. She felt the immense loneliness in which he lived, in spite of his renown, in spite of the prodigious fame which had begun to come to him since the performance of *The Mastersingers*. There is also a strongly personal touch in this letter to Klindworth; for not only had he had a share in arranging the pianoforte scores of the Master's works, but he was also an intimate friend of Hans von Bülow and remained so up to the last years of the latter's life. And that is why she speaks to him of Hans in almost as cordial terms as of the Master: " I was very glad that you kept Hans company for a little while longer. The poor fellow is overwhelmed with work at present, though the results seem to be gratifying. The concert must have been a real refreshment to you; how overpowering it must have been to make the acquaintance of the Prelude to *Tristan*! I am absolutely vegetating here, but it suits me very well. When one has had more experience of the world than would seem requisite or desirable, complete retirement does one good. Besides, I felt it an absolute necessity to treasure here for ever in quiet and tranquillity such a matchless impression as is produced by *The Mastersingers*. Wagner's creations are in such contrast with our world of today and its bustle that they have the power to make one feel quite dazed when one is still in the midst of it all." In these words, too, there is, as it were, an underlying motive: for the great success of *The Master-singers* would have been impossible without her, since it was only through her self-sacrifice that the work itself was brought to completion. We must not underestimate this wonderful woman's inward excitement during this period which followed *The Mastersingers*. For her its effects were of quite a different order, and that not an egotistical one; but its success was, as it were, the great and solemn answer to the question which she had put to fate. Not that she hesitated, or shrank from her solemn resolution, but it satisfied all her feelings as a woman that, through *The Mastersingers* itself, she saw her love for its creator glorified, consecrated, and hallowed.

Immediately after the last performance of *The Mastersingers*, on the other hand, we see signs of an agitation in Hans von Bülow so vehement and passionate that only with difficulty was he able to cope with his duties in Munich up to the end. Nor should we forget that, just at this time, he absolutely rejected the highly tempting offer from Pasdeloup and the impresario Ull-mann to conduct *Lohengrin* in Paris, which was from every point of view an honourable one. For the moment he regarded himself entirely as the servant of his master, King Ludwig. But never did Peter Cornelius say or write anything so true as what he said of the conductor of *The Mastersingers*: "Filled as he is with a priestly enthusiasm for art and its chosen exponents, their gallant performance lends him a heroic aureole." And now, too, he behaved like a hero. He hastened to Wiesbaden, indeed, to find succour at the side of Joachim Raff, to whom he had always had recourse at those moments when, so to speak, the effect produced upon him by the Master had been too much for his strength and he wanted to touch earth again, a purpose for which Raff's un-emotional and reserved Swiss temperament made him highly suitable. Here Bülow gambled and practised pistol-shooting. For the rest, however, his household was scattered and absolutely broken up. His mother had returned to Berlin, and now Frau

Cosima took a step — indeed, she was forced to take it — which was perhaps the most fateful in the whole course of this dramatic denouement. Its significance was undoubtedly more than merely symbolical, and even by Richard Wagner it was regarded as " the end." He proposed to her a visit to Italy, which was absolutely necessary to him after the unprecedented agitation of *The Mastersingers*. Such a powerful mind as his could not simply emerge from Triebschen, direct all the rehearsals of a work whose performance inaugurated a new epoch in the German theatre, and then retire once more to the solitudes of Triebschen and the confines of this old country-house which, wide as was the prospect which it commanded of the Lake of Lucerne, were yet unspeakably narrow. He invited Frau Cosima to go abroad with him, so as to clear up the whole situation thoroughly from Italy. But the veil of mystery extended to this journey as well, so that when Hans von Bülow became aware of it, it seemed to him to hide nothing but treachery and lies. He could not but take it in this way, and so, as a matter of fact, he did. His pistol-practice, too, had more than a merely symbolical significance. By opening a letter in the most innocent way, he became aware of this journey and of the full import of the Master's relations with Frau Cosima, which were known to all the world and hidden from him alone. Upon this he laid aside the conductor's baton, which he had wielded in Richard Wagner's behalf, and took up the pistol. In the manner traditional among gentlemen he discussed with a friend, who appreciated him and Wagner's music equally, how the matter was to be cleared up. He wanted to obtain satisfaction by the pistol for what was in the circumstances an unheard-of state of affairs, which he at first regarded as a monstrous outrage. But his friend replied: " You cannot fight a duel with the Master," upon which he collapsed on a chair and burst into a fit of passionate sobbing. Then he once more took up the threads which threatened to become hopelessly entangled. He gave out to his friends as the truth the explanation of this journey which had been intended to deceive himself — though only with a view to sparing his feelings — that is, that Frau Cosima had got to go to her step-sister, the Countess de Charnacé, at Versailles, for some considerable time, in order to take care of her health, which was seriously affected, and, in any circumstances, to visit Italy with her. He did so with such decision and confidence that some of the hostile reports which were going round were silenced at once. But he poured out his heart to the Countess de Charnacé, and perhaps he also divulged something of what he had gone through to one of his friends and more distant acquaintances. His letter to the Countess de Charnacé is heart-rending, as is, indeed, the whole correspondence which he carried on with Frau Cosima's step-sister. The Countess, who, like Cosima, was a true daughter of Marie d'Agoult, had, indeed, the profoundest comprehension of him, and while the denouement was in progress, she had also offered her services to her step-sister in the capacity of mediator. Unfortunately, with the exception of a single letter, the correspondence between him and his wife's step-sister is still inaccessible. But in this letter he revealed his knowledge of the journey to Italy and went on to say: " The affectionate reminiscences of me that you preserve, together with the deep tenderness of your words, could not but have touched me profoundly and given me confidence, and even courage, if I were not at present in a state of utter moral and physical weakness. By an unavoidable fate, the carrying out of my final resolution to break completely with my past existence, as a man and an artist, is still delayed for several weeks. I have to purchase the absolute rest which my utterly ruined health has required for long past, by prolonging a state of affairs which is as impossible as it is inevitable. Finally, in order to bear this inward agony, I have had to feign an unnatural insensibility, the enforced maintenance of which I deplore when I think of the real good which you have done me, madame, by your beautiful letter. On the other hand, I take so little interest in myself at present, or in my more than problematical future. I am now too old to build up my life again out of any materials but the remains and ruins of that which is past, and these stand in glaring contrast with an object in which I cannot understand how such a superior nature as yours, madame, can interest yourself. But please do not measure by the coldness of my words the depth of my gratitude, which I am unhappy enough to be unable to prove or put to the test for the moment. But though I have little confidence in my recovery, yet I do not doubt that I shall find it possible later."

It was doubly hard for him to come to this decision and put into action his resolve to obtain a divorce. Most of all, the parting with his children was unspeakably hard for him. But even in his most vehement and passionate moments he could not think of taking them from their mother; for from the first there was one thing which he had had to observe: that he could find no better mother for his children. And though his own mother had always behaved to Frau Cosima like a harsh stepmother and treated her, in her own house, in a way which no other woman would have endured, he had always had the feeling that the grand, maternal element in Frau Cosima must be defended even against his mother. There can be no doubt whatever that by her petty, violent, and morbid behaviour this lady had turned the life of her son's wife into a hell, and that in the most critical hours of her life Frau Cosima had moved about her own home as restlessly as a soul in torment. We should not forget that the birth of her second daughter had almost ended in a tragedy owing to the unexampled neglect of her mother-in-law. Frau Cosima was left all alone in her travail, and by the time help at last came to her, and it proved requisite to send for the midwife, the child was already born. In spite of this, the inward bond which attached Cosima to Hans was an extraordinarily strong one, and marked by real passion.

But now, after her return from Genoa, where the Master had tried to persuade her to remain, merely asking that the children should be handed over to her, an explanation ensued of the most heart-rending and impassioned description on both sides. She did not emerge from it until she had explained to him with the utmost clearness the relations which had constituted such a dramatic development in her life. As we have said, Hans von Bülow was a man in no way cut out for marriage. His violence was often so great that, long before Richard Wagner entered their house, a Berlin doctor had said it was wonderful that Frau Cosima could stand such a state of affairs at all. But she was far too much of an artist's child not to do so. She had experience of her own father's violence and was able to see beyond the indefinable irritability which was really the outcome of his artistic production and activity; so that she carried off the most vehement scenes with a sort of coolness, even displaying a certain humour in them. This, together with Frau Cosima's unreserved appreciation of the chivalry of her husband — whom, it cannot be too often insisted, she loved with all her heart — had undoubtedly been the salvation of their marriage; so it is not at all correct to assume that, in the long run, it would have been quite impossible for the Bülows to live together. But it was at this very time, immediately after the performance of *The Mastersingers*, that an indomitable conviction of the fatality of her great and mighty mission took shape of its own accord in the young woman's mind. It was in no sense of the word an act dictated by the senses and by supreme passion that led her to the Master, but the clear consciousness that without her he would be lost, and that without her helping hand the mighty works which he had in view as the aim and object of his life would never attain their consummation. Such was the substance of these last explanations in their home at Munich, when Bülow and his wife said farewell to each other for life. Nothing, perhaps, can be more affecting than this scene. We should be reminded, not of *Tristan*, but far rather of Brünhilde's farewell to Wotan. Her sentiments were fully analogous to the great emotions of Wotan's daughter. For Bülow had given her one thing which had, indeed, long been dormant in her, but had also come to life: " *zu lieben, was du geliebt* (to love what thou hast loved)." [1] But Bülow was no Wotan, nor was he a King Mark; far from it. His feeling of devotion to the Master had been so unreserved that it dominated, not only his artistic, but his personal sensibilities. All the harder and more profoundly did he feel this parting; for Frau Cosima had been to him not only his wife and the mother of his children, but in some sense, too, a pledge confided to him by his master, Liszt. On the other hand, it would be doing him an injustice to represent his attitude towards his master as too completely that of a disciple. In his relations with Liszt his own personality as an artist always came into very decided prominence. In particular, he always preferred to hold quite aloof

---

[1] *The Valkyrie*, III, iii.—TR.

from Liszt's relations with the Princess, however much she had extended her protection to him for a time. In his eyes her influence was, so to speak, anti-musical, and he inveighed furiously against her interference in Liszt's work on Chopin. But the daughter stood higher in his estimation than the father and was really in part a sister to him. Nothing could be more touching than the fact that, after the parting with Frau Cosima, he took the son of the Brussels musician Servais from his own home and had him live with him, welcoming him and treating him as a disciple, largely because of his astonishing likeness to his deceased brother-in-law, Daniel. This clinging to the beloved dead, which almost amounted to a resurrection, has something heart-rending about it just at this moment. It was as though his grief for Daniel formed an outlet for his deepest emotion. But Frau Cosima's heart bled no less than his at the parting. Throughout his whole life she always continued to honour him most highly and in her innermost heart she felt as much pain as she did gratitude at his consent to the divorce. This was no ordinary parting. Besides, they were far too intimately bound up with each other, and both their natures — above all, that of Frau Cosima — were far too deep, too honourable, and also, it must be said, too religious for them not to have suffered unspeakably from the parting. When the idea of a separation became imminent, she took counsel with her confessor, like the pious Catholic that she was, and revealed all to him; and, with a profound understanding of this great nature, he declared that she must follow the promptings of her heart. Thus the severance took place amid infinite suffering and ineffable agony, and with such a burden Frau Cosima started out for Triebschen, now never again to be parted from the Master till his death.

From the very moment of her arrival at Triebschen, she began to keep a diary, which she inaugurated by the following words addressed to her children: " You are to know every hour of my life, so that you may one day come to know me, for, should I die early, others will be able to say but little about me, and if I die at an advanced age, all I shall be able to do is to keep silence. Thus you shall help me to do my duty — yes, children, my duty. What I mean by this you will see later. Your mother will tell you all about her present life, for she believes that she can do so. 1868 is the turning-point of my outward life: in this year it was vouchsafed to me to carry into action what had been the inspiration of my life for five years past. I did not seek this action, nor try to bring it about; it was destiny that imposed it upon me. In order that you may understand me, I must go back to the hour in which I realized my true and innermost mission, when my life was a desolate, unlovely dream, about which I am able to tell you nothing; for I myself do not understand it and reject it with all the force of my soul, which has now undergone its purgation. Outward appearances were calm and remained so, but inwardly all was waste and desolation, when the Being revealed himself to me through whom it was soon made clear to me that as yet I had never lived at all. My love was a new birth, a redemption, the death of all that was worthless and bad within me, and I vowed to myself to seal it by death, by the holiest renunciation, or else by complete resignation, that might be worthy of the miracle of love which has come upon me, if ever I am able to requite it. When it was so ordered by the stars, by events which I had to experience in a different connexion, that I saw my only friend, the tutelary genius of my soul, the revealer of all that was noble and true, driven out into solitude alone, abandoned, joyless, and friendless, I cried unto him: " I am coming to you, and I mean to find my highest and most sacred happiness in helping you to bear your life. It was now, too, that I parted from my two dear eldest children. I have done it and would do it again at any moment, and yet I miss you and think of you day and night. I love you all alike; in your hearts I seek a sanctuary for my memory upon earth when I shall have gone hence; and I would have sacrificed all for you — all but the life of the Only one. The parting will be but a passing one, and you are still so small that you do not feel it as your mother does. Such is my hope."

With thoughts such as these she hastened to the Master's retreat. But it was the Master himself who spoke the memorable words about this step: " To this refuge (*Asyl*), too, the woman next fled who was to establish it as a fact that I could indeed be helped and that the axiom of so many of my friends, that it was impossible to help me, was wrong. She knew that I could be helped, and help me she did." This is the true inwardness of the Triebschen period, and the Master's artistic achievement bears witness to it. But even had this not been so, these days at Triebschen were none the less hallowed: hallowed by a love and sympathy beyond compare. And so she ruled the house at Triebschen, which, with its garden, field, and coppice, is commonly represented as a considerable property. Yet essentially it was small and confined; their thoughts and emotions alone extended afar. But one thing above all: he was infinitely happy. When he offered her his New Year wishes at the beginning of 1869, she had to write in her diary: " I am still so overwhelmed by his goodness to me that, thanks to my deep and incessant perception of his greatness, I could be for ever melting into tears in his presence." Yet she had delighted him by the two youngest children's New Year wishes, which they had come in their little white frocks to offer to their father.

This first of January was a fateful day. The first thing into which he initiated her was his pamphlet *Das Judentum in der Musik* (*The Jews in Music*). He discussed with her the bearing of this article on his position — that is, on that of his art. But she listened with some alarm to his lucid and unflinching arguments, and one thing above all affected her deeply: that is, the picture which he sketched of Felix Mendelssohn-Bartholdy. " For the first time Mendelssohn appeared to me as a tragic figure." This was a completely new world to her, in which she had first to find a footing, though for years past, at Hans von Bülow's side, she had lived in the midst of furious controversy. She was now uncertain how to advise Wagner, for she felt too much biased in his favour; indeed, she herself says: " I cannot advise him, for whether I were to be told that he is involving himself in the greatest annoyances, or that he will be utterly ignored, or that he will produce a good effect, I should believe anything." But her other impressions were all far greater. A telegram arrived from the King, and letters from the children, which set both their minds at rest. " And then," she writes, " he played me the Spring Song from *The Valkyrie*. When once you hear these strains, my children, you will understand me. I cannot

335

hear them without swooning." Then she settled down and asked him to go on dictating his biography. This she did out of a glorious superstition, for she imagined that what one did on the first day of the year one would continue to do. And so she took down the chapter on Schopenhauer, which was immeasurably precious to her, and wrote it with the golden pen with which he had written *Tristan and Isolde* and *Siegfried*. He had given it to her, and with it she also intended to write her own diary; for the pen " which wrote down the most sublime things traced by a supreme mind shall be dedicated to none but the deepest and most womanly heart." And with it she wrote a blessing more touching than any that has ever been conceived or uttered by a mother: " My blessings upon you, then, my children, upon those of you who are near and those who are afar, and upon thee, too, my unknown child, still resting within the womb. Your mother's love is a friendly light to you throughout your lives. Never misjudge your mother, though you may never act as she has done. For fate has here ordained a thing such as does not happen twice."

And now began a wonderful intellectual life: he occupied in supreme creation, in which he conceded her a full share; she preoccupied with shielding him from all cares and outward hindrances, and keeping him strong and healthy for his great work. It is touching to see how they now chose the same things to read at the same time: " Platen — no, *Wallenstein* — no; Calderón is too pathetic . . ." and the Master took down the Odyssey, which made the most glorious impression upon her and gave her a really sublime evening, which left indelible images imprinted upon her soul. For a time, indeed, Homer occupied her entirely; for he had exerted the deepest influence over the Master's art and the whole of his earlier life, but most of all over his ideals. From Homer he drew spiritual peace, as he did again now, with which was associated in beauteous harmony the peace of nature. But it is curious that it was precisely out of the frame of mind induced by the Odyssey that his feeling for the German heroes developed. Through his grandiose conception of the German nature as a whole, he led her to understand his beloved Bernhard of Weimar and Gustavus Adolphus of Sweden. Nay, more, he went on to speak of the horsemen's songs (*Reiterlieder*) of the Thirty Years' War. Day by day the great wealth of his learning was revealed to her, and now that there was nothing to disturb her, as he peopled her solitude with the figures which occupied his mind, this unprecedented knowledge naturally produced a quite peculiar impression upon her, and in the evenings she listened to him with all the more pleasure as he caused all the books of the Odyssey, all the great scenes of the nymph Calypso and the healing Leucothea, to pass before her eyes. And, like a truly loving wife, she says that her sole distraction while he was reading to her was to contemplate his radiant face and delight in the music of his voice. And so it pained her when at first he would leave her nothing to attend to by day, but in his courtly way did everything himself; and she wrote sadly in the evening: " He does not yet know how gladly I do everything for him, the smallest and the greatest things alike."

But most beautiful of all were the hours when he played her his works. When he played her the Prelude to *Tristan,* she was profoundly agitated — in fact, she could scarcely preserve her self-command. " At such moments all I know is that, in Elsa's words, ' *für Dich möchte ich zu Tode gehen* (for thee would I go to meet death),' [1] and even this I am powerless to express."

These were wondrous days, days rapt from the world, and it was only sorrow for her children that brought her back to earth. We see her standing high up in the garden, overcome by the deepest emotion: " As I stood on the hill-side, I was enraptured at the circle of snow-covered mountains, which represent to me the mysterious phenomenon of a motionless dance. As I gazed long upon the scene, my spirit became aware of the music through which exalted natures reflect themselves for us in sound. I felt the transience of all personal existence; the eternal essence of all greatness rises, a radiant message, from the pale mirror of the lake."

Only thus, indeed, was it possible for him to obtain the mighty power to continue his *Siegfried* and to succeed in casting it in his wondrous mould. For all their impressions from the outside

[1] *Lohengrin*, III, ii.—Tr.

world were painful and alien to them both. The news from Paris
was gloomy and depressing. Its doings and bustle seemed more
strange to them than ever, and they really wanted to hear no
more of the state of the world, " where everything is going on in
its normal way (*wo jetzt das Diapason normal ist*)." And so
they were really quite cut off from the world. As she said:
" There is such a thing as happiness, but we do not know it.
I know it and know how to value it. All the suffering and misery
in the world has a happiness deep hidden in its heart, like the
pearl in its shell. No pain can touch it; and in the most grievous
hours the pearl of ecstasy was resting tranquilly in my soul."

In spite of this, her position was by no means an easy one.
In accordance with a wish of her husband's — a wish which
was, however, rather pedantic and formal — she was to live in
concealment at Triebschen. She had complied with this wish
and had now to realize that it was not so easy. The servants of
the Bassenheim family, which was otherwise very friendly, spied
upon them, and there was a danger lest the secret of their where-
abouts might transpire in Munich. She set her mind at rest,
indeed, with the thought that in concealing where she was from
the world, she had had nothing evil in view, but only consideration for others. " And should the trials which I expect arise from
this, I will tell you all, my children, in God's name — how it
came about, and how it happened, and how I endure it." And
her dreams were of them; in spirit she spent her time in the
nursery at Munich, yet on awakening from such dreams she went
her way firmly and confidently in the house where she had to
guard the treasure entrusted to her charge. It was a wonderful
alternation between dream and reality: for both she and Wagner
were natures which felt the closest connexion with the spirit
world. It is touching to read how they told each other their
dreams, and how these were, so to speak, complementary. She
shared his every care, and also his every joy. When, in his
degenerate journalistic way, Fröbel published an article against
Oper und Drama, which could only be read with disgust, she
remarked: " There is no question here of a conflict in which one
opposes one's adversary courageously, nor even of a martyrdom.
This is a mere case of mud-throwing, against which there is no

resistance." But Wagner was naturally depressed by such in-gratitude. For it was he himself who had opened up the way to Munich to Fröbel.

But there was no lack of friendly communications from the outer world. She was deeply delighted with the letters of her eldest daughter, Daniela, and her relations with Frau von Schleinitz, too, were not severed at all. She received really touching letters from her friends the Countess Mouchanoff and the Countess Krockow. Yet, as she said herself: " But I do not know what I have to do with friendships now. None will follow me when they know where I have gone; it is only by you, my children, that I now want to be loved and known." Her whole heart was stirred by the Master's works, and by the Odyssey, too, to a quite peculiar degree. With truly feminine sensibility she read the passage in which Ulysses returns home and is recognized by none save his faithful old dog, Argus. And she remarks: " How near we are brought to the deep mystery of nature when Ulysses' sick old dog is the only one who recog-nizes him under his changed aspect, and then dies after twenty years of waiting! "

Next came round Hans von Bülow's birthday, January 8. He might well be proud of the spirit in which Frau Cosima recalled it. " I wish that he might spend it in a peaceful mood of recon-ciliation, though I can do nothing to contribute towards this. It was a great misunderstanding that united us in matrimony; I still feel the same for him as I did twelve years ago: great sympathy for his destiny, delight in his gifts of both mind and heart, a real esteem for his character, together with a complete incompatibility of disposition. In the very first year of my marriage I was in such despair at our misunderstandings that I wanted to die. This was the cause of many errors, but I always plucked up fresh courage, and your father suspected none of my sufferings; and I think he will not refuse to bear witness to the fact that I stood by him in both joy and sorrow and helped him to the best of my power. He would never have lost me had not destiny brought me into contact with him for whom I was bound to recognize it as my mission to live and die. I have not a single reproach to utter against your father, though the last few years were beyond measure hard for me. I wanted to make the attempt to amalgamate my previous existence with my new life; I believed this to be possible — that there might be a fusion of such utterly different feelings. Insults and mortifications have proved to me that I am a fool, and all that remained to me was to make my choice and to suffer."

During the whole of this period she was a prey to a deep melancholy, and though she passed the hours spent in the company of the lonely artist with a cheerful face and touching sympathy, she poured out her heart in her diary, and her dejection was reflected in her dreams. She saw her sister Blandine, and awoke, after a long conversation with her, thinking that she was already dead. And her comment is: " Children, draw close the bonds between you! It is only when one has drawn both joy and sorrow from the same source that trust and love are kindled. The friendships which life in the long run brings with it are all subject to doubts and misunderstandings. The unflinching faith which rest upon full knowledge dwells only in the love of sisters."

They were both concerned about their relations with the King, and the thought that the allowance settled on the Master might be stopped was ever present in their minds. But what affected Wagner most were his spiritual experiences with the King, and this made him far more afraid of the possibility that he might be faced with the necessity of declining the allowance than of any hostile step on the part of Ludwig. But they weighed the consequences: " We discussed the possibilities of living in a garret in Paris for the future. One living-room and two bedrooms for us and the children! God knows what fate has in store for us." But it was often his own ideas that plunged him from the greatest optimism into the deepest pessimism. Nor was it outward circumstances that forced such cares upon him. For he quoted Calderón to the effect that happy love is the most terrible thing, for then one has everything to fear. But the curse of his life, he said, was poverty and marriage. Naturally this gave Frau Cosima cause for grave reflection too. But she had to say to herself that such of the works as were completed must secure them against want, even without the King. She did not think of herself, however, or of the future — only of the completion of *The Ring of the Nibelung* — and this is why she said: " When he is away, I am a prey to apprehension and care; we shall be given no rest, I see us abandoned to misery and spiteful mockery. But so soon as he is there again, the evil thoughts vanish. It is a real pain to me to be parted from him even for a short time." It is no wonder that she gave herself up to such thoughts, for she was lonelier than ever. Hans von Bülow was silent, and so was her father, who was now staying in Germany. And she sighed: " How alien everything connected with this world has become to me! " And what news she did hear of the world was of hatred, calumny, and insults, which were heaped chiefly upon herself and her portrait. " The sole remaining consolation is that what is worthless is also incapable of founding anything." The Master divined what was in her heart, and tried to comfort her, and in his presence she entirely revived. How touching it was when he said to her: " Poor woman — but, after all, you have me (*Arme Frau, da hast Du nun mich*) " !

It is interesting to see how their opinions differed upon some things. It was the news from Munich that actually set them talking about Lola Montez. Cosima's comment upon her end, of which she had heard recently, was: " Poor creature! " But he sternly rebuked her with the words: " Such dæmonic and heartless beings are not to be pitied and regretted." Of course he was right, she said, but evil was always lamentable, and a miserable end was pitiful beyond all things. Lola Montez was, indeed, not so entirely unconnected with her own destiny. For a time Cosima's father had been held as fast in her bonds as King Ludwig I had been, and fundamentally it was on her account that the breach between her father and mother had taken place. And now in the campaign against the Master in Munich the parallel between him and the Spanish dancer always played a prominent part.

For the rest, the whole of this time was filled with her anxiety about Hans von Bülow. She herself says that perhaps she tortured herself about him far too much. But his artistic activities had been a source of delight to him; and since the frustration of their great artistic enterprise this source had dried up. Besides, she dreaded the alienation of her elder children. How different was the Master himself — how much more lively! He could not believe that she would have to atone for her devotion to him by the alienation of her elder children. He tried to make Triebschen a veritable paradise to her, and she became more and more at home in this dream-world. As she herself beautifully remarks: " The play of mist and sun makes the opposite shore seem like a dream-vision. The trees covered with hoar-frost give me a kindly greeting; Pilatus, with his golden cloud-halo, is like the sublime king of this dream-world. ' *Alles Vergängliche ist nur ein Gleichnis* (All that is transient is but a symbol) ' rings in my ears as I reach the high ground and look about me. No happiness upon earth, but in our hearts the imperishable essence, which sounds within us at every sublime strain of music, at every profound poem, at every beautiful picture, at every sight of nature, or at every great and high-hearted action."

But a strange mood came over her, for he was now dictating to her the part of his biography dealing with his experiences in Zürich, and the image of Mathilde Wesendonck dawned directly upon her spiritual vision. It was no petty jealousy of this woman, so kind and yet so weak, that involuntarily assailed her. After taking down Wagner's account to his dictation, she afterwards wrote in her diary the memorable words: " It seems to me that the year 1858 was the real turning-point in Richard's life, and that if Frau Wesendonck had borne herself well then, he would have been spared all the perplexities which lasted till the appearance of the King. Then, too, it would have been superfluous for me to become a burden upon his life, though we should always have become deeply attached to each other. The consciousness of this has saddened me." Thus she was forced to live in the past and yet to look out with dread and sorrow upon the present. For that February on the lake was indeed symbolic of her outward life. Not a word came from Munich, while she received sad news about her mother from Paris; and at first what she most needed, in spite of all, was lacking — that is, the companionship of some outside persons. Everything caused her the most violent agitation — most of all, if he became despondent about his work — not about his own ability, but about people

RICHARD WAGNER'S HOUSE AT TRIEB-
SCHEN

Photograph by Wehrliverlag, Kilchberg-Zürich

and the times. When he spoke of the pointlessness " of such great and impassioned work for this paltry, petty Puritan age," she was seized with despair: " It is terrible to hear him say this, it is as though there would be no blessing upon our union if *The Nibelungs* were to remain unfinished." Oppressed by these thoughts, she wanted to go to him in the night, and, in the anguish which was dawning upon her soul at her powerlessness to help him, to tell him that she was going away and now meant to live for her children alone. " But I did not do it! How readily would I have made the sacrifice of my life and happiness! But I thought of his life, his destiny, and fell into a faint. When I came to, I went to him, and in the morning I was able to tell him that I had slept well. But on the next day a strange conversation sprang up, as though of its own accord. I asked him whether he had ever really wished for death, upon which Richard said that he had indeed longed for it, but had never really seen himself faced with it; only when he had thought that we must part did he feel that his life was at an end and that he could do nothing to help it. I quivered and trembled, for what he told me followed, as it were, the trend of my thoughts during the night." She felt how lonely he was and how she alone stood by him.

Indeed, circumstances were depressing enough at the moment. The thought of Paris and the garret kept recurring to them, and so, on the other hand, did her fear of madness, not for herself, but for her husband. As the result of an article which had appeared about her husband, a letter arrived from him, demanding, in the most singular terms, an explanation about the days at Zürich when he had first entered Richard Wagner's house. The article had stated quite correctly that Richard Wagner had cared for him like a father at that time, while his own family had left him without resources. " This seems to have wounded him," adds Frau Cosima. " How petty! " The Master drafted an explanation and sent Hans the rough copy. On top of this came another thing, about which Frau Cosima writes: " Whether from lust of possession or religious scruples, the Wittgenstein woman (*Die W.*) refuses to give up the manuscript of *Jesus of Nazareth* which was lent her. Whatever her reason may be, the cynical insolence is the same." Next she heard that Hans was playing nothing but Rubinstein at Hanover. This affected her violently, for she knew his nature and opinions and could not conceive how he could have changed them so completely all at once. And she reflects: " I do not know whether I am getting more and more receptive or more and more morbidly susceptible. But there are certain powerful impressions that I can hardly bear any longer. I stand in absolute dread before the might of genius, which suddenly discloses to us the unfathomable mysteries of existence, as though we were seized in the grasp of this divinely dæmonic power. What Richard said on the death of Schnorr comes into my mind: ' Perhaps art is a great curse (*Frevel*), and those are indeed to be esteemed happy who, like the beasts, have no notion of it.' But suppose that this happiness, too, seems like eternal darkness! I gaze till I am blind, listen till I am deaf, and feel all the beauty till I can feel no more, and the glittering starry abyss draws me down, I gaze into it powerless to resist and am swallowed up unconscious in its depths. We poor women, who can do nothing but love, are indeed to be pitied when we divine the mystery of genius. Yet without this co-operation with genius, what are we? And upon this, exhausted as by a sort of swoon, I sank into a deep sleep."

But now came a fresh alarm, occasioned by Hans. He wrote the Master a letter requesting that his wife should pay a visit to Versailles, there to await the further progress of events. The Master fell into a state of extreme agitation. " He rushed wildly out of the room (*Er taumelte förmlich hinaus*). I at once grasped what Hans meant by his last communication." But without a break she immediately goes on to write the wonderful words: " The most sublime atmosphere both around me and within; my unborn child stirs within the womb, and I bless it. May its spirit be clear and mild as this glittering night-sky, august and tranquil as the mountain shrouded in its mantle of snow! May its disposition be as deep and peaceful as these lightly rippling waves, may it gaze into the gloomy darkness at its feet as unmoved as the sombre forest at the foot of the mountain, while the summit is bathed in light! May the fortunes of the future shine tenderly upon it! May it ever think with love of the mother who bore it in love! " This marks her great and mighty transformation. It is like the emotion which suddenly awakes in Sieglinde when Brünhilde, her saviour, announces to her that she bears within her womb the most glorious hero in the world. And now, strong and great, she went her way through these days of suspense and apprehension, which her husband had certainly not meant to cause, but which were none the less due to a certain narrowness in his point of view, as well as to the difficult position in which he stood towards the State.

She suffered, too, from the fact that the Master was profoundly agitated at his friend's letter and said that it seemed to him that nothing but magic kept him alive, and that he could really bear no more. But she was able to bear everything. She, too, was haunted by premonitions and cares, and all natural phenomena seemed to her, as it were, symbolic. One evening, as she paced the shore of the lake, a single star glittered down upon her from the dark clouds; and she exclaimed to it: " Guide my destiny in friendship, shine kindly upon my children." " As I spoke these words, it suddenly disappeared. Was it that tears clouded my eyes, or that the light of the rising moon dimmed its little light? ' Ah, thou art inexorable as the other great one, like him thou dost bid me be resigned.' Then suddenly it appeared once more. ' If thou art now appeased, vouchsafe me a friendly sign, that thou wilt be a friend to my children! ' And suddenly I saw Richard standing before me, having sought me everywhere and called to me, like Siegfried, from every side. Joyfully I hailed this sign, the whole landscape was bathed in light, the clouds were vanquished by the moon, the sombre mood had passed away. My little friend I saw no more, but I had before me my great friend, who was to me the pledge of this mad crisis in my fate. Richard said I should but know all the things he cries out to me when I am not there! Ah, I know that he loves me! " This is a wonderful night piece from the dramatically eventful idyll of Triebschen, which brought with it fresh pictures day by day, and even hour by hour, and stands before us in all its great and unique beauty and deep sensibility, in all the radiant purity that streamed forth from this woman

and her love! That evening the Master read some history to her
— the passage on the help given by the Platæans — and then
the fight with the dragon out of Schiller. In all this she had the
profoundest sense of the great and beautiful. Tears, and yet more
tears! The Master was indeed right when he said: " There is
only one danger for us — that we love each other too much."

They lived remote from the world, and yet it was for ever
near them. It is strange how the greatness of Bismarck intruded
itself upon the solitudes of Triebschen, how Wagner saw none
save Bismarck who could help Germany and art, and how he
wanted to write to the statesman's wife to induce her husband
to become a patron of art. But Frau Cosima warned him against
such a step and such a letter. She herself had ideas which she
did not impart to her friend; though it cannot be said that
Johanna Bismarck would have had no comprehension for such
a letter. In the depths of her soul she had, indeed, artistic tendencies, and when music spoke to her, her prosaic view of life
vanished, just as it did at her husband's voice. Yet Frau Cosima
was right. The letter would not have found a response from
views like those in which it had its origin and for which it called.
But she indulged in reflections on the subject, and wrote in her
diary: " Why has all courage died within me, even the courage
for suffering? " And she looked through her letters: " During
the morning I read again the first letter which Richard wrote me
from Starnberg, and the poem on the sunset enclosed in it." She
was living in the present, yet seeking strength for this life in the
past. She would not have needed this had she not felt alive within
her the mighty conflict between duty and sin. And so she began
to see visions of a parting and a return to Munich, of once more
meeting with indifferent persons, from whom she was bound to
flee, in order, as the vision directed her, to seek a paradise for
her beloved. And she remarks: " The world of today — how its
music grates upon our solitude! " In her greatness of soul, she
had abandoned everything and sacrificed everything. How
touchingly it sounds when she writes: " Today is St. Richard's
day. In earlier days I should not have let it go by without jestingly reminding my beloved of his supposed patron saint's day
by a little present. But now I cannot, for I handed over all my

small resources to the house at Munich, and I must deprive myself of this joy. Ah, gladly will I do without it! It seems, indeed, to have been my natural vocation to give up everything and desire nothing. I can quite well imagine that a different age might have seen me a religious visionary — but love has taken hold of me and fulfilled itself, I know nothing but love, and will gladly suffer in it and through it."

It was in this frame of mind that they both read Danner's book of ghost-stories, and in it the touching story of the dumb child who forgets its sisters; but the spirit of their mother appears in her stead and takes care of the brothers and sisters while the child is dying. "We were deeply agitated. 'The important question is whether we are in communion with the spirits of those dear to us,' said Richard, who has a great leaning towards those realms, and perhaps, unconsciously, a great connexion with them." Not only did their hearts cling to each other, but their imaginations too. They had to take everything seriously and discuss everything thoroughly in order to arrive at a clear understanding of it. There is a self-torturing element in the nature of this wonderful woman, yet it was only by this way that she attained her full greatness. Thus one evening she asked him whether her love seemed to him to be in itself a wrong. " He does not understand me, he thinks I meant what the world sees to be wrong in it: the treachery of a friend. Then he said that he knew one thing only: that, since the world existed, no man of his age had so loved a woman as he does me. And so the wrong which I had mentioned bore no relation to the way in which it might be right for us to act, in accordance with our knowledge of life and of the highest virtue." Over all these thoughts and feelings there floated an exalted love: " I dreamt that I bore a son, and when I awoke and rose from my bed, I found that my camellia was in bloom. Since I had involuntarily connected it with Siegfried, I am overjoyed. If only the souls of my children might bloom as sweetly and as silently! " And even had she not felt herself that she was indispensable here, she must have learnt it from Wagner's own words, when he said " that if I were to go away, his life and work, his composition and endeavours would be at an end; and so I did not persist

347

in my idea of a two months' separation." For she had thought things over, and intended to write to Hans that she would come to the children in Munich for two months, and then, at the beginning of May, return with all four children to Triebschen. Her object in this was to avoid a scandal, on account of the children and also of the King. But the Master saw but one thing — the two months' parting, which was in his eyes a painful thing to be dreaded and which he could not endure. Thus, both on her side and on his, every thought was permeated with a sense of duty, a sense that she alone could sustain him, herself, and his art. The idea of a separation was impossible to him, and, as a matter of fact, with the exception of a few short days, they never left each other again.

But he charged these quiet days with infinite emotion for her, and an instruction which was constantly touching upon every province of art and existence. Thus they read together a letter of Albrecht Dürer's, written while the news that Martin Luther had been taken prisoner was fresh in his mind. They perceived the profound and sorrowful religious sentiment that was to be felt in its words. How different was such a nature from the gay *joie de vivre* of the divine Italian masters, they said, and the heavy, ungainly language only added to the effect. But it was wonderfully moving. " No such son, certainly, was ever born in Italy." And once more a discussion arose in this connexion of the idea of a comedy based on the life of Luther, which forms such a wonderful undercurrent to all the Master's creative work. It was not the parallel between Luther's affianced bride and Cosima which prompted him; for he felt that Cosima had missed her vocation, which should have been that of a sister of charity; indeed, when on her solitary walks she met poor convicts, or when tramps knocked at the door of the solitary house, her kind heart always showed itself, not in the capricious charity of a good and happy woman, but always with that religious tendency that sees in the poor the image of Christ. Thus she was really happy, yet every day her deeply religious nature reproached her gravely. She had to turn over the whole situation in her mind and could not accustom herself to the consciousness that she was expiating sin, but only to the full consciousness of her guilt. But, side by side with this, what upheld her was her sense of Wagner's genius, and the idea that it was her vocation to protect and guard it. She bore all his outbreaks of vehemence with calm, and when he afterwards came and begged for forgiveness, she could not understand why he did so. " I can only press his hand in silence. How should I ever presume to forgive him? It is my duty to be good and amiable to Richard, just as the hours come round and strike. I think over my merits, but I also think over my faults. I have hurt many people without meaning it; I had to wound Hans, and the children miss me." But her mind was busy with the idea of genius, and she was grateful when the Master enlightened her upon this point too. Thus, apropos of her impression of Mendelssohn, he said prophetically: " Such a shadow does not increase. It can only fade away. But genius must become legendary as soon as it has ceased to be. Then one believes that one has known it. In this respect the immortality of the works even communicates its impress to the person, so that one feels as though life and death can have absolutely no power over such men as Weber, Beethoven, and Mozart, and that from all eternity they have been round about us as spirits, just as they still are now. But to men of inferior talent life is all. They can but be forgotten, they cannot be lords of the world of shadows."

This was her world, in which she lived and beheld the Master. How small was everything that happened outside it! What though her mother-in-law made mischief, and that in the most unbridled fashion? And when, as afterwards happened, she showed Frau Cosima's maid the door, with ill-bred remarks directed against her daughter-in-law, Frau Cosima endured it with pain, but dominated by her noble sentiment: " One thing I feel, that, come what may, I must remain courageous and cheerful, so that I may be a real help to him. Peace will come one day, and for this day he is blessing me and the children." But she was most affected when he played her extracts from his works. Once, after listening to *The Valkyrie*, she writes: " I could really faint. God, what a work! Whosoever possesses a deep faith receives as guerdon of this faith a beauteous hope. Today, as I felt to the depths of my being how utterly I believe in Richard — in his mission, his genius, his goodness, and his love — gradually, from my ardent sensibility, which, though shadowed by unspeakable suffering, yet stands impregnable, there rose an impalpable emotion, pallied and delicate as a crescent moon against a blazing sunset. Not of happiness, not of success, nor even of tranquillity and peace. Silent and indefinable there dawns as the sweetest reward of my supreme emotion the fairest hope."

It is touching to see how now in all her tribulations her heart cried out for her mother: " How happy I should be if I had a mother — a mother who should understand all things, who should gauge the depth of my love, understand my cares, and say to me: ' Give me your children, I will take care of them and make them happy ' ! " But the news which she received from Paris was melancholy indeed. The Countess Marie was ill, and when her illness came to an end, she was cold to her daughter and alienated from her. And Frau Cosima writes: " My soul is like a bud, which can bloom only in the sunshine of his music." But the Master's leading theme, to which he recurred every day, was that parting would be his death! But then again he said gaily that by the time he had finished *The Nibelungs*, she would deserve the order *Pour le mérite*. But everything agitated her violently. When they read Tasso together, and the closing words of the hapless poet fell from his lips: " Thus does the sailor cling at last even to the rock on which he was to find shipwreck," her comment is: " I cling to the rock of his love, on which my ego — that is, all that is evil, self-willed, and sinful — is shipwrecked. To live for him is my redemption." Indeed, a hundred times did she anticipate the emotions and experiences of Parsifal.

Meanwhile, however, the outer world was in a turmoil. Though *The Mastersingers* aroused rapturous delight everywhere, the essay *Das Judentum in der Musik* caused a prodigious uproar which it is hard to realize in the present day. Even *The Mastersingers* was now hissed off the stage, and a letter arrived from Breslau in which it was said that seven thousand Jews were threatening the Master. On the other hand, Bülow championed the cause of his Master's essay as of old. But Wagner cared nothing for the world. He thought only of Cosima and said jestingly that he would throw over anybody — God knows whom, even Shakspere himself, if he came to have a chat with him; he wanted nothing but her. And with his characteristic kindliness he said of her father, who was holding aloof in an almost hostile spirit: " Your father's nature could find harmonious expression only in a woman! " But the news which arrived from abroad made a deep impression on her. When she heard of the death of Berlioz, the old scenes of her childhood rose up once more before her. She recalled those who had died during the year — the Reaper had been terribly busy: Lamartine, Genelli, Rossini, Berlioz; and almost simultaneously with this news a copy of the *Liberté* containing the letter which she had written about the Master was sent to her. Her sensibilities were so acute, and her memories of all that she had been through in Paris so striking, that some ripple from them could not but stir the quiet waters of her secluded retreat.

But the Master's influence was stronger still. He initiated her into the music of Beethoven, he read the Edda with her, and she watched the third act of *Siegfried* growing before her. Once, as she was playing Beethoven, the Master came into the room and said: " My angel is playing from the celestial ether," and then he went on to speak of the great Wala scene and gave it as his opinion that, at the words: " *Um der Götter Ende zehrt mich die Angst nicht, da mein Wunsch es will* (No care for the end of the gods devours me, for my will intends it)," [1] he could produce an extraordinarily dramatic effect by means of a recitative. " But then," he added earnestly, " there would be the end of the whole thing as an art-work." It should not be forgotten, too, that during this prodigious further development, both in the Nibelung drama and in his own mode of writing, nobody stood by him or witnessed it save Frau Cosima. But what he needed at this moment was to absorb himself profoundly in the Edda, to which he now introduced her; though her comment is: " What delights me most of all is the sight of his face as he sits opposite me; his eye grows dark and flashes, and his resonant voice stirs my heart to its depths." The way in which this work came into being in this utter isolation is a thing unique, and she

---

[1] *Siegfried*, III, i.—Tʀ.

is right when she says: " Seldom indeed have two people been so solitary as we." Yet she vibrated in response to every moment. " There are certain sentiments which I cannot hear expressed in his voice without an inward thrill, and then I have to look at him, and realize in my soul how unworthy I am of him, and swear to him a fidelity that endures all sufferings with exultation and can never falter." And so essentially the appalling storm that was then raging in the outer world was only serious to her on his account. She writes: " They will drag us in the mud. Gladly will I suffer all if only I stand at his side. Let them heap insults upon me from generation to generation, so long as I have helped him, so long as I have been permitted to hold out my hand to him and say: ' I will follow you till death.' My only prayer is that one day I may die at the selfsame hour as Richard. My highest pride is that I have cast all things away, that I may live for him; his joy is my fairest happiness. Without him, as Cleopatra said, the world is a mere sty."

And now came a letter to her from the King, sent on by Hans. But how very differently did she now receive the letter! " I cannot express the misery which takes possession of me on reading these ecstatic phrases." It is true that the letter arrived at a time when gloomy and most depressing thoughts were giving her cause to tremble. Once again in memory she lived through the birth of her second daughter and recalled how she had awaited her time all alone. " With what insensible silence was the child received by her father! Nobody troubled about me save Richard far away, and I did not know it; how dreary, empty, and spiritually wrecked my life was then! How can I ever thank Richard enough for what his love has done for me, I felt so miserable then! I scarcely dared to tell Hans; he took it so unkindly, as if it disturbed his comfort. I have never told anybody this; and I do not write it now as a reproach to Hans. The trials of his life were great, and he did not know what things hurt a woman or make her happy, for I never said anything; but [I write it] because I think with a shudder of that night in Berlin, and the fulfilment of my destiny has become fully comprehensible to me."

352

Now, indeed, she was living through a real and touching springtide of love. How charming and gay it sounds when she writes: " Yesterday, when Richard saw me with flowing hair, he said that I had hair like a perfect Geneviève, and added: ' God! If I could carry you off to the wilderness like that! But there are no wildernesses left, there are pensions everywhere. The wilder the place, the more luxurious the pension.' " And so Eastertide came round, and she writes about these days: " I went to church, simply so as not to offend people's sentiments, for they do not understand that such a day is best spent quietly at home. At four o'clock I was at the church of the discalced Carmelites. I was told as a child that this is the time when one ought to wish, and one's wish would be granted. So I wished for the children's and everybody's welfare, and, for myself, I wished for the forgiveness of all those whom I have hurt. I forgave in spirit all those who have done or wished me harm or are still preparing to do it." So she was still living in the mental state of which she had received the impress in childhood — one which was not only religious, but strictly devout. And she made a remark which was great indeed: " In our love is truth, but in this world are but lies and treachery." She quoted most feelingly the words from one of Shakspere's sonnets: " 'Tis better to be vile than vile esteemed." But her mind was also occupied with the important question of creed. She discussed it with the Master, who said: " Your father would certainly have no objections to make to our union if I were to become a Catholic in order to facilitate it." " Upon which I asked him whether, had it been necessary, he would have turned Catholic in order to marry me. He replied that that was a deuce of a question (*verteufelte Frage*), he simply could not imagine the situation. At first I was dashed, and for one moment I felt that, after all, I was giving up religion and everything else in order to be united with him. But then I understood. The woman may and ought to sacrifice all for the man whom she loves. But the man can and ought to have one point on which he neither weakens nor hesitates. Besides, as Richard remarks, the transition from Catholicism to Protestantism is quite different from the reverse process, by which the Protestant is required to make a formal acknowledgment of heresy. But the whole subject threw me into a very serious frame of mind. It is hard to arrive all at once at that insight into things which enables one to rise superior to the pain caused by a perception of the distinction between a man's and a woman's love. And since with me everything takes a long time, the case has exercised me for a whole afternoon."

It was indeed a way of the Cross that she had to travel, and she did so " *himmelhochjauchzend, bis zum Tode betrübt* (exalted unto heaven, cast down unto death)." For the news from Munich, too, was highly agitating. Hans von Bülow's condition, it is true, was now reassuring, but, on the other hand, demands were now made upon the Master which cut him to the quick, and she felt that the slightest contact with the world was unbearable to him both physically and morally. First came the announcement in the papers of the impending performance of *The Rhinegold.* She therefore lived in mortal dread lest this performance might destroy his pleasure in the rest of his work. " The worry," she writes, " has crushed us both. I well realize that we can live only for each other and with each other, and all contact with the outer world, even through the friendliest medium, is fatal to us." One consolation was that in the question of the children, as she learnt in a roundabout way from Paris, Hans was prepared to adopt a chivalrous attitude and had entirely shaken himself free of his mother's promptings. The return of the elder children to their mother was pending. So it is affecting to read her description of how she played at hide-and-seek with the two little ones, and with them discovered the first violet. But she felt all the influences which worked upon her solely on his account and, as it were, through him. How cold and positively absurd Tausig's telegram from Berlin sounded to her: " Colossal success of *Lohengrin,* all the Jews reconciled." What was the petty controversy about the pamphlet on the Jews to her, compared with this work and its creator? She was reading the biography of Goethe by Lewes. And she observed what a terrible thing the fame of the man whom she loves is for a woman. " It seems strange to me, too, that women who are loved by great men do not realize that they are all that they are through these men and this love, but imagine that they are also something in themselves over and above this."

On April 8, however, she made the journey to Zürich in order to take over the care of the children. She did so with a melancholy joy. She found them changed and not well, though not exactly ill. But the journey home was already more cheerful, and the two girls, who had now been away from their mother for so long, gradually came to feel at home at Triebschen. She naturally watched them with an anxious eye. But it was infinitely touching when the elder of them dictated to her a letter to their father, and she became, as it were, the mouthpiece of their affectionate childish feelings. She writes: " I am grieved at the sight of the elder children, for they do not look so well as the little ones," and because she fancied that they had missed her at a critical age. But her solicitude was exaggerated, and she was right when she remarked that she had to swallow it all by herself, so that Richard should not suffer from it. On the other hand, both she and the Master felt it most acutely that Hans should be living in isolation among all the utterly contemptible Berlin intrigues: " Then my heart broke, I wept and sobbed and meditated for the whole morning. In the afternoon I wrote to the King and informed him of the whole situation." She thought that she could never be cheerful again, and it was only her duty to Wagner and the children that sustained her through this moment. How touchingly she writes in her diary:

" *Gute Nacht, meine Kinder,*
Gute Nacht, mein Geliebter,
Gute Nacht, arme Hans!

(Good-night, my children,
Good-night, my beloved,
Good-night, poor Hans!)

" If tears are of any value in the eyes of God, then must you all be at peace now, for I have indeed wept bitter tears on your behalf." Her mood was really swayed partly by the children, whose education occupied her whole time, and partly by the development of *Siegfried.* She undertook the entire instruction of the two elder children and did it in such a fashion that nothing more exemplary could be imagined. It had, indeed, a sort of calming effect upon her; but at the same time she regarded it as an act of expiation, too. Nothing delighted her more than the praise of the Master, who watched her activity with respect and reverence, not unmixed with chagrin, and a touch of envy of the children for the time which their mother devoted to them. But he also recognized the true greatness of these maternal sentiments and even said once that it was not only the children's good dispositions but their good education that impressed him, and that everyone who saw her with the children must be filled with awe; upon which she writes: " How happy these words made me! " And yet the very presence of the two elder daughters was a constant source of melancholy to her. When Lulu dictated a letter to her, and she was glad at the beautiful way in which the child wrote to her father, she thought of him all the while with anxiety and trouble — more, indeed, than was necessary. She says, indeed, that she had been very little to him, " but it costs me dear to deprive him even of that little." Both she and Wagner suffered from this; for the Master lived in constant dread lest she should return to Munich out of a sense of duty, because she was anxious about Hans. And yet she met with the most painful insults from that very quarter, caused by the harsh behaviour of Hans's mother, who had made all sorts of arrangements on behalf of the children, as though they were not in Frau Cosima's charge. The latter had indeed the right to reproach Frau Franziska with not having taken at all good care of her own children, either physically or morally. But she kept silence about all these insults, which were quite certainly not to be ascribed to Hans von Bülow. The whole month of May was clouded by a slight melancholy, which was, of course, due to her condition. Even when they made an excursion from Grütli to Fluelen with the whole band of children, when they drove along the Axenstrasse to Brunnen and came home by steamer, her anxiety did not leave her, in spite of the happy mood to which she surrendered herself entirely. For from Paris, too, came news of the saddest description. Her mother seemed to have fallen a prey to insanity — indeed, to violent mania — and had had to be removed to an asylum. For weeks on end she hung between life and death until an improvement set in, which, it may be said, ended in a complete cure.

But Wagner felt a great and momentous inclination towards work. When he played her excerpts from the third act of *Siegfried*, which had just come into being, she felt as though she must faint for mingled pain and bliss. Then did she realize the object and duty of her life at Triebschen. But he rose and pointed to her portrait, saying that " this was what he had beheld as he had written it all; life still remained upon the heights." Meanwhile she was making all preparations to celebrate his birthday, in spite of the fact that her own condition filled her with constant anxiety, indeed with thoughts of death. Yet she lived in a wonderfully uplifted frame of mind. She really felt that this third act of *Siegfried* was intimately bound up with her and with her whole being; for the Master was now drawing upon the themes which had come into being during that period at Starnberg when she had come to him. At the time, they had intended them for quartets and trios, but now they found their true application, for they formed the setting of Brünhilde's song: " *Ewig war ich, ewig bin ich* (I was from all time, I am for all time)." And in this is revealed a wondrous mystery of love and creation. But it also bears witness to all the deep and pure greatness of this woman's nature that, amid her supreme triumph at this artistic creation, she should at the same time have felt grief for the sacrifice which she had been forced to make. And she writes: " I realize that if death were to approach me now, I should not grieve. It seems to me cruel that I should have abandoned Hans. So I have to tell myself that, if I too feel this cruelty, then it is clear that there is a God who controls me and determines my action, and that the will and choice were not my own. But I do not take it amiss in anybody that they should not see this as I do, or share the faith which I possess, and which is my condemnation. Gladly and lightly will I endure the abhorrence of the world. But Hans's sufferings rob me of all joy."

And now came May 22 and the Master's birthday, when she had a surprise for him in the shape of a string quartet from Paris, which particularly delighted him because it played Beethoven's E minor Quartet. He was deeply moved by the sacrifice which she had made for him. Richter had previously awakened him in the morning with the Siegfried motive.

Then solitude once more descended upon Triebschen, and cares crowded in upon her as she thought of the dark hours which awaited her. She was the Master's good companion to the last. While he lay sick, she read him his uncle Adolf's pamphlet *Theater und Publikum* (*The Theatre and the Public*), in which occur a number of ideas which are to some extent an echo of the Master's views, though he did not know of them till now — that is, long after he had committed his own views to paper. It is moving to read how they now played the Haydn and Mozart symphonies together. This was in some sense a distraction from his prodigious creative work at this mighty third act of *Siegfried*, which stirred his whole being and devoured his vital force. But there was one curious scene which took place during these very days in May. Jakob, the faithful servant who managed the house, came during the night and announced in alarm that his boy was ill. She writes: " I went in and laid my hand on him, and the child became calm. Jakob told this to Richard, who said that he had experience of my hand and knew that I could call a man back from death to life by its touch." Indeed, he venerated the element of clairvoyance in her, recalling that of the women in the *Germania* of Tacitus, and if at times his violence broke forth, he could not apologize to her enough, and she writes on one occasion how he had said that " I ought to know that everything in me is high and holy to him, and that if he used such expressions occasionally, it was like the Saturnalia, when it was permitted to jest with the gods. For him I was already floating in the empyrean. I could not help weeping violently when he said this, and I tried to change the subject, for I simply cannot understand or endure that he should set such store by me."

At the beginning of June the performance of *Tristan* by the King's command brought fresh worries to Triebschen. Bülow wrote in a perfectly correct spirit, with all the devotion of an artist to the Master. But on the one hand he could not oppose the King's will, and, to be just, the King had the right entirely on his side, though, in memory of Schnorr, the Master would not hear of a performance. He wrote to Bülow and begged him to decline to conduct *Tristan*. But this was impossible, and it must be said that the performance, with Herr Vogl and his wife, was fully worthy of the Master.

Next came a period during which Richard Wagner himself made the entries in the diary. At first this caused Frau Cosima deep alarm, and she regarded it as an absolute *coup de grâce;* but these were but the dark and ominous feelings which crowded into her soul immediately before her great ordeal. It is wonderfully significant that during the last few days the Master read her the passage on the birth of Parzival out of Wolfram von Eschenbach's poem. She was profoundly affected by its beauty. Then came the night of June 5–6. Friedrich Nietzsche had invited himself for the night of June 5, and the Master wanted to put him off; but Frau Cosima thought it would be better for him to come. She herself was in a state of the deepest lethargy, which she was powerless to shake off. She was aware of all that was going on in life as of a far, distant echo, and she felt as though things would melt into a mist before her eyes.

So Nietzsche came and they spent yet one more quiet evening together. But at four o'clock in the morning the boy Siegfried was born. It was the Master himself who entered this in the diary. He heard a cry of " *Ach Gott in Himmel!* " from Vreneli, the good spirit of the house, and in his anxious dread imagined that something terrible had happened. But then she said with a laugh: " It is a son (*Ein Sohn ist da*)! " — and a deep emotion swept over him: " Then he was surprised by an incredibly splendid glow as of fire, which blazed upon the orange wall-paper beside the bedroom door with a glow of colour such as he had never seen before, and was reflected on the blue casket with my portrait on it, so that the picture, covered with glass and surrounded with a narrow golden frame, was transfigured with an unearthly beauty. The sun had just risen above the Rigi and cast its first rays into the room. The most glorious of

sunny days was shining. Richard melted into tears; and now
the chime of the bells floated across the lake from Lucerne,
ringing for the early service on Sunday morning." As he approached the happy mother's bed, both of them were overcome
by a solemn emotion. " I was merry and cheerful. The gift sent
to us by fate in the birth of a son at once appeared to me of
immeasurable worth as a consolation. A son of Richard's is the
heir and sole representative of the father of his children, he
will be a protector and guide to his sisters."

And it was as though all gloomy thoughts now faded from
her mind, and as though she herself had in some sort been born
again in her son. It is infinitely touching to see how during these
days the Master kept the diary quite in the style and according
to the ideas of Frau Cosima, closing with the notes of that wonderful passage in the duet between Siegfried and Brünhilde:
" *Leuchtende Liebe, lachender Tod!* (Radiant love, laughing
death!) " [1]

As early as Sunday the 13th she herself made the following
entry in the diary: " Oh, hail to the day which gives us light,
hail to the sun which shines on us! How can I, the poorest of
creatures, write down the feelings with which I once more take
up this book. When the woman said to me: ' I congratulate you,
it is a boy,' I could only weep and laugh and pray. May God,
who gave me him, preserve him for me, may he be the support
of his sisters, the heir of his adored father. Now that my happiness lies so sweetly tangible before my eyes, it seems to me more
and more nebulous and incorporeal. I see it floating, rising
high above all distress, and can only thank the world-soul, which
announces to us by such a sign that it is friendly. The day was
radiantly glorious, I did not sleep all night, but I feel well, and
I thought over the letter which has to be written to Hans, in which
I mean to set forth my past, present, and future relations to
him, if he will consent to this. May God inspire me with the right
words, that I may help him a little. I hear Richard working.
On coming up to see me, he told me how wonderfully it has
come about that his triumphant themes (*Jubelthemen*) fitted
themselves splendidly, of their own accord, as an accompani-

[1] *Siegfried*, III, iii.—Tr.

ment to the motive, ' *Heil dir, Mutter, die mich gebar* (Hail to thee, Mother that bare me),' so that this exultation is heard uninterruptedly in the orchestra till the point at which Siegfried himself joins in. By tomorrow he will probably have finished the sketch. When he came up, he called me ' the great Zenobia.' This name for me had come into his head during his work. In answer to my questions he said that I was great, truly great. But all the greatness that there can be in me is the reflection of his nature. He went on to say that I do nothing but sympathize with all beings if I see them troubled and in need of me, but that when I see him glad, then and then only am I happy; and this is indeed the truth. As Richard was looking at our son by himself, the child appeared to him as he will be one day, gravely kind. He told me one thing with deep emotion: it seemed to him as though he had seen the eidolon of our dear boy. May God preserve him to us. I am writing these lines during a wonderful sunset, lying at the window. Could I but sing a hymn to the Godhead! Richard sings it for me. My hymn is my love for him." And she describes the little bird twittering before her window, which the Master called Siegfried's bird, for it announced his arrival and was now inquiring after him. Then he came himself with the completed sketch of the third act. He remarked, indeed, that it had come exactly at the right time. " For not till now has our child been born. He is the pride of his father, which finds expression every time he approaches the cradle." Nor was there any lack of romance. Speaking of Wilhelm, the worthy Jakob's son, who was eight months older, he says that the child should have been called Kurwenal, so that he should have grown up with his own son, as that faithful retainer did with Tristan. And now, during these very days, came Hans von Bülow's farewell letter in answer to that of Frau Cosima. This letter, written on June 17, may be regarded as a christening-present to Siegfried, though of a curious kind. It is a wonderful letter in its way, and shows us Hans von Bülow's noble and profound character: " Dear Cosima, I thank you for taking the initiative as you have done, and I will not go out of my way to find grounds for complaining of it. I feel too unhappy, through my own fault, not to avoid everything in the way of unjust reproaches that may be wounding to you. In the unspeakably cruel separation which you feel to be your duty, I acknowledge all the faults on my side, and I will continue to lay stress on them in the most marked way in all the unavoidable explanations on the subject with my mother and your father. I have made you a very poor and unkind return for all the devotion that you displayed towards me during our past life. I have poisoned your life, and I can only thank Providence for having granted you a compensation at the last moment, when the courage to go through with it must have abandoned you. But, as a matter of fact, since you have left me, the only support of my life in my broken-down state has gone. Your mind, your heart, your friendship, your patience, your indulgence, your sympathy, your encouragement, your counsels, and, above all, your presence, your glance, your words, all these have formed and determined the basis of my life. The loss of this supreme good, whose value I now recognize for the first time now that it is lost, and which crushes me both morally and as an artist, makes me realize that I am a bankrupt. Do not think that there is any sort of irony or any disparagement of you personally in these laments; I am suffering so much that I may allow myself to complain, while I none the less abstain from casting the blame on any other than myself. You have preferred to devote your life and the treasures of your mind and heart to a being who is pre-eminently superior in every respect, and, far from blaming you, I approve your step from every point of view, and fully admit that you are right. I vow to you that the only kindly and consoling thought that has at times penetrated my inward darkness and outward agony has been that Cosima at least is happy."

Bülow could not have felt the separation or expressed his feelings in a more idealistic and noble way. Frau Cosima, too, felt this to the full, and though grief overcame her at times, an intense calm now descended upon her.

The letter contains a remarkable outburst about *Tristan*, against which all Hans von Bülow's resentment seemed to have turned. He saw in it in some sort a source of harm, not only for himself, but also for other people, and he even hinted that the prodigious force of the music ruined the nerves of those taking part in the performance. Frau Cosima and the Master smiled together at this curious indictment of a great and mighty work, in the service of which nobody had laboured so nobly or so congenially as Hans himself.

But another year had still to go by before the great question of the divorce, which was in itself so simple, could be settled as regards outward formalities. Frau Cosima suffered unspeakably from this. Though during the day-time she rejoiced in the Master's work and in the stimulus that it constantly yielded her in ways that were ever new, her nights were full of boundless grief at her husband's sufferings, and most of all at the fact that she now really learnt for the first time how greatly he missed her. And so she lived in two worlds, one a world of sorrow and the other of infinite happiness, in which her glance fell upon Richard and her son. When Wagner stood by the cradle and maintained that the child would be a genius, she remarked: " All I want is that he should be a man." And when he then played her *Siegfried,* her whole life was bound up in the greatness of his work, and from this arose, as it were, the realization and, above all, the justification of her happiness. It is extraordinarily melancholy to observe how, during the whole period of the divorce proceedings, a heavy cloud hung, as it were, over both of them, though Frau Cosima did all she could to allow this undercurrent of her feelings to be as little apparent as possible, still less to disclose it to the Master. But he did not shrink from explanations at all, and even said that he would " not be troubled about the form which our happiness was to take, were it not for the existence of what separated us. Once more we went through all our sufferings at Munich — but we could not have done otherwise." This conviction is constantly appearing and was Frau Cosima's firmest support during the whole of this period.

It is touching to read how he tried through with her the French song which he had once written in Paris, and of which he had given her the autograph manuscript as her last Christmas present. He was, indeed, overcome by a profound bitterness when he recalled how he had then taken the songs to Madame Viardot and had had to wait for a long time outside till he was at last admitted and requested her to sing *L'Attente.* But she had refused his request with an ecstatic smile. " And he added: ' I had too much to bear, I did not find a single man.' I asked him whether he had been more fortunate with the women. Yes, he replied with a smile, for he had met me, and he added later that he felt nothing save praise and glory for me, but sorrow and bitterness about everything else."

Isolated though they were, they none the less took a great interest in the destinies of the world. With deep comprehension they watched the progress of the Vatican Council, and he felt that the resistance of the Germans to its decisions was the expression of a powerful force, from which he drew the conclusion: " Once more it is probably reserved for the Germans to redeem the honour of humanity. The French and English will simply clear out or else ignore the whole thing."

But the real grandeur of these days lay in the fact that, in their utter isolation, they maintained the deepest sincerity towards each other, and that Frau Cosima above all succeeded in drawing a right distinction between her infinite love for Richard and her infinite pity for Hans. Every night she turned it all over in her mind and made the most touching reflections on the subject. And how nobly she writes: " God treats me graciously and with goodness, it is only the world that is hostile to me. I see nothing but goodness around me, yet sorrow is in my heart. I hope, all my little ones, that you will have an easier life than your mother. No such poor, unhappy being as Hans exists. He feels miserable at my absence, yet I could never make him happy, or even cheerful." But once more she found consolation in exchanging ideas with the man whom she loved: " In the evening we discussed the remarkable, mysterious character of our union. How shy, yet at the same time how overwhelming was our first approach to each other, how aimless our first union, how we thought in silence of nothing but resignation, and how circumstances and people forced us to recognize that our love was genuine and that each of us was indispensable to the other! The world-spirit intended that I should receive my son from you, and disposed all things accordingly. We ourselves were forced to follow it without understanding it." This filled her with a feeling of extraordinary resignation, and never, indeed, did the philosophy of Schopenhauer find so true and genuine an echo as in their two souls. But the greatest consolation came to her from the Master's own works, both those which he had already created and those which were then coming into being. They had a characteristic discussion of *Lohengrin,* in connexion with an assertion of the Master's that he was incapable of writing a national hymn (*Volkshymne*); " Upon which I said to him that I should have known the whole of his great art from the summons of the trumpets in the third act. Once when I was depressed by the close of the scene between Lohengrin and Elsa and really thought that I could not follow out the further course of the drama, the trombones thundered out, like a voice from the subterranean regions, proclaiming that Elsa was to have an answer to her question. Then came the piercing summons of the trumpets — once more I was enchained, and the music helped me to bear the shattering effect of the drama. And so in the second act, when Ortrud enters Elsa's abode and Telramund declares that evil is visiting the house, the trumpet-call which salutes the morning succeeds in giving us the necessary alleviation, which nature always provides for the agitated feelings." After one such dissertation he remarked that, not he, but Frau Cosima ought to have been appointed an honorary member of the Berlin Academy.

Thus their moods were subject to constant ups and downs, the simplest natural feelings and the deepest philosophical knowledge being alike revealed in them. Add to this their constant preoccupation with music and literature, in connexion with which Frau Cosima's mind and feelings found brilliant expression. On the arrival of the wonderful portrait of Beethoven, which still adorns Wahnfried today, she remarked: " We have joys quite unlike those of others. Few have a life like ours! " And they read Goethe's *Torquato Tasso* and *Don Carlos,* Cosima drawing a distinction between the feminine characters: the Queen had always been the ideal of womanhood, the Princess, on the other hand, merely a charming form of feminine character."

She, too, suffered from the misunderstanding of the outer world, though she did not speak of it; so she was correspondingly delighted when the Master repeated a remark of his Russian friend Seroff's about her: " *Quelle femme héroïque* (What a heroic woman)! " and she said that the remark quite unnerved her, for she had grown so accustomed to the idea of hearing nothing but abuse. There can be no question that it was her grief about Hans von Bülow that aggravated and threw a gloom over the whole circumstances. But this was all part of her deep, grand, pure nature, and once, when her daughter Lulu was dictating her a letter to her father, she summed up her fate, as it were, in the following words: " The serpent lies hidden in paradise, it lurks in my heart, while all around is happiness, so radiant and beautiful. Let us pray — destiny is deepest sorrow and supreme happiness! My poor heart grasps them both. Union with the loved one spells unbroken happiness — grief for the pain that one has caused spells sorrow inconsolable! " Yet she had at once to add: " How childishly my father talks about remorse! How could I feel any? It is pity that weighs upon my heart; I know, too, how Parzival is suffering and seeking for Amfortas. Shall I ever know unmixed happiness again? " And the Master himself called her " the nun of Triebschen."

For a time it seemed, indeed, as though her father wanted to raise obstacles to the divorce proceedings. They themselves knew too little and had no clear insight into the legal proceedings in divorce cases; so that in many ways Frau Cosima troubled her heart more than was necessary. But it was still only in lonely hours that she brooded over these things; otherwise she discharged her social duties in connexion with the house admirably and was an understanding companion to the Master in all his free hours — even when he talked about her father as an artist, though in so doing he was always prompted by purely musical considerations. When they both sat down to the piano and played the Haydn symphonies as duets, he was led to speak of that master's greatness in respect of form. From this it was only a step to Liszt's symphonic poems, and the Master said that he was worried about the turn which Liszt's mind had taken. Yet he spoke with a certain predilection of the *Faust Symphony*, and also of *Mazeppa*, on account of the big impulse that runs through it; but he deplored Liszt's dreadful apotheosis-mania, his use

of the triangle and the tomtom, the chain jangling in *Tasso*, etc.
And his church-music, said Wagner, amounted to no more than
an absolutely childish playing with intervals. He regretted all
the more that he had never lived in real union with Liszt, and
deplored the influence of the Princess Wittgenstein, who, he
said, like a savage, was only accessible to the crudest effects
in music.

But now there was another who frequently took part in these
discussions: Friedrich Nietzsche, who had made his first stay at
Triebschen on that memorable evening of June 5, and whose
relations with the Master and Frau Cosima had become more
and more intimate from that time onwards. I should not go so
far as to say that there was any absolutely positive outcome of
what he said; but the profound intellectual power latent in him
produced a strong effect upon them both, nor should he be too
much underestimated spiritually. When, for instance, in speaking
of Liszt and his *Saint Elisabeth*, which is so full of poetry and
poetic fragrance, he remarked that it was the scent of incense
rather than of roses that went up from it, there was something
academic about his remark, which was also strongly in evidence
at other times. Thus Nietzsche was a vegetarian on principle. The
Master rebuked him for this, saying that the conflict of all against
all ran through the whole of creation, so that it was necessary for
man to gain strength from his food in order to be capable of
great achievements. Nietzsche entirely agreed with him, but
persisted in his abstinence, which made the Master quite disagreeable. There was another thing, too. His magisterial attitude made him feel it his duty to draw Wagner's attention to all
comments coming from the outer world and to point out the
intemperate character of these attacks — though he did so, it is
true, with the most honest indignation. As though silence and
reserve in face of these contemptible attacks had not been a
necessity of Wagner's nature, if he was to preserve his peace of
mind for his work!

It is quite certain that the couple at Triebschen regarded the
world from quite a different point of view, as regards both contemporary and past history, when they discussed it alone. His
views on the State, her feelings about people, were so clear and

definite, and so clever, too, that the two might well have been sufficient company for each other. They read the memoirs of the past without discussion, but discussed the personalities of contemporary times and their position in public life. Thus, for instance, in talking of an article on Pius IX in the *Augsburger Allgemeine Zeitung,* she observed: " The author certainly speaks quite otherwise than he would do in conversation. He places the Pope in a noble light, though he has to mention the futility of his plans and the cruelty of his measures. Thus you, too, have had to idealize King Max and King Ludwig I in art and in politics." To which he replied: " You are right. They are false portraits! The present does not belong to us! We ought not to try to describe it." And he added: " How will Siegfried feel one day, when he sees the third act of *Siegfried* and learns that this very scene was written at the time of his birth! " And he played the third act of *Siegfried* and explained to her, as she listened with deep emotion: " The kiss of love is the first intimation of death, the cessation of individuality. That is why Siegfried shrinks from it in such alarm."

And now came his sister Cäcilie, whom he had not seen for the last twenty-one years. His feeling for her was particularly intimate and warm, though his relations even with her were haunted by the idea which he had once expressed in the words: " We do not need any love, all that we need is honesty." She now joined the circle which included Nietzsche: a curious association, which, however, turned out very well and spoke well for the Master's sister. But this ideal state of affairs was disturbed almost daily by the news from the outer world. Thus Marie von Mouchanoff sent word that Liszt had dissuaded Hans von Bülow from the divorce, and suggested to Cosima that she should go to her father without delay and speak to him in person. This seemed even more necessary because an unpleasant scene had just taken place with Bülow's mother. Hermine, nurse to Frau Cosima's children, had gone to Munich and been to the Bülows' house. The old lady, who was at home, received her with abuse and forbade her the house. In connexion with this episode Frau Cosima made the following memorable entry in her diary: " So this is how the good lady has revenged herself for those ten years during which I treated her in such a way that Richard was quite sure she was fond of me and could not but be so; he was quite flabbergasted when I said to him: ' Ah, the woman is only waiting for a chance to do something nasty.' " And she now revealed something of her martyrdom, and something, too, of the mother's fatal influence, which prejudiced Hans von Bülow's development throughout his whole life. As was her way, she could not help turning it all over in her mind. She did this while strongly under the impression of the happy feelings to which the Master gave expression during these days: " As the sunset was dying away, he said how well and happy he felt, how his health was restored and his whole nature steeled, as it were, and how it was I who had accomplished all this. I should like to fall on my knees in gratitude to God, and lest my soul be corrupted by presumption, I recall the thought of him to whom I had to cause suffering, and I grieve with him, afar off and in silence, over the grimness of earthly destinies. The happier I am, the more deeply I feel it that there is one who is not happy, and all my sensible arguments, and all my knowledge that I could not have done otherwise, are of no help to me — or, rather, I do not appeal to such help." For a moment, indeed, she did consider the idea of going to see her father and asking for his support; but Wagner declared that he simply would not let her go, saying that " people would be quite capable of shutting me up in a convent, like Barbara Ulbrich." But this was not true. Bülow had surmounted his feelings and was actually thinking of coming to Munich to attend the performance of *The Rhinegold*.

This performance, indeed, had caused the Master infinite care, annoyance, and, above all, pain. He could not understand the young King, who was eager to hear and see the work and was endeavouring by every means to make its production possible. As a matter of course his entourage and the staff of the Hoftheater did all they could to bring about the performance, even against the composer's will. But, equally as a matter of course, Bülow declined to conduct it, and Hans Richter also withdrew at the critical moment, so that they had to have recourse to such poor abilities as those of Wüllner. This made very little impression on the King, for he could not see how insignificant and pitiable the performance was — reminding one of an ordinary theatre rather than a court theatre. But the Master felt that the performance of his work without his consent touched his honour and therefore petitioned the King by letter — and he wanted to do so in person too — in the hope of inducing him at least not to have it performed in public.

For the rest, the whole world was in suspense about this performance. Liszt, who had received an invitation from Munich, meant to be present, though he had declined the invitation to *Tristan,* at the very time when his presence might have cleared up all difficulties. The other friends of them both were naturally present too. Georg Herwegh made his appearance, the Countess Mouchanoff arrived in Munich, and the Countess Krockow, too, was not far away. In short, everybody had a part in it except the Master himself. During these very days, indeed, serious debates had been exercising both the head and the heart of Wagner and Cosima, on the subject of whether they ought not for once to omit to draw the yearly subvention. Frau Cosima was the last person to dissuade him from this, though, owing to the impossibility of inducing Wagner to economize in any way whatsoever, she often passed difficult moments. The papers were full of reports of every possible description, even seeing in the performance an intrigue of the Tuileries, alleged to have been set on foot through the connexions of the Countess Mouchanoff and her daughter. There was a sinister accumulation of errors and confusion, and it is characteristic of Nietzsche that, with academic accuracy, he was tireless in sending information about the press attacks and their reckless allegations. But at last Frau Cosima succeeded in silencing Wagner's scruples and complaints. She talked over the whole situation with him thoroughly. If the royal subvention ceased, or was forced to cease, he thought of a visit to America. For the rest he recovered his calm, and when a demand arrived from another quarter for permission to perform the piece, his reply was that this was the business of the King of Bavaria alone, and that if the King wanted to amuse himself by having a performance, he himself could not prevent it. For at the back of his mind there was always a great and vehement anxiety lest without him the work would simply cease to exist.

It was immediately after such a serious discussion as this that the Master drew out a sheet of music-paper and said: "I have something for you, something has come to me." "And upon this he showed me the beginning of the Norn scene. 'Nobody in this world,' he said, 'has shown any courage in my cause but you. People might at least have some respect for that.' I had to reply that I had not had courage, but only love. Ah, well do I know how feeble is my strength!"

Schuré, too, had come to Germany, and visited the two recluses at Triebschen, on which occasion he had a conversation with Frau Cosima about the Master. He said that the anomaly of such a phenomenon as Richard Wagner in their day was an event in itself. In Wolfram von Eschenbach's day he could not but have brought happiness to the world; but nowadays he felt compelled from time to time to clear up the inextricable misunderstandings existing between him and the world by a manifesto, and the more he explained matters, the deeper the gulf became. The theatre as he conceived it was a temple, whereas the theatre of the day was a booth at a fair. He spoke the language of priests, and then shopkeepers were expected to understand him! For her these remarks were a triumph, and her comment upon them is: "I had to devote my whole life to him, for I realized his position."

During these days the faithful Vreneli gave birth to her second child. Frau Cosima was a true friend to her and had a tender feeling for the new arrival. She nursed her trusty servant and spent much of her time at her bedside — another instance of her warm-heartedness. While still quite young, indeed, she had said that she was really cut out for a sister of charity, and this feeling never left her throughout her whole life. Every poor person who knocked at the door of their house received, not only a gift, but also the deepest expression of pity and sympathy for his condition. Just at this time, for instance, a musician who had played under Wagner during his Zürich days came to Triebschen. He had taken to embroidery of the most lamentable description; yet with what compassion and pity did she receive him and accept his wretched work! Next came a poor student, and he too found comfort. Or they would watch the convicts working on their landlord's property and always treated them humanely. This extended even to the children, and one day, on appearing in the garden, Frau Cosima saw her daughter sitting among the convicts sharing their scanty prison fare. Humane sentiment radiated forth from her, and from the Master too, and during her whole life it showed itself in the most touching and affecting ways. She was always self-sacrificing and good-hearted when she could be — not only when she had to be. The bent of her whole nature made her philanthropy a deep and almost sacred obligation.

And now arrived a letter from the King, quite in his old style and with all his former cordiality. He absolutely begged to be forgiven for the performance of *The Rhinegold*; but, he said, his longing had been too great. The Master learnt, indeed, with alarm that this letter was intended to prepare the way for his intention to produce *The Valkyrie* as well, and Frau Cosima now writes: "It is really terrible. But we agreed that Richard really lives by grace of the Nibelungs. He owes them his existence, and so we must also thank God that a being such as the King should have such a queer whim in his head and simply will see and have the things, though of course without connecting them with any grandiose conception. Richard says: 'He cannot ruin the work. I only can ruin it, if I am interrupted and cannot complete it. The fact that he is spoiling the things now will not impair the effect if once the work is performed according to my intentions.' He even added: 'People will always be indebted to me, at any rate for *Tannhäuser* and *Lohengrin*. But the whole performance of this demands a higher general level of culture. If this is not forthcoming, then the most consummate performances in Munich will be of no avail. It is all fate.'" For this reason he also refused to go to Vienna, saying that it would be better for him not to do so, for he had only to appear for an ominous feeling to be stirred up, which jeopardized everything. But when the news really arrived that the King was set upon the performance of *The Valkyrie*, he felt thoroughly out of temper and was ready to throw away his pen and never write another note of *The Ring*. It was an unspeakably hard time for him, and no less so for Frau Cosima; but she succeeded in pacifying him.

FRIEDRICH NIETZSCHE

From Elisabeth Förster-Nietzsche's
The Life of Friedrich Nietzsche

It was with this object in view that she desired frequent visits from Nietzsche. He had produced a deep impression at Trieb-schen by sending Wagner his lecture on Homer. There can be no question that there was a certain element in his conception of the Greek world which owed its origin to Richard Wagner's views on art; so we may safely say, as the Master's nephew, Hermann Brockhaus, did in after days, though rather in a nega-tive sense, that " when Nietzsche has finished with Schopenhauer and Wagner, he will lose himself too." But at this time his ap-pearance and, above all, his boundless devotion to Richard Wagner's work meant the introduction of an element of positive importance into the solitary house. Frau Cosima herself, it is true, recognized the pedantic, academic element in him; in fact, she actually gave the young scholar good advice about this on many occasions. We shall be able to review this more thoroughly below. However that may be, for a time every letter from Nietz-sche counted as a real pleasure though Frau Cosima could not avoid some anxiety lest he might be working in too proud and arrogant a spirit, becoming engrossed in things instead of allow-ing them to react upon him clearly and directly. But the impres-sion of Nietzsche's personality as a whole belongs to the Trieb-schen period, as do those of Schuré and of the exquisite and accomplished Judith Mendès and her husband, who, until the days of trial in 1870, displayed in their way a great and pro-found understanding for Wagner and Frau Cosima, as well as for the Master's art.

Nor is their intercourse with the Bassenheim family without interest — not only with the Countess, but most of all with her father, the old Prince Öttingen. The Bassenheims lived in Switzerland as in a refuge, which they had established there upon bidding farewell to Bavaria. Relations with them were thoroughly cordial, though a certain haughtiness on the part of the Countess occasionally introduced a disturbing and chilling element; for Frau Cosima was not inclined to accept any sort of humiliation, and at this moment the mistress of Triebschen should be regarded as a *grande dame*, who was perfectly capable of playing towards everybody the great and momentous role which became her so well both intellectually and as a woman.

Though by night she might writhe with pain, care, and grief, by day she was a proud and confident woman, a mother, earnest, yet always kind, who herself instructed her children in every branch of knowledge, and thus gave them a solid foundation for life. It is remarkable how she managed to observe every trait in her children's characters, how the slightest untruthfulness troubled her, or a glance that was not perfectly limpid caused her the gravest heart-searchings. For she could be severe, too, even to the point of injustice. This was an echo of her own bringing-up, the value of which she now realized to the full; for she was learned in every sphere, and so she gave her children no mere scholastic instruction, no mere cold introduction to elementary subjects, but succeeded in making her teaching wonderfully animated. When one day she told them the legend of St. Elizabeth and the miracle of the roses, or another day introduced them to St. Anthony of Padua, with a fervour which would have enchanted her father, she was giving them a revelation of life itself, with all its character, its sorrows and its joys. But she was also their best playmate. She acted in their toy theatre the fairy-tales and plays which she had read out to them from Jakob Grimm, and she observed, not without satisfaction, that the children took a greater pleasure in Grimm than in Andersen's fairy-tales.

Thus Frau Cosima's life was filled with affectionate duties and tasks dictated by her mother love. The life she led was a great and serious one, and the Master himself watched it from day to day with a reverence beyond compare, though not without anxiety at her excessive toil and a slight envy of the time and emotion which she sacrificed to the children, thereby, as he imagined, robbing him. But his whole being was stirred by something young and childlike, for he had never seen at close quarters all these manifestations of the truest and greatest womanly feeling, and so they now hovered before his eyes all the more evidently and clearly.

On the other hand, her duties as hostess of the house at Triebschen fell rather into the background. But all who had the good fortune to be admitted to it — such as Catulle Mendès and his wife, Judith, who afterwards resumed her maiden name of

Gautier, their Russian friend Seroff, Count Villiers, and Richard Pohl — have much to say about the charming life there. Frau von Mouchanoff, too, came to Triebschen several times, and once Frau Cosima read her the draft libretto of *Parsifal*, which moved her most deeply and, by sweeping away the somewhat worldly impression which she had formed of the Master and his works during the days at Munich, once more turned her into an unqualified and reverent appreciator of his greatness, though a trace still lingered in her of the rich young man in the Gospel, of whom we are told that he " went away sorrowful." It was to her that the Master dedicated his *Das Judentum in der Musik*. This was a distinction which, though she bore it with dignity, had been a little painful to her, in spite of her independent position and character. We cannot blame her for this, however, for we know what a prodigious effect was produced by this pamphlet, and what a flood of answers appeared to it, which were not inspired by such pure motives as those of the Master and tried to drag him and everything connected with him in the mud.

In the mean time, however, he had written the pamphlet which forms a pendant to this work and had, like the other, a great cultural task to fulfil, entering, perhaps, even more deeply into questions of the same kind. This was the pamphlet *Über das Dirigieren (On Conducting)*, which appeared about the turn of the year, creating an equally great sensation and arousing intense bitterness, though at the same time it met with considerable recognition; for it formed in some sort an introduction to that development in the Master's thoughts and feelings which reached its climax a few years later at Wahnfried and on the hill of Bayreuth with its festival theatre. At the same time he had also composed a strong rejoinder to the attacks which had appeared upon him in the press after the luckless performance of *The Rhinegold* in Munich. This was the article "*Das Münchner Hoftheater* (The Court Theatre of Munich)," which we must reckon among the official documents concerning the foundation of the theatre at Bayreuth.

But these were only outward happenings. His inner life went its way. Frau Cosima tended the Master faithfully, doing all she could to anticipate his thoughts, and trying to fulfil his every wish. She wrote the difficult letters to the King and Cabinet for him and celebrated with him every notable hour and intellectual anniversary. It is moving to read their conversation on Schiller's birthday. She said that it was not right of them to have forgotten him on the previous day; but he replied: " I looked at his portrait with pleasure." Next they read *Don Quixote* and the life of Cervantes together. But she called a halt in these readings, because she came upon a passage alluding to an engraving of the poet which she intended to offer to the Master as a Christmas present.

The question of the divorce dragged on almost intolerably, so that even their residence in Switzerland came into question. As a matter of fact, both of them thought for a while of accepting a friendly offer from Italy and moving into a villa in the neighbourhood of Milan. But day by day Frau Cosima came to realize more what it meant to be with him. For, fond as he was of jesting, and great as was the merriment which he caused both in the house and in her heart too, he was again and again possessed by those great thoughts whose expression is indeed like a revelation. This is all the finer because his utterances were free from the slightest doctrinaire taint and were really only possible when he was speaking to her, though they were and are of universal significance and application. She was deeply stirred by all that he had to say to her apropos of literature or of works by Beethoven and Mozart. It was a great thought greatly expressed when he said: "Music is the direct effluence from Christianity and the saints, such as Francis of Assisi, who uplifts the whole Church and the whole world." Or when he said of Socrates that he was the purest type in the history of the development of the human intelligence, while he characterized Plato as absolutely the first of philosophers, all the rest, his predecessors, having been mere empirics. But the ethics of Socrates, as revealed in the *Crito*, are so sublime, he said, that even Christianity itself could go no further. It breeds ecstasy, and even a sense of the nothingness of the world. But nobody who has achieved anything while living among men can ever go further than Socrates. And he said of himself that he, too, wanted to be the gad-fly, for ever acting as a stimulus. In this respect, it is true, there were others who undoubtedly surpassed him; and all that came from the outer world, concerning the performance of *The Rhinegold* and his other works, or else the divorce, was of so painful a nature that it caused both of them severe suffering. But their great consolation was in their love, and in this sense he set love above everything: "Love works like an eruption, it upsets all strata, raises up mountains, and then stands there as an ideal. Revolution is its supreme law."

But great trials still awaited this love, and none but a nature as strong and valiant as that of Frau Cosima could have borne them. When, for instance, she saw a personal attack on herself in the *Kladderadatsch,* in the shape of an article and a picture, with the motto "*Così fan tutte,*" she was sad, not so much on account of the attack itself, as because this paper had been edited by her friend Ernst Dohm, and she would never have believed him to be capable of such a gross action. The Master remarked, indeed, that he had simply succumbed to the fate of those who were mere journalists; but she was consoled by the news, brought by Richard Pohl, that, some nine months before, Dohm had had to flee from Berlin to Weimar before his creditors. So he, too, had been overtaken by a grievous fate.

And so Christmas-time came round, and she was filled with her delight in giving. She had devised all kinds of things for her husband and, most of all, too, for the children. But on this still December evening she could not help thinking sorrowfully of poor Hans. "It is curious," she writes; "Hans really disliked Christmas, and now that I know he is alone and am thinking over the festivities beforehand, I am overcome by an inexpressible melancholy when I compare his lot with mine." December was always a sad time for her; the image of her brother, Daniel, rose up again before her, and with it that of his lonely grave, of which she took care, and the upkeep of which had been entrusted to Konstantin Frantz. It was in this connexion, and with a deep sense of her love for him who was dead, that she wrote: "Children, cling close to one another. Nothing can take the place of the love of brothers and sisters." She suffered more than she would say. And so, while all the news which went forth into the

world from Triebschen at this time, including the Master's letters, was, if anything, cheerful in tone, she had to say of herself:
" I must only take care that Richard shall not notice how weak
I feel. I am happy about his work; but this is just what he does
not notice." So he was quite in exuberant spirits, and when a
high order from the Bey of Tunis arrived, he ordained that the
glittering star was to adorn the roof of the puppet theatre, rib-
bons and all. Nietzsche, who had also arrived at Triebschen for
Christmas Eve, helped with these decorations.

But the festivities were worthy of Frau Cosima. She had
chosen a poor girl from Bamberg to represent the Christ-child,
and now on the evening the Knecht Ruprecht appeared first and
scared the children. The Master pacified them and then rolled
the nuts into the room. The Christ-child appeared next, all glittering with light. He advanced, and the whole household followed him, including the children. The Christ-child disappeared
beneath the tree, and the children now flocked round it for the
distribution of presents, in which the whole household, including Nietzsche, joyously took part. He had himself laid his lecture
on Homer under the Christmas-tree, while among Frau Cosima's
presents was an almanac in which was printed the comedy written by Wagner's stepfather, Geyer. The Master was full of delight and now withdrew into the dining-room with Nietzsche,
while Frau Cosima remained behind with the children and knelt
with them beneath the Christmas-tree, on which the candles had
now been extinguished. And now she uttered a prayer: " Beloved Christ-child, Thou hast come to us and brought us happiness. We thank Thee, and think the while of all who are unhappy,
and pray Thee with all our hearts to visit them this evening and
bless them. Send food to the poor who hunger in cold and darkness, and bring them to Thy kingdom, give consolation to those
poor souls who weep alone and joyless, and speak happy words
to them. Greet the little children for whom no mother has lit up
a tree, and tell them that Thou art their best friend. As Thou
hast given us these many lights, so shine Thou upon all men with
Thy great light, that they may be as happy as we! " And after a
quiet time she took the children off to bed. Deep and sorrowful
thoughts of the distant Hans rose up in her. Then she returned to

the dining-room, where she found the Master in friendly and intimate talk with Nietzsche.

On this evening Nietzsche, too, had made a deeper impression upon her than before. She had not found it as easy as the Master had to feel at home with his nature, and the strongly pedantic tinge in him had repelled her, till he himself succeeded in showing himself a more and more trusty friend. On Christmas Day itself she read him the sketch for *Parsifal,* and her entry in her diary consists merely of the words: "A terrible impression *(Furchtbarer Eindruck).*" We know that later Nietzsche took not the slightest interest in this piece and maintained a positively hostile attitude towards it. But the plan itself must have produced a very strong effect upon him now. At this time, indeed, he was still inspired by quite other thoughts than later, when they had had to give way to cold and sombre ones. The Master himself had a "sublime" conversation with him in Frau Cosima's presence on the philosophy of music, and expressed ideas which she cherished the hope that he would develop further. They were, indeed, the germ of his marvellously penetrating essay on Beethoven.

But Nietzsche felt that he quite belonged to Triebschen — indeed, his sister calls him a "Triebschener." "The cordiality with which the Master's house was thrown open to his disciple gradually led to a deep and close friendship, and they spent precious days and hours remote from the world. They bore all their sorrows, great and small, together loyally, they suffered at the performance of *The Rhinegold* and *The Valkyrie* in Munich, and Nietzsche took the deepest interest in the genesis of *The Twilight of the Gods.* They had both assigned him the task of buying presents for the Christmas-tree in Basel. He brought with him not only Dürer engravings, antiquities, and works of art, but also dolls, a puppet-theatre, and other toys." Frau Cosima, we read, always felt quite abashed when she approached him with such requests. She could only find courage to do it by entirely forgetting that he was a professor, a doctor, and a philologist, and remembering nothing but his age, which was twenty-five. For the rest, she made things very convenient for him, out of consideration for his unpractical nature: all that he had to do was to hand in cards at the shops with the necessary descriptions. But he took such a pleasure in doing this that he refused to let himself off so easily and looked with a scrutinizing eye not only at the works of art, books, and other things that he understood, but also at the children's toys. For instance, he had cause to find fault with the figures for the puppet-show, on the ground that the king did not look enough like a real king, and that the devil was not so black as might have been desired; he also developed views of his own about the robe of the angel for the Christmas-tree. Such were his preparations for Triebschen. But we hear more from Nietzsche's sister about the Christmas festivities themselves: "During the holidays the snug old country-house was transformed into a lovely Christmas fairy-tale, in which the children forgot time and space for ecstasy, and the grown-up people for wistful emotion. The presents exchanged were all sorts of beautiful, cleverly devised things, with an especial appeal to the heart. For instance, my brother received a beautiful edition of Montaigne from Frau Cosima. On the other hand, Nietzsche had received a confidential commission to get six copies only of the biography printed and to supervise its production" — which he did in the most careful and touching way. We can see from the simple entry in her diary on January 3 of the fateful year 1870 how much he occupied Frau Cosima's thoughts even during this Christmas-tide: "Have written nothing for a whole week. Spent the whole time with Nietzsche, who left us yesterday. On New Year's Eve we lit up the tree again." And now in traditional French style the Master presented her with *étrennes* (New Year presents) as well, so that she was quite overcome.

For the rest, the old year closed and the new year began with anxiety; and the Master truly remarked that: "Life is like Brünhilde's flames — from time to time a hero strides through them and subdues her, but for the most part men perish in them." And with regard to the slow progress of the divorce proceedings he said:

"All rights and laws are still transmitted
Like an eternal sickness of the race.

Nature and love alone are prompt, but the laws simply crawl."

They celebrated January 8, Hans von Bülow's birthday, in silent melancholy: " I lay awake at night thinking of Hans's birthday. If I had thought of him alone, if I had lived for him, too, would it have been better? I think not. I firmly believe, moreover, that that was not my vocation. I have set my heart upon it that for my sake Lulu will love her father above all things and devote herself to him." And rhymes are wrung from her soul, such as these: *" Ihr ruhigen Sterne, grüsst aus der Ferne des Armen Nacht* (O tranquil star, greet from afar the poor one's night)."

Meanwhile the Master had completed the orchestral introduction to the Prelude of *The Twilight of the Gods* and seemed to be progressing splendidly. But now, all of a sudden, news arrived that the King really meant to have a performance of *The Valkyrie*. Both of them were seized with deep alarm. " When I told him that I should not be able to be present, he declared: ' Then on no account.' And once again he returned to the point that it was unthinkable that one of the works should be performed without my being present. I kissed his hand in deep agitation, upon which he laughed and said: ' So my life has been a necessity of nature.' " But Wagner was quite as upset about this affair as he had been before about the performance of *The Rhinegold*. On that occasion he had hurried to Munich and Starnberg on August 31, in order personally to win over the King to his views; but he had only been able to negotiate with Düfflipp and Perfall. Now even this link seemed to be entirely severed, and the King, in a sense, completely estranged from him, devoid of understanding for the desires which he cherished and was bound to cherish with regard to the performance of his work. Frau Cosima suffered and grieved with him. But on the other hand he had gained a necessary support in her and found in her not only the fullest sympathy with his ideas, which had now reached complete maturity and stood forth in a clear and definite form, but also an assistance based on conviction. His anxiety at having now to abandon *The Valkyrie*, too, to a separate performance in a theatre, though this took place under the ægis of the Bavarian King, was painful to him for the reason that the great plans which were now afoot would again be put in the shade — might, indeed, prove impossible to carry out, owing to the dismemberment of the tetralogy. For a time Wagner and Frau Cosima, too, interpreted this desire of the King's as a piece of unparalleled hostility, not only to his work, but to himself, though in reality it was due to his longing to hear and know the work; and this interpretation hurt Wagner beyond measure and pained him more than he could say. His grief was indeed checked by the incredibly brutal language which the directors of the Munich Hoftheater, not to speak of the official press of the Bavarian capital, began to use against him. It was the old story: an apparent loss of favour with the royal master was the signal for the utmost brutality on the part of the underlings! It was under such auspices as these, then, that the performance of *The Valkyrie* in Munich was initiated and carried out. For the rest, he and, most of all, Frau Cosima rightly observed that the work itself could not be injured by such proceedings and measures.

Moreover, they refused to let their inner life be disturbed, and the intellectual level on which they exchanged their ideas was as wonderful as ever. Thus she once said to him that, on reading Lessing's essay upon how the ancients represented death (*Wie die Alten den Tod gebildet*), she had been reminded of Isolde, who, as she extinguished the torch, appeared at once as a heroic lover and a goddess of death. The Master expressed his agreement with her opinion in high delight and next went on to talk of the skeleton in the Middle Ages. The Germans tried to derive from it a sense of something cheerful, he said, because they are so original and come closest to the Greeks in this conception. — Everything roused her to great thoughts! They played the Ninth Symphony, and she was overcome by the powerful effect that this work produced upon her. She saw in it an exhortation to the necessity for faith, both on the part of Schiller and, above all, on that of Beethoven. But, as she remarked: "Who can give himself faith? My father, for instance, is certainly a convinced believer, but I do not call that faith at all." It is interesting to see how she now carried on a most animated correspondence with Nietzsche. And yet we should be wrong in imagining that she was full of respect for the philosopher and professor; for she none the less managed to give him a certain feminine guidance in all things and approached the intellectual element in him with a certain critical spirit that she in no way concealed from him. In the mean time she, too, underwent a powerful intellectual development through her relation with him, and it was a momentous thing to occupy the place that she did, between the greatest musical and poetic genius of the age and a philosopher who was likewise developing more and more into a poet. No wonder that the Master once said: " If I only knew a being in the slightest degree comparable to you, so that I could say to myself: 'That is what I call a talent, that was developed in Cosima'! All that I fear is loss and sickness. Even now I do not realize how happy I am, even now I do not enjoy it enough." And she wrote modestly: " Who can measure how my heart receives such words? I never want to leave the house again."

One consolation was that her father's goodness of heart could not be banished for long, and that, though he did not write to her herself, he did to Daniela, whose description of the Christmas festivities touched him deeply. Through him she wanted to influence Hans, who was now at Florence, not far from Liszt, and who, when once he had recovered from the first attacks of indisposition which are invariably caused by a visit to Italy, began, as his letters clearly show, to feel extremely happy there, both as a man and as an artist. Wagner's comment was: " That is right, for it is not what one is that cuts one off, but how one sees things and expresses oneself." We must also admire the extraordinary tact with which he watched the development of this question, in relation both to Hans and to Franz Liszt.

Once more he was seized with a mood of supreme creation. The Norn scene had been a brilliant success: " It sounds like the fluttering of night-birds " — so Frau Cosima describes her impression of it. " It all depends upon the impression of nature. Here in the Norn scene I can see the tall firs by the crag and hear the soughing of the wind in them by night." And his comment was: " Only since my union with you have I acquired an unbelievable confidence in myself. I know that I am growing old, but life is only just beginning for me." And there is something extremely charming in seeing how in the evenings, as a relaxation from such mighty creative work, he went back to the books of his youth and read her König's *Hohe Braut,* upon which, as we know, was based the libretto of *Die Franzosen vor Nizza.* They both found more pleasure in this charming story than in the impressions recently produced upon them by the imitations of his great libretto of *The Ring of the Nibelung;* and, on reading Ettmüller's *Siegufried,* Frau Cosima remarked in some wrath: " Since Richard has forged the myths of the Edda into his *Ring* by the sweat of his brow, anybody who likes can try his hand at making a piece out of it. And they are praised and talked about for it, while Richard's eternal and unique work is being killed by silence. But what does it matter? "

The great political events of the year 1870 were also casting their shadow before them. For a long time past she had had hardly any dealings with her brother-in-law Ollivier. Meanwhile he had become Napoleon's minister and had gained a momentous influence over his foreign policy. This naturally exposed him to fierce attacks in the Chamber, and it was these attacks which induced Frau Cosima to resume her correspondence with him. For, as she said, he could not think now that it was his rise in the world that had led her to approach him again.

In their political views, too, the noble pair were in significant agreement. They were already alive to all that was going on at the Tuileries and the constant restlessness that revealed itself in Napoleon's policy. But they were equally interested in the Vatican Council, especially as it affected Germany and in particular Bavaria. Richard Wagner had certainly no special reason to esteem Ignaz von Döllinger, the Bavarian champion in Rome, for, though Döllinger was not an opponent of his, yet his whole nature ranged him on the side of those tendencies which had made Wagner's development impossible in Munich. But his courageous attitude in Rome made an impression at Triebschen. What is more, in spite of the errors and confusion arising out of the King's desire to see the first part at least of the tetralogy performed in Munich at all costs, the King's political attitude

gave them both sincere pleasure. At first, indeed, the ultramontane victory aroused some anxiety. But they were greatly pleased
at the way in which the King at once extended a protecting hand
over his minister, while even his conflict with the Reichsrat made
them realize that in this sphere, too, the King had steadily pursued his own way. In these views, with which was also mingled
their delight in Bismarck, they both took up a perfectly definite
standpoint and were filled with a conviction which made them
recognize that the subsequent development in German affairs
was the only right one. The situation was quite different in
Munich, where, under pressure from Rome, the ultramontane
left were already talking again of putting the King under guardianship and, in their opposition to his political views, harped
on the power and obstinacy of the Bavarian peasantry. For a
time, indeed, the Master had fears for the King and was even
afraid, not altogether without justification, that he might be
deposed — and this at a time when Wagner stood at the opposite
pole from his royal protector, while the latter, deaf to all the
Master's supplications, besides those of Frau Cosima, was insisting in his headstrong self-will upon the production of *The
Valkyrie,* the premature performance of which was bound to
have as fatal consequences as that of *The Rhinegold.* Perhaps
Wagner took this business far too much to heart; but it is evident
from what he said to Frau Cosima towards the end of January
that his agitation was not feigned: " If I had not got you, I
should simply not know for what purpose I am in the world.
I think I should go mad: on the one hand, to be incapable of
being other than what one is, and, on the other hand, to be absolutely at loggerheads with the world — it cannot but make one
bewildered about oneself." He regarded the performance of
The Valkyrie as a shadow upon his life and said that this affair
cast a gloom over all his ideas about the world. " If I were not
sustained by the fire of art and the ardour of love, I should cease
to live." He became far too much absorbed in these ideas, just
as Frau Cosima daily found a fresh source of pain and sorrow
in Hans von Bülow's sufferings and the whole question of the
divorce. Yet she might have set her mind entirely at rest
about Hans. His letters from Florence had a note, if not of

cheerfulness, at least of courageous vitality, and, thanks to his brilliant qualities both as an artist and as a man, he soon felt at home in the Italian world and in Florentine society, so that he was soon perfectly happy there.

Meanwhile we must draw a distinction between Frau Cosima's silent, melancholy musings and her household activities, in which sphere she allowed none of these feelings to be apparent, but had as her only object Wagner's peace and quiet and the success of his work, besides the education of the children. But every word of love that he said to her blossomed like a flower in her heart. It is affecting, too, to read in what terms he spoke to her of their first meeting, in Paris in 1853: that journey, he said, had really been in order to view his future wife; for she had been as Tristan, who had noticed nothing. Thus she drew rapture and happiness from both past and present. She watched his prodigious work *The Twilight of the Gods* grow before her eyes, while at the same time she saw how his mind was occupied with those ideas on the philosophy of music which we have mentioned. He said, indeed, that the whole of philosophy might be constructed out of a single movement of a Mozart symphony, just because it was so simple and the treatment of the melodies so infinitely subtle. Beethoven was a much more difficult instance: the first movement of the *Eroica* simply defied definition. He was eager to discuss his philosophical ideas with Nietzsche; he drew them entirely from within himself, and the latter too entered into them with all the ardent zeal, though at the same time with all the one-sidedness, of a young scholar. He coined an epigram on the spot summing up his views on *Figaro:* " Mozart has invented the music of intrigue (*Intrigenmusik*)"; to which the Master immediately rejoined that, on the contrary, he had sublimated intrigue into music; one had only to compare Beaumarchais's pieces, admirable though they were, with Mozart's operas. In the former one found wary (*scheu*), witty, limited people talking and trifling cleverly together; but in Mozart the characters are glorified beings who suffer and lament. Frau Cosima saw to her astonishment, but to her delight and interest, how in all these things the Master was the young philosopher's teacher. And a few days later, when the latter wrote in a perfectly cheerful tone of the delight of the French papers over the fall of Hohenlohe, his letter filled both of them with real alarm, and the Master said that, after all, Schopenhauer's philosophy might have a bad influence upon such young people, owing to their application of pessimism to life, and the hopeless attitude towards practical matters which they deduced from it. Both of them felt a real friendship for this young man of learning, which found expression not only in their intercourse with him, but also in their profound understanding of his nature. For their insight was clear, and they refused to be dazzled in any way.

It was only with regard to his son that the Master indulged in delightful Utopian dreams. Thus he asked her once: " You do really wish him to be a sort of Parzival? " And she replied with a merry yes. And he said that since everything about them was concerned with music, it would not be at all surprising if he were talented, but only a natural outcome of it all. But she answered with deep emotion: " So long as he but continues to be healthy, and the children flourish." Not a day went by without its labours and cares about their education. She was filled with alarm if the children unintentionally offended the Master, and at such moments she had none of that deep maternal confidence and calm which Gottfried Keller has described in his wonderful short story, *Frau Amrain und ihr Jüngster*, dealing with the bringing-up of a child. But she entered into their life wonderfully, only next moment to become engrossed once more in the progress of the Master's ideas and feelings. He was for ever touching new stops. Once when he was playing a chorale from a Bach cantata, which moved them both deeply, he remarked that a Jew had made a French opera out of it; and that was characteristic of the whole problem. But she replied: " And yet it is these strains, though desecrated and distorted, that made the success of this opera." " And Bach is Luther. See with what equanimity he writes the boldest, most audacious things." Thus the whole of life was constantly present to them. Yet, side by side with this, the old trance-like strain pervaded Frau Cosima's daily life and work. She dreamt that her sister Blandine came into her room looking exactly the same as when she died, and she felt

that she must talk to him of Blandine's death. He nodded gravely
and said: " One's whole nature is changed when one has lived
through such experiences. To think that such a being as Blandine
should have disappeared! And Schnorr! One has survived it,
but one is changed." But he added with a sigh of satisfaction:
" Instead of Schnorr we now have Fidi [Siegfried]."

There is no doubt that the postponement of the divorce caused
her deep depression, which constantly revived her old train of
thought about her guilt and Hans's sufferings. She had written
to her old friend Lothar Bucher, and he replied very reassur-
ingly that Bülow's lawyer was absolutely honest, and that Hans
would come to Berlin about the end of March to settle the business. But Heinrich Porges now appeared at Triebschen to act in
some sort as agent for the King. He gave them an account of
affairs in Munich, of the shocking performance of *Tannhäuser*
under Wüllner, and his utter incapacity. He was pleasant company for them, but he never succeeded in penetrating to the
holy of holies of this shrine of art. The Master amused himself
by talking philosophy with him in the Socratic manner, but at
the same time expounded his own views. Thus he set up the
Grail as the symbol of liberty: it was renunciation, the negation
of will, and vows of chastity that forced the knights of the Grail
away from the world of illusion. The knight may break his vow,
on the condition which he imposes upon the woman: for if a
woman is so far mistress of her natural instincts as to ask no
question, she is worthy to enter the Grail. It is in order that he
may be able to find this out that the knight is allowed to make
advances to her. This discussion arose, it is true, from Porges's
article on *Lohengrin*, but it led him into another world, into
which, esentially, nobody but Frau Cosima was able to follow
the Master. For on the next day the Master found her sad, simply
because she was thinking over what he had said about *Lohengrin*,
and the emotion which this had caused her was still present in
her, as his words continued to echo in her mind. For the rest,
it was a great consolation to her when, on a solitary walk which
he took with her, Porges talked with her about the past and said
how happy he was at seeing the Master as he had never seen him
before, so calm and full of life, and how he felt sure that Wagner

would never have taken up *The Nibelungs* again had not this great revolution taken place in his life. When she repeated this to the Master with tears, he agreed and said: " Not a note should I ever have produced again if I had not found you. Now I have a life."

Spring came in with the roaring of storms, and with it came stimulating ideas of every kind. The Master thought of his " heroes," with whom alone he wanted to associate — Bernhard of Weimar, Luther, Frederick the Great, and Oliver Cromwell, whom Cosima added to the list. Thus he put to flight his daily recurring thoughts about the performance of *The Valkyrie*. Yet this caused the Master and Frau Cosima quite different feelings from those which the King had intended. We can quite well follow the King's train of thought. *Tristan* and *The Mastersingers* had appeared upon the boards of his court theatre to his own extreme satisfaction, as well as that of his friend, the great composer; why, then, should not the same be possible with the other works? But he did not consider that the tetralogy made far more exacting demands, and that the first thing necessary was to meet these, as regards both accommodation and technique, but especially as regards the technique of singing, before proceeding with the production. Every day of the preparations for *The Valkyrie* ought to have shown him this; but it did not occur to him. And now the Master was once more intent upon his old idea of producing the tetralogy at some other place, remote from the bustle of the world. And, recalling the Master's visit to Bayreuth, mentioned in the autobiography, Cosima asked him on the evening of March 5 to look up the article " Bayreuth " in the encyclopædia. Later, too, he mentioned this place quite of his own accord as the one which he would like to choose. " To our delight we found that the encyclopædia mentioned a splendid old operahouse." It was one of Frau Cosima's original and intuitive utterances, which so often flashed into her mind at critical moments, that formed the starting-point for the development of the Bayreuth idea. March 5, 1870 was its birthday. And in a certain sense it was Frau Cosima who gave birth to this idea too.

Next they plunged with the greatest enthusiasm into Droysen's *History of Alexander the Great*, in which the hero of the

389

Hellenic world rose up before them clearly and in all his power and raised them high above all the pettiness of the present, including the well-meaning and constantly repeated explanations of Porges, who did not succeed in gaining his ends and now, with touching submissiveness, allowed himself to be absorbed into the spirit of Triebschen. But the present day began to bore them too. And it is curious how, perhaps through the fault of the Wesendonck household, a shadow began to fall even over his former connexions. Wagner had sent the first manuscript book of the autobiography to Wesendonck, who thanked him cordially, but advised him with a touch of condescension not to continue to go into the details of his life so minutely. The Master was seriously put out, and Frau Cosima shared his feeling, though both now and in after days she tried to avert a coolness between the two households. But this was yet another sign of how far they had both risen above the world and now had to bear the consequences, as expressed in Goethe's words: " *Wer sich der Einsamkeit ergibt, ach, der ist bald allein* (He who chooses loneliness, alas, is soon alone)." Nor did she hesitate to tell Porges, too, something of what had decided her to break with the world; and the Master remarked: " People are so false and treacherous that nobody believes in magnanimity and sincerity. Not a soul would believe in you." And when they were alone, he added: " Not only do I love you (*liebe Dich*), but I live in you (*lebe Dich*). When you are in the least troubled and depressed, I am crippled, like a bird wounded in the wing."

But there is a peculiar fascination in watching the pains which Councillor Düfflipp took in his attempt to bring about the production of *The Valkyrie* so urgently desired by the King; how he wrote to Hans about conducting it, and how greatly it was desired to hurry on the divorce, so that the King might once again summon Wagner back to Munich and associate with him freely. But it all met with an obstinate resistance on the part of Bülow. He would not hear of returning to Munich now, for, as he explicitly remarked, it would be suicidal. He himself was a sick man, he said, but there was one who was strong, and his name was Klindworth. But Düfflipp was doubtful about approaching Klindworth again, for he would refuse. Thus they were in the greatest straits and even tried the experiment of installing Heinrich Porges in the conductor's desk. As he had just returned from Triebschen, this appeared most odd, and Porges had every reason to make excuses to the Master.

Yet the waves from the outer world were powerless to wash over the solid rampart behind which Frau Cosima brooded over her gloomy thoughts, in which she was confirmed anew by reading Gottfried of Strassburg's *Tristan*. What most went to her heart were the following words of the poet:

> *Trug jemals einer stetes Leid*
> *Bei währender Glückseligkeit,*
> *So trug Tristan dieses stete Leid.*

> (If ever man bore deep distress,
> Along with lasting happiness,
> 'Twas Tristan bore this deep distress.)

These verses seemed to fit her own case exactly: " For I am happy, yet I cannot forget that there is one who has suffered and is perhaps still suffering." In spite of the spring, much also happened that was the reverse of gratifying. She rejoiced to hear and see the arrival of the starlings, which settled on the house, scattered themselves about the different trees, and circled round the house, chattering loudly and joyously. But now news came from Vienna that Beckmesser's song had been recognized as an ancient Hebrew melody, of which, it was alleged, the Master had meant to make fun. The result had been an outbreak of hissing during the second act, and shouts of " We won't hear it." The Germans, however, got the better of this uproar in the theatre, about which the Master said: " Not one of our social historians has noticed that the Jews are actually daring to say: ' We won't listen to it ' in the imperial theatre." Far profounder were the effects of their evening readings, in *Faust*, for instance — especially the Second Part, which seemed to them to mark a veritable rebirth of the poet. Or in *Hamlet*, which produced totally fresh impressions upon them both, especially Frau Cosima: " For the first time I have grasped the fact that Hamlet

391

is lifted by his experience of the world far above revenge, and
even suicide. The hideous deed which should have spurred him
to vengeance causes him to realize the nature of the world and
consequently the fact that nothing but the King's death can
expiate the crime; besides, to one who has communed with spirits
reality appears but as a terrible dream."

The Master also initiated his companion into Buddhism. In
this connexion he says what a pity it is that the Jewish religion
should have been grafted upon Christianity and entirely corrupted it: " There is no getting away from it: a state of equilib-
rium as regards the world could only be achieved through this
absorption in the best and greatest that the world has hitherto
produced." In these matters the Master really appears in the twofold character of Hans Sachs and of Tristan, instructing and
initiating this already highly cultured woman into all these fresh
spheres. He had but one serious trouble, and that was her excessive devotion to the children, which he remarked with some
chagrin, saying of it: " I can already see myself at Marburg,
standing under the gate before the Convent of St. Elisabeth."
Yet she was anything but this, especially when she knew that
the fullness of his creative power was upon him. She entered
into his feeling, as it were, in the genesis of every new bar, and
with passionate devotion she watched *The Twilight of the Gods*
come into being.

It was from this, moreover, that she drew her hopes and ideas
for Bayreuth. Just at this time Richter came to Triebschen again,
and she spoke to him of her hopes: " The only thing for which
we will give up our refuge will be this blossoming of art at
Bayreuth." And all that they heard, thought, or read tended to
influence them strongly and powerfully in this direction. When
the strange news came from Munich that the King meant to have
the forms of the galloping Valkyries, conceived by Wagner
merely as nebulous shadows, represented by his grooms, this
could only strengthen their determination to secure a complete
representation of the work at Bayreuth, which should be sceni-
cally perfect as well. But she felt the spell of the music rising from
the Master's very manuscript, and in the course of a discussion
about the nature of music she said of him and his work: " It is

not the representation of an idea, but the idea itself. All the feeling for beauty in the world has taken refuge in music! " With such sentiments as these, they sought refuge in Plato's *Symposium*, from which Cosima obtained one of the deepest impressions of her life; and she was, in some measure, revived by the thought which finds expression in the *Symposium:* to engender the beautiful in the beautiful. On the other hand, Wagner declared that it was under just such an impression as that in the *Symposium* that he had written his book *Kunst und Revolution* (*Art and Revolution*).

On the whole, however, matters were progressing. Richter met Liszt in Munich and went with him to Hungary. He had satisfactory news to write about Liszt's changed state of mind; indeed, the latter usually judged matters more calmly when he was away from Rome and the influence of the Princess. But what affected him particularly was the news of Bülow's successes in Florence. He had already received an order from the King of Italy, and the papers were praising him and his influence upon the musical conditions of the Italian capital. This was a great consolation to Cosima, too; while on April 13, in order to arrive at a compromise with the King, the Master himself tried as a last resource to move him by his fine and well-known poem:

Noch einmal mögest du die Stimme hören,
Die einstens aus dir selber zu mir sprach.

(Oh, mayst thou hear once more the same voice speaking
That from thyself was wont to speak to me!)

But this last resource also failed, and on May 4 the King gave orders to proceed with the production of *The Valkyrie* regardless of Wagner. On the 14th Wüllner was charged to produce the work with such resources as he possessed at home. On June 26 took place the first performance, which produced an immense impression, and the piece was repeated, together with *The Rhinegold*, on July 7, 10, 14, 17, 20, and 22. Liszt and all their friends were present, and the former expressed his impression of the piece beautifully, though still with decided reservations.

The period of preparation and development preceding the performance was naturally bound to produce quite a different effect upon Triebschen from that which it did upon the world at large, not to speak, of course, of the hostile newspapers, which chiefly attacked the enormous cost of this production.

Frau Cosima lived entirely in the narrow world of Triebschen, which was none the less so wide. She rejoiced at every word of Wagner's, and her heart exulted when he paused before her picture and said: " Here is the only being upon earth who means anything to me." " So long as I behold your dear face, I shall not die." And from *The Twilight of the Gods* he managed to find his way back to the *Œdipus Tyrannus*, when she observed that she would like to hear these Greek classical choruses. Upon which he pointed in the direction of Bayreuth and said: " They will be taught in our school! " And she added: " But the piano must not be taught there at all. The pupils must know just so much about the piano as is necessary to become good musicians. But no instruction in it must be admitted in our school. For virtuosity stifles everything of the sort." To which he answered: " You are right, but how daring you are! " Yet they were absorbed almost exclusively in each other. She herself says: " Not much that is pleasant from without. The children alone give us comfort and support, otherwise we would gladly die. People have held every conceivable opinion about our union, but it scarcely occurs to them that we were swayed by an overmastering love, and that it was no mere chance that we discovered each other! " So the cry came from the heart when she called to him in the morning: " Are you friendly to me? " and he replied gaily: " Nothing but friendly, and I grow fonder of you every day." And when the conversation turned upon women, he said that " if they lose a certain timorous modesty, and want to be anything more than wives and mothers, how unpleasantly stiff they become! " And in connexion with these arguments he went on to discuss love among the Greeks, with whom, when it did not degenerate into vice, it displayed the highest æsthetic tendencies. " But reverence for women is a new force, which makes an entire breach between us and the antique world. Among the German races women have something more mysterious about them, something closer to nature." And this mysterious quality she undoubtedly possessed. How easily she was alarmed by a dream, when she started up out of her sleep, and Richard stood before her! " I think with anguish of how I awoke just as abruptly as this at the death of Blandine. Who is suffering? Who is dying? Is it my father, or poor Hans? God help us! I cannot and will not think of Richard in such a connexion. I do not even like to hear the cuckoo, for three days ago he questioned it and only heard three calls in reply. O everlasting care, when wilt thou disappear? Only with our life! "

The only news from the outside world that affected them at all was that of the Vatican Council and the performance of *The Valkyrie*. And now he received a letter from Levi in Munich, asking him whether he would mind his accepting the conductorship, or, since he had heard that the performance was against the Master's wish, would he like him simply to decline? And the Master said: " I respect him, because he really calls himself Levi, as in the Bible, and not Löwe or Lewy " — and, in fact, he continued to have a high esteem for him during his whole life. It was about this time that Frau Cosima questioned him about his diary, for she was anxious that he should continue to keep it. He answered in the negative: " It has stopped. Now I am enjoying my happiness. I vow that I am no longer surprised at anything, now that I see that the old power has not left me at all, and that my imagination is always inclined for creation — perhaps too much so. Whom have I to thank for this? " " The King of Bavaria," she answered jestingly. " It is the answer to his recent letter." But he grew serious and replied: " Believe me, in my weariness I would have renounced this favour, had I not found you."

He was in fact living through his most creative period. *The Twilight of the Gods* advanced quietly and surely, though accompanied by the deepest inward agitation; for every step forward not only was a prodigious feat of creation, but also marked a steady progress in technique. He explained this to her from day to day. For instance, when he reached the point where Brünhilde is seated alone upon her rock gazing at the ring, instead of a parenthesis he introduces a cadence, for this is not an interlude.

But his thoughts went on far beyond *The Twilight of the Gods,* to *The Victors.* On May 1, on returning from his walk through the wind and rain, he said: " If ever I compose *The Victors* in my old age, I shall write a prelude to it, in which the first part of the action is to take place (the rejection of Ananda by the Chandala maiden). Nothing but music can render this — the mystery of regeneration." And now the *Amselthema* (thrush theme) suddenly occurred to him, which he used later in quite a different fashion. But in this connexion he said, not without a slight touch of irony: " How glad I should be to compose a libretto now! What easy, quick work! What is it compared to the scoring? " But in the evening the two of them played together the first act of *The Twilight of the Gods.* It is not surprising that in these circumstances he declined an invitation from Vienna to conduct the Ninth Symphony, and said to her: " Wherever I have my home one day, I will perform the symphony for you. But I will have nothing to do with all the rabble." " Home " was again an allusion to Bayreuth, for which he had other tasks in store besides his works. For once when he was reading *Wallenstein* with her and was led on to talk of the relations between Thekla and Max, he found fault with certain historians of literature who absolutely condemned this scene. To him it seemed very much to the point, as signifying the abruptness of true love. It is owing to magnetism that the sheep unerringly finds its way to the right herbage. And they discussed having these pieces performed in the school at Bayreuth, for it was the disgraceful acting, they said, that spoils them for one.

They lived, indeed, in the pure springtide of love. One morning she appeared by his wish dressed in white. He called her the *Dame Blanche,* or, better, Thekla: " In all that is beautiful I have you as my prototype; that is why I am so happy. It is you who realized that it was possible to help me." How different are her feelings in the dark hours of her suffering: " If only we could tame passion, if only it could be banished from life! Its approach now casts a gloom over me, as though it were death." But at the same time she was engrossed in her preparations for the Master's birthday. She had devised all kinds of surprises and retained the regimental band, forty-five men strong; while the children, and especially the eldest, Daniela, were also to take part in the surprise. She spent the whole night before his birthday decorating the staircase and hall, and when she had finished, she wrote in her diary in the small hours of the morning: " But I am no longer any good for festivities, and even before the day has begun, I sit here writing this and crying. God grant my children happiness today; those who have suffered much can no longer laugh with a whole heart. On festive occasions especially, one realizes how sad life is. For the wounded heart the insensible passage of time, the silent flight of the days, is best. May God vouchsafe his blessing and soon grant me peace! " But joy put her melancholy mood to flight. At eight o'clock the children, adorned with garlands of roses, burst into Wagner's room, the band struck up the *Huldigungsmarsch,* and Richard sobbed with delight at the surprise. Next Daniela went to her bird-cage, which had been given her on her birthday, in October, and set her beloved pets free. Frau Cosima had written her the following verses, suited to her childish sentiments and way of speaking:

> Little birds, now fly away,
> Think of me where'er you stray.
> Each one build a cosy nest
> Where the little ones can rest.
> Small men sing in gayer mood
> While their wives hatch out the brood.
> When the white snow covers all,
> Come in answer to our call.
> If the cold distress you thus,
> Come and make your nest with us!
> And the little ones bring too,
> We will welcome all of you.
> If you come not, then farewell!
> For love is not an empty shell,
> Nor worthy of the name would prove
> Where to possess is more than love.

So fly away, far out of sight!
With loving eyes I watch your flight.
And if tears fall, a gentle shower,
They'll change our parting to a flower.
Pretty finch, away, away!
Dearest siskin, don't delay!
The door is open, do not stay!
This is a day without alloy,
Since that the birds should share its joy
The children wish with all their heart.
So, little birds, depart, depart!
Fly away fast, for you are free!
My thoughts pursue you joyously.

The opening of the cage cost little Daniela some tears, it is true, and all her pets flew away except the little wagtail, which remained behind, but was found dead next morning. Frau Cosima had been glad that her eldest girl had made up her mind to sacrifice her pets for the occasion. But she said: " How I give praise to the children's star, because I know that they are here, in this peace and solitude to which Richard has removed them in their childhood! No struggle for life, no hardships can impair their happiness."

On the 20th the household had already been in great excitement. One of the King's equerries had appeared, leaving a horse, Grane, who was a delight to them all for a time. The little Siegfried was put on his back and kept his seat with proud delight. A telegram also arrived from Liszt, quite in his old tone: " With you for ever and ever, in bright days or in dark." Touched by all these festivities, the Master called Frau Cosima " the conductress (*Kapellmeisterin*) of his life." And in this birthday mood he talked to her beautifully and affectingly about life and its manifestations. " I felt," she says, " as though through him — but through him alone — I were penetrating to the essential nature of the world." He went on to speak in his own fashion about the transmigration of souls, describing the whole idea as a kindly one; death alone was a grave matter, as a test of life, but all that came after it was as kindly as possible. Though, as he said: " Thank God, a deep mystery still lies over it all." And another time — though still in connexion with the same great question — conversation turned upon Fairyland. " Shakspere had his head full of these fairies, the elfin world of ' Old England ' was alive within him." They read alternately Shakspere, Schiller, and Sophocles, and, as she comments: " Each of them caused us the same emotion and surprise, for the work of such a genius always bears upon it the stamp of something which defies comprehension." Shakspere, they agreed, was a natural genius (*Naturgenie*), Schiller a genius developed by conscious art (*Kunstgenie*), who had to achieve pathos by deliberate effort, that he might deliver the German stage from its universally prevailing realism. Goethe had of course done the same, and just as he moves us by his objectivity, so Schiller moves us by his subjectivity. Wagner was particularly fond of *Die Jungfrau von Orleans*, of which he said: " All this cries out for music."

About this time appeared the memoirs of Hector Berlioz. They were written entirely in that spirit of bitterness which had darkened the unhappy musician's last years. Frau Cosima felt hurt and almost repelled by them, for she had formed quite a different impression of him as a result of her childish reminiscences. But the Master said that after those memoirs he renounced all relations with France. Indeed, his opinion of the French became more and more severe. It is almost as though he had had a premonition of the approaching war. He spoke once of the strange influence of the French upon costume, how they spoilt everything, and how all their powers and innermost instincts tended towards degeneracy.

He had now completed the first act of *The Twilight of the Gods*. When he played her the scene of the *Tarnkappe* (cap of invisibility), she remarked: " The inhuman apostrophe to his wife has a terrific effect; at any rate, the great tissue of themes has created a language of which the world has no idea." And when it comes to the snatching away of the ring, she writes, in allusion to the parallel between Alberich and Brünhilde: " The most noble of beings suffers exactly like the ignoble one. The will is one and the same thing in every creature." And once, on June 4, when she sat down to the piano quite as an exception — for till the day of the Master's death she hardly ever touched it without him — he came to her and sketched out the music which accompanies the drawing forth of the sword. Thus it was on the eve of his son's first birthday that he completed the pencil-sketch for the first act. On the morning of this memorable day she makes the following entry in her diary: " My child, your birth — my supreme happiness — is connected with the deepest injury to another. My existence was to blame for this! Never forget this, but see in it an image of life and atone for it as best you can. But receive my blessing as the realization of my sweetest dream." Early in the morning she was " sweetly " awakened. " Richard heralded the hour of his birth at the piano. The children brought flowers and stars, and Richard said: ' What a beautiful morning! How happy I am! ' " And Frau Cosima celebrated the day in the following verses:

> When in sweet mourning all the earth reposes
> Lulled by the sun's departing kiss,
> We loved in mingled pain and bliss,
> And thou didst blossom with the roses
> That now luxuriantly growing
> On Tristan and Isolde's grave, and glowing
> With golden grapes entwined with roses blowing,
> A lovely garland round thy being drapes.
> Thy face brought blessing into Tristan's night,
> In which beneath death's shadow once we lay,
> Father and mother woke to new delight
> When Siegfried's singer laughed toward the day.
> By the roses and the grapes,
> By Tristan and Isolde's rest,
> By the last kiss of the departing light,
> Possess, my Siegfried, what should be possessed
> And be thou clear as day, as deep as night!

Lauter Gesang
von Luther vom Schwan

tönet so lang
dem Himmel hinan

als Freund und Herz lebendig offen
bekennen: Glaube Liebe und Hoffen

———

It is curious that at this time the Master was thinking about the past and also came to speak of the days at Zürich: " Yet how much of my past is dead! When I think of Zürich, where I spent nine years, which have not left a trace on me! I conducted Beethoven's symphonies, and it is all blotted out. But it is mutual." And turning, he added to Cosima: " You are all soul, love, and spirit! " And she remarks: "When he says that, I feel like Gretchen: ' *Weiss nit, was er an mir findt* (I can't think what he sees in me).' "

During the following days their solitude was broken by the visit of Nietzsche with his friend Erwin Rhode. The latter had also been appointed to a chair at Basel and came to Triebschen imbued with a deep and strong love for the Master's works. His nature was possibly a far more gifted one than that of Nietzsche, and he had an amazing and unbounded knowledge of Greek antiquity, accompanied by a touch of real genius. " I should be inclined to describe him without qualification as a more considerable man even than Nietzsche," says Frau Cosima, and it is not surprising that he made a lasting impression upon them both. At any rate, Frau Cosima always remembered him with warm friendship; and, as was natural, his love for *Tannhäuser,* which he, too, rates very highly in his diary, produced a strong effect upon her. When she visited Heidelberg in 1892 for the performance of (Liszt's) *Christus,* she had a long *tête-à-tête* conversation with her old friend of Triebschen days. Nietzsche now read them his lecture on the Greek music-drama, not without encountering certain doubts on the part of the Master, who expounded them to him with clear and searching arguments, though, as Frau Cosima remarks: " The lecture is a fine one and shows that he has a real feeling for Greek art." Nietzsche had brought her a Dürer engraving, entitled *Melancholia,* which, after the departure of their Basel friends, suggested a comparison between Dürer and Sebastian Bach. As the Master observed: " They are both to be regarded as the conclusion of the Middle Ages. For it is nonsense to regard Bach as being one of us. Both are equipped with a rich imagination, full of mystery, lacking beauty, but achieving the sublime, which transcends all beauty. Dante may be regarded as a third, though he is less sympathetic

to us, because he is not so human — in fact, not Protestant."
They next began to read *Wilhelm Meisters Lehrjahre*, and the
influence of that work was in the ascendant during the days
which followed. They read it, to be sure, in a most singular
frame of mind; for they were expecting every day to hear that
the divorce was now completed, and this was to be followed as
soon as possible by their marriage. Frau Cosima's wedding-
clothes were already arriving and naturally caused them both
pleasure, accompanied, however, by serious reflections. They
spoke of their son's future, and the Master played to him and
was delighted when the little boy listened with an earnest expression. And out of this, again, arose thoughts of the future
performance of *The Ring of the Nibelung*, about which the
Master said: " What I think is that if the work were once in
existence, it would be there for ever for humanity; and though
I know that the masses will not change and cannot remodel anything that is already in existence, all I ask is that what is good
should also have a place of its own, a harbour of refuge. People
are bound to take up and retain what is vulgar and bad, all
that the good can still find is, perhaps, a refuge." And arguing
from the greater to the less, he concluded: " You will see: *The
Valkyrie* too will turn out to my advantage. Something or another will happen which will perhaps be more favourable to me
and my plan than if there were now an eternal silence." During
the whole of this period they were both in an exalted mood.
Once, when it was moonlight and they had finished the third
book of the *Lehrjahre*, he said: "How things have turned out for
us! Did we know how our union came about? It was ordained
by God." And, gazing at the moon, he asked her: " Do you know
what prayer I made to the moon? That I might be spared ever
having to be parted from you in order to provide for our existence. If we were forced to part in such a way, it would be terrible." Yet his relations with the King, too, caused him some
anxiety, not so much on account of outward circumstances as
from personal considerations, and his comment was: " One
stands between one's genius and one's dæmon. You are of the
nature of the genius, and the King of the dæmon. Love and creative work are all in all to me, and creative work only because

I love. You are the central sun round which everything moves. If you are only happy once more in all that affects you, then I shall be glad and happy. But you cannot cast spells (*hexen*) — the outer world remains just what it is — and yet you have cast a spell." And on another occasion he exclaimed as he came to her from his work: " My work — what a luxury! I only do it so that you may not be cross! "

And now news poured in about the performance of *The Valkyrie* in Munich, and her comment was: " It is like daggers stabbing my heart, and I ask myself whether this outrage will really go unavenged." But Wagner said with a smile: " You are the sister of the King of Bavaria; you both joined hands to sustain my life. He, it is true, like a foolish creature; you, like a good woman." And she adds a curious observation: " I cannot unravel the mystery of the King's feelings. But there is a common saying that this is never at all possible where a king is concerned."

Wagner now gave orders to the household that all letters from Munich were to be handed over in the first place to Frau Cosima. " I am glad of this rule," she wrote, and at once began to carry on the correspondence behind the Master's back. She was still able to use her old connexions for the benefit of others. The Countess Bassenheim came to her with a petition that the tenure of her father's, Prince Öttingen's, property might be changed, so that it might be inherited in the female line. Frau Cosima at once wrote to Munich to this effect, and after a short interval the Countess's petition was granted. For the rest she was able to help him through these days with brilliant success. The reports from Berlin about the performance of *Tannhäuser* spoke of it as an unprecedented success. At the end of the first act there had been an immense outburst of enthusiasm. And she wrote in her diary: " We are discussing Bayreuth and forgetting Munich." It was just now that she was herself reminded of Paris, through a fresh channel: Richter had arrived at Triebschen from Paris, and related his experiences there. He had not been to Notre Dame, but had only done some commonplace sightseeing. He was quite inoffensive where music was concerned, and in the evenings during his stay at Triebschen played Haydn symphonies with the Master: "It reminds me of the time when I used to play them with Blandine." And she quotes Madame de Staël: "*Ce beau temps, où j'étais si malheureuse* (the beautiful days when I was so unhappy) — my melancholy youth — fatherless and motherless — yet so happy."

And so July came round, and the last formalities in connexion with the divorce had to be complied with. In spite of this the Master started writing his work on Beethoven, besides discussing his projected comedy, a possible *Luther's Wedding, Bernhard of Weimar,* and *Frederick the Great.* But it is remarkable that at this very time all their conversation and thoughts tended, so to speak, towards Paris. Thus one day Frau Cosima discoursed upon the Paris fashions: "They are the most perfect picture of fashions with which we have nothing in common. Yet the German women cannot help copying them. The Parisian knows to a nicety what she is and what her style is, and dresses accordingly. But the German woman looks at her neighbour, envies her, and wants to imitate her. And that is why beauty is lost. After the Wars of Liberation there was a moment when a new impulse should have been given to the whole nation, but at that time people were as much afraid of the word ' German ' as they were of the Red Republic."

Such was their conversation on July 7. On the 8th the first news of a war forced itself upon their solitude. Frau Cosima was seized with deep alarm, but also with deep resentment. "The French are furious that anything should be done without them." Those were days of extreme tension, but were beguiled by an excursion to Pilatus, to which the Master had looked forward with delight for a long time past; for the mountain peaks belonged to the world in which he conceived his great works and to which he always returned and sought strength to carry them out. And so, in spite of her doctor's warnings, Cosima took part in the ascent of the mysterious mountain. She, too, felt the grandeur of the heights, and the deliverance from all burdens which it brought, and said that: "Love alone rules and reveals itself in the high, pure ether." The silence and solitude produced a sublime impression upon her, all the more so when the Master explained that it was such impressions which had inspired his representation of the life of the gods in *The Ring of the Nibelung*. The moonlight and sunrise stirred her emotions and lent her fresh life; but she had to pay for her exertions by spending a day in bed, when he sat by her side and read to her out of Tieck's *Dichterleben* and Byron's *Manfred*. And now the guide brought the news of the ultimatum presented by the French to the Emperor William, and she writes in the utmost agitation: " I am absolutely beside myself at the insolence of the French. That nation deserves to be punished without mercy." They returned home, and the Master's good-natured remark on this rather unsuccessful excursion into the mountains was: " Such an outing will never be a success for us, but we have our own happiness instead." And when she " asked him childishly " whether he loved her, he replied: " I should like to know what else I do but love you."

In Lucerne they met Karl Klindworth, who had arrived there on a visit. This was a great comfort to Frau Cosima, for he had come from Berlin. " In Berlin he saw Hans, who is getting on well, and was content with his stay in Florence and is planning a visit to America. If only I may be vouchsafed the consolation that things are really going well with Hans, then, O God, never indeed has there been a happier woman than I." And their friend, quiet, but faithful as ever, gave them an account of his impressions of Munich. *The Valkyrie* had been overwhelming; her father had been present and had gone on to the Passion-play at Oberammergau; upon which she commented: " How different such a life is from ours! How taken up with externals, how desirous of distractions! How great is the gulf between us! " Yet she was impressed when Klindworth described how her father had sobbed incessantly during the whole of the scene between Brünhilde and Siegmund, and how the Countess Mouchanoff, too, had been unable to listen to this moving scene a third time. Klindworth found Wagner rejuvenated and in such spirits that he could hardly recognize him. Hans, too, had said to him that if Wagner ever wrote a single note more, it was only thanks to her. She then had a confidential talk with their old friend, who was returning to Germany and would meet Hans there: " I am asking him to tell Hans everything which I had intended to write him."

There is no doubt that it was the warlike events which did most to help the Master, and Frau Cosima too, out of their depression about *The Valkyrie*. She really lived entirely in and for the day's happenings. She was indignant at the outrageous behaviour of the French, who could not be content with the Prince of Hohenzollern's disclaimer, but demanded a promise from the King of Prussia to Benedetti. She was glad when King William duly refused to receive the ambassador. During the night of the 15–16th she could not sleep for her anxiety to hear what would happen next. She was relieved that the French friends whom they were expecting, Villiers and Mendès, did not arrive. " For," she writes, " it would be very unpleasant to see French people now." What is more, the newspaper further brought the sensational announcement that the Emperor had been perfectly well aware of the Prince's candidature and was only indignant that he should have declined to marry a niece of the Empress Eugénie. The ministers had actually not known this, but had been misled by their own Emperor! Wagner gave it as his opinion that they were a gang of knaves who had started a conflagration in Europe, and the populace in Paris was celebrating this by singing the *Marseillaise*. How curious, on the other hand, was the news from Munich, where they did not know what attitude to take up towards the directors of theatres in other parts who were trying to purchase the right to produce *The Valkyrie*! Indeed, as she rightly says: " They seem to be in such a muddle at Munich that they would be glad to have Bülow back again and change everything round."

During these days, too, a slight breach between Triebschen and Nietzsche can be noted. Out of consideration for the Master, indeed, he had not been to Munich for *The Valkyrie*, but he did not know what attitude to adopt towards the war. Frau Cosima writes: " I answered him and am doing my best to make him enthusiastic in favour of the Prussians as the champions of German rights." For she was full of enthusiasm for the German people, and also of deep apprehension. " What is before us? How is this terrible war to end — how can it end? " At this moment a terrible storm broke over Triebschen, and she says: " I maintain that the gods are angry with the French. War has been declared, Paris is full of nothing but phrases, but the Prussians are calm, steady, and resolute." The Master's comment was that the Frenchman is an odd creature. He will not keep his word, but if you remonstrate with him, then you have got to fight him. The French were the incarnation of Renaissance corruption. But she said: " I am so absolutely beside myself that I am afraid of boring Richard. Yet, kind and affectionate as he always is, he called me his life-giver (*Lebensspenderin*). It is curious how our French friends will not let themselves be put off. Villiers sent his piece, and with true French insolence made fun of the ' exellent Prussians.' Richard asked them not to visit us and explained that all our sympathies were on the side of the Prussians." Frau Cosima could not help writing to their old friend Lothar Bucher to express her unreserved sympathy with Prussia. Her diary now becomes a regular chronicle of events. She mentions the disturbances in Lucerne, where great anxiety was felt. The conduct of the French was more and more revealed as an infuriating tissue of lies, ignorance, insolence, and vanity. " Grammont and Ollivier give as their reason for the declaration of war Bismarck's circular note to all the foreign courts. But no such note exists, only a telegram, as it appeared in the papers. And so it is in everything, nothing but lies and treachery. As I say to Richard, ' The war is a Beethoven festival. War was declared on July 17 and Beethoven was born on December 17, 1770. God grant that the magic seven may be of good omen here.' Richard says that he is beginning to hope. War is sublime, it reveals the insignificance of the individual. It is a regular dance, which will be executed with a most appalling finale — like those of Beethoven, in which he unchains every supernatural force, as in some grandiose ballet." She was put out because Nietzsche wrote that he was going to Allenstein. He seemed to want to escape from both the French and the Germans. On the other hand, she rejoiced to hear from Munich that the Bavarians were joining Prussia, while her heart felt a pang at the news that " the Austrians, in their usual shameful way, are coming to an agreement (*paktieren*) with France. . . . But Richard is in good spirits. Conditions in Germany were getting too bad, he says. This war may again show what there is in the Germans." She was correspondingly delighted with the reports of the German Army brought by Baron B., who informed them at the same time that Colonel R. had already been staying in Paris for the last four weeks by Bismarck's command.

They were now upset by the arrival of Villiers and Mendès, who had escaped from the war and from France and taken refuge in Switzerland. The painful impressions that prevailed in spite of their personal amiability were surmounted by making music. She told them outright her views on the war, which were tactfully received, especially by Mendès. The Master played them the Norn scene and then *Siegfried* and last of all the scene with the Wala and with Frigga. It was in this connexion that he gave her the following beautiful explanation: " Do you know what I was thinking about in connexion with Brünhilde's great *arpeggio*? Of the movements of your fingers when you are dreaming, when your hand moves through the air. And that is why I am still dissatisfied with it." And on another occasion he said to her: " Since you have been at my side, I have an unbounded confidence, an unashamed faith in myself. Even this frightful war will, I believe, turn out a blessing to me." It bears witness to his strong artistic conscience and the reaction of these great events upon him as an artist that amid these impressions and their daily increasing sense of good fortune he continued to work at his *Beethoven*. This state of mind reminds us of Milton, who, while the storm raged through the streets of London, and stones were flying through the window, went on dictating his *Paradise Lost* to his daughters. Wagner felt the war to be something holy and great. As he wandered about the garden with Cosima, he said: " One suddenly feels where one belongs, and that sense of community which cannot be felt in times of peace, since it is only what is bad that comes to the surface; one feels something that cannot be put into words, but is stirring in everything, and this stir accompanies all one's desires and hopes." With such feelings did they greet every piece of news: " When the University of Kiel wants to march as one man, when the commercial class is making the greatest sacrifices, when

Bismarck tells the Chamber that he did not communicate the report of Grammont's interview with Werther to the King, because he had found the demand for a letter of apology absurd; when the students of Vienna want to join Germany, when the Chambers behave disgracefully in Munich, and when they go on lying and boasting in Paris in fine style." On receiving the news that her step-sister's son had had to join the Navy, she regarded it as no more than necessary. But the French fleet caused her great alarm, as did the advantage over the Germans possessed by the French owing to their position and their network of railways; upon which Richard scolded her for having so little idealism. False reports arrived, too, which were calculated to alarm her: a report that the Turcos had already burnt down two villages near Offenburg in Baden, or that six thousand Austrians were fighting on the side of the French. Fresh from these impressions, the Master demanded point-blank of his French guests that they should realize " how we hate these characteristic qualities of the French." Then arrived the first news that the troops had joined battle, and she writes: " The children and I are praying for the Germans." Wagner was meditating upon the German character, in connexion with his work on Beethoven, while she was apprehensive at each fresh piece of news. It was, of course, obvious that in a neutral country a large part was played by false reports from the French side, calculated to spread alarm. Bismarck's methods were very different. Through the agency of *The Times* he revealed the proposals which, he said, Benedetti was constantly making to him for an invasion of Austria by the French, in order that they might then conquer Belgium, when the southern states would be drawn in so as to gain French Switzerland — and more of the same kind. It is highly characteristic to read how the Master expressed his sentiments to his French friends, though this did not in the least deter Villiers from reading them his work, the meretricious execution and theatrical style of which simply exasperated them both. " Richard says how detestable this rhetorical poetry is, and as a matter of fact both the Mendès, with their fine perceptions and high culture, share these feelings."

And now their old friend Malwida von Meysenbug once

more appeared on the Sonnenberg. She had come, in some sort, for the wedding, which was to take place immediately. All the arrangements for the marriage had been discussed with Pastor Tschudi too. It is touching to read how Cosima asked Richard whether he was quite content, and he replied that he knew no being in the world with whom he would have united himself save Frau Cosima; but for her he would have entered a monastery. She was deeply moved, and torn between joy and sorrow. With such emotions as these she ordered the wedding-rings of the sort traditional in Lucerne. Both of them were deeply agitated, and this is reflected in their strange and almost Shaksperian dreams. In the morning they both laughed over these, but they felt how the ideas which occupied them during the day met again at night in the visions of their mutual dreams. But the day was given up to outward impressions, and these were more concerned with Bismarck than with what was happening at the front. She remarks: " We are more and more delighted with Bismarck, whose revelations show more and more plainly how shrewdly and honestly he has acted. He says that he had to keep the French in play, if only to have peace for a few years. The narrow-minded diplomatists had been the French, who had thought it possible to make such proposals to a German minister. It is the first time that we have heard such language; and how noble and proud is the minister's attitude! At last, too, in spite of England's incessant insults and the way in which she has behaved, he has succeeded in forcing her to deliver no more coal or cartridges to France. How uplifting it must be for Bavaria, Saxony, and Württemberg to fight as the German Army! " On the other hand, she is indignant at the false reports from France, and the terrible effects of their machine-guns: " Machine-guns for our men, and their finery for our women — that is what the French have in store for us." The news of Weissenburg affected them deeply: " Richard and I look at each other in tears, and will say nothing. The situation is too great, too terrible. Blessings upon Germany and the German Army. We hardly dare to think of the importance of our cause." On the other hand, the news of how the Empress Eugénie had been to the Church of Notre Dame des Victoires — " *Notre Dame des Mitrailleuses* (machine-guns) Richard calls it " — to pray before the image of the Madonna seemed to her trivial. She was infuriated to hear that the people of Weissenburg had taken up arms against their brothers the Germans: " Oh, shame! I could spend the whole day in prayer. As each piece of news comes in, the heart composes itself for worship — how glorious is the fraternization between north and south Germany." Nor was there any lack of idyllic little scenes in Switzerland. The *gendarme* discussed the situation with the jovial Master and said: " Yes, the King of Prussia is a good gentleman. He is the only one who will come to the help of the Pope. The Pope has said that he would yet have to ask help of the Prussians." But Richard said: " One thing I know: who tells lies and who tells the truth. The French do the former, and the Germans the latter." And now came persistent rumours about Bismarck and the way in which Beust and his creatures were working against him; on which the Master declared: " He is a true German; that is why the French hate him so much." Next they heard with the utmost emotion the news of the victory of Wörth and the flight of the French. A rising in Paris was already being mentioned, and it was even said that Bazaine had been routed. But she set to work like all German women: she and the children scraped lint, and prepared bandages and linen. The news brought to Count Bassenheim by the Viennese banker Tedesko was curious and significant. He had already, he said, lost thirty millions on account of France. This suggested a suspicion that Beust had been accepting money in secret, and that Austria would now join France; for Tedesko was an intimate friend of Beust's and said: " As for this Bray, look at what he is up to now. We all thought that his sympathies were on the right side — that is, the French." These reports were not altogether inventions. Up to the battle of Wörth the Austrian Government had really had thoughts of intervention. Count Bray's sympathies were not French, but we know that he had asked Beust for instructions, and that these had only been rendered illusory by the truly soldierly attitude of von Prankh, the Minister for War, and by King Ludwig's loyalty to his engagements.

While she passed her days scraping lint, in which the

children also took part — for they preferred working for the soldiers to playing — she shrank in alarm at every report which was favourable to the French. But Richard was sure that the Germans would win. Her own comment, indeed, is: " I have the belief, but the dread as well." But he explained: " Just as the Indians believe that every unfulfilled desire gives rise to the life of another soul, so the longing of all good men that the German nature may now at last begin to bloom forms a basis for our victory over this much-dreaded France and her apparently incredible organization." But even at this time insults to the Master were not lacking, and one such letter from Brussels was signed: " *Les manes de Meyerbeer et Mendelssohn* (The shades of Meyerbeer and Mendelssohn)." But he was in high spirits and said on one occasion, throwing his arms round Cosima: " Yes, a charming wife was what Beethoven never had. It was reserved for a poor old man like me — that is why I have this irrational belief in myself." And one fine morning in the garden he picked her a pansy and offered it to her with the words: " I was thinking about our love! I do not know what to call it, but I know that it is the most ardent of things, and will never allow us to leave each other."

And now Malwida von Meysenbug came on a visit to them with her pupil Olga Hertzen. She was able to give them a minute account of Hans's position in Florence. It was all highly gratifying. He was said to have remarked that " if I become more agreeable, I have Florence to thank for it." Then came August 15, Napoleon I's birthday, of which she had once witnessed the celebrations in Paris. And now came the news that Bazaine had been defeated, and that King William in person had led the cavalry. " A terrible day of judgment! What will become of the French? What indeed? And Napoleon? Rome, Boulogne, Strassburg, Mexico, must they not all appear to him now as the real seed (*Kern*) of his destiny, and the Empress, on the other hand, as the worthless and even ridiculous husk? " But in the evening, so as to lead the conversation away from the war, which was repellent to her in every way, Malwida introduced the subject of Minna and the days in Paris. " With tears in his eyes Richard spoke of these connexions and said how to him Paris was an abyss of utter vulgarity." And so what had mainly constituted his earlier life, and everything connected with it besides, had ended in utter derision. " I must be patient and indulgent with him, he said, for I could have no conception of the atmosphere in which he had lived. ' The first person who gave me an impression of nobility,' he added, ' was your father.' What must such words not mean to me, who never cease to admire and revere him! " Thus Paris appeared doubly terrible both to him and to her, all the more so since the neutral papers in Switzerland were constantly full of pro-French news. On the other hand, a *Times* correspondent who had witnessed the battle of Wörth from the tower was bound to say that the Germans, when repulsed, retreated in admirable order, as though at the word of command, whereas the French fled headlong, each one pressing upon his own fellow-countryman in front of him, in order to escape more quickly. Upon which Richard remarked: " Every army has some distinctive feature. The Macedonians had their phalanx, Napoleon's warriors their dashing attack, but this calm steadiness is the distinguishing mark of our Army. But what did the French Army of today possess? " The news that the whole French nation was to take up arms alarmed her. She considered that the Germans were giving the French too much time. But the truth always prevailed, and so they heard of the successes at Gravelotte, and there was already talk of an advance on Paris. Richard said that the French capital, the " *femme entretenue* (kept woman)" of the whole world, would be destroyed. As a young man he could not understand how Blücher could have desired it, and had disapproved of him. Now he understood him. The burning of Paris would be the symbol that at last the world was to be set free from the oppression of all evil. In 1815 the Allies had refrained from doing anything to the city, because what they all meant to do was to go there again to amuse themselves. Richard wanted to write to Bismarck and beg him to bombard Paris.

While they were in this warlike frame of mind and filled with a full realization of their national sympathies, their marriage was celebrated, on August 25. She was full of mingled joy and sorrow. On August 19 she writes in her diary: " Thirteen years ago today was my wedding, in just such rainy weather. I did not know what I was promising then; for I did not keep my promise; but I know what it was that swayed my feelings. Never will I forget my sin, and I will look it constantly in the face, in order to learn humility and resignation." No wonder that, with all these feelings, she said: " Paris has become indifferent to us all. The French may do or not do what they like, provided only they are humbled." And they were well on the way towards this. When news arrived of the decisive victory of Metz, by which the French were cut off from Paris, she wrote: " May God vouchsafe to our glorious German tenacity that the prize may be adequate to these terrible but glorious battles." On one and the same day the Master wrote his wonderful poem to the King, and the title-page to the first act of *The Twilight of the Gods*, which he sent him for a birthday present. News poured in from all sides, including the manifestoes of D. F. Strauss and Freiligrath, and, above all, the information that Mazzini had been arrested, about which she writes: " And so the three figures whom my father honoured are in an enviable position! Mazzini in prison, the Pope in a thousand troubles, and Louis Napoleon in the gutter, just as Doctor Wille foretold long, long years ago, to the indignation of my father, to whom, in view of our approaching marriage, Richard referred with emotion as ' My good spirit.' " The banns were now published on the 21st. " All preparations had been made: Richard's splendid letter to my mother, mine to Frau Wesendonck. I asked him whether he was content with this letter, and he said that it was excessive, that he had cast a veil of poetry over his relation with her, so as not to make its commonplace character too plainly apparent. But all the poetry had died for him, and he had rather not be reminded of it. He said that I should receive an unpleasant answer. But I do not believe so, for I do not think that I have behaved with anything but delicacy." The witnesses to the marriage were already making their appearance, and the Master said " that he would have to laugh aloud like a child on reading my signature, Cosima Wagner. It was like a dream to him. I pray God for grace that in my joy I may not forget him who is mourning and suffering."

Thus everything at Triebschen was already overshadowed by the approaching wedding, which of course produced a remarkable and uncommon effect on the outer world too, for the life at Triebschen in itself aroused curiosity among the widest circles. Frau Cosima asked with justifiable surprise what people imagined Triebschen to be like. The Master confirmed her wonderment: " Why, about five minutes ago I received an anonymous letter from a lady, saying that she had laid a wager that I should not marry you, and that I was to put an advertisement in the *Neueste Nachrichten* to say yes or no, for my friends were anxious about it. She says that you are a schemer, and that the King is very angry at the rumour." Frau Cosima wrote very sadly about this: " People's malice always horrifies me. I have done the woman no harm; what does she gain by insulting me? How can anyone go so far as to throw mud like this at somebody she does not know? It cannot be envy, for nobody in the world can envy me, since I have retired from the world." But she was really too much occupied with her own concerns, and all that these people could do was to cast a slight shadow over the ceremony which solemnized their love. She had also the task of announcing to the two children the step which she was about to take. " They laugh with me and weep with me." But when she left her eldest daughter, the child threw herself down on the grass and wept bitterly. And so August 25 came round, which the Master had hailed in his wonderful poem to the King, opening with the words " *Gesprochen ist das Königswort, dem Deutschland neu erstanden* (The royal word is spoken by which Germany has risen anew)," and closing with the promise: " *Es strahlt der Menschheit Morgen, nun dämmre auf, du Göttertag* (The radiant day of humanity is dawning; now break, thou daylight of the gods)."

They were married in the little Protestant church at Lucerne by Pastor Tschudi, Hans Richter and Malwida von Meysenbug having been invited to act as witnesses. Nobody else was present but the children and, naturally, the inquisitive crowd who could not be kept out. And so destiny was fulfilled, and, in spite of all the crushing accumulation of obstacles, the pair were united. Wagner himself was deeply affected. But Frau Cosima wrote

415

in her diary: " Our marriage took place at eight o'clock. May I prove worthy to bear Richard's name. My prayers have been concentrated upon two points: Richard's well-being and my hope that I may always be able to promote it, and Hans's happiness and my hope that it may be his lot to live a cheerful life afar from me." The Master himself expressed the whole depths of his emotion in a letter to Frau Eliza Wille, in which he sang the praises of the woman who, casting aside all scruples and hesitations, had devoted herself to him. " She has braved every insult and borne every condemnation." Frau Eliza gave her a ready and feeling welcome. But for the present they remained in complete retirement. Congratulations came in from all sides, including the King and Councillor Düfflipp, and their faithful friends took the deepest interest in the occasion. But she lived in complete retirement, absorbed in her feelings for him. When he played her *Lohengrin,* a few days afterwards, her sentiments were not only for the man she loved, but also for the artist who, though she had grown up entirely under French influences, had Germanized her, in the fullest sense of the word. It was, indeed, the Master's work, and especially his *Lohengrin,* that had decided her destiny. She wanted to belong to the land which alone could produce such things. But he saw in her only his helpmeet. One morning shortly afterwards he exclaimed: " You must be called Cosima Helferich Wagner, for you have indeed been a helper."

They next paid a visit to Zürich and Mariafeld, where she was greeted by Frau Eliza with the words: " I have followed you with real sympathy, you have assumed and borne an enormous task, and you are so young with it all." And she was able to repeat to her the following words of her father: " My daughter has now got the husband who is worthy of her." That, too, was a comfort to her, and she said of this day, which was otherwise devoted entirely to politics: " It makes me happy to see that an old and tried friend is glad to confide Richard's fate to my hands." On this occasion the Master still continued to avoid any personal contact with Mathilde Wesendonck, though on her wedding-day Frau Mathilde had significantly sent Frau Cosima a wonderful bouquet of edelweiss; but this flower, which blooms on the edge of the abyss, had already a real and profound symbolism in Frau Cosima's eyes.

Yet this great and fateful day did not throw all warlike impressions into the background. Frau Cosima was deeply stirred by the news, which now arrived from the front, of how hymns had been sung after the battle of Wörth, as after Leuthen. She was all the more sensitive to the French lies about alleged German atrocities: that they ill-treated the wounded, and compelled all the young people to fight in the first place against their fellow-countrymen. She observed the destiny of Napoleon, which now began to be fulfilled. He was said, she writes, to have desired to return to Paris and die before the walls of the city. But he had met with the answer that he would be of no use there, and that if he was really anxious to die, he could meet his end just as well at Reims. But really the French papers had nothing to report but lies, about alleged dissensions between the German generals, French victories, and serious conflicts between the troops of Prussia, Württemberg, and Baden. All Germans, on the other hand, were represented as robbers, and all the while, secure of victory, the French ministers were smiling and saying that the outcome could not be in doubt.

While their friend Malwida was at Triebschen, Richard Wagner read her his essay *Was ist deutsch?* He was astonished to find that Frau Cosima knew it by heart, and was delighted at this, as he was at everything that now came his way. He felt his happiness to be complete and could not express it tenderly or candidly enough. " I believe," he said once, " that it is your calm, soft sleep, my dear, good angel, that has brought me such tranquillity." And he added: " You are my whole existence." And she says: " It is like a dream to me that I may really make him contented, and even happy."

And now came the news of the battle of Sedan. The victory over MacMahon at Beaumont had already caused her to rejoice, but now Colonel van Rhyn brought the announcement of the capitulation of the whole Army, and the surrender of Napoleon to the King. The Master said exultantly: " This is a christening-present for Fidi. Nine battles in the last month, all of them victorious, and now this as a conclusion! God in heaven, what a

September 1870

destiny! I am fatal to the Napoleons. When I was six months old, there was the battle of Leipzig, and now Fidi has made mincemeat of the whole of France." Little Siegfried's baptism followed on September 4, while they were still fresh from the impression of this victory. The Wille family had come over for the occasion. At the beginning of the service a violent storm broke, and as Pastor Tschudi pronounced the opening words, there was a terrible clap of thunder, which they hailed as a lucky omen. But during these very days Frau Cosima lost her wedding-ring. Hardly anything could have given her such pain or affected her delicate sensibilities so much as this loss. She looked for the ring herself in vain, but a few days later she heard that a woman had found it, in a place where Frau Cosima had never been during the whole time. And now she confessed to him that, according to her old habit, she had prayed to St. Anthony of Padua, and lo! he had helped her again. The Master smiled, and said that it was love that was the true and genuine miracle, and worked miracles. But she saw in the incident a salutation of fate and a sign that by it, too, her feeling for Richard had in a certain measure been blessed. And she remarked: " My union with Richard is like a palingenesis, a rebirth, which brings me nearer to perfection — the redemption of my former erring existence. But I feel — and tell him so — that our perfect union will not take place till death, with the dissolution of all the limitations of the individuality. When I try to tell him how I love him, I feel the full impotence of being and know that not till I am in the arms of death shall I be able to tell it to him. And that is why I always weep when I want to approach him and tell him how my soul adores him." He had but one care and slight annoyance; he begged her not to devote herself too much to the education of the children: " No mother brings up her children all alone." " To which I rejoined: ' I think my children will be grateful to me for having been so much to them.' He retorted: ' But you were never brought up by your mother.' ' I should have turned out better if I had had a mother about me.' He would not hear of this and became disagreeable. We parted with tears and smiles." And then she called after him: " ' Do you love me? ' and he replied: ' I have nothing else to do, no work (*besogne*) save to love you and you alone in the world.' "

And so these days of newly-married happiness passed by in jest against the grave background of the great war, while, as of old, the Master filled these quiet moments with the deepest intellectual animation through his music and the stimulating effect of his literary gifts. He completed his finest work, that on Beethoven. He read her this work, and she was stirred to the depths of her being and entirely carried away by the profundity and lucidity of its ideas, though Wagner said he regretted that he had not compared Beethoven and Schopenhauer. " There would have been a general outcry then! And yet he came near to the rational principle of Beethoven's world. Lately again I have been quite overwhelmed by the genius of Schopenhauer, as I read what he says about the differences between human beings and characterizes them as one of Nature's insolences that she should not have created another type of man, the result of which is that there is a greater discrepancy between talented men and men without talent than between mankind and the beasts. One has only to look at the public in a theatre and see how one part of it is full of emotion and concentrated interest, while the other is inattentive, restless, and foolish. No understanding between the two is possible — hence the torture of the man of talent in this world, where he has to regard as belonging to his own kind beings who have no more resemblance to him than an ape." It was this book and his complete absorption in Beethoven that turned him, and perhaps Frau Cosima even more, away from the French and gave her a terrible impression of that world with which she had once been so intimate.

On the other hand, she too came to understand Schopenhauer better; and to some extent she viewed her relations with the Master, in particular, in the light of his idea of resignation. It was for this reason that she was unwilling to accompany him on his visit to the Berlin Academy, of which he had become a member. But he wanted her to take part in the excursion, and make a detour to Bayreuth, and even failed to understand her motives when she said that she had better stay at home. " He thinks that it is social considerations, my previous connexion with Hans's family, that deter me, whereas it is my inner voice alone that says to me: ' You have no more to do with the world; at the time when you were the cause of grievous sorrow, you made up your mind to live in future for nothing but the children and the Only one in the retirement of home.' I do not want to explain that to Richard, lest I may grieve him, and God will help me to do what is right." And she comforted herself with Schopenhauer: " How his teaching grips me! When I went to bed, I asked myself whether I should not have acted better in life if such ideas had been impressed upon my mind in youth. But soon I had to say to myself: ' You had the teaching of Jesus, which was enough if you had not been just weak and sinful — so *mea culpa*, then, from the depths of my soul, and may I accept every sorrow as an expiation of my existence."

Such thoughts as these were the accompaniment of her life, just as shadow formed the complement of all the sunshine which poured down upon Triebschen. They had many visitors, and among them came Frau Stocker-Escher, in whose houses Richard Wagner had lived in Zürich, and in whose garden his dog Peps was buried. She greeted the young wife most cordially, while Wagner said: " It seems to me so commonplace to call you simply ' my wife,' and I think how people must feel who saw me in earlier days, too, with *my* wife." " But to me it seems the height of pride to hear myself called his wife, and I can only face my feeling of unworthiness by recalling in the morning with fervent gratitude all that has happened to me, while at night, as I meditate on my unworthiness, I plunge myself in penitence." Such words, indeed, read like the diary of a nun who is devoting her whole life to penitence in her convent cell. Yet she enjoyed her retirement, the quiet of Triebschen and her children, to the utmost. And once, when they were taking a walk to the Fontaine de Soif, the Master remarked that without the children they would be far too serious; but the children beckoned, uplifted, and drew them into the world of their own merry existence. It was on their account that he chose fantastic tales and ghost-stories to read and so turned to Hoffmann's *Tales*. He asked her whether weird stories did not frighten her. " I smilingly answered no; but then I began to think about ghostly apparitions and about Daniel, and the latter with deep feelings of self-reproach: for he was sacrificed, owing to the fact that my father sent him to Vienna on the advice of the Princess Wittgenstein, so that I blame myself now for not having saved him by going with him to Cairo. I am also afraid that I may not have consulted the right doctor when he lay sick at my house. All this was in my mind, and now, as chance would have it, on the first appearance of the ghost in the story *Das Majorat*, the name of Daniel is uttered twice, and Richard pronounced it in the meaning and penetrating tones that are all his own. I trembled, not with fear, but with unutterable woe. The tale itself fascinated me by its pregnant style and fine colour." And she had to beg Richard to sleep in her room, for otherwise she might be unable to sleep for sorrowful thoughts. For her dream-world, too, was very much alive and not only reflected the events of the present, but also enabled her, to some extent, to look into the future.

And now very practical matters came under discussion. Thus Frau Marie Mouchanoff once more appeared to talk over the Bayreuth scheme with him. He was not much pleased at this, and the very news of her impending arrival dashed his spirits; for he did not like to see an outsider concerned in his enterprise, and one, too, who was to play an important part in it. Frau Cosima encouraged him and kept referring to the grand qualities of their friend's nature and the lack of aim in her enthusiasm, for she thought it was only this strange woman's French manner, which was so unpleasing when she was discussing things with him, that jarred upon the Master. But his present happiness kept this idea in the background for the moment. His happiness made him to some extent a sceptic, so that she said of him: " Such rapture would be impossible without a great need. Besides, true love is as rare in this life as genius. The best thing is to recognize that life is a task, an irksome punishment (*Pensum*). All that enchants us in it comes from elsewhere." For this reason she wrote to arrange a meeting with the Countess in Bayreuth, though, as she said, " God knows what will happen there, we are setting about it without much faith."

It is characteristic, but comprehensible, that amid all the news from the front, and all the vicissitudes which were to be seen, not so much in the events of the war as in the *communiqués* about them, the Master was absolutely horrified at the composition of the *Wacht am Rhein* and remarked: " If a clever Frenchman were to see it, what an ironical view he would have of our German Fatherland, marching into battle to such a melody as that! " Richard was obsessed by the idea to the point of tears: " We have sunk too low! " he said. " It is only our troops that redeem us, and they are great — and Beethoven," he added with a smile, " he will certainly not sing the *Wacht am Rhein*." He had himself thought of writing a funeral composition, not a symphony of victory, for an expression of grief for the dead seemed to him the only thing worthy of such prodigious and mighty feats. But he remarked in the same connexion: " We will put the German Fatherland to another test with Bayreuth." Thus we see how deeply and closely this idea of Bayreuth was bound up in the minds of this noble pair with the war and the resultant regeneration of the German people. And so their mood changed daily, and even hourly. News came from Paris of her mother, who was naturally in absolute opposition to her children's views. She wanted to come to her daughter in Switzerland, in the hope of recovering there; but Frau Cosima felt that the solitude of Triebschen and the views which they held could not be very gratifying to her mother. For she and Wagner were withdrawing more and more into themselves, and living for each other and for the children. When she went for a drive with the children, he gazed after them as though in a trance. And when they stood together before the toy theatre, watching the Faust puppet-show, he recalled his own childish impressions, dating from the times of Karl Maria von Weber, and the dæmonic fascination which the performances of Weber's works had exercised over him as a child. He even remarked that nothing could replace such artistic impressions for those who had not enjoyed them. The *Freischütz* and the *Egmont* overtures, too, had a permanent influence upon his life. Their terseness always produced a great effect upon him. " In Schumann," he said, " *forte* is constantly recurring, and then *forte* again, and then a few traits which might belong to the greatest of masters, yet which efface the whole effect."

It is touching to see what pains Frau Cosima now took to learn to knit, so that she could make leggings for Fidi. She worked at things of this sort while the Master read her the *Persæ*, through which the whole misery of France was, so to speak, reflected back upon her. " Yet the distress of France could not form the subject of a tragedy such as Sophocles wrote about Xerxes and his defeat." But the picture which Lenbach painted of Frau Cosima gave them great pleasure: " Vreneli, to be sure, was horrified at the black frame, and so was Richard too, who expected to see me dead, or my father in the monastic habit. In short, the black frame had a strong effect upon his imagination, and it was only gradually that the picture came into its own, till at last he became unspeakably fond of it. But our mood continued to be deeply serious all day "; and her comment was: " There are no more joys left for us save noble, solemn ones such as these." For the picture really produced a great effect upon him. Moved by gazing upon it, he resumed the instrumentation of *Siegfried*. It is wonderful that during these stirring times he was always able to go on living for his work, while all the time paying full tribute, both intellectually and spiritually, to what was happening. We stand amazed at his clear and sure judgment of the changing situation, and at his penetrating characterization of the persons concerned and their actions, which no historian could surpass. When he read Jules Favre's account of his meeting with Bismarck, he at once recognized the sentimentality which dominated him, as it did the whole of France. He quite genuinely considered that the French could never have any other feelings again — at once devoid of sympathy for the sufferings of others and quite unworthy to bear their own.

But all that they tried to do outside their home seemed to go wrong. An excursion which they made to Brunnen went off very badly, and both drew the conclusion that they ought not to venture upon anything outside. As they returned home in the dark, in a mood of rather humorous resignation, she offered him her hand in silence, and he said: " Thou only hand — well do I know what I am grasping when I take this hand." She was deeply affected by this, as well as by a little incident which took place on the next day, when the faithful Kos fell into the water and was just about to drown, but was saved at the last moment. Richard greeted him with sobs, upon which she remarks: " I was as though turned to stone by my anxiety for him. It is always my voice which calls to him: ' Stay in the harbour where you have taken refuge.' " And he said: " Such a free nature, which sees all, knows all, and has a deep pity for all, yet remains so cheerful that it is always a help to all, cannot be conceived as anything but German." But she recalled memories of long-past years: " Seventeen years ago today I saw Richard for the first time," she writes on the 9th, adding at once: " I was wrong about the date. The anniversary is tomorrow." And now, before the door of the house, between the poplars, there appeared a wonderful rainbow. " Rhinegold! " she cried; but he replied " Bayreuth! " and at that moment Prell, the Lucerne bookseller, entered the door, to deliver the notices which he had promised about Bayreuth. " The good fellow says that houses will be easy to rent there and spoke highly of the situation of the town. Richard said that this was a good omen. But Prell also brought portraits of Bismarck and the leaders and heroes of the war. Richard admired the portrait of Moltke and said that he would like to make the acquaintance of Bismarck and Moltke, without their knowing who he was. He would like to be near them as a perfectly obscure subordinate. He thought he found something of Frederick the Great in them, the same high courage, caution, and concentration of ideas."

But every day brought a fresh *communiqué*. None were conclusive, all were exciting. The Bavarians occupied Orléans. Then came the flag controversy between Bavaria and Prussia, which appeared more important than it really was in the accounts of the foreign papers, but at the same time pettier. During these days he played her the scene of Siegfried with the dragon, and sang Fafner's last words, which affected her unutterably. " I said that my emotion was the same as though I were looking at a dying animal, which is perhaps more touching, or in a way, at least, moves us more, than a dying man." He agreed and said that with an animal resignation is more instantaneous, because death comes upon it unexpectedly, whereas with a man the whole of his vital force is struggling against it."

But his mind ran upon Bismarck in other connexions too. After the war he wanted to send him his pamphlet *Deutsche Kunst und deutsche Politik.* " I judge him aright, for such a powerful mind must see the importance of the theatre at once." In their leisure hours they read Byron's *Don Juan.* This mock-heroic poem attracted and repelled her equally. The scene in the harem seemed to her like part of a comic opera. But he remarked: " This Lord is always in such a hurry; the ardour which inspires his works is an arid one, for though he has warmth, he lacks dramatic power. He describes, but cannot represent scenes dramatically (*darstellen*)." They returned to the book every day, only to drop it while they talked about the war, when the Master sang the praise of Prussian organization in connexion with the proceedings at Metz and in connexion with what Gregorovius had written: " Where would Europe be without the power of Prussia, this despised hole-and-corner place of which nobody expected anything, but where preparations for this have really been going on ever since the fall of the Hohenstaufen. Because the country is sandy and unproductive, the people were forced to have recourse to the most rigid organization, and it is this which has achieved this miracle of providing supplies for six hundred thousand men. What would Germany be without Prussia? And for this reason we can understand why they will not give up their Prussianism. For they may well say: ' We do not know what Germany is.' Old Fritz [Frederick the Great] showed foresight."

In such moods as this he even had dreams of a friendly interview with Moltke; but they both agreed that there was nothing to say to such a man, and that " the likes of us would be very much embarrassed if we tried to express our sentiments to him. Nothing save the acclamation of a whole people can do that." Or, she added: " A king." " Yes, and that is why the instinct of the people has prompted it to adopt a chosen representative, who must surrender much of his liberty in order to represent the people as a whole in given circumstances." At that time these were great and clear-sighted ideas, which only slowly, with the

425

progress of time, became common property. But both of them were entirely of Bismarck's way of thinking with regard to the bombardment of Paris: " We do not rejoice that Paris is not yet being bombarded. For the longer this goes on, the more our poor troops suffer."

Then came October 19, and Frau Cosima writes sadly: " I recall my betrothal fifteen years ago under the auspices of the *Tannhäuser* Overture in Berlin. How I wish I could make amends for what Hans has suffered through me! Perhaps the children will be able to do this — I hope so." But Wagner playfully helped her over such days of sombre memories. " You are my all," he would say in his pleasing Saxon dialect, " I am your — all sorts of things (*Ich bin Dein allerlei*)." And he sang her the scene between the Wanderer and Mime, which affected her deeply.

Then he came to her bedside in the evening and said: " I simply cannot say how I love you, it is still like a dream to me that I am wholly yours." " He thinks that I am only lent to him. This makes me want to pray. What evil can I say of life when, without merit of any kind whatsoever, without any claim, without anything to account for it, I have found such happiness, while I see other splendid people bearing such sufferings. I do not lack sufferings, it is true, but they are concerned with Richard and Hans, not with myself." In such a mood as this she celebrated her father's birthday on October 22. She was anxious about his health and happiness, but Richard said laughingly: " I have not acted like Wotan and Sachs. I have married Brünhilde and Eva too. I have confidential talks with them both, but I take care not to follow their advice." And he added: " In this bed lies a melody, a great and beautiful melody."

Owing to the events of the war, their relations with Nietzsche had suffered a serious set-back. He had no such deep German sentiment as they possessed; for this genuinely national spirit was altogether foreign to his nature. Moreover, he had fallen ill as a result of his service in hospital and had only just recovered. He then returned to Basel, where he let himself be swayed by the daily reports. His letters to Triebschen speak of his fears for the time which was coming. The heavy hand of militarism and pietism, he said, would be upon everything. The Master was naturally much exasperated by these ideas: " I admit it all — *gendarmes,* soldiers, the muzzling of the press, the limitation of parliamentarism — but not obscurantism. The one thing of which a man can be proud is his intellectual liberty, the one thing which raises him above the beasts."

On October 26 they next ventured on a visit to Mariafeld. They were met in Zürich by Arnold Wille and had to see the wearisome Polish festival at Rapperswyl and look at Polish antiquities, which had not the slightest interest for them. But at Mariafeld they were welcomed by Frau Eliza's warm heart and her great and profound intelligence. Professor Hellwig, a friend of Liszt's, was also present. In the evening Wagner read them extracts from his autobiography, arousing deep sympathy in this woman who was such an intimate friend, and the interest of her able husband. But on the next day Frau Cosima had a mission of her own. She went alone to see Frau Mathilde Wesendonck. " In spite of my persuasion, Richard would not accompany me. He was greatly displeased by Frau Wesendonck's poems *Aufruf an das deutsche Volk* (*Appeal to the German People*). Besides, he maintains that at the last she behaved very badly to him. And so, for the first time for eleven years, I entered the rooms in which I had played, as it were, the part of a mediator and confidential friend. I found the amiable lady transformed into a brunette, whereas she was still fair when I saw her in Munich four years ago, which was bewildering. I was delighted at her friendly reception, looked at the pictures, and on my way home mused on the curiously dreamlike character of life. If anyone had told me ten years ago, when I was trying to bring her to a gentler state of mind towards Richard, that I should myself become involved in a great crisis of destiny with Richard, I could quite have believed it, but it would have alarmed me terribly." From the Wesendoncks' house she next went to the Hotel Baur, where the Master's old friends had gathered together: Sulzer, Hangebuch, and Colonel Müller. Sulzer in particular pleased and touched her greatly. His acute, decided, yet never abrupt remarks, added to his blindness and his reserved yet high-minded nature, fascinated her beyond

427

expression. He had lost his wife and was now left alone with five children, who had suffered greatly from the part which he had played in public life. She asked him to bring his children to see her own. It was a touching yet merry evening, and they returned to Zürich in cheerful spirits. She could not, indeed, get rid of the uncanny effect produced upon her by the change in the colour of Frau Mathilde's hair. This journey had produced a peculiarly tender and emotional mood in the Master: "After dinner Richard lavished his heavenly love upon me. He maintained that I grow more beautiful every day. He is ready to die of happiness. Little that is divine exists, he said — only Cosima. And then, when I behold myself, I feel that I am like the most insignificant of buildings, which becomes a splendid spectacle in the rays of the setting sun. When he left me, he played a wonderful theme, which I begged him to write down." We shall see into what work he afterwards developed it.

But now arrived the news that Bazaine had surrendered with a hundred and fifty thousand French. "It sounds like a fairytale," she writes, "though it has always been said that he was trying to cut off the Prussians." But Richard said in his gay fashion: "It is a fine thing that we have got Bazaine, but still finer that I have got you." And in the evening he played and sang the second act of *Tannhäuser*, which filled her with inexpressible emotion. "Biterolf, Wolfram, and the Landgrave all move me to tears, but Elisabeth's words: '*dass auch für ihn einst Der Erlöser litt* (that for him too the Redeemer suffered once) '[1] stir me to the depths of my soul." Richard explained to her that Christianity was summed up in these words; but, noticing her profound agitation, he was almost shocked and could not approve her emotion. "You are Elisabeth, Isolde, Eva, and Brünhilde all in one," he said jestingly, "and I have married you." "But as for me," she adds, "I feel as if I could die of such an upheaval of emotion." She could not but share Gretchen's feelings, and it was with a like feeling that he quoted Gretchen's words: "*Und küssen mich, so wie ich wollt', an Deinen Küssen vergehen sollt'* (And kiss me as though I would die of thy kisses)." But then, considering the situation and the prodigious

[1] *Tannhäuser*, IV.—Tr.

successes and events of the war, he said: "Nothing but silence befits us duly in view of the fearful grandeur of what is happening — no boasts of victory, no laments over our sufferings, but a silent, deep realization that God orders the world." Both of them, indeed, were indignant at the insulting words spoken by Gambetta about Bazaine and his army, who had fought and suffered so terribly and only yielded to inexorable necessity. On All Souls' Day came the news that the bombardment of Paris had been decided upon: "Those who will not hear must feel," she writes in her diary. But at the same time she composed a prayer for the dead for the children to repeat in honour of the day. He too was in a serious mood and had in a sense suggested this idea to her by what he had said about the chorales sung by the soldiers: "If anyone were to ask me: 'Is there a God?' I should reply: 'Do you not hear Him?' At this moment, when these thousands of men are singing His praises, God lives, He exists. To represent Him to oneself as one who looks on and approves or disapproves is absurd; but for peoples and individuals alike there are moments at which He exists: it is then that He awakes."

Their thoughts also turned towards the King of Bavaria. And she writes: "But the King, the King! How can one explain such a nature, how can one comprehend it? None but a dramatic poet could render him, inexplicable as he is." In this mood she heard that Richter was conducting the B major Symphony, and her comment is: "Music always inclines me towards worship and the understanding of life, it is in itself a penitential exercise to me, but one which brings salvation." And she thought of Hans and her father. For she had heard from Marie Mouchanoff that, owing to his French sympathies, Liszt was not going to Weimar: "And thus the breach has become quite irrevocable." As a matter of fact, in these great sentiments too, to which Wagner had been able to surrender himself so utterly, the Princess had exerted a painful and disturbing influence. She had herself no home, and the religion which she was seeking and believed herself to have found was no true one, but only a phantom, which, reaching forth out of the past with its withered hands, had taken possession of her. How different were the pair at Triebschen!

In the evening they read *Othello*, of which she said: "Every syllable of it is a real experience"; while she was indescribably affected by the last act: "I told Richard that I should never really know the piece, for I am far too agitated to impress the precise details upon my mind." But she felt all the force of Richard's theory that Shakspere did not belong to the sphere of mere literature at all, and simply could not be compared with a poet or artist like Calderón. "Through Shakspere one can to some extent explain a phenomenon like Homer. For the relation of Homer to the priests may have been something like that of Shakspere to the cultivated literature of civilization. And I add: 'and like that of Richard to our literature and music of today.'" But during this period he also read another of the Greeks with her — Aristophanes — and tried to initiate her, to the best of his ability, into the strange subtleties of Greek comedy. In so doing he was in some sort leading up to a curious piece of work with which his mind was occupied at that time, which was no more nor less than an imitation of Greek comedy. On November 8 he called her and told her that he had something to read her. It was *Die Capitulation*, a farce for which Richter was to write the music, and which was then to be performed in the little theatres. She was well able to enter into the atmosphere of the piece and saw with pleasure that this work distracted the Master from the grave and gloomy thoughts that prevailed in him at the time in another connexion. But to her personally he remained a young and impassioned lover. "Ah," he said, "even now I cannot believe that you have been given to me; you are only lent — the maiden from the world of faery, who will shortly vanish away." And he added: "We are really in paradise." On waking up one morning, she found upon her bosom the loveliest roses with their buds, which he had laid there while she slept. Such were her consolations during these November days, and while she herself was timid and reserved, she felt that he was inspired by the most ardent feelings, and said that it was precisely the fact that nature had blessed their union which had given him such great confidence and calm. This was the point at which his new life began. Till then, he said, he had wandered in an abyss, haunted by phantoms.

And now came an infrequent guest, Alfred Meissner, her friend of Berlin days. He had been to see her before, it is true, while she was in Munich, and had profited by an interview with her to write an article which he had published in some newspaper or other. She said that she had recovered from this and was delighted to see him; but he was the cause of some most unfortunate experiences: " When Richard came in, the unfortunate man of letters began to talk about the performance of *The Rhinegold* in Munich, of the admirable libretto, of how wrong it was of Richard not to go and see such things, and of the splendid scenery. I was on thorns. Richard withdrew with a laugh, and I begged the good man for God's sake not to talk about such things. But he stayed and brought his young seventeen-year-old wife to dinner with us. Both of them behaved in a good-natured and amiable way, but when, once more, Meissner started talking about *The Rhinegold*, the Master enlightened him fully on the subject."

Nor had Wagner's recent experiences with Nietzsche been particularly fortunate, either. He had sent him his *Beethoven*, and Nietzsche had returned the manuscript with the remark that but few people would be able to follow it. This marked a deep cleavage between him and Wagner, who had really been the first to initiate him into Schopenhauer and was in the fullest sense of the word his master. But now his ways led him on beyond Wagner to the antique world, and in losing Wagner he lost himself too. But Frau Cosima was pursuing grave reflections. The second anniversary had come round of the day upon which she had said farewell for ever to Hans von Bülow. "Richard says that my religion dates from that hegira, I pray with my whole heart. But he recalled the first morning two years ago, and how touching it was. ' Yes, that is what impresses people like Wille. You are the dot on the *i*, the glory of my life, the cause for which they envy me.' I recalled yesterday how I had arrived with my two children, trembling and scarcely able to speak another word. I had banged the door of the world behind me and parted from it for ever."

But the fortunes of war were accomplished, in spite of the prodigious resistance developed by France, which was, however, bound to be in vain. And in this deep confidence the Master shook off his monstrous burden of suspense. For if bad tidings arrived, it was put in the shade again by news of a victory. One day she read the news that a German merchant-ship named the *Hans von Bülow* had been seized by the French. This made her sad, and Wagner remarked that she was not the same as usual; "but it must not depress me, for he is absolutely dependent upon me." And she comments: "Whenever I contemplate life sadly, I am uplifted by the thought that I am able to be necessary to him, that he was really in need of me if he was to endure life here below." And she was quite at home on their little peninsula, which she felt to be so charmingly secluded: "To enter this house, which shelters all that I love, gives me a divine feeling. I rejoice in our quiet, full life." And he said with a smile: "'You will always remain a young woman, that is your age; for every man has an age at which he is all that he is ever likely to be.' I laughed and said: 'Then I shall become an old maid.'"

But he had turned to another piece of work, which he did not divulge to her. She imagined, indeed, that he was sketching out the second act of *The Twilight of the Gods:* "But he does not like to be observed, otherwise he is put out; I notice it by his excitable state of mind. But he is indescribably good to me." Then one day he heard her playing the piano and came in softly to listen. When she noticed him, she at once left off playing, upon which he said that "when I played the piano, I put on such a serious face that my eyes became dark, and I was so absorbed in what I was doing that he was afraid of me." She almost regretted having played, in her anxiety lest it might not have pleased him, though he had desired it. And the next day, St. Catherine's day, the maidens' festival, she thought of what he had said to her on the evening before. Thus every day had its quiet charm, which was still further enhanced by Wagner's mysterious creative work. He did all he could, indeed, to hide the great surprise which he had in store for her. But he was amused when she told him of the children's questions about religion, and said that their childish gaiety ought to be left entirely unclouded. He talked to her of her father, to whom he had once complained about his troubles. Liszt had gazed at him and replied: "The fellow wails about his life and then writes such things as these." And the Master added that her father was the most original man he had ever met, and possessed the greatest genius; and next to him came Hans, for the latter had fire. And so, he said, one revolves in the most intimate circle, but this circle had been pretty well broken up. "For when women join in, they turn everything upside down which had previously been going on well, as Herwegh says of my Nibelung poem." For the rest, at this very time they were plunging into French history. They read Ranke's book on France and came to the great age of the Wars of Religion. She was deeply fascinated, and remarked how amazing it was that no Frenchman had chosen Coligny as the hero of a play. But they were all Jews, they knew nothing but the Old Testament. And apropos of the Massacre of St. Bartholomew he observed that since Catherine de' Medici France had really only been governed by factions who had fought among themselves. But from every subject and, so to speak, from every period he came back gladly and joyfully to the woman whom he loved: "You are so dear (*traut*), so proud, so noble, you are such a confidante to me, you are the only soul in whom I confide, all others are so alien to me. My life would no longer be possible without you. If you had hummed and ha'd and held back, I should never have left you, and that would have been a pretty state of affairs." And in this mood he played her Siegfried's wooing, from the third act, and said: "It really is fine, and the cry ' *Heil dir, Mutter* (Hail, Mother)! ' — do you see? — that is religion, when man, forgetting self, refers everything to the universe as a whole."

And now Nietzsche arrived; but as a matter of fact he no longer fitted in at Treibschen, and so he was not shown *Die Capitulation,* and the discussions of war and rumours of war took a different turn. Nor did he understand the Master when he came into the room singing the tune: "*Mir ist auf der Welt nichts lieber als die Stube, wo ich bin, Denn mir wohnt aneinander meine schöne Nachbarin* (In the world there's nothing fairer than the room where I abide, For my pretty neighbour too is living here, close by my side)." Nietzsche now retailed alarmist reports about the hundred and twenty thousand men forming the Army of the Loire, and its good leadership, and said that he and his colleagues at Basel were seriously anxious. The greatest battle of the war was expected. This certainly damped the spirits of the household at Triebschen, but only for a moment; for news immediately arrived of two victories, that of Amiens and that over Garibaldi, and Nietzsche's academic timidity was in no way able to shake Wagner's Olympian mood, caused to some extent by his delight with little Siegfried. And when in the evening, fresh from these impressions, Richard Wagner played the third act of *The Mastersingers,* they were once more filled with joyful emotion. On the following day, however, Frau Cosima was greatly agitated because the Master complained of his eyes; but her anxiety was soon appeased, and though the outer world tried to blacken this radiance, and the attacks on him were more violent than ever — especially that of the Augsburg musician Schletterer, who had proclaimed the dogma of his own infallibility — it did not matter, nor did he worry about it. His joy at the defeat of the Army of the Loire was too great, and now, above all, he perceived the greatness and significance of German organization, which originated in one side of the German nature. He said that Gambetta and Bismarck were busy courting the Holy Father, for Bismarck desired an order from Rome that the nations should yield to force. But Europe was again admiring France. The wretched nations, dazzled by the great French Revolution, to the memory of which the Old World had once more been awakened, expected perfect felicity upon earth from the Republic and imagined that evil would vanish with its coming! It was for the Republic that they were fighting, and they looked upon it as the resurrection. " The German, on the other hand, indulges in no chimerical visions; above all he realizes instinctively that no rogue can bring salvation to the world, and so when the King commands, he obeys. The obedience of the German officers, which of course seems shockingly absurd and narrow-minded to the French, is the outcome of a profound instinct and a deep intuition, about which it is impossible to talk to half-insane people. I have been through all these illusions and have now reached the point of being able to understand the meaning of this narrowly defined sense of duty."

It is really wonderful to see how new ideas were for ever being suggested to them, both by facts and by their daily work, of which their reading may be reckoned a most profitable part. While they drew great thoughts from the present, and from the bearing of the German soldiers, whom the Master celebrated so gloriously in his address to the German Army in Paris, they were also able to arrive at most original conclusions from reading books which created a sensation at the time, though they are now as good as forgotten. Thus out of his dissertation on a narrowly defined sense of duty arose a very subtle discussion of Frederick the Great, which started in connexion with David Friedrich Strauss's book on Voltaire. And here the diary reports the following remark of Wagner's: " A king must be great in endurance, he must prove the quality of his heart by remaining unmoved by many things. Kings have become like this owing to their exceptional position. I know perfectly well that when the King summoned me to his box at *The Mastersingers,* he only did so in order to show the people who thought they were going to influence him that they were not; and the arm which he turned against me on other occasions, he then turned against other persons." All thoughts of the King now caused them both a growing melancholy, though they still had a deep sense of gratitude. There was no need for her to exhort him to be mindful of this gratitude, but rather to advise him to remain what he was, for no king could take this from him, still less destroy it. But never was the monarchical idea in itself stronger in him and Frau Cosima than at this time.

But the way in which she was irradiated by Wagner's mind, and her unlimited capacity for assimilating all that he gave her, were wonderful. There is genius in love as well as in other things, and this found the most beautiful expression during these winter days; in the Master this happened in such a way that he succeeded in deceiving even her keen eyes, rendered keener still by her strong intuition. She imagined him to be deeply engrossed in the instrumentation of *Siegfried,* and he contrived over and over again to play her the great passages, especially those of the third act, and the scene of the awakening, to which they both constantly returned. It was this scene, too, which stirred her so

435

unutterably and which without her he would undoubtedly have been unable to write as he did. For it was Frau Cosima's wonderful womanliness that first really revealed to him the direct connexion between this awakening and his new artistic development. And so we read the following words about this scene of the awakening: " This birth of love in the young man, who has no idea what a woman is, and who is carried away and rejuvenated by this woman, who has already sat at the loom of life and is superior to him — it seems to me to be unique. And then the music! " And her husband replied gaily: " Yes, I can still do it. It is really not long since I composed that, and since then I have been through the most fearsome experiences [Act I of *The Twilight of the Gods*]." But she had no idea that fresh, so to speak, from the Valkyries' rock, he had felt the stimulus to create another work, which he was writing in absolute secrecy and which was to offer to the world quite a new way of conceiving and executing a poem in music. To do this was, as it were, pure sport to him, but when he rose from composing, his heart was full of the profoundest joy and emotion, and in the midst of winter the springtide of love bloomed for them both. And when he received news from the outer world — for there was no lack of friendly signs — he would say: " Do they know what they are at? All those who have come to know you can have no doubt about you. It was written in the stars that you were to devote yourself to me. Yes, yes," he continued, gazing at her portrait, " this proud little woman was resolute. ' You will have something to wonder at,' she thought to herself." Next morning he said that the reason why she looked so serious that day was her redeeming loyalty. And he went on to say that he would like to be rich and take a villa in Italy with her and there study at leisure and in peace. " I never read anything at all now, yet I live for this, I have you and the children."

But life went on, and it was Nietzsche who always kept her in touch with it. He sent alarming reports from the front and described the alleged mobilization of four hundred thousand French troops, and the continuance of these bloody events, which, it seemed, would be endless. And then again he wrote that a professor at Basel had asked him whether Wagner's *Beethoven* was written as an attack on the creator of the Ninth Symphony. This at least justified Nietzsche's remark that, though this work was the supreme expression of the Master's views on art and humanity, it would only be understood by the few; for never has an artist received such a tribute from another. But this work, too, could only have been written at Triebschen and in this wonderful loving seclusion. The information arrived on December 17 — that is, on Beethoven's birthday — and they asked each other how they should commemorate it. Whereupon, recalling the days at Zürich, the Master said that he would have liked to conduct a Beethoven symphony there to please her; and they discussed how they could make up for this. As a matter of fact it happened at the laying of the foundation-stone in Bayreuth. The idea of Bayreuth was not often mentioned, nor, indeed, was anything that involved leaving their retreat. But once any such project came under discussion, it ended in a regular vow that only together would they retrace their steps into the world, and that they would never part. In this connexion the question of their leaving Triebschen had also to be discussed, and he observed that there had always been moments of this kind in his life, at which he had been as though dead, yet which contained the germs of a new life: for instance, at Paris after his musical directorship, then at Dresden with his conductorship, lastly at Zürich, and to end up with, Triebschen. Upon which she said that flight had been a decisive factor in his life: " Flight from Riga, flight from Dresden, flight from Zürich, and flight from Munich twice over. It is to be hoped that this law has at last lost its force."

And so Christmas came round, both politically, in the sense of national peace, and in the narrow world of their house. On the 22nd, again, he told the story of a rector of the consistory at Bordeaux, who, in speaking of the German nature, maintained that the opposition of the Saxons to Charlemagne — that is, of the Germans to the Roman principle — could be traced up to the days of Luther. And he said that at the time he had followed this argument with lively interest and had been an ecstatic disciple of Frau Jessie Laussot, who " did not wear blue spectacles then." This, too, was a reminiscence of his period of adventures.

But the Christmas festivities quite relieved the great suspense with regard to public affairs. On December 24 she wrote: " My day is spent in arranging the things, which I do in a melancholy mood; for the war-reports dictate my mood; besides, I am thinking of Hans. At five o'clock Richard brought in Nietzsche, and at seven we lit up the tree. This is the first Christmas that I have not given Richard a present, nor he to me. And this is right. All is contentment and happiness, the children in ecstasies." Next came the morning of her birthday, about which she made the following beautiful and touching entry in her diary: "I can tell you nothing, my children, about this day, nothing about my feelings, nothing about my state of mind — nothing, nothing, I will only tell you quite drily and barely what happened: As I awoke, my ear caught a sound, which swelled fuller and fuller; no longer could I imagine myself to be dreaming, music was sounding, and such music! When it died away, Richard came into my room with the five children and offered me the score of the symphonic birthday poem — I was in tears, but so was all the rest of the household. Richard had arranged his orchestra on the staircase, and thus was our Triebschen consecrated for ever." The work was entitled *The Triebschen Idyll.* And she continues: "In the afternoon Sulzer arrived, which was a real joy to Richard. After lunch the orchestra came into the house downstairs, and now the *Idyll* was heard once again, to the profound emotion of us all. Next came the wedding-march from *Lohengrin,* Beethoven's Sextet, and the symphony once more to end up with — this symphony which had never been heard before. Now I understand Richard's mysterious work, and the good Richter's trumpet, too; he played the Siegfried theme gloriously and had actually learnt to play the trumpet on purpose, which had brought down many remonstrances upon him from me. 'Let me die,' I exclaimed to Richard. 'It were easier for you to die than for me to live,' he replied. In the evening Richard is reading us his *Mastersingers.* Dr. Sulzer and I are enjoying it as if it were quite new. I spend the whole day as though in a dream, my spirit is still listening to the vanished strains, and as it recalls them, my heart, oppressed by its emotions, seeks relief in music. Twilight dreams arise. Ah, to see no more, but to listen in deepest stillness to the triumph of love, the disappearance of all limitations, the supreme ecstasy of losing all consciousness of existence!"

She felt the full greatness of the work. For, coming in the midst of the composition of *Siegfried*, it was like an echo of the great experiences at Triebschen and was also at the same time a new revelation of the Master. For if in future the symphony or the symphonic idea is to strike out new paths, it must take its departure from this simple, yet infinitely rich *Idyll*, which was in some sense the expression in artistic form of Wagner's gratitude to Frau Cosima. He has expressed this in words as follows:

> Thine was the high, self-sacrificing will
>   That found a refuge where my soul could thrive,
> Hallowed by thee it lay remote and still
>   Where art could grow apace and so achieve
> That world of heroes which, as by a spell,
>   Is now the dear homeland in which we live.
> Then to my life a joyous message came:
> "A son is there!" Siegfried must be his name.
>
> Might I in tones give thanks for him and thee,
>   For loving deeds could there be fairer pay?
> These in our home were ever wont to be
>   And quiet joy, to music turned alway.
> For those who ever loved us faithfully
>   And smile on Siegfried and our son, I pray
> That through thy kindness they too may possess
> The music of our quiet happiness.

No more beautiful token of love could have been devised, and it formed a grand and glorified conclusion to the bitter struggle of this heroic couple, the great and impassioned artist and the infinitely self-sacrificing woman.

APPENDIX

Frau Cosima's Abstract of the Oresteia *of Æschylus*

THE EAGLES of Zeus devour the hare with young. In atonement for this wrong Artemis demands the purest of sacrifices. The King sacrifices his daughter, and by this very expiation incurs guilt. Her mother avenges the outrage demanded by the divinity, and Apollo calls upon the son to avenge his father. Gods and men are alike enmeshed in bloodguiltiness, which begins from Zeus, from his eagles — that is, from the discord of nature. Nor do the Erinnyes (Furies) fail to appear, and Apollo is powerless to master them; he can only put them to sleep for a time. Who is it that appeases them, that breaks the fatal chain? Who shall check what grows out of this bloodshed? It is Pallas Athene, knowledge, who founds the State, establishes justice, and opposes to the rage of natural forces the reign of sacred human order. Mercy arises from justice. The matricide whom his divine instigator was powerless to clear of guilt is delivered by the tribunal of discerning men, the avenging goddesses become Eumenides (gracious ones) in the State founded upon the law, and the poet, who had transported us back to the primal chaos and turmoil of becoming, leads up to the present and gives his people a share in his poetic conception by showing them that their institutions are sacred and bound up with all the sacred mysteries, thus creating a living work of art in association with them.

But in *The Ring of the Nibelung* Brünhilde judges the gods through the knowledge of love; she does not discern, she knows; she does not establish, she destroys; the poet does not lead up to any present, for he has no place in time, his people did not see through his eyes, and so he created alone the eternal work of art, unbloody, tragic, and redeeming, in that it emancipates from life's realities. In the former everything is drawn from life and turned to the uses of life; in the latter art is everything.

Cassandra

Apollo loved her and endowed her with the prophetic gift. As a prophetess, and so holier than the god, she frees herself from the vortex of deception and " deceives Loxias." The god punishes her: if she wants to be superhuman, then men shall be unable to understand her, they shall not believe her, her gift, bestowed by an accursed thing, is turned to a curse. Divine is Apollo demanding love's surrender! Holy is the prophetess who transgresses against him; all this is seen by the poet, who knows and proclaims the " loveless longing for love," and catches every voice through which the mystery of being is revealed.

The Chorus

They enter just as the watchman has left his lonely watch, gladly and with mysterious allusions. They have not yet seen the beacon-fires, but recall how long it is since the princes went forth against Ilium, and the rage with which they started out; they express a pious confidence that a god will punish the infamous wretch, though much has yet to be suffered because of the woman " whom many a man would have wed "; and they conclude their observations, which explain the situation to us, by an account of themselves: they are staying at home because even ten years ago they were prevented from joining in the expedition by old age, which makes them like " a dream-vision wandering by day." Thus we know everything in outline, and through these first passing allusions we are already full of forebodings when Clytemnestra appears to prepare the sacrifice and divide the offerings among the altars. The Chorus question her and beg her to assuage their " fever of care," which is already lightened by the sacrifice, as by " hope's radiant smile," and looses the burden of fear from their " hearts deep-gnawed by pain." Clytemnestra leaves the stage in silence, in order to make further preparations for the ceremony, and in an atmosphere of ominous suspense the Chorus celebrate the departure of the captains, for to them there is left the trust in God, "unabated by years . . . in whose strength I sing." And here begins, as it were, the religious motive, for which we have been prepared by the trust in God expressed in the first chorus; for the deepest mysteries are revealed by them in this solemn chant: the impious meal of Zeus' eagles, the recognition of the eagles devouring the hare as the captains of the host, this recognition being due to the seer, who proclaims that the wrath of Artemis is kindled against her father's "winged hounds." The cry of "Yet oh, may the Right be triumphant yet!" goes up from the whole Chorus in tones of prayer and supplication between the strophe and antistrophe, in which the leaders of the two parts have sung of the meal of the eagles and its interpretation by the seer. Next comes the prayer of Calchas to Artemis, and the seer's prophecy of another victim, "the seed of a feud that shall cleave to the house," for the crafty Queen is lying in wait, with "the treacherous wrath that forgetteth never . . . set on revenge for the child that was slain"; and here for the third time the cry goes up: "Ailinon, Ailinon — Yet oh, may the Right be triumphant yet!" For the voice of Calchas foreboded "such doom, albeit with blessings blent," and shuddering apprehension and grim memories go side by side with joyful expectations; and with trembling awe the Chorus absorb themselves in meditation on the name of Zeus, "who brings peace to the mind." For they want to "cast aside the burden weighing, all to no profit, ever on [the] mind." But this very absorption in the nature of the godhead leads them back to present sorrow, and the second strophe proclaims that the favour of the gods enthroned on high is stern and remorseless. After declaring that Zeus "unto men the path of wisdom showeth," making them learn through suffering, the second antistrophe reverts to the Greek leader, and shows him, afflicted by the distress of the Army, yielding to the seer manfully and without wrath. The third strophe, which is again entirely devoted to past events, still further expatiates on the trials of the Greeks at Aulis and the anguish of Agamemnon, next proceeding to his inexorable resolve and to the sweet, pathetic figure with her virginal grace, upon which it dwells with pleasure mingled with pain, only gradually to relapse into gloomy silence as Clytemnestra once more approaches. It utters one last wish — no prayer, no appeal to the gods, but just an impotent, well-meaning old man's wish:

> "*And then* — O, I saw not, I tell not! Fair issue
> Had Kalchas' devisings! The fateful tissue
> Of instruction from Justice's loom down-sweepeth
> On such as have suffered: — but what is her dooming
> Suffice it to know in the day of its coming.
> Who knoweth beforehand, beforehand weepeth.
> With the dawn's forthshining shall come revelation.
> That the end may be well is the supplication
> Of the near one, the dear one, who this land keepeth." [1]

Clytemnestra appears, is questioned, and announces the good news. In this dialogue, under the strong impressions of the moment, dread forebodings melt away as night before day: twice do the Chorus, in their confidential alternating dialogue with the Queen, ask to be told the glad tidings, and as her account comes to an end and she moves away, they sing " glad thanks " to Zeus. This motive, first introduced by the Choragus, develops in the strophic song of the Chorus into an earnest admonition to the people: " His hand herein all men may trace "; jubilation over the victory passes directly into contemplation of the chastisement of impiety.

> "But O, be mine a lot kept free
> From suffering: mine be feet that pace
> Paths that the steps of wisdom trace:
> So shall content companion me.

---

[1] The poetic quotations are from the translation of A. S. Way, in *Æschylus in English Verse*, by permission of the publisher, The Macmillan Company. — TR.

For riches shall be no defence
Unto the man who from his sight
Spurns the great altar of the Right
In pride of full-fed insolence."

Thus ends the first strophe, and the antistrophe draws a picture of temptation and punishment: here speaks Æschylus the judge, here we have the religious motive again; but at the close the poet once again returns to life ("Even such was Paris," who "heaped on that guest-table shame"); only to give a deeply moving picture of Menelaus' love and mourning in strophe 2 and its antistrophe. But the poet brings his song to a close on the same note as that of the first chorus; he directs our eyes from the mourning of the Prince to that of the people in the "lands of Hellas," which is "greater still," and from this the survey rises once more in the religious vein to him who is unjustly fortunate, for to him "Fame above measure given brings man but woe." We feel that we are at the parting of the ways between history and saga, the present and the past, reality and poetry; and the stream of the song, swelled by the tributary streams of religious feeling, poetic vision, priestly judgment, and prophetic warning, ends, as in a peaceful lake, in the repeated wish for "unenvied weal."

The transition to the action of the play is effected by means of certain of the Chorus, who express doubts about the news: the religious motive is, so to speak, broken off, the stage enters into its rights, and on this note of doubt there appears, doubly welcome, the homely watchman, still full of dark allusions, and after him the herald. The latter's last speech, his description of the storm and of the disappearance of Menelaus, by which, we may gather, the poet was preparing the way for his satyric drama — this description gives the Chorus occasion to muse upon the meaning of the name Helen, from which they pass to the "tears of mourning" which the wrath of the gods sends with her to the Trojans. Like a lion-cub, brought up with a lamb,

"Even so on Ilium-town
Floated a spirit down
Of peace, by seeming,
Of windless peace, a crown
Over her wealth-renown
Soft splendour beaming;
An arrow of desire
That archer-eyes were winging;
A flower soul-thrilling, springing
Out of love's bed of fire"

— and with it came "a Fury ruin-fraught"! Impressed by this fatality, antistrophe 3 quotes "a hoary saying," to the effect that insatiate woe grows rank in the garden of Fortune, regardless of right or wrong; but the poet, in his effort to order life aright by his admonitions, represents it to his Chorus in another light:

"That sin it is, the godless *act*, that bears
Spawn like itself, foul offspring of foul mother:
But they whose straight path righteousness prepares
Fair is their lot, and goodly issue theirs."

And the fourth strophe develops the theme that "Arrogance, in sin grown grey," brings forth "impious Hardihood," but

"In smoke-fouled huts doth Justice shine,
On virtuous lives she still hath smiled:
From gold-tricked halls and hands defiled,
She turns with her averted eyne."

Justice "guideth all things to their goal." And once again the fate of the Trojans is unfolded before us — a fate brought upon them by impiety: the past, the fate which guilt still has in store for the captain of the host; and the present, the reality, appear, conjured up by the poet and veiled in threatening admonition, producing by the glory of the poetry a wondrously spectral effect. — In a religious service the priest's sermon, but doubly effective here in the realm of vision and saga!

Agamemnon enters in triumphal procession. The Chorus express their desire to honour him duly, neither overjoyed nor crushed by the fullness of their gratitude. For this purpose they decide to be candid and confess to the King that they considered him unwise in proclaiming war on behalf of Helen. The fine simplicity of the relation between the people and primitive royalty finds expression again in their closing words:

> " . . . Thou at last shall see
> By inquisition made shalt know,
> Who righteously, and who in perfidy
> Hath ruled thy folk for thee."

As soon as Agamemnon has given thanks to the gods and expressed his agreement with the sentiments of the Chorus, Clytemnestra appears, and this scene seems to be dominated by her and the shameless revelation of her hypocrisy. She spreads beneath the King's feet the crimson carpet, over which he approaches the palace as though along a path of blood; she pours out her final assurances of her joy, only at the end, in grimly ominous fashion, to call upon "Zeus the Accomplisher" and beg him to " take thought for that thou meanest to fulfil." And as though we could actually see the horror of the Chorus at what they have understood and divined in this, we now hear them questioning one another with bated breath:

> "Why and O why doth this terror insistently haunting me still
> Like a bird of black doom hover nigh to the heart that is boding
>   ill? "

With their own eyes they have seen the King's return, yet the " Avenging Spirit's keen Peals as from the choir of my thoughts " and they cannot be happy.

"Mine heart would outstrip my tongue,
Would pour forth its hidden tale;
But darkness around it is hung
For a shroud: it must wait and wail."

And now their hearts are athrob in the darkness, while the flame softly mounts. Clytemnestra breaks in upon their despondent, melancholy brooding, with the harshness which is at once the mask, the essence, and the protection of her distraught and anxious spirit. Insultingly she calls Cassandra, who is lagging behind. "Follow her," say the Chorus sympathetically. "It is the best thing you can do." Yield to compulsion and "Consent to feel Fate's yoke, unfelt before," is their advice, as Clytemnestra moves off, furious at her silence. And now begins Cassandra's heart-rending lament, which discloses the real tragedy. Here is the wholly guiltless victim, already undone by the god before her death, who, though knowing all, is entirely dumb, and now and now only raises her vain lament:

"O frenzied heart, O demon-possessed, who touching thyself hast chanted
A tuneless strain like the sad refrain of the nightingale tawny-golden
Who for Itys, Itys, with burdened breast, with spirit misery-haunted
Wails on and on, while the long days run of a life with woes enfolden."

So sing the Chorus, before whose boding senses she evokes the hideous deed which is about to be perpetrated in the palace. But who could possibly give the remotest idea of this scene, even with the help of extracts? We stand amazed at all that the poet calls up before us, almost as though he were endowed with supernatural powers: the vision of the unseen, created, as it were, out of nothing, the ordered march of the action as though dominated by him, and the impetuous unchaining of all his powers. Cassandra breaks into lamentation. The Chorus are horror-struck that she should approach the sun-god with cries of mourning; she repeats her cry, and the Chorus recognize a divine inspiration in her "thrall's soul," but desire no prophecy. She, however, gazes upon what is inevitably to happen within, she cannot but utter it, and through her we are present at the action, the horror of which almost vanishes for us, thanks to the passion of sympathy aroused by the prophetess:

> "Now let the unglutted Furies yell
> O'er the sacrifice that she sacrificeth!"

she shrieks, as she sees the "lion in the mesh"—Agamemnon in the deadly net. But once he has fallen, she bewails her own fate, and in answer to her own question to him: "Why didst thou lead me here?" she replies in bitter grief: "For nought but to be here slain with thee!—what other can be the end?" And she envies the nightingale, with whom the Chorus compare her, for her "shadow-cool lament," adding: "But for me doth wait a merciless fate—the stroke of the two-edged blade!" And the Chorus, quite carried away by a passion of sympathy for her, ask:

> "Ah, whence be the god-given visions that crowd on thee, horrors
> rashly boded?
> This tale thou hast told hast thou shaped in the mould of song
> where is death's voice crying!
> Thine ominous strains are shrilling loud with an utterance terror-loaded.
> Where be they found, the limits that bound the paths of thy
> weird prophesying?"

Her answer is a wail of "Woe for the wedlock of Paris!" And for the second time she announces her approaching death. The attitude of the Chorus is now entirely changed

to one of pity, and, after once more bewailing her city, for
the third time she prophesies her death. The Chorus question
her about the " malignant God " who constrains her to pour
forth these woeful strains and wailings of death. When they
insist, she collects herself, as it were, she sees no more
visions, she utters no more laments, but she tells them her
story:

" Nay then, no more the oracle through veils
　　Shall shyly peer, like some new-wedded bride."

But she demands that the Choragus shall swear to bear witness
that she was aware of the impious guilt of this house. The Choragus asks how an oath can unravel this coil of woe, and expresses
his surprise that she, coming from a land of "foreign speech,"
can tell them of everything exactly as if she had seen it all, and
in secret, confidential dialogue (stichomythia) she replies:
"Prophet Apollo made this office mine." "A God," he asks
tremulously, "yet smitten with desire of thee? " And with
maidenly gentleness she answers: "I shamed to speak of this
tale heretofore." Gentle in his turn, the Choragus, who as her
chosen confidant has now become quite a distinct personality,
does not probe into the question, but exclaims, as though to restrain her: "Too tender, in general, are all who are happy, and
with prosperity goes ever pride." Upon which she continues:
" A fervent suitor he, who breathed fierce love." To this complete
confession he rejoins: " Came ye together by love's ordinance? "
And she: "I promised Loxias — then I broke my troth." He
makes no comment on this, but presses her with the question
upon which everything turns: whether she was already in possession of the god-given power. Yes, she was. Next he wants to
know whether the god did not punish her. "No man believed
me — my sin's wage was this," she wails like a child, to which
he replies: "Yet seem to us these thy soothsayings true." Upon
this she is once more seized with a wild exaltation of grief, like
the " bufera infernal (whirlwind) " which sweeps Francesca
and Paolo away again after they have told the poet the fate of
their loves; and now she sees in a vision the banquet of Thyestes

and Clytemnestra's hypocrisy: "All-reckless . . . she feigns rejoicing for his safe return."

And, turning to the Choragus, Cassandra continues:

"Heed me or not, 'tis all one: wherefore fret?
That which shall be will come. Right soon shalt thou
Pitying confess me all too true a seer."

Yet he only half understands her. And now she speaks with terrifying plainness:

"Agamemnon's doom, I say, thou shalt behold."

He will not understand, but she persists in her words, and says almost scornfully: "Thou dost but *pray* — at murder's work are these!" Once more the frenzy seizes her, and she casts away her priestly robe, her staff and prophetic wreaths, with the words: "Make rich some other lost wretch in my stead!" Apollo, who has inflicted all these sufferings upon her, is stripping her of their very insignia. She next sees the deed that Orestes is to do, and greets the portals that are to lead her into the realm of shadows, for she will utter no more laments: "Down from the chariot! There will I suffer death!"

Yet she raises another wail as "the house reeks all adrip with blood." To the omnipresent poet she appears no longer as foreseeing things, but also as scenting them in advance, like some super-beast; a fetid breath floats up to her as from a grave. But she goes forward composedly, with the words: "Enough of life." The Choragus tries to hold her back, but she has already told him that her time has come, and that if she shrank back once more in terror, it was due to an overwhelming instinct of the mind and senses, a last surging up of the will to live which had overcome her. Now all that she asks is that the Chorus shall bear witness one day to what she has spoken, when the time of fulfilment shall have come, for she is anxious that men should know of her prophecies. But she calls upon the sun-god for revenge, and adds:

" Ah, human life — when most it prospereth,
A shadow can transform it; if unhappy,
Oblivion, like a wet sponge, wipes away
The picture. And 'tis this oblivion
That pains me more than clouded happiness."

Thus this scene closes on quite a personal note, with a lament over the fleeting transience of all things, even sorrow. By this revelation of a being of whom, but for the poet, we should have known nothing, and by the disclosure of her fate, the poet enables us to gain such an insight into the very essence of tragedy that all destinies appear before us in their inexorable necessity, exhorting us to fortitude and at the same time inspiring us with it. Sublime, heart-rending, and salutary, the tragedy here interrupts, as it were, both the drama and the religious service: the innocent victim goes to her death, the image of knowledge scorned, the enslaved daughter of a prince, Cassandra, the beloved of a god, sees her last vision and utters her last lament. No song, no prayer, no invocation accompanies her, and no moral is drawn from her fate. The people gaze upon the prophetess and look on in silence at the revelation of the mystery, as at the miracle of the mass; once this is accomplished, the human action begins again. And the poet, who has heard her lament the oblivion into which she will sink, consoles us, as it were, by the creation of this imperishable, unforgettable, ineffaceable picture of the maiden prophetess, thus refuting his own words.

Reverting to the fate of Agamemnon, the Chorus give themselves up to the contemplation of happiness. Shouts of distress ring out, and the old men, whom we had seen from the very beginning to be incapable of action, vehemently discuss what is to be done, until Clytemnestra appears. And now her frankness is as horrible as her hypocrisy:

". . . This is Agamemnon, late
My lord, a corpse. This hand that did the deed
Wrought righteousness. The truth is as I say."

Such is the situation now. The Chorus threaten her with exile: she retorts with mocking words about their silence at Iphigenia's death, and with threats. The Chorus note how the drop of blood shines thick beneath her eye and now threaten her with the future. She vows that she knows no fear so long as Ægisthus is at her side; and she uncovers the corpses. The Chorus turn from her to them and begin the dirge: they curse womankind, and, above all, Helen. Clytemnestra stops their curses. The Chorus mournfully apostrophize the dæmon of the house of Tantalus; " True word was that same," rejoins Clytemnestra, and pictures the raging of the dæmon. The Chorus at once take up this deeper interpretation, and turn to Zeus:

> " Ah, 'twas done as He willed
> Who is First Cause of all!
> When is purpose fulfilled
> Of man, save as thrall
> Of Zeus? — what thing of all these did not
> He foreordain to befall? "

Having thus changed to a note of resignation, the two hemi-choruses go up on the stage and approach the corpse of the King.

Leader of first hemi-chorus

> " Oh my King! oh my chief!
> For thee how shall I cry?
> How shall love wail its grief,
> While thou so nigh
> Foully slain in this web of a spider outgasping
> thy life dost lie? "

Second hemi-chorus around the bier

> " Woe for yon bed!
> Tamely slain like a slave

453

There my King lieth dead,
Thrust down to the grave
By the steel in the fingers of treachery clutched,
    by the two-edgèd glaive! "

Clytemnestra persists that it is not she, but the wrathful
avengers of Atreus who have punished Agamemnon, the husband being offered as a sacrifice for the children; upon which
two of the second hemi-chorus exclaim in indignation:

" Who shall witness for thee
That thine hands are clean —
Ah, how can it be? —
Of this murder, O Queen? "

They admit, however, that the ancestral avenger was her ac-
complice, and, after picturing how the stream of blood is swallowed up in the morass of guilt caused by the murder of the
children, the second hemi-chorus mounts on to the stage, and
the leader repeats:

" Oh my King! oh my chief!
For thee how shall I cry? . . ."

Whereupon the first hemi-chorus in its turn repeats:

" Woe for yon bed!
Tamely slain like a slave
There my king lieth dead. . . ."

Engrossed in the justice of her deed — or else anxious to
prove it — Clytemnestra now recalls the death of Iphigeneia, the
child whom he gave her, and whom she has never ceased to
weep for:

" Is this child-slayer's doom not
The child-slayer's meed? "

is her conclusion, and at these words two of the first hemi-chorus
wonder in vain whither to turn in their anxiety, for: "Fate on
new whetstones is whetting the vengeance of one wrong more! "
   The Choragus lifts up his voice in lamentation over the death
of their lord and asks who shall dig his grave, who shall weep
for him. And, turning boldly to Clytemnestra, he asks:

" Wilt thou dare such a thing —
   Even thou who didst slay! —
   With thy death-dirge to wing
   Thy lord's soul on its way?
   For his mighty achievements such graceless grace
      wouldst unrighteously pay? "

To which the full Chorus reply with plaintive questioning:

" Ah, who shall upraise
   O'er the godlike dead
   The death-chant of praise?
   What mourner shall shed
   Tears, and with sorrow unfeignèd the path to
      his grave-mound tread? "

But, proud and unmoved, Clytemnestra rejoins that it was by
her hand that he fell and was slain:

" I will bury him, I — but not with laments of
      his household-train;
   But his daughter shall meet him,
   As fitting it is,
   With embraces shall greet him,
   And welcoming kiss:
   By the swift-flowing River of Anguish shall
      Iphigeneia do this! "

This sinister candour meets with no response, but the two members of the second hemi-chorus break into the reflection:

" Lo, how the spoiler is spoiled, how the slayer
    atonement pays!
Stands the ordinance sure
While the years of Zeus run,
That in suffering the doer
Pay for all he hath done.
From this house who shall banish the curse-
    brood? — with ruin 'tis knit into one."

And here the Chorus proper comes to an end and makes way for Ægisthus, who, exulting over the vengeance exacted, tersely relates the story of the banquet of Thyestes. For this insolent evil-doer the Choragus has nothing but the announcement of strife upon earth, no reflections upon fate, no wise saws, no meditations on the reign of God, such as he had indulged in to Clytemnestra. But the Queen, as though she had now come under the protection of Justice, whose instrument she proclaims herself, next expresses her wish that the dæmon may henceforth leave this house and torment another race. She is weary, and as Ægisthus and the Choragus become more and more violent in their dispute, finally grasping their weapons, she steps between them to restrain them. She does not want to see a fresh accumulation of woes, and she waves the old men homeward. "What we did, must needs be so," she declares curtly, and when Ægisthus and the Choragus still continue to exchange threats, the latter even threatening him with Orestes, she says:

" Reck not thou of these, to heed their empty yelpings: thou
    and I,
Rulers now of town and palace-halls, will rule them royally."

With this insolently outspoken contempt for all that might be capable of standing in her way, and uttering an impiously audacious wish for a pleasant life, now that the work of vengeance is accomplished and she is satisfied, Clytemnestra closes the first part of the tragedy.

The Libation-pourers (Choephoroe)

Once again she rises up directly before us, full of alarms and disturbed in her rest at night, a figure of incomparably grander stature now, as described by the Chorus and her own daughter, whose actions reflect the mother's fears. And we know that her anxiety is justified, for it is the returned Orestes who opens the second part of the tragedy. Sent forth on his mission by Loxias, he first invokes the Hermes of the underworld and then offers up a lock of his hair on his father's grave — " a poor gift, but rich in mourning! " " the faithful tribute of deepest sorrow " — and a token that he has come as avenger. He has just performed this act of piety when he catches sight of the chorus of handmaidens, and Electra, his sister, who joins them, also in the dress of a handmaiden. He conceals himself, and we learn from their laments that the Queen came rushing at night into the quarters of the handmaidens in a frenzy of terror, and that the diviners had interpreted her dream as meaning that the dead were raging against their murderers. Strophe and antistrophe 1, which draw an impassioned picture of this sinister woman's terrors, are followed by strophe and antistrophe 2, which announce the certain doom of the guilty. Upon this, strophe 3 informs us that the godless woman is sending offerings to pour upon the grave to avert the evil. This impious act, inspired by terror, draws from the Chorus wails of horror and the promise that justice is sure, and in antistrophe 3 once more re-establishes a sort of ghastly calm; the epode of this wonderfully constructed chorus next pictures for us the plight of the Chorus, for whom the gods have ordained that they shall be handmaidens here, and who are weeping for Electra. The King's daughter herself is alluded to as a slave like them,

" and my heart seems dead,
All frost-benumbed by grief."

457

After this incomparably poetic introduction, she begins to speak. We know all: the disordered state of the house, her own plight; and so her speech is concerned with the act which she has to accomplish. With divine simplicity she asks the handmaidens how she is to perform it. With equal simplicity and sincerity the Choragus counsels her: "Pouring, speak solemn words for loyal souls." And so the name of Orestes comes to be mentioned. "You remind me of him who is dearest of all," replies Electra to her who has named him. And with his name the Choragus now warningly couples a reminder of those who were guilty of the murder. The girl hesitates, the warning adviser insists, and, overborne by her, Electra begins her earnest prayer to the Hermes of the underworld; she implores her father to send Orestes home, then prays for herself, that she may be more virtuous than her mother, and lastly follows up her pious words of blessing by an allusion to the accursed one, adding: "Thus I confront the sinners' wicked prayer." She demands of her father an avenger for her father, and, triumphing splendidly over the doubting, despairing horror with which she appeared to fulfil her mother's impious command, she signs to the Chorus to pour the sacred funeral libation. The Chorus respond with a lament and an appeal to the deliverer of the house; and as they are calling upon him, Electra finds the lock of Orestes' hair. She knows at once whose it is. "He shore, and sent, in homage to his sire," she cries as one inspired, and conviction breaks from her lips in a "heartsurge of bitterness." She wishes that the lock of hair could speak, she will appeal to the gods; and as she mounts towards the altar, she recognizes footmarks which exactly correspond to her own. She is overwhelmed with bewilderment, her senses faint, and Orestes appears. He solemnly calls upon her to pray the gods "that all the rest may be vouchsafed." His presence breaks the spell of her conscious foreboding. She does not recognize Orestes, he has to make himself known to her, till at last she greets this god-sent deliverer with a passionate outburst. With exalted solemnity, mindful of nothing but his mission, he calls upon Zeus; and when the Chorus counsel prudence and silence, he rejoins, in the consciousness of his divine mission: "Me verily Loxias' mighty oracle will fail not." He relates the words

458

of the oracle, from which we see that, whatever he may do, he is inexorably handed over to the Erinnyes. To the promptings of the gods he adds, like a true Hellene, those of reason: his needy state and the impossibility of abandoning the citizens of Argos to the rule of a woman. Once more the Chorus intervenes as advocate and promoter of justice:

> "Aye for the stroke of murder the stroke of murder shall
> smite . . .
> ' Doers must suffer ' — so sayeth the immemorial saw."

Orestes thereupon breaks into a lament and recalls the darkness in which his father lies. Firm and unmoved, the Chorus point out to the " child " that wails of lamentation for the dead are a cry for vengeance upon the murderer. Electra joins her lament to that of her brother, bewailing their own fate, from which the Choragus deduces the promise of a happier future. Orestes describes how different it would have been had Agamemnon fallen before Ilium, and as though a transition had now been found from mourning over the dead to that action against the living for which they are longing, the Chorus amplify the picture, supplementing what Orestes has said. Gentle but impassioned, Electra intervenes with the words:

> " Nay, rather that even so
> By their own kin slain amid peace
> Were those who have laid thee low."

This gives the Chorus, who are ever bent upon action, an opening for pointing out the vanity of the wish. And when they have prophesied a like fate for the children, the brother and sister transform their lament for their father into a supplication for righteous vengeance, and, intoxicated with enthusiasm, the Chorus cry out:

> " O might it be mine, o'er the murderer foeman
> Murdered, to chant the triumph-song,

As he burns on the pine-logs, and over the woman,
The traitress, to hymn the avengèd wrong!
For why should I hide how the vengeance-vision
Aye hovers before me? . . ."

till the expiation seems actually to have been accomplished, while once again we hear of the misery of this accursed house, for which no stranger can find a balm.

After the Choragus has prayed to the Blessed Ones of Night to hear her and grant victory to the children, an antiphonal chant in invocation of their father begins between the brother and sister, like a sort of litany, which the Choragus once again interrupts by inciting them to action; whereupon Orestes, recalled to reality, inquires why, since Clytemnestra never thought of the dead man, she has now sent these libations. The Choragus narrates his mother's dream in all its details. " In sooth, this dream was no deceptive vision! " cries Orestes; and his dread of his fearful mission is apparent to us from the vehemence with which he greets this dream as a confirmation of it. In reply to the questions of the Chorus he now tells them how he thinks of proceeding, and gives instructions to his sister and the women; but " the rest " he leaves to " him who sent him."

And now the Chorus depict in strophic song the monstrousness of the approaching crime:

" Tell the passion uncontrolled
Aye with human ruin joined —
Loveless lust of female kind
That doth wedlock's tree disroot
In the man as in the brute."

They compare it with the hideous deeds that have already been done, and find it more terrible still. The fourth strophe foretells the victory of Justice:

" The deep-brooding Erinnys brings home
The child Retribution, of whom
Shall the blood-pollution, that haunted
The house, be avenged thus late."

Thus ends this scene, rigid, firm, and inexorable as the law, in which lamentations, curses, tears, and supplications have poured forth in inconceivable variety, in a resistless, surging flood. The action now proceeds, simple and intense: Orestes knocks at the portals of the palace, he summons Clytemnestra, she comes, he announces the death of her son, she breaks out into hypocritical laments as though in pursuance of some law.